THE FEMININE GENDER

FROM GODDESS TO SLAVES

Dr Maan Khalil Al-Omar

Editor: Jihan Asim Al-Taie
Translator: Kais As-Sultany

Table of Contents

DEDICATION

I dedicate this book to:

My mother, the inexhaustible source of her motherhood

My sisters, the gracious and the friendly

My wife, the complete and the wise in her thinking

My daughter, the kind and prudent in her decisions

My granddaughter, the passionate about her family's love

ABOUT THE AUTHOR

Professor Maan Khalil Al-Omar is one of the most prominent Middle Eastern sociologists known for his research and theories about the stratification of the Middle Eastern and Arabic societies and their interaction with other societies. He is a theorist of Arab sociology and the founder of the theory "Towards an Arab Sociology".

He is a highly qualified researcher and theorist. He received his Bachelor of Arts degree in Sociology from Baghdad University in 1965, then he obtained his master's degree in Sociology from Eastern Michigan University, USA, in 1968, and culminated his academic studies in 1976 by obtaining a PhD degree in sociology from Wayne State University, Michigan, USA.

His rich career journey as an assistant professor began in the College of Arts, Department of Sociology, University of Baghdad, where he progressed until he reached the rank of Professor in 1988. Besides his work in Baghdad University, he taught sociology at Muhammad bin Abdullah in Morocco, Yarmouk University - Jordan, Emirates University - United Arab Emirates, and Naif University - Saudi Arabia. Currently, he is an advisor to many governments as well as to non-government organisations in the Middle East, focusing on the development of different social aspects in these societies.

He has written a staggering 70 books and published more than 50 studies on various social topics covering the sociology of crime, juvenile crimes, family, education, youth, childhood, women, poverty, and the sociology of revolution. His writings varied between theories, methods, applications, and fields of sociology, focusing on the critical and evaluative aspects of contemporary social events. His latest publication – the dialectic of the individual and society in sociology – is an outstanding read in which he clarifies a new horizon in the development of sociology science with the development of human societies.

INTRODUCTION

Throughout the history, the woman has never been isolated or singled out, she is the mother, daughter, wife, friend, and sister. The objective of studying the feminine is to explore the depths of knowledge about half of humanity and human life in the past, present, and future. The woman has been subject to huge social suppression throughout history at various levels. Religions, cultures, politics, industries, and trade collectively came together on her to exploit and enslave her to be a cheap commodity and easy target to be seized. On the other hand, when sociology literature is reviewed from its birth until the last quarter of the twentieth century, it can be seen that it is the mirror that depicts human society with all its elements.

Sociology is a new science and has passed different characteristic stages since its establishment. In the initial stage, it focused on major topics such as society, civilisation, change and social construction. With its progress and when it assumed solid foundations and converted from fantasy to necessity, it became a vital tool in the development of society. It, therefore, started to deal with more medium topics such as gradual, classes, groups, social movements, and the family social problems. In the maturity stage, it went further and deeper to diagnose, theorise, model, and simulate the more diversified social aspects. In this respect, its main concern was the role of social behaviour, such as crime, delinquency, corruption, and gender. It continues to add extra aspects to its portfolio whenever a new social issue emerges. Parallel to such addition, sometimes it is necessary to go back in various steps to refine and enrich whatever was added. The gender topic, which is the concern of this context, is no different in its requirement for further adjustment. It needed refinement and tunning to match the

1

gender's role in developing the society. Moreover, gender became the main balancing element and one of the important measures for the health and advancement level of society. It was noticed that the available sociology literature concerning gender was found to display quick and side issues regarding the suffering, problems, and aspirations of women without tackling the roots of each of these aspects. Although this is not a flaw in sociology's literature and its scientific research approach, neither ignorance of sociologists, it is the exact reflection of the advancement and the changed speed of the society. This is absolutely right because sociology is the only mirror of social life. Therefore, if the movement to the change of the society is slow and its culture is more traditional and moral than the urban or industrial, where intolerance and discrimination against women existed and still continues even in modern and capitalist societies, sociology follows its pattern in its response and reaction. Accordingly, it has not neglected the feminist movements and their contribution in enriching its literature with new facts, particularly those that emerged from western society. That is a fair statement as the western society, ahead of other societies, managed to remove some prejudice against femininity as part of its scientific objectivity. Moreover, it did not leave developments and changes affecting the individual whether this individual was female or male, child or elderly, mother or father, wife or husband, poor or rich. In this respect, serious literature emerged on issues of biological and gender differences of individuals. The impact of these studies was found to be influential after the rise of the voice of the women's movements supported by the ethnic bias movements and some liberal political parties that were coupled with the spread of democratic principles, the increase in the

2

participation of women in formal and customary activities, and crowned by the society's need for the women expertise, competencies, and skills.

This book consists of twelve chapters that begin from defining the concept of the feminine, passing through her upbringing, identity, location, powers of slavery, struggle, the third type, phases in ancient civilisations, her place in ancient human history and her positioning in the present societies, ending with means of liberating her from social slavery. It was not written out of intolerance against men or as advocating for women, but rather because the woman was and is oppressed, despised, suppressed, and subjugated in all historical stages, and in many heavenly and earthly religions. She is a human being who takes care of housekeeping, the transmission of the social and religious heritage of the ascending, and she is the first sacrificial generations to serve the family, but she does not have authority, power, wealth, and influence in the society, therefore, the man raped her rights and doubled her duties as if she were a slave to him and to the society. This is the social, cultural, and religious slavery, family enslavement, and career exclusion. These types of enslavement made me record my observations against this intolerance and discrimination emanating from society, culture, religion, and government.

At the end of this introduction, my pen is incapable of expressing my thanks, gratitude and appreciation to my wife and my life companion Jihan Asim Al-Taie for the strenuous efforts she made in reviewing and correcting the Arabic text of the book, May God bless and protect her. My special thanks also go to my friend Dr Kais As-Sultany for his efforts in translating and publishing the book in the English language.

Finally, I ask Al-Mighty God, who has given all the right and His existence, to guide our steps and to culminate our endeavour with success and to guide us to knowledge, which is our first and last goal in all that we pursue for.

Professor Maan Khalil Al-Omar

INITIAL THOUGHTS: FEMININE GENDER - STRUGGLE AGAINST LATENT VIOLENCE

The Keys to the Gender Field

Each sociology field has its main theoretical and procedural keys (concepts) that it uses in its research and studies. The keys of the family field, for example, are represented by upbringing, marriage, divorce, cellular family, extended family, family disintegration, family violence, spinsterhood, widow, etc. The keys of the crime field include but are not limited to delinquency, deviation, suicide, white collars crimes, administrative and financial corruption, addiction, terrorism, smuggling, fraud, and forging, while the major keys of the field of urban sociology represent migration, environmental pollution, crime-endemic areas, marginal cities, urban areas, and tin cities, etc.

Since the gender field is still a virgin topic in its overall presentation, its keys have not yet been classified or defined well. They are limited, and some of them have been borrowed from other fields of sociology. This book is, therefore, a sincere attempt to participate in the establishment of the roadmap of the gender field where the following can be labelled as its main keys: gender barometer, gender motivator, gender incubator, gender identity, the gender role, and the gender stratification. Before proceeding further, it is imperative to define the above keys to enable the doors opening of this very pristine topic so that its horizons can be featured and the course of its historical and its social events can be clarified, as follows: -

5

1. **Gender Barometer:** it is the criterion or the measure which is going to be devoted for the assessment of the inequality in the social life of most of the societies of the world at their various development stages for the two poles; feminine (woman) and masculine (man). Often the feminine is stripped from most of her rights and loading her multiple varied burdens that are more than her capacity. Such abstraction and downgrading make her positioned into the lower reaches of the society stratification, and its hierarchy makes her "voice" inaudible and her decision impermissible. The items of the barometer are: -

A. Her servitude in return for her liberation; that is, her enslavement via the restrictions and the controls of male power (paternalistic), the Indian "mano" laws, and the principles of Confucianism in China. To achieve equality between the feminine and the masculine, it is necessary to free her from this enslavement, which deprived her of her rights.

B. Her fairness in carrying out periodic duties by letting the male participate in bearing them.

C. Equalising women's rights with men's rights in the family, work, wages, inheritance, and electoral voting.

D. Approximating the man's and woman's duties in family and work.

2. **Gender Motivator:** That is, the factors that provoke, motivate, or drive the rise of the feminine to deserve her rights, reduce her duties, lift her grievances and deal with her as the main pillar of the family and the good half of the society, and the trustworthy guardian to raise the current generation to be healthy, righteous, and productive in the future. The drives of the motivator depend on the social development degree and in general they are:

6

A. Preference of men on women in terms of interaction, reaction, attachment, relation, and rights.

B. Overloading her with the heavy burdens of daily and future family, cultural and social responsibility.

C. Deprivation of her from making decisions about herself, her family, and her future.

D. Exercising physical and verbal violence against her.

E. Stripping her of the family inheritance.

F. Preventing her from casting her vote in political and municipal elections.

G. Disrespecting her opinion on choosing her life partner.

These are the most prominent motives that make the feminine stand up and demand her lost and usurped rights.

3. Gender Incubator (Her Positioning): in which the feminine lives and works like the family and society, but they do not share tasks and responsibilities in a fair or equal manner with her. Enslavement "at work for a low wage that was out of proportion to her effort. Likewise, she is not allowed to have advanced and developed education but is restricted to elementary and primary education so that she is left to work in the nursery, doing nursing, service, and social care more than engineering, advanced technology, medicine, and communications. The situation is manifested in the disbursement of salaries and wages as she is paid less than the man who works with her at the same level and efficiency.

In brief, these three keys work in a prominent way in studying the role and position of the feminine and the masculine in social life. Their relationship rises and falls according to the development of society and its use of science and technology. As society advances in these tracks, the need for femininity increases and the items of the barometer rise in its tube, the items of the motivator are manifested, and the doors of the incubator are opened, and vice versa.

However, the genesis formation of the gender does not mean rebellion, revolution, or uprising of the feminine against the masculine, because they are both subject to restrictions beyond their control, such as inherited cultural controls, Manichaeism and gender laws, Chinese Confucian principles, and the way of life of the society (agricultural or feudal). It is a social condition pushed by the motivator into the barometer to express interaction and intersection, attraction and contestation of their interests and rights in each phase of the social change movement, which is subject to the two poles of change (abandonment and adoption) in both the feminine and the masculine.

4. **Gender Identity:** Social culture determines the content of gender identity through the upbringing of the family, peer group and school of the individual according to its biological sex according to the conditions and requirements of social culture for the role of the female or male.

5. **Sexual Identity:** It is the reflective image of the correspondence of biological sex (male or female) with gender behaviour specific to the biological gender. The features of this identity appear in the period of adolescence or the sexual puberty period.

6. **Sexual Dualism (Hermaphroditism):** It includes physical characteristics that are not clearly masculine or feminine. They are not limited to visible sexual characteristics such as the genitals, but rather features within the body such as hormones and genetic materials.

7. **The Transsexual:** It is the individual who has been converted during surgery for his genitals. He is originally male or female, but he psychologically believes that he

8

belongs to the opposite sex, so he is transferred according to surgery for his genitals.

8. Intersex: It refers to the intercourse between the two sexes in which the male and female characteristics overlap.

9. The Transgender Converted: Those who have acquired a social role in contradiction to their biological sex are called "third type gender".

10. Gender Stratification: It means the gradual distribution of social and economic resources on a scale that reveals the biological differences associated with the qualitative differences (gender). Its sources are wages, education, type of work inside the home, participation in family, political and economic decisions, and political positions, but not class regression or ethnic or religious, partisan, or regional affiliation.

11. The Occupational Gap: The gap or the widening difference between a woman's work and a man's work where the man is appointed to a higher professional position than the woman's position though both have the same qualification, experience, and professional competencies.

12. The Wage Gap: The gap or the widening difference between the paid wages to the men and the women who occupy the same position on the professional ladder and hold the same qualifications, experience, and professional competencies.

13. Feminine: She is the new-born who was brought up and interacted within a different style from that used with a new-born male. She is exposed to more restraint in her behaviour and thought than on her male brother, while they show less interest in her desires, ambitions, and hobbies. She is in charge more of housekeeping and is less liberal in her behaviour than her male brother though both are of the same parents, society, culture, and religion. This is not because of their biological differences but due to what was established by society, religion, and social culture.

14. Her Enslavement: Taking the feminine as a slave for his service to satisfy his selfish interests, ambitions, and desires. He treats her in rough with severe cruelty and exercises all types of humiliation, submission, and contempt against her and then considers her a dishonour.

15. Her Struggle: The feminine resistance against her enslavement by society, culture, religion, and government. She is confronting all of them to stop her enslavement through her social, economic, and political struggles in life.

16. The Spinsterhood: The feminine who prolonged her celibacy and did not marry. She stayed at her parents' house for a long time after passing the age of marriage without getting married.

17. Rape Her: The man, society, culture, religion, and government stripping the legitimate rights of the feminine woman as a wife, mother, citizen, and nanny by oppression and injustice, imposing their authority over her while using violence on her to obtain their need from her against her will.

18. Supporting: In the sense of defending the rights usurped from the feminine and supporting her right in her struggle against the rapist and the enslaver (man, society, culture, and government).

19. The Victim: The feminine who is subject to the usurpation of her legitimate rights by force and injustice by the man, society, culture, and government to convert her into prey.

20. Liberation: Eliminating injustice, persecution, and slavery, and take her out of the circle of servitude to set her free from the restrictions and pressures of enslavement of men, society, culture, government and religion, and ridding her of them in order to be free and independent.

21. Becoming: That is, transferring from one state to another to reach what she wants to end up with clearly.

22. The Marital Gap: A high rate of illegal sexual intercourse between a man and a woman outside the marital relationship in exchange for a low rate of legal marriage.

23. Single Parent Families: Families that include the mother only with her children or only the father with his children.

24. Total Slavery: The collective and not the individual slavery practised by society, culture, religion, and government, which is considered a legitimate customary state.

25. Situational Slavery: Individual and factional slavery imposed by emerging global conditions such as globalisation or global trade or the collapse of a political system.

26. The Glass Ceiling: The high-profile professions and the higher positions that are monitored by men in official organisations. Feminine is not allowed to reach them as occupying such positions is considered as an exceed of her limits.

27. The Glass Ladder: That is, a self-moving elevator without human effort used by the man to reach the highest professional ranks in the major official organisations without allowing the feminine to use it in the civilised, technologically advanced, and capitalist countries.

28. The Eunuch: He is a male whose genitals have been removed to perform female acts. He exercises non-male roles and is not stigmatised by shameful or contemptuous stigmas but rather by the ruling elite and the affluent class.

29. The Improvised One: She is a female who performs roles that are not feminine but rather masculine. She wears men's clothes and adorns the male dress and deals with females in a masculine style.

30. The Third Type of Gender (Feminine): This is a male by biological origin and works as a prostitute in the practice of sodomy in addition to his work in domestic services. He wears distinctive clothes different from those of normal men and has his hair cut in a special style that does not resemble men's haircuts.

31. Divorce Without Guilt: A divorce in which no partner blames the other for a sin he committed or guilt he conducted. Rather it is a demand made by both of them.

32. Pink Work: Any non-manual work with elementary skill and an undifferentiated position, such as clerical jobs, a section to receive customers or a section of customer requests in restaurants and hotels.

33. Conditional Works: It is full-time work but for a limited time and used when there is a need or demand for these unfixed jobs.

34. The Crushed Feminine: She is the Soviet Union female whose roles and positions in society have been crushed between the jaws of a grinding mill. The first was the downfall of a political system that was supporting and elevating her, while the second was the overwhelming chaos that followed the fall of the political system and the advent of a new regime contrary to it. She has been raped by several perpetrators who have appeared with the new regime represented by employers and international mafias that specialised in smuggling and the trading of the white slave. Neither the government nor women's organisations or partisan organisations extricated and protected her from the grinding action between these two mighty jaws. A gender congruence has therefore occurred with biological differences where she was exposed to injustice, oppression and poverty and became a victim that has been crushed between political and economic chaos and family burdens.

35. The Temporary Commodity in Japan: The single feminine who is viewed by the Japanese cultural belief as an emergency and temporary commodity until her marriage, after which she leaves the work. Therefore, she has no real effect on the professional and economic life as much as she has on the Japanese family.

36. Patriotic Sacrificed Woman: This is the Indian woman whom Prime Minister Indira Gandhi featured as the "Mother of India" as a national symbol imbued with national history and struggle against British colonialism, backwardness, and illiteracy.

37. The Wise Feminine: She is the Indonesian wife who organised her gender and made it an influential force on the Indonesian government and society in not disputing or opposing the teachings of the Islamic religion in marrying more than one wife at one time. Instead, she imposed her decision on the government to not appoint an employee married to more than one wife in its departments. The government responded to such a decision, and she was wise as the religious and political system responded positively to her.

38. The Submissive Feminine: She is the Latin feminine in Latin American countries who has been subjected to traditional teachings of the Roman Catholic community and the domination of the manly feudal system over there. She is forced to kneel to them because she cannot resist them as they represent strict moral forces.

39. The Double Veiled Feminine: She is the Muslim woman who used the first veil as an expression of national solidarity against the Shah's regime in Iran, and the second veil expresses the oppression and domination imposed on her by the Islamists of the Taliban in Afghanistan and the Shiites in Iran, Iraq, and the Houthis in Yemen.

40. Paper Equality: That is, the issuance of model laws on equal rights between women and men, but they are not implemented by the government onto by society as it happened in Israel, Japan, and India.

41. Ideal Equality: It was achieved in the Scandinavian countries in making feminine rights equal to those of men in education, work, popular representation, health care and cultural activities.

42. Matriarchy: The matriarchal system represents an ancient stage in time in which the power of the woman/mother prevailed in society and monopolised the economic and political leadership, as well as the religious authority. This corresponds to the patriarchal system that later replaced the authority of the mother. Although women are physiologically weaker than men, they have occupied high social positions in the family, society, and power. They also assumed a high spiritual position in an ancient historical stage in which liberal sexual relations prevailed where the children's affiliation to their mothers were higher as they belonged to the mother's line as it was impossible to determine the true father of the children.

Anthropologists have called this system matriarchal, meaning the power of women in society. Since the children at that stage were related to their mothers and there was no kinship system that defined sexual relations, the women were the only known parent with confidence and affirmation of the children. The women, therefore, enjoyed a great deal of respect and acquired high social and religious status.

Such a high status in the beginnings of human stability had been driven from nature because women were the first to settle in the land, and they were the ones who discovered the agriculture and domesticated animals, as well as the principle of land fertility mimicking the principle of women fertility. The women's power in society was, therefore, acquired and developed as their natural right.

Because of the woman's acquisition of spiritual significance, the religion has resulted and developed as a duty to return the bounty of giving birth. Therefore, the human being sanctified the earth just as he sanctified the female featuring her as an image and successor of the mother earth. The earth did not imitate the female, but the female did imitate the earth. She became sacred like the earth, and the religious respect and reverence became the basis of her authority, the rise of her religious and social standing, her state policy, and her administration of the religious rituals.

The female is the origin. She takes precedence over the man by her giving, and the man is the result of that giving. Naturally, the son is the future husband, who in turn fertilises a woman and becomes a father and so on. The kinship organisation finds its place in the arms of the women, and all social organisations have stemmed and developed from her. Thus, the mother's right become a natural right for her.

CHAPTER 1: GENDER – ITS CONCEPT, INCEPTION, ORIGIN, DIFFERENCE, AND STRATIFICATION

INITIATION
A. THE CONCEPT OF GENDER, ANCIENT AND MODERN
B. GENDER'S INCEPTION
C. GENDER'S ORIGIN
D. DISTINGUISH IT FROM SEX
E. GENDER'S EVOLUTION
F. GENDER'S STRATIFICATION

CHAPTER 1
GENDER – ITS CONCEPT, INCEPTION, ORIGIN, DIFFERENCE, AND STRATIFICATION

INITIATION

The issue of the sexual kind (gender) is subject to two influences that cannot be avoided, namely: the biological body and social culture, which make equality between them non-existent or impossible, regardless of intelligence, genius, temperament, and gust of each of them. In the light of these two variables, the man does not accept the woman to be equal to him, whereas the woman demands such equality as it gives her a preference in rights, duties, power, influence, work, and wages. This is the crux of their contention.

With the development of technical life and the change of societies, and their transformation from a historical stage to another, there were calls, demands, and women's movements to eliminate the injustice and prejudice which have afflicted their role in the family, society, work, education, and the like. The higher the level of education and the acquisition of scientific knowledge, the more women called for their equality with men. However, the biological and cultural obstacles (inherited values, customs, and norms) challenge them to obtain the same.

In this respect, it is clear that the theory of Essentialism is biased towards male as it states: "the advance of essence over existence", which is the antithesis of existence. According to this theory, the existing differences between the male and female are attributed to innate differences that cannot be skipped as they stem from physical (biological) differences inherent to each other in a natural way reflecting human nature.

17

It is appropriate to point out that the advanced social, psychological, and educational research on the sexuality of the sexes has confirmed in an intensive and focused way the rejection and refuting of the "Essentialism" in attributing the difference between the sexes to innate biological differences. At the same time, such research does not reject the role of biological characteristics in the development of gender, but it confirms that the difference between men and women is due to the socio cultural obstacles that emphasise the inequality between them more than the biological obstacles.

The development of social life and scientific and cultural advancement allowed the woman to utilise her desire, intelligence, and instinct, and hence brought her closer to the available opportunities to fulfil her objectives. Such advancement has also provided the woman with strong incentives to demand equality with men so that she can get rid of the restrictions of the traditional role imposed on her. But when this movement and the exit from the traditional controls have widely spread in developed societies, the existing differences between the sexes started to become ambiguous and lacked clarity. This is because the separation between men and women in the premovement stage was prominent and clear, where the preference of the role of men over women was the norm. In a post-movement stage, however, the gender seemed to become mixed and interwind, particularly when the society advanced and developed culturally and scientifically from the traditional, conservative, rural, nomadic, religious, and ethical stage. Such advancements have initiated an appreciable increase in society's need for women's jobs outside their homes in official and scientific institutions, organisations, and associations. Therefore, she has been pulled out from her domestic, educational, and marital duties to become

18

financially, scientifically, and professionally independent, which in return freed her from the restrictions of her traditional role in the family and the society.

A. <u>THE CONCEPT OF GENDER, ANCIENT AND MODERN</u>

The term gender is used to express the social, cultural, and psychological qualities of a person (male or female) associated with masculinity (masculine) and femininity (feminine). These expressions have been defined and described by the society in which we live and are carried in our thinking. In this sense, the behaviour of the female or the male is not determined by our own thinking. Instead, it is created, featured, and defined by society and our minds are only vehicles to carry such a description as given by society. For example, in Eastern societies, the traditional meaning of the male is the masculinity concept whose contents have been formulated by the society and taught by family and companionship (friendship) throughout the generations. He has the following features:

1. strong and brave, able to defend himself.
2. firm and assertive in his opinions, words, and ideas (not hesitating about that).
3. rational rather than emotional.
4. tends to move and do group sports rather than individual activities.
5. has difficulty expressing his emotions and love (that is, he stutters and gets confused).
6. is brave and has high dignity and high stature of generosity.
7. supports friendships and kinship relationships.

As for the social meaning of the word female in eastern society, which is reflected in the minds of orientalists, it refers to the following:

She:

1. is beautiful, lovely and has great taste.
2. is emotional, affectionate, and friendly, who loves to help others.
3. is patient, forgiving and generous.
4. is smart, but her affection overrides her intelligence.
5. is talkative, likes to debate and chat with friends and people.
6. loves to do housekeeping and making food.
7. puts her family before her friends in her love relationship and friends after her relatives.

This is very interesting as it shows the difference between the societies depending on their advancement. While Eastern society attributes the difference between the male and female to the biological difference, which determines the sex (gender), Western society has the opposite view as it believes that gender determines biological differences. In the beginning, the biological and gender determinants are the same, and both represent a natural state in that the biological difference is a clear and undeniable difference, as the female has a womb and breast and gives birth. Accordingly, she is tender and emotional and loves children and household chores, while the man has muscles and genitals that differ from the female, so he is strong and competitive, violent, and more rational than emotional.

Through the family upbringing, the family teaches the new-born his role as specified by society, and the mother cannot override or manipulate those teachings. If the new-born is a female, she will be labelled as female, and the mother does not dare to interact with her as a male or name her a boy and buy her clothes and toys for male children, and the same is the case with male new-borns. Therefore, the parents are the link between the socio-cultural determinants and the new-born in the assignment of the social role to her or him. Deviation from cultural determinants faces criticism, rejection and reprimand by the family, relatives, neighbours, and acquaintances. Harold Garfinkel, 1967, stated that the sex is male and female, and there is no third sex among them, and they remain that way until they die. Neither the boy turns into a girl, nor the latter changes into a boy, but the social structure determines the gender identity of the male and the female and does not confuse them. A child at the age of eight months begins to realise his gender as he realises the difference of his sex through his haircut, clothes and name.

The term gender began as an abstract linguistic term, then its use evolved into a theory and ideology, where the first stage began with the definition of gender as a linguistic term used to classify nouns, pronouns, and adjectives, or as a verb based on gender-related characteristics in some languages and in purely linguistic forms. Then a second trend emerged for defining gender as: "It refers to characteristics related to men and women that are socially constructed in exchange for characteristics that are biologically based (such as reproduction).

The issue of separating the biological and social dimensions was not addressed. Rather, the priority of the leaders of the feminist movement was to work to demolish the prevailing concept at the time, which is that the biological, genetic characteristics of both men XY and women XX are the only decisive factor in defining the roles that men and women play in society. Accordingly, gender was based on sex, and thus it is shaped biologically more than socially. During the second phase of its use, the term crossed the boundaries of the interconnectedness between the terms sex and gender, as the radical trend of the Radical Feminism movement began to present a new definition of gender that distinguishes it from the word sex. It came to be called the role and position of both men and women that are socially formed and are therefore subject to change. The concept of gender has become a new trend in women's studies. Some believe that it was proposed to replace pre-existing concepts such as Feminism or Womanism, which referred to the struggle of women to bridge inequalities between them and men. Gender is a departure from the sacred goal pursued by women in their struggle against the hegemony of the patriarchal society. Others believe that the concept of gender is devoid of descent and has no origin or history, and whatever the case, the addition that distinguishes gender studies is that it is directed at both men and women in order to eliminate the qualitative gap between them.

The term (gender) is now the most common one in feminist literature, which refers to the specific characteristics, the mutual recognition and acceptance of the roles of men and women within society. Focusing on gender rather than focusing on women is closely related to the vision that says: The problems of women are not primarily due to the biological differences between them and men, but to a greater extent to social obstacles and cultural, historical, and religious differences. Therefore, the gender division according to the concept of "gender" is not a biological division. Rather, it is based on the broad general context within which the social division of work takes place. Gender also means a set of behaviours and concepts related to females and males that are created and spread by society and that all cultural societies transform biological differences between females and males into a set of concepts about discrimination and activities that are considered appropriate.

Gender philosophy also sees the divisions and roles assigned to men and women, as well as the differences between them from the culture and prevailing ideas of society that can be changed and cancelled completely so that women can play the roles of men, and men can play the roles of women. This means that gender philosophy repudiates the influence of differences in innate biology in determining the roles of men and women.

In sum, gender philosophy seeks to achieve complete similarity between male and female, and refuses to acknowledge the existence of differences, and rejects divisions even that can be based on the origin of creation and innateness. This philosophy does not accept equality that considers the differences between the sexes but calls for the similarity between them in everything. Gender has a social and historical dimension, so gender should be perceived not only as a fixed characteristic of individuals but as part of a continuous process by what actors often construct in contradictory ways, just as gender is a cultural discourse, and as such, it is subject to continuous struggle and practice.

De Laurelitz also went on to say that the concept of gender is a social and cultural construct as well and that this is a continuous historical process that is managed in all societal institutions every day of life, the media, schools, families, courts etc. She also emphasised that the concept of gender technology is a socio-cultural and semantic system and a representation system that determines the meaning of individuals in society by following them.

Her Thoughts and Opinions

Van Zoonen summarised that the media is the only and continuous site for the practice of gender, and it can be seen as a social technology for gender, remodelling, readjusting, rebuilding, production, training, and contradictory cultural aspects of difference in sex.

Gender Definition in the British Encyclopaedia, Gender Identity

It is the human feeling of himself as a male or female, but there are cases in which the human feeling is not related to its organic characteristics, and there is no compatibility between the organic characteristics and his gender identity, the gender identity is not fixed by birth, but rather psychological and social factors affect it by forming the nucleus of gender identity and change and expand by the influence of social factors as the child grows.

Defining Gender by World Health Organization

It is a term that is used to describe the characteristics that men and women carry as complex social characteristics that have nothing to do with organic differences.

Definition of Gender in the United Nations Document

Chapter Five, Paragraph 2, 15 defines the objectives of the document as follows: "To better support the family and consolidate its stability, taking into account the multiplicity of its patterns."

Gender and Women: the process of realising the meaning of gender requires that we not only listen to women. Focusing on women may be part of the problem, as men and women can suffer from a lack of empowerment. There are many transformational projects that bring about a radical change and rarely pay attention to gender or support a current situation that is not justified. Negotiating structural change with women and men requires time and courage, which makes the task unattractive for donor countries and many NGOs. The process of linking this development with a feminist agenda imposed by the West has imposed hostility towards addressing structural change in gender relations.

Gender and Sexuality

Gender, an English word that descends from Latin origin, has meaning in the linguistic framework Genus in terms of masculinity and femininity, but the true synonym for gender is the social sex, social kind, or social role.

The sex aspect is characterised by a minimum of biological factors that make us distinguish a certain body as a woman's body or that of a man.

As for gender, it is the social, psychological, or cultural story of the body, meaning that it is the social or psychological view of sexual difference, and it is a group of culturally specific characteristics. If we go back to the definition of (Oakley), a professor of anthropology who introduced this term to sociology, we will find that she translates the word sex into biological form, that is, the biological category in terms of whether is it male or female. In contrast, the word gender refers to parallel and socially unequal divisions of masculinity and femininity. In this way, gender refers to a set of behaviours and concepts related to females and males that are created and spread by society.

Symmetry and Equality

Gender equality is a fundamental human right, and society alone can guarantee that all women and men realise and benefit from this right.

Equality: Equity for women in rights, duties, and life opportunities in terms of education, services and jobs that lead them to decision-making positions.

Symmetry: It is the product of the gender theory, which the feminist gender adopts as its basis, namely the abolition of all-natural or specific differences in the life roles between men and women, and the claim that any difference in characteristics and roles is made by society.

Despite the recognition of the lack of equality between men and women, and the attempt to work towards equality between the sexes, ideas about what equality means and how to reach it are still the subject of widespread controversy and permanent conflict. However, by analysing the discourses that deal with equality and symmetry, it is revealed that the difference between the two is not clear.

Gender and Development

There are international efforts to raise the economic level of the family and to ensure that woman has an income to help raise her level and to support her role within the family and society. Yet, it does not necessarily mean that the woman is the decision-maker within the family because she has money, as the ties have become more complex.

Equality in social type (gender) is a core issue in development and necessary to eliminate poverty permanently and effectively, as indicated by the World Bank strategy.

Gender, Theory, and Feminism

The women's liberation movement, or what is referred to as the first wave of feminism, began in 1830 and continued until the year 1920 AD. The focus of the participants in it was on obtaining civil rights for women in their societies. That is why the trend of the movement at that time was a liberal one that sought to emphasise equality, while the second wave of feminism was dated around 1963 CE, and this stage was characterised by the spread of awareness-raising groups in England or France and America, as well as the gradual inclusion of feminist issues in academic institutions.

26

The starting point for feminist thought assumed that all women have common experiences, which are based on the oppression they are subjected to in different societies due to gender. Over time, a pivotal shift occurred in the general attitudes and feminist concepts when the American black fighter Sojourner Truth challenged nineteenth-century feminists and rebuked them for ignoring the problems and concerns of black women. She said, "Am I not a woman also?". This phrase became a recurring slogan in the writings of black feminist critics, and groups of women questioned the assumption that all women have common experiences of oppression. In 1972 AD, the Black Feminist Manifesto was issued by a group of feminists who met in the city of Boston and criticised the American feminism that expressed the interests of the middle class of white women and had adopted the idea that political positions that sought to bring about radical changes in society stemmed mainly from identity.

The decade of nineties, however, witnessed a remarkable shift in the assumptions on which identity was based, as feminist research went beyond the stage of describing the specific positions of identity politics and entered a phase of critical engagement with the complexities resulting from power, struggles, and the vague boundaries of identities in the postmodern context.

In continuation of the idea of the differences that exist between feminist projects in different countries, Mohanty says that the feminist policies of non-western feminists take upon themselves to confront the racial and colonial historical legacies, and they also address the role those professional systems play in reducing the opportunities available to them on the level of daily life.

These critical contributions reinforce the recognition of the existence of multiple feminist movements, not one feminist movement, by considering the implications of differences in determining priorities for feminist action. It is worth noting that a large number of feminist researchers are working on crystallising concepts and terms that help build bridges across cultures and languages while respecting differences and forms of discrimination. In this context, many critical attempts have been made to formulate the appropriate term to express interlocking and complex relationships at the same time, so we find the concept of multiple feminism as multicultural feminism, multinational feminism, or feminism movements.

Thus, feminist thought represents multiple challenges in the twenty-first century, represented by the prevalence of conservative trends in the world and the preceding period of the revolutionary liberation tide that reached its peak in the sixties of the twentieth century, which was a fruitful cradle for national liberation movements in the third world countries, and social liberation movements such as the feminist movement in the West. Then came the events of September 11, 2001, which provided the historic opportunity for conservative governments to reduce the civil rights of citizens and narrow the space for freedoms available in public and private spheres.

Feminist thought has succeeded in becoming an integral part of the cognitive fabric in academic institutions in the world, and on this basis, it is possible to engage with and review feminist thought, but it is not easy to ignore it.

Gender and Post-Feminism

More than a hundred years after the start of the feminist movement, the word "gender" in the 1980s began to find its way as one of the most prominent terms used in the dictionary of feminist movements, and this term appeared in the United States of America and then moved to Western Europe in 1988. This expression was not the only renewal in the feminist discourse, as the so-called "post-feminism" has finally emerged as a framework for new theses and demands, or different readings for women's demands, and in search of a new definition of the concepts of femininity and masculinity after women have acquired the right to vote and work, and to enjoy her rights as a citizen in many countries of the world. [http://www.alnoor.se]

B. <u>GENDER'S INCEPTION</u>

The issue of gender has come within the framework of a global agenda that talks about human rights, women, and children since the collapse of bipolarity. There is an indication that the term gender began to appear for the first time in the West in the early seventies in development studies. It was used as a contrast to the expression of women. It was then moved to the Eastern countries in the second half of the eighties. Since then, it has become known in the debate about development frameworks through the literature of international organisations working in the fields of development which consider the issue of social type (gender) as a Western feminist philosophy that expresses the crisis of Western thought in the post-incident stage. The literature indicates that the term "gender" was used for the first time by "Anne Oakley" and her co-authors wrote in the 1970s to describe the socially defined characteristics of men and women as opposed to those biologically determined.

However, some believe that the use of the term and its spread in international literature was during the eighties of the last century, a period characterised by intense discussions about the impact of structural adjustment

29

policies on the status of women. Actually, the use of the term "gender" is due to the International Labour Organization, which used it to refer to relations. It attributed the differences between men and women to the difference between societies and cultures, which are subject to change all the time.

As a general trend, the term refers to the distinction between males and females based on the social role of each of them as they are influenced by the prevailing values and customs. They look to this term as if it refers to the cultural stereotypes of masculinity and femininity, which in turn indicates that the prevailing cultures are the ones that bring about the change in the idea of the female about herself and her role in society and vice versa. Thus, the stereotypical thoughts are what subject women to injustice, low status, and not obtaining their rights. At the same time, the issue of inequality is the basis of the international debate about women's issues, which has necessitated allocating many studies and research to find out why the issue of discrimination and inequality exists so far. Since women are the sacrificial party in the life process at all levels, it was inevitable that a so-called study of the status of women appeared, which turned to the study of women's issues and ended with the need for the advancement of women as they represent half of the world's population.

The Convention on the Elimination of All Forms of Discrimination Against Women at the end of 1979, which was ratified by most countries of the world in 1981, aimed to ensure that women obtain equal rights with men in all fields. The inclusion of a separate chapter on equality, gender, equity, and women's empowerment in the International Conference of Population and Development (ICPD) held in Cairo in 1994 is evidence of recognising the importance of gender-based analysis. That is right because the old approach did not separate women from development and considered both as an entry to point for eliminating discrimination against women. This is what was meant by many studies, especially accompanying the International Women's Conference in Beijing in 1995 CE. However, the modern analysis tool is known as gender appeared, and the women labelling in development was replaced by the social type, gender. This is a serious attempt to formulate a global theory - about the conditions of gender inequality. [Http://www.alnoor.se]

C. __GENDER'S ORIGIN__

In order to understand the meaning and dimensions of the term gender (social type), it is necessary to be familiar with the history of the feminine movements to which the term is associated. It is also important to explain the stages that these movements went through from the beginning of their appearance on the political, social, and cultural stage until they reached their current form. Meanwhile, their known claims and how their narratives have developed and affected by the concepts that prevailed in those stages are looked at.

Two different calls have been appeared and adopted by two types of women movements. The first call was wise and concerned with women's liberation and fairness. It was adopted by the moderate women movements around the world. The second call, however, has an extremist tendency and concerned the extreme feminism that crystallised in the West in the 1960s and was imitated by a small minority of oriental women. The difference between these two calls, the two movements, and their philosophy and demands is like the difference between reason and madness!

The most issue that the calls and movements for women liberation aspired to; was to be fir with her from the social and historical injustice that befell her and from which she suffered from. They do not want to have a separation between man and woman. On the contrary, they insist on preserving the instinctive distinction between femininity and masculinity. Such a distinction is extended to the differentiation and integration of work in the family and society that achieves the equality of the two complementary rifts between men and women. At the same time, it maintains the longing of each sex for the other, its need for it, and enjoying each other by their differentiation without which neither sex will be happy in this life. These movements believe that all this can be achieved without declaring war on religion or on the instinct that God created people as males and females ... and also without declaring war against men.

As for the extreme feminism (or radical feminism) that crystallised in the sixties of the twentieth century, it is defined as: "An intellectual, political and social movement with multiple ideas and streams, which appeared in the late sixties. It is seeking social and cultural change and changing the building of relations between the sexes in order to reach absolute equality as a strategic goal. Its theories differ; its objectives and analyses are according to the cognitive principles it adopts; its ideas are characterised by extremism and perversion, and it adopts the conflict and hostility of the sexes. Its aim is to provide new readings on religion, language, history, culture, and gender relations. These philosophies, ideas, and claims pervaded in an unusual way in Western societies during the last three decades of the twentieth century.

These western feminine movements succeeded in putting pressure on Western religious institutions that betrayed their message until, in 1994, they issued a new edition of the Old and New Testaments, called the Corrected Edition, in which terminology and masculine pronouns were changed and transformed into neutral pronouns.

I.   The Trends of The Feminine Movement and Their Influence on Philosophical Schools

1.   **Liberal Feminism Movement:** Liberalism can be launched on any feminist movement that seeks to improve the status of women in legal terms, health, education, and political participation, and to improve the standard of living of women with a clear demand of their legitimate rights without introducing extremist concepts. No anti-women movements appeared against the liberal feminism movement because what it called for was an agreed-upon collective destiny.

2.   **The Communist Feminine Movement:** It adopts the following ideas:

i.   The woman is a human being, equal to the man and has all rights of the man. She must be free in all of her choices, and her femininity does not prevent her from anything that a man can do.

ii.   The freedom of a woman requires that she be free in her sexual relationship with men, and marriage does not prevent her from that because she is not the individual property of a man. So, after communism abolished individual ownership of things, will it go back and accept it for persons?

iii.   The need to create the appropriate environment and opportunities to empower women economically. This would remove them from the home to be employed and become productive and ridding them of the duties of the home and the husband and what were called the stereotypical and traditional roles that could hinder this matter. For this, collective restaurants and nurseries and public washing machines were established while raising children was considered as the state responsibility rather than of women. Lenin called collective restaurants and other nurseries and kindergartens as buds of communism that did not need anything of pomp and grandeur. They would, in reality, liberate women, reduce or erase inequality between them and men, and respond to their role in social production and public life.

3. **Existential Feminism:** Existentialism is the philosophy of personal and individual experiences, the philosophy of doubt and rejection before acceptance and certainty, and among the pioneers of this philosophy are Jean-Paul Sartre and his lover, Simone de Beauvoir, the author of the book (The Other Sex), which adopts sceptical ideas. In this book, the most important part is: The reason, the profound thing that restricted women to domestic work at the beginning of history and prevented them from contributing to the reconstruction of the world, is their enslavement by the reproduction function. Simone says about the role of upbringing in creating the status of a woman, "A human is not born as a woman but becomes so." She proceeds: "A woman's behaviour is not imposed by her hormones or the formation of her brain, but rather is a result of her condition." Finally, she encourages women for rejection, revolution and rebellion against this reality and calls for, "A world in which men and women are equal ... women will work, educated, and trained just like men, under the same conditions, and with the same wages, and customs will establish lustful freedom, but sex enjoyment will not be

a wage-paid service, and the woman will be obligated to secure another source of livelihood, and marriage will be based on a free association that the spouses can cancel whenever they want, and motherhood will be free in which birth control is allowed. "

4. **Radical or Gender Feminism:** Radicalism can be considered as a tendency and method of approaching and treating rather than being a philosophical school. It was characterised by unreality, distance from the gradual, excessive bias towards women without regard to the social context, and interests above men and women. It has demanded a radical change in the total of gender relations within the family and in society alike, with the demise and eradication of patriarchal authority to reach absolute equality and the supremacy of gender relations in society or what is called genderization of society.

II. The Philosophical Environment in Which Femininity Was Raised

In the following section, the most important principles and ideas that have influenced Western thought since the emergence of the Renaissance, Enlightenment-era, then modernity and beyond, and consequently affected feminism as a nascent part of this intellectual system are given:

1. **Secularism:** it means the primacy of the human mind over the divine transmission and the rejection of religion as a supreme reference to cut in matters and return to it upon disagreement. Rather, the matter went beyond that to atheism and the total denial of the Creator and other ideas. It seems that this was a natural result of the church and its practices, which insisted on presenting crooked human ideas in the name of the Christian religion. Many scientific discoveries have created a state of suspicion in religion and

the people trying to forge their way away from God and religion, so what is known as secularism and secularism has occurred and the exclusion of religion from life. Religion, therefore, has lost its reference, dominance, and authority in defining good and evil, truth, falsehood, virtue, and vice.

The feminine movement has been affected, like other movements, by the mentioned reasons for the orientation to secularism. It was also encouraged by matters related to the inferior and bad religious view of women and their rights in the two prevailing religions in the West, Christianity and Judaism after they were affected by distortion and human change.

2. **Rationalism:** It is the lineage of secularism and its essential or central philosophy and a natural result of it because, after the rejection of religion as a reference and source of knowledge, belief and legislation, there must be an alternative. The contemporary Western world in all its fields must have left important and fundamental effects on the reality of women and the feminism movement upon which the feminine philosophy depends. However, with its extremist extensions, it was a disastrous affliction on woman, as it degraded her status, as will be described below.

3. **Materialism:** It came to the surface in various forms after the Renaissance, such as the rejection of the unseen and everything that does not enter the circle of the senses, including people's attachment to their world, their benefits, and the withering of the spiritual, faith and emotional side of people. The matter worsened in the philosophies of what was called post-modernism.

This tendency had an impact on the feminist movement and the quality of those demands that stemmed from reality. It was a harsh reality for women that did not secure their living except after wasting their femininity and exhausting their energies, and in many cases, they were sexually exploited by the employer and enslaved in another way. It led to the spread of prostitution and then the white slave trade and the sale of women and girls in the market of slavery and prostitution.

4. **Individualism:** it is the glorification of the individual as a single entity and considers himself as the centre and the scale of all things within the scope of competition and collision with others.

Secularism and rationality were the reason for establishing individualism in the human being and its pivot around himself, even in the field of law and rights. The liberal formulation of the human rights idea in the West looks at the individual as if he was independent of the group in his original conception from the beginning as an individual. Then he entered the group conceding some of his rights to protect his remaining rights. This is how the idea of rights appeared in an individual conception. Individualism is one of the basic premises of femininity, which emphasises the individuality of the woman, stripping her from the social context, highlighting her as the equals of man without linking her to the family, society, or children.

5. **Utilitarianism and Hedonism:** This tendency is a feature of the individual and Western society, and it is a natural result of materialism and individualism. It is an ancient tendency in Western philosophical thought and goes back to centuries BC according to the Greek philosopher (Epicurus) who called that good is pleasant, and any act is good in the measure that it brings us pleasure.

Then came the philosophy of pragmatism, which became an American religion that affirms; that the right or wrong of any idea lies in the extent to which it realises benefit in practice when trying it out. In the postmodern period (Michel

Foucault) said: "Pleasure constitutes an end in itself. For fun, for morals, or for any scientific fact. "

In these atmospheres, the female cries also rose with scepticism about moral standards (norms), the woman's right to own her body, to refuse childbearing, breastfeeding and motherhood, the woman's right not to raise and care for her children (as will be detailed later), and the right of the woman in releasing her sexual desires, free love, and even homosexuality and same sex marriage.

6. **Absurdism and Scepticism:** (Charles Frankel) mentions: "In modern culture, everything is relative and there is nothing absolute. We do not have primary principles, no final values, no firm beliefs that are indissoluble, and no belief in the existence of a teleological meaning of life."

This rejectionist scepticism was embodied in the so-called postmodern period, where (Michel Foucault) states: "The work of thought is to make everything that is well established into trouble." Thus, extremism reached its peak when the demolition of the established became important for thought and philosophy and a fundamental act for it, regardless of the type of that well-established concept.

The feminine movement has also adopted these concepts and has been affected by these sceptical and rebellious tendencies in its various sects, to varying degrees of course, and this influence led some of these streams to summarise their principles in sentences such as:

    a. Death of metaphysic
    b. Death of man
    c. Death of history

When the female radical stream arose, it arose in the light of these concepts and questioned all existing sources of knowledge: (religion + social and psychological theories + law ...) and considered it as masculine biased, and questioned the prevailing moral systems, values and customs and considered them backwards, outdated and in need of radical changes. It questioned the language and considered it biased that needed to be reformulated and called for the reconstruction of language. Even the biological nature of women was denied, questioned, and linked to the cultural environment and upbringing rather than to the reality of the nature of women and their creation in a specific way. Motherhood as a natural function for women and the family as an essential institution for life and gender relations have also been questioned as it will be detailed.

7. **Conflict:** since its first inception in the time of Greece the western thought was based on the principle of conflict, lack of harmony and creating contradictions between things instead of realising complementarities and similarities. It is built on the fact that the dichotomies in the world have no room for coexistence and complementarity, but rather the struggle must be manifested in order for one to survive, which must be for the fittest and the strongest.

It was devoted to the situation of the woman in the West, so her rights were applied in confrontation with the man as if the gain came from the struggle against him rather than the cooperation with him even in the marital relationship. Therefore, many important family cooperation values were absent of this perception mainly; the idea of housing, affection, the joint building of the family as a social institution in which rights were generated by solidarity, and synergy between spouses without detracting from the rights of each other.

8. **Sexism:** within the scope of this aspect, sexual pleasure is made as a supreme goal. The roots of the gender

idea as pornography and sexual communion go back to the time of Greece and specifically to the ideas of (Plato) who stated for his republic: "The women of our warriors should be communal for all. Also, it is common so that the father does not know his son, nor the son knows his father." Some researchers say that (Plato) was a promoter of homosexuality or homosexual marriage, which was common in Greek society. Judaism came next to instate the fornication of the prophets. Christianity invented monasticism and considered sex as filth and an impurity unworthy of those who seek the sacred.

Communism, however, called for communal sex concepts and pornography, considering sexual acts in its doctrine as a very personal matter and easy to get. It is nothing more than a drink of water, as per Auguste Bebel, a German communist thinker who stated that satisfying the sexual instinct is a completely personal matter like the satisfaction of any other instinct, and no one should hold accountable to others.

In the 1960s, the sexual revolution started, and Western societies completely changed, as the son took his mistress to his father's house, the daughter accompanied her lover to her bedroom in front of her parents, the family disintegrated, and sexual relations outside marriage spread. It is due to the tyranny and predominance of this tendency and the female demands for civil marriage, the marginalisation of the family institution, the de-sacralisation of the marriage contract and the family bond, and the constant disregard for the chastity of women. All this is because it is part of the male culture that views women as a source of enjoyment and specific for men.

III. The Most Prominent and Most Dangerous Views of (Radical) Feminism

1. **Advocating Gender Enmity and Declaring War Against Men:** Femininity declared a brutal war against men and raised slogans such as (men are an enemy class) and (war between the sexes), and even reached the point of calling (to fight for a world without men).

These ideas were not just a verbal argument or an exchange of slogans, but rather their prominence in real practice in various forms, led first to a terrible deterioration in social relations between men and women, especially in sexual relations, and the family institution was attacked intensely as an institution of oppression and oppression. For women, there must be free association and sexual freedom. Rather, it goes beyond calling for homosexuality (lesbianism), as it is a possible appropriate form to get out of the control of the enemy man.

When it talks about empowering women, we should not forget that the feminine movement means empowering women in their struggle with men.

Usually, a question is asked in the gender training of women's and men's gatherings: What was the first moment in which you became aware that you were male or female? Another question is: When was your first realisation as a male or female that you have to do or not do things? Or, what are the things that are imposed on you because of your gender and hate to do, and the things that are imposed on the opposite sex and would you like to do!!

2. **Reconstruction of Language:** Contemporary feminism, in its endeavour to reformulate language, set off from the saying (Michel Foucault): "He who has power owns the language." Thus, they interpreted European languages and the texts of the Bible and questioned them

41

because they are (made by men). In order to prove what can be called male prejudice, the following words can be observed in the English language, which indicate a woman's subordination to man and the inability of her independent existence as a human being except through the man: a human (Hu-man), mankind (man-kind) even a woman (Wo-man). If the word "man" is omitted, the means of the woman will be lost in the language, analysing the word "Hi-story", which means the history of the man without the woman, and they demanded a reformulation of history to tell the story of the woman and is called (her-story).

The danger is not in reviewing certain words or inaccurately worded terms or writing texts that favour women with feminine pronouns, but the danger lies in the fact that the feminine tries to impose certain words and special and new terms expressing her vision of the world and her own thought about all the issues that we have raised (which are comprehensive and multifaceted). In this way, it wants to falsify human and introductory knowledge to establish a culture of its own, create new values and consecrate them through the linguistic shell and the interconnectedness that exists between the signifier and the signified.

This is what made the approach of cultural conquest and empowerment of foreign domination to replace the concepts of the nation with the concepts of the other that are marketed politically and academically so that the nation's mind and awareness can be occupied in preparation for the occupation of its buildings and the dispossession of its civilisation.

They demanded a reformulation of the language and a reformulation of the Bible and the pronouns in it. In this endeavour, women's movements contributed to encouraging the issuance of a new edition of the Old and New Testament

42

books called the politically corrected Bible in 1994, in which many terms and masculine pronouns were changed. Converting them into neutral pronouns is considered fanatic as it reduces the influence of words describing homosexuality for people.

When femininity introduces words such as 'gender' instead of a man and a woman to describe the relationship of the two sexes or the word 'partner' or 'spouse' instead of the husband, and the word 'feminism' to express the movement of women, and 'biological father' for father, and calls any intervention by parents in the interest of their children and their upbringing' patriarchy', and use 'empowerment' for provision of rights, marital obedience is called a power relation, and the concept of the family is expanded so that there is a traditional and an unconventional or non-stereotypical family. Specific to homosexuals or pornographic groups that live together, the word 'stereotyped roles' is used to describe the basic roles of men and women in the family, for what has changed is not letters and words, but contents, meanings, culture and thought.

The matter is more dangerous when it comes to drafting international covenants related to population, women, children and so on because after ratification, they become binding, and the words contained in them are interpreted according to the feminine lexicon. The authors of these texts are those who name things without their names in preparation for their permissibility, so they do not say abortion and killing the fetus, but rather say (A woman's right to choose) and more.

3. **Abolishing the Role of The Father in The Family by Rejecting (Parental Authority):** Patriarchy means: the rule of the absolute father within the family, and the whole decision is concentrated in his hand, and this is a concept specific to the West.

The Christian religion has further entrenched the concept and legitimised it through many ways, including emphasising the concept of God the Father and the Son (meaning the remembrance) and naming and likening the Lord (the Almighty) to the Father.

Patriarchy is linked to the reality of the founding of the time of the Greeks and Romans, and all this is headed by an influential, dominant father, whose powers include:

a. He has the right to get rid of a disabled, deformed, female, or unwanted child by immersing, strangling, or throwing monsters.

b. The head of the family is the only one who owns, and the rest of them are children, wives, slaves, horses, and furniture ... all of them are considered his property, and he is free to dispose of them.

c. The wife is stray in their eyes and is treated like a child or a minor.

d. After marriage, a woman enters into the religion of her husband and leaves her religion, her clan and everything that precedes her marriage, and bears the name of her husband, his clan, and his religion ...

The danger of the feminist movement adopting the slogan of anti (patriarchy) lies in:

a. Femininity did not stop at the limit of attacking the pre-Islamic patriarchal system but rather went beyond that to attack the family, its system, the origin of its formation, and questioning its usefulness.

b. This transcended to the rejection of any type of father's leadership of the family, considering it patriarchy, and in this context, I welcomed the family managed by the mother alone (Family Mother - only)

c. Influenced by the secular and Marxist movement, feminism also made this concept a comprehensive analytical framework. She spoke about patriarchy in religion and that it appeared to justify and establish patriarchy. The state is also considered an extension of patriarchy.

This anti-patriarchal literature contributed to creating a state of aversion and hostility to the father and sensitivity to accepting any of his directives and rebelling against him, and also contributed to the drafting of very harsh western laws preventing parents from disciplining their children, and this is a violation of the right of parents and depriving them of their right to raise children.

4. **Rejection of the Family and Marriage:** The Communists believe that the one who resorted to the woman in order to accept marriage is the economic factor, and the woman's need to live for herself and her children and this is what does not remain in the communist system, because all are taken over by the state, so the basis on which marriage and the family depend is dropped and the woman is freed from her restrictions.

We can summarise the matters that resulted from this call to annul the marriage and the family as follows:

a. A huge increase in the number of people living with others without a legal bond. In Britain, for example, the percentage of women who live with a man without an official bond increased from 8% in 1981 to 20% in 1988.

b. The large number of marital infidelities by the spouses and the accustomed people to it, so that it is neither considered a serious threat nor a crime, and this indicates that the family, even if it remains, is only formal.

c. Raising children with one of the parents, or the so-called single-parent family, and women - 9%.

d. A terrible increase in the rate of divorce: One of the most important indications of western feminist movements' rejection of marriage and the family was their relentless pursuit of overthrowing the Personal Status Law and the demand to facilitate it more and more to the extent that marriage and the family are only formal so that women can obtain a divorce and destroy the family more easily. It is a way, the shortest of which is the cost, and sometimes the complete conviction of the utility of demolishing the family in liberating women. The beginning of the sixties is the real date of the start of the family's collapse.

5. **A Woman's Ownership of Her Body:** The feminist movement, especially after the 1960s, called for the slogan that a woman owns her body, or your body is your own, and this dangerous call requires several things, including:

a. The advocacy of sexual pornography and among the problems left by this phenomenon:

Unmarried mothers, most of whom are in their teens.

The huge increase in illegal births or children of adultery. This is one of the difficult problems that exist in contemporary societies due to the large number of crimes that come from behind these children, as they raise a distorted generation that suffers from many psychological complexes and is raised on the hatred of others, darkness and cruelty, and not mercy, only rarely knows a way to their hearts, and they often become easy prey for gangs and networks of sex and crime regulation. Therefore, there are now two well-known global phenomena that these children form a great basis for; sexual trafficking or the sexual exploitation of children, and juvenile crimes and their violence and problems, and they teach them the arts of banditry and terrorism.

b. Refusing to have children.

c. Intense showing off and nakedness.

46

d. The most important problem that arises in the secular discourse is that it considers the veil backwardness and thus calls for removing the veil because its unpopularity is a path to progress, and from here, the veil comes outside the circle of exercising freedom, because it is backward, and there is no freedom to practice backwardness.

e. The woman's right to abort her fetus.

6. **The Permissibility of Abortion:** When Westerners considered that a woman owns her body, the incidence of illegal pregnancy increased, and it became a multifaceted and multidimensional problem, and instead of westerners thinking about treating the origin and root of the disease, they looked for solutions to its symptoms, as if adultery and pornography were an untouchable, constant origin of society. The constants of society do not change, and in their endeavour for a solution, they put forward several issues, including:

a. Facilitate access to contraceptives and lift the ban, provide them in universities and schools at symbolic or no prices, and enable teenage girls to obtain them.

b. Among the solutions that I have raised is the issue of sex education and making it a requirement of schools even at the primary level to introduce children to the safe sex process and methods of contraception.

c. However, it seems that this was not enough. Abortion was also presented as an acceptable and even necessary solution by feminist movements and those who supported them. Feminism called on governments to issue lenient legislation on the right to abortion.

Statistics indicate that about 40 to 60 million women in the world try to abort an unwanted fetus, which means killing 40 to 60 million fetuses.

The delay in some western countries or their reluctance to legalise abortion is not due to moral or religious reasons as much as it is due to their severe fear of population shortages, compared to poor developing countries that witness huge population increases that threaten the demographic future in the world from the point of view of the rich in the West. The evidence for this is not the support of these countries but rather their drafting of international covenants calling for family planning and population determination, whether by contraception, abortion, or other means. The goal is to reduce as much as possible the number of people in developing countries so that the poor do not crowd at the tables of the rich.

7. **Rejection of Motherhood and Childbearing:** Supporters of the feminism movement ask whether it is really a woman's duty to burden her with caring for children in addition to pregnancy and childbearing. The questions extended to the meaning of femininity itself, and about the fact that there are those distinctive organic differences for men and women, and whether it is possible. It is attributed to environmental and cultural factors, and thus it loses its biological basis, and it becomes social aspects that do not deserve all the attention that is raised around it, and this means that the new movement does not target anything less than the emergence of a new woman or a type of woman completely different from what humanity has known until now.

Only by abolishing both the physical and psychological responsibility of women in having children will the emancipation of women be achieved, Eisenstein H. says.

This female rejection of childbearing and motherhood comes in the context of a total and categorical rejection of the existence of any difference between male and female that

48

can be based on assigning a specific role to a woman or a man, and this is one of the convictions of the movement and upon which basic things are based.

In this context, feminism talks about the concept of gender to define and characterise the relationship between the sexes in order to avoid and marginalise the concepts of male and female, and to emphasise the aforementioned concept of rejecting any kind of discrimination between them or rejecting any kind of distribution of roles even within the family on the basis of sex. Feminism now seeks to generalise relations and the concept of gender, that is, it implements 'gender' or 'genderization' in all walks of life and the institutions of society, which is called the institutionalisation of gender or 'gender mainstreaming'.

8. **Homosexuality and Building A typical Family:** While this obscenity was individual and secret, since the sixties, it has become collective and public, and its people organised themselves into multiple organisations with multiple names to claim their rights or rights, both males known as gay and females known as lesbian and demanded two things:

a. Recognition of this act as a natural matter and viewing it as personal freedom, rather a special kind of cohabitation, and that it is a human right. Recognising it is considered a legal achievement and an addition to basic human freedoms (in their view and the view of those who support them).

b. Issue laws that recognise these as legitimate families who possess all the natural rights of the family.

With regard to feminine movements, it looks at the issue as:

a. A way for women to get rid of their subordination to men.

b. The woman is rid of the power and violence of the man. She should get rid of the problems of childbirth, childbearing, and motherhood.

c. Through the stop of giving birth, the woman proves that she can be independent of herself and completely dispense with the man in everything, and by this way, she proves her purity and absolute equality.

d. Lesbianism (also called sapphism) is a matter of native instinctual women have, as they claim.

e. To achieve this goal and provide such a community, the women's cell publications included principles such as urging unmarried women to remain unmarried, married women to leave their husbands, and warning women against sexual relations (with men), pregnancy, and the purchase of cosmetics.

And the matter developed after that, and the feminine escalated its tone and considered normal sexual relations (Hetero Sexual) something categorically rejected because it is imposed on women by the patriarchal authority (Patriarchy) because the woman can satisfy her desires through the woman as (Julia Kristeva) says. Still, the matter aggravated to the extent that lesbianism is considered a condition for a woman to be considered a supporter of a woman's cause or to be a true female when Adrienne Rich said in her article on legal sexual practice that if a woman wants to be a true feminine, she must be a lesbian. She must become a lesbian, and she should give up all thoughts that haunt her and make her feel gay, sick, and crazy just because she has sex with women instead of men.

To support this idea, the term gender equality has been included in order to ensure that gays get the same rights as normal or traditional, and this was recently evident in the decision of the United Nations Secretary-General in March

2004 that allowed gay married couples to obtain the same rights as traditional married couples in terms of inheritance, taxes, social insurance, etc. [https://www.maghress.com]

IV.   Distinguishing Gender from Sex

There is confusion, ambiguity, and lack of attention among many people about the use of the phrase gender. They regard it as sex, and they do not pay attention to the essential differences between them. The term "sex" means the biological difference between a female and a male, whereby the new-born receives his biological identity when he is born and is said to be a girl or a boy, and from here, the distinction between them begins.

As for gender: it is a cultural and social description that distinguishes between the female and the male sex on the basis of meanings, beliefs, norms and judgments associated with femininity and masculinity that have nothing to do with the biological structure. An example of this is that for many individuals, masculinity is associated with: aggression, independence, lack of shyness, boldness and lack of affection, while femininity is usually thought of as being affectionate, nostalgic and dependent on the man in her life.

Understanding these differences between gender and sex is very important from a sociological perspective because many people think that sexual differences are the basis for gender. However, that is not the reality. For example, the male child is expected to be self-assured, reliant and strong, to defend him all by himself. These determinants and specifications represent a socio-cultural vessel that society provided to individuals for the boy. These descriptions have nothing to do with the male members at all. So, there are some major differences between sex and gender. The first is a biological structure, and gender is a socio-cultural structure.

The Biological and Social Bases of Gender Roles

Sociologists begin to study the male versus female gender from the angle of choosing the biological and social rules determining the role of the sexual type in order to identify who determines right and wrong, responsibilities, expectations and relationships for men and women in society because gender roles have both biological and social bases. The biological basis for the role of gender is rooted in different chromosomes and hormones. In response to this, the female releases an X chromosome only (as the female carries XX chromosomes) but (the male has XY chromosomes). If the Y chromosome is released from the male and pairs with the X chromosome of the female, it will produce a male fetus, but if the X chromosome is released from the male and combines with the chromosome X of the female, then the fetus is a female. It is worth noting from the scientific point of view that the ratio of determining the sex is 50% for both parties. Once the sex of the fetus has been determined in the mother's womb, the hormones carried in the blood through the chromosomes begin to be determined too. During pregnancy, the glands begin to secrete their respective hormones. With time, some internal organs develop, including the reproductive ones. Thus the doctor distinguishes the gender of the fetus after birth through the external sexual organs visible to the eye. When the child reaches puberty, hormonal differences appear in the male and the female. The female exhibits secondary sex characteristics such as menstruation and breast growth with expansion of the hip, narrow shoulders, and skin with a fatty layer in the body, while the secondary sexual characteristics of the male include large size of the reproductive organ and a large growth in the body muscles with coarseness of the voice and its depth and hair growth on chin and cheeks, with more body hair and more length. [Kendall. 2012. P. 70]

In the context of the aforementioned presentation, the following question shall be asked: Are there biological and genetic influences for both males and females that make them aggressive or peaceful? Judith Lorber 1994 answered this question and stated when the boy runs (the child) and makes noise, we say to him, "Boy, do not do it." This means that the (Y) chromosome had appeared in his body early on, making the defining male characteristics his distinguishing identity. The same is the case with the girl when she does not throw the ball with sufficient force. We tell her, "That's a typical girls' throw". According to Lauber's interpretation, this child carries the XX chromosome. However, Lauber asks: Is this condition general and comprehensive for all, at every time and place? Are there groups that stimulate and encourage their vitality and activity, or not? Or only when there is a presence of fans who encourage the freedom of movement outside the home in space and exercise and move freely as an expression of foot and boldness?

Lauber gives another example of knowing whether the boy or girl is aggressive or non-aggressive due to the presence of a biological or genetic factor or influences that push them to do so. She says if we give a tennis ball to the boy and the girl when they are three years old and encourage them to compete with each other in this, the result is that their vitality will be high, their body energised, and they will grow forearms and strong arms, and this, in turn, activates their motor energy and makes their body more flexible. In fact, these encouragements provide acceleration, enhancement, and stimulation of physical differences. In other words, the social culture is the one that stimulates and activates the movement and vitality of the boy and the girl, and there is no effect of the biological and genetic influences in that. Competition and aggression come from the fans surrounding the individual (family, friends, school, and the media), as no child or girl is hostile by heredity or because of the enormity of the body or its strength, but with the presence of motivators, excitement, and encouraging the use of physical force in humans.

Analytical logic of the foregoing states that the social base upon which a gender role is based is known as the "gender belief system" and that the idea of masculinity and femininity is to be carried and applied as legitimate and acceptable in society. The pattern of gender belief, however, reflects what is known to sociologists as "gender division in work". In response to this, the tasks and responsibilities are separate according to the role of gender. But the question is, how do people decide and define the work of the woman and the man? In answering this question, let's consider the events of several cultures as presented in various studies on these cultures. All of them confirm that the social factors are more influential and effective than biological factors in dividing the gender work in societies.

Many examples can be given here; in poor agricultural societies, women work in fields and farms to meet their family members' daily needs, while men usually produce products that are sold directly in the market - for cash - but they spare no time to work in the management and household. In high-income societies, there are a large number of women who do jobs outside the home while keeping their work inside the house, managing it and caring for family members. Across cultures, the field of work for women is private - personal and family, while the field for men is general and lies in the economic and political spheres. These differences raise the question of how did this split

54

happen? How is it rewarded? And how does access to scarce resources such as wealth, influence, and prestige affect this split? With regards to granting the field or practising in it, men have more opportunities and greater access than women by entering the field of wealth, influence, and prestige. This situation leads to inequality. However, genderism is manifested in areas other than those mentioned above (wealth, influence, and social consideration).

For gender inequality, some sociologists used a "gender role approach" in their argument, focusing on how the process of upbringing contributes to making the male dominant and the female submissive and follower. Other sociologists have relied on a constructive approach, which focuses on how the wide interaction and the continuation of the social structure threaten the boundaries of individuals' behaviour. Let us look at how upbringing can make gender stereotyping prevail and eternal.

D. <u>GENDER'S EVOLUTION</u>

In (July) of 2010, the United Nations General Assembly formed a new United Nations agency for women, called the United Nations Entity for Gender Equality and the Empowerment of Women, or the United Nations for women. The decision was to create a separate body to deal exclusively with gender-related activities after years of the United Nations specialised agencies working with specific issues. This United Nations Agency for Women began work in January 2011. It is important to know the concepts and dimensions of the concept of "gender" and the emergence and contexts in which it was born.

Insinuations: In 1949, the book "The Other Sex" was published by the French writer (Simone de Beauvoir). This book is considered as the preparer of the constitution that launched the feminist movement in the world. De Beauvoir argued that the man exerts emotional power over woman, which made her suffer from deep persecution; because, in the end, she accepted the transformation of the man from a real human into a deity-like symbol. De Beauvoir believes that a woman does not give birth to a woman because of a biological, psychological, or economic lack of determining one's personality as a female in society.

De Beauvoir believes that the emancipation of the woman depends on the extent to which she can change the image in which the man views her, and her physical and psychological characteristics, plus the extent of her liberation from the cultural heritage that negatively shapes her unconscious lives. The woman is in his "other" sex, as the female transforms into a woman within a domineering male reality whose personality was formed on the basis of the concept of power whose features and boundaries have established economic power through the ages.

Simone de Beauvoir exclaimed, "A person is not born a woman, but becomes a woman." She worked, with her intellectual and literary production, to question the identity of the woman. She confirmed that the woman's original and natural identity was stripped away from her, and the current identity is man's creation, and her liberation depends on her ability to break out of the shackles of the stereotypes created by society. Thus, she paved the way to theorise the concept of "gender".

E. GENDER'S STRATIFICATION

This term refers to a concept that includes a gradual distribution of social and economic resources on a scale that reveals biological differences associated with qualitative differences (gender). As for the criteria for this progression, they are wages, education, type of work within the home, participation in family, political and economic decisions, political positions. It is not class isolation, ethnic, religious, party or regional affiliation. This is a reality. As for the second truth about gender hierarchy, it is prevalent and present in all human societies, but it varies by degree, not by gender. Civilised societies have their gender hierarchy slightly varying in degrees of peace, in contrast to conservative, traditional, feudal, military, and religious societies, whose hierarchy includes peaceful, divergent and sharp hierarchies. It is very rare to find a contemporary society that includes balanced equality between feminine and masculine in work, wages, education, positions, and decision-making because that depends on the need for places for them, their skill levels and education, the culture of the man and the type of political system in it.

However, there are criteria that can be used in measuring the degree of equality between feminine and masculine, such as:

1. The work of women in the economic field.
2. Women's fields of education.
3. Doctrinal and religious support for the issue of equality between them (is it strong or weak?).
4. The extent of the man's contribution in helping women in housekeeping and childcare.
5. Separation of a woman's work from a man in the workplace, or lack thereof.
6. The extent to which women are allowed to ascend the official ladder of influence and make official decisions.

These are the social simulations and criteria that can be used to determine the gender hierarchy in any society. For example, Swedish society is considered one of the most modernised societies of our time. It has a high degree of gender equality through the participation of the woman in the labour market, housekeeping and childcare supported by the government, in addition to her active and proactive role in the political system. However, their wages are lower than the wages and salaries of a Swedish man.

In other countries, women still have fewer educational opportunities than men, and illiteracy rates are still high among them. But in Japan, the woman is highly educated, and she participates in the labour market more intensely. Her status in the family is characterised by a rigid and restricted role, but the rate of violence against her is truly little compared to other societies. At the same time, some of them are sex workers in homes, bars, and clubs, but their wages are not equal to that of men. In fact, this unequal situation represents a gendered phenomenon that prevails in all parts of the world without exception.

There is no harm in referring to another type of society that includes an extremist and severe gender hierarchy, such as Afghanistan during the rule of the Taliban in 1996, which stripped women and girls of their most basic human rights, withdrew them from the labour market, forbade them from getting education, isolated them in their own schools, and prevented them from going outside their home unless accompanied by a man (guardian) with her and painted the windows of her home with black paint in order to remain isolated so that none of the people saw her. This separation and segregation is called gender apartheid in sociology, and then there is a severe gender stratification like the Afghan that is prevalent in Saudi, Kuwaiti and Qatari society. [Andersen and Taylor. 2013. P262)]

CHAPTER 2: THE GENDER UPBRINGING AND CULTURAL DIVERSITY

INITIATION
A. CULTURE AND UPBRINGING IN GENDER INEQUALITY
B. GENDER UPBRINGING BY PARENTS
C. GENDER UPBRINGING BY PEERS
D. GENDER UPBRINGING IN SCHOOL
E. GENDER UPBRINGING IN SPORTS
F. GENDER UPBRINGING IN THE MEDIA

CHAPTER 2
GENDER UPBRINGING AND CULTURAL DIVERSITY

INITIATION

It may be asked why these two topics were coupled in the title of this chapter? The answer is because the formation of gender in our present contemporary society consists of several diverse social cultures. Each of them has its own distinctive gender upbringing patterns that are different from each other and hence require such conjunction. The first step of upbringing in contemporary society, such as the American society, starts by labelling the gender. Gender difference begins from the moment the newborn is delivered. It is wrapped in a different colour. For males, a blue wrap is used, while a pink wrap is used for females. At this moment, the difference is manifested between them, followed by their different clothes of distinguished colours, patterns, separations, and the toys they receive, from which the interactive differences continue from birth to death.

Social upbringing is a long-term process. It starts with the social interaction between the child and the society when the child starts to learn the culture and realises his roles to be able to function in the society. Each generation transmits the essential elements of the culture to the next generation through a Primary Socialization, which involves the teaching of the family role and the necessary skills that suit the society such as language, acceptable behaviour, and the control on the permissible and forbidden, right and wrong, liked and hated, preferred and detested, and so on. After Primary Socialization, the second stage of social upbringing comes. It involves the Continuing Socialization that starts when the individual learns the rules of social roles, he is going to use throughout his life stages.

Upbringing does not only refine the personality of the individual and allows for the development of skills and energies. It also moulds the beliefs and behavioural patterns of each group. In turn, it teaches its members the gender socialisation through which they acquire the cultural behaviour of the feminine and the masculine associated with the biological sex of the male or female. In this respect, there are certain exceptions related to social change that usually clash and stand in contrast to gender education at the general level. It is, therefore, necessary to understand cultural diversity in all of its forms in order to understand gender upbringing in contemporary society.

A. <u>CULTURE AND UPBRINGING IN GENDER INEQUALITY</u>

The society is an incubating vessel that accommodates unique cultural characteristics that are gained and adopted by the members of the society as social inheritance, like a train that runs on its rails. It provides the members with general and appropriate guides for their behaviour, beliefs, and relationships. Such cultural acquisition can only take place through social organisations and integrated institutions that live within society and are represented by the family, religion, school, political party, media, and other accessible means that satisfy members essential and basic needs. Every institution plays certain role(s) and has a special type of upbringing that complements the needs of other institutions without interference between them. In elementary upbringing, the parents educate their children with what they inherited from their previous generations, that is practised differently on the boy and the girl, i.e. the girl gains inferiority and influence over her male brother, then the school and the rest of the economic, political, governmental, sports and media institutions begin to reinforce the family's disparity in the gender upbringing. In a second term, social organisations transfer the cultural heritage to the younger generation in order to pass it on when they grow up to the next generation, who distinguish between feminine and masculine in their family influence and social consideration.

It is a fact that culture provides its members with standards of social control in order to conform to its standards and identify those who violate them. Among these standards, there are criteria for gender roles that are informal, unwritten, but customary such as sarcasm and mockery by peers, loss of family support, disapproval, and criticism of everyone who does not identify with its standards for both males and females without distinguishing. For example, the girl avoids acting violently and loosely as she will hear criticism, disapproval, and ridicule of her behaviour by her friends and family members because her cultural norms favour a gentle and affectionate disposition in her interaction with others. At the same time, if the boy acts in a weak or hesitant manner, he will face criticism, ridicule, and disapproval from others around him because his culture has provided his society with special criteria for males, such as roughness, audacity, and taking that should be reflected in his behaviour. This is on the childish level, but at the adult level (maturity), the standards do not allow the man to work in nurseries or care for children because they are specific to women, and the women are not allowed to work as a plumber or as a blacksmith because it is specific to the men. These are cultural norms that persist as long as they are nourished by society's culture. However, it may change if the culture changes its standards on feminine and masculine measures, meaning gender scales.

There are stereotypical ideas that the general culture uses on the subculture, such as the culture of ethnic, national or age groups that are often offensive and discourteous to them like the spinster, the divorced, the widow, the elderly who want to marry a second time. They face stereotypical names that the general culture gives because they represent the subculture to make fun of and mock them by describing their behaviours as naive, stupid, or fool.

Most research, studies and theories confirm that the first stage of upbringing (gender childhood) has strong effects on the persistence of stereotyping of the role of gender in old age. An example of that is raising the female to obey, submit, accept and be dependent on the behaviour of the male in his controlling and domination role more than teaching her to be a pioneer and leader. At the same time, the male is brought up on a leadership model that leads and presides over the behaviour of the female in many fields such as education, religion, administration, politics, and other public fields. It is known that from the very beginning of life until later that the role of gender is acquired through active participation in social life. Among the most prominent developmental agencies of gender roles are parents, peers, teachers, school, sports, and the media.

More clearly, what has been acquired and learned in the first stage of childhood gender, particularly in the first five years of the child's life (male or female), will continue with age progress. In this stage, the girl is up brought to be submissive to the power of the boy or his representative (father, uncle, maternal, grandfather, or brother), and the domination of the boy over the girl (his sister or the relative girls). After this age, when he goes outside the house to play with his peers, learn in school, participate in sports teams, or watch him on television, all of these social upbringing agencies promote and support how he has been raised in his family. This is because the culture of the society generalises this gender pattern on everyone. Neither the biological nor the genetic factor has an effect on it. However, individual violations occur in societies that call for equality and raise their children on gender equality, such as the British society, as there has been a case of intolerance against pregnant women in Britain. Many affirm that the countries of the West have achieved equality between women and men, but the British (Julie Brierley) saw otherwise. For this reason, she led a campaign to encourage a sit-in at the Federal Court building in London. Her campaign collected more than 60,000 women signatures and 103 MPs from Parliament. As per Julie, 38, her and other women's anger was due to the discrimination and unfairness they were treated with at the workplace. She called the campaign under the slogan "Pregnant then screwed", starting by her experience as she received unfair treatment from her boss when she told him she was pregnant. She got his answer the next day to inform her via voice message that he had dispensed her service, and she was considered resigned. This behaviour prompted her to discuss the situation on social media with other women who had gone through the same experience and perhaps even harsher. That led her to think about leading a campaign calling for equality in the workplace, an end of discrimination, having fairness for women, and not punishing her because of pregnancy, childbirth, and breastfeeding. Many of the protesting women carried banners that read (The March of Mummies) in reference to the attempt to mummify them and freeze their ability to work. Some of them experienced great difficulties during pregnancy, including Liz Monroe, 26, who became pregnant with her first child and, after giving birth, tried to return to work, but no one welcomed her return, as her employer hired a man in her place. Rita Lateng, 33 years old, has a similar case as her boss tasked her with overtime work inconsistent with the time she allocated to her infant, and when she objected, he fired her. With all this unfair treatment the women received, the man is rewarded and gets an increase in wages and promotions when he becomes a father. The campaign leader believes that women are in real distress because they are not protected by the state and have no support from anyone. If the woman returns to work shortly after giving birth, she is accused of neglecting her baby and labelled as selfish, and if she takes full maternity leave, the employers label her as uncommitted, incompetent, and undeserving of the salary. In her opinion, the reason is attributed to that the men believe that the woman's place is in home, cleaning, cooking and making bread and pastries, and she should stop working as soon as she sees the blue colour in the pregnancy test. If the woman tries to object to the employer's unfair decisions, her preoccupation with childbirth and her poor health may prevent her from instituting the legal case in a timely manner, thus losing her right. This is what actually happened with about 14% of the affected women.

Statistical data on sex discrimination at work in British society:

- 19% is the difference in salaries between men and women in Britain.
- 100,000 is the number of women who have faced discrimination at work in Britain.
- 54,000 women drop out of work sites annually in Britain due to pregnancy and childbirth.

- 40% of employers prefer to employ women of post-childbearing age [Saidity Magazine No. 1924 dated 20-1-2018]

B. GENDER UPBRINGING BY PARENTS

The first agent that sows the seeds of discrimination and difference between a boy and a girl is the parents through the following channels:

1. Their humour and concern.
2. Choose their clothes.
3. Choose their toys and games.
4. Training them to perform housekeeping.

And through these channels, the soil of differences is cultivated by: -

1. Reinforcement of biological differences.
2. Crystallising a system of gender division of role.

Seeding and cultivating the soil were not done by or through cultural and community feeding, but rather through:

1. Mother and father behaviour back in the childhood stage when joking and caring for their children.
2. Delegating them to help in housekeeping.
3. Manufacturing and factories that produce children's clothes, toys, and games.
4. Visual media (TV and cinema).
5. Electronic devices and their smart and entertaining innovations. All of them nourish human cultures (may it be likened to children) with biological differences.

In other words, the biological differences represent the principal base of gender that parents use in teaching and training their children on the characteristics of their biological type in childhood as a first stage in the different gender roles that they will develop. Such a gender role crystallises inequality of rights and duties in building a society that is intolerant and distinguished from the male against the female by birth. Exploitation and enslavement of the female by the male are supported by the social culture, the falsifiers of religion for their service, and by feudal lords and non-national politicians.

Therefore, the parents' behaviour which represents the first channel, seems to follow the biological difference between the boy and the girl, which determines the discrimination and gender difference as it is seen through their humour and concern for the child since birth. They practice and crystallise gender discrimination (boy or girl) through their interaction with the child without realising it. The boy, in their eyes, is more robust and durable than the girl. Therefore, parents are more active, livelier, and resilient better when they carry and play with him, while they tend to take gentle care with their daughter when they carry her, hugging, embracing with kindness, sweetness, and leisurely. They repeat vocal caresses and phrases expressing the indulgence in singing her songs, repeating her name with the song's lyrics and rhymes. These conversations, songs, and assonance are not the same with the boy, though, as they are specific to admiration and expression of strength and manhood. This is the first enhancement of the gender role of the new creature.

The second channel, however, includes choosing the clothes through which the second reinforcement and support for the gender role is achieved without realising that this choice will subsequently generate inequality in gender rights between their son and daughter. Parents buy bright and attractive shirts with a feminine character on which are drawn flowers, roses and a heart, or a picture of Cinderella or Barbie for the girl's shirt. As for the boy's shirts, they have drawings of superheroes and distinguished ones, such as soccer and basketball heroes, Mickey Mouse, Superman, or Spiderman. This is a distinctive reinforcement between boys and girls from birth that tells them to behave differently.

The third channel, on the other hand, is the selection of toys and games, which reinforces the parents' gender stereotypes and the difference between them. For example, a set of cubes, vehicles, sports equipment, and military weapons such as a gun, a pistol, a tank, and a plane are for the boy, while for the girl, the selected toys are much more tender such as models of cartoon houses and decorative tools (makeup) kitchen and sewing tools. These toys are the most enjoyable, entertaining, and nurturing for gender differences because they develop skills and hobbies by which the children are encouraged to participate in different gender activities.

Assignment to housekeeping represents the fourth channel in gender discrimination activity by parents as it concerns the upbringing mechanism. For example, house entrance cleaning, lawn cutting, carrying garbage bags outside the house are designed for the boy to train him to be independent, self-reliant, and bear family and household responsibility. The girl assignment, however, is focused on washing and drying dishes and clothes, cooking some foods, preparing salads, or ironing clothes. These are the first seeds that parents sow for their children, which grow later and are adopted by peers, school, teachers, media, government, books, and other things. Later, the fruits of these seeds are reinforced by the patriarchal authority, the non-patriotic politicians, and the debt brokers. Note that the parents' practice of gender differentiation among their children does not stop at the stage of childhood. It continues after their marriage and the birth of grandchildren as if it were an interconnected chain of gender differentiation whose foundation and basis were biological differences.

C. GENDER UPBRINGING BY PEERS

The group of friends has a strong influence on gender nurturing in reinforcing the renaissance of gender stereotypes and pressuring individuals to engage in gender-specific behaviour. A peer group or comrades is a group of friends interconnected through common interests that reflect their similar ages. They accept all that comes from their peers, especially those who confirm their observations and ideas about the behaviour of their age group. The male friendship group puts more pressure on males than females put on females to be feminine. An example is that most girls today wear jeans and play football, basketball, and tennis. As for the males, they wear clothes that are decided by their group members and enhance their sentimentalism and support the spirit of loyalty to the group and affection among its members. If one of them fails to do so, he will be alienated. In fact, the importance of peer groups is in nurturing the behaviour of females and males to enhance the gender differences in their identity and future ambitions and to encourage the trial of everything new. It nourishes the spirit of cooperation between the members of the group and crystallizes their concepts, terms, attitudes, and tastes because they have the same developmental spaces that the parents did not dictate or that they avoided, such as romantic love, passionate emotions, idealistic and extremist ideas, and tastes that reflect their age. It is a gender upbringing but different from the upbringing of the parents. It pushes the juvenile towards behavioural independence and pride to develop new capabilities and skills that the parents did not develop. Therefore, it is complementary to what was preceding it (parents' upbringing), and sometimes it contradicts it because it is a generational upbringing rather than a family.

D. GENDER UPBRINGING IN SCHOOL

In mixed American school education, the difference between males and females in elementary, intermediate, and secondary schools reflects the teachers' prejudice and intolerance against females. It is like parenting and peer upbringing in reinforcing gender differences starting from: -

1. Paying attention to the school male activity more than the female school activity.
2. Appraise the performance and achievement of the boy more than of the girl.
3. Sexual harassment is prevalent without shame.
4. The boy's opposition to school standards more than the girl.
5. The female student's grades are higher than the male student.
6. The tendency of the male student to leave school more than the female student.

Gender discrimination is clearly manifested in education, where the interest in educating males is more than that of females in terms of devoting enough time to the males and listening to their problems, criticisms, and suggestions. The teacher does not pay enough attention to the questions posed by a female student or the suggestions she presents. Just by saying (yes) or responding by silence, or moving to the next question. This is neglect with no praise for every positive performance or encouragement when the female proposes ideas or observations. It is in contrast to what the teacher or the female teacher does towards the male student when he completes work as he gets praise from the teacher.

Not only that, but the teacher often tends to divide students into two parts (a section for male students and another for female students). When the class performs a sporting or classroom activity, the teacher calls the female students' team "chatter" and calls the male students' team "the strong." Hence, there is educational feeding to distinguish the role of gender in mixed education in American society.

Verbal and physical sexual harassment exists in these schools, and the boy often calls the phrase (prostitute) or (bitch) to the girl student. In 2001 the US government surveyed 2000 public schools in which 83% of females were found to have been harassed by male students, and 79% of male students were harassed by female students. However, the school faces many effects of gender stereotypical behaviour on boys more than girls, such as rebellion against school standards, non-compliance, and violent activity without responding to male and female teachers, and their grades are often lower than that of female students. This means that the mixed school does not address gender discrimination; it rather deepens and promotes it through the interaction of male and female teachers and through school activities that separate the sexes. Thus, it is an integral link to the chain of gender upbringing after the parent and peer circle. [Kendall. 2012. Pp. 70-74)

E. GENDER UPBRINGING IN SPORTS

The only field that highlighted gender equality is sports in schools and universities. Both of them practice most games and activities continuously, and sport has proven that it represents play and entertainment and teaches equality between males and females. In American society after 1972, the law of gender equality was passed in academies and sports. It allowed the boys to start playing games that girls used to do, such as jumping rope, gymnastics, and skating. At the same time, it gave way to the girls to enter the field of sports monopolised by the boys, such as soccer, basketball, volleyball, arena, field, and so on. This means that the physical sport has clearly opened the door to equality between the sexes because it expresses the tolerant spirit, athleticism, and free competition. This is a positive activity in favour of gender equality that had not been seen in the upbringing of parents or teachers.

F. GENDER UPBRINGING IN THE MEDIA

There are many and various media outlets (newspapers, magazines, television, and cinema),, all of which support gender upbringing. It nurtures the biological roles of males and females, which reinforces gender stereotyping. In other words, it does not advocate, does not demand, and does not address the issue of equality in women's rights with the rights of men. Rather, it is dedicated to programs that blatantly reflect gender differences without criticism or demand to change them even though television programs have the ability to refine and develop ideas among viewers (male and female) staring from animated films (cartoons), adult movies, and ending with educational programs that display equality characteristics. It was noticed that when there are educational programs, they are miserable and useless but rather deceptive, delusive, and failed. They are meaningless, dishonest, and have no influence in their treatment of gender issues.

Then there are presentations that reflect and address the problems of domestic life, especially the problems of women within the home and the family, dealing with the traditional role of women in the home and the workplace as well as their relationships with individuals in both places, focusing on

72

gossip and confusion about rumours and scandals. They are dealing with personal problems or envy and intrusion on the affairs of others while reflecting and visualizing the role of the man who directs, advises, and commands the woman. It is transcendent over her and who is dominant in her destiny. At the same time reflects the mistakes of the woman in everything she does. Moreover, there are episodes in television series about the events that happen in hospitals and the nonsense talk of nurses evaluating the patients, doctors, and the personal lives of others. They highlight male doctors and display their competencies in conducting subtle surgical operations, treatments of patients, and wise administrative leadership. It is opposite to how they describe the female doctor's performance, who their accomplished, brilliant, and successful performance is not portrayed. On the contrary, they intentionally reinforce the traditional role of women as dominated by men and attribute bad behaviour of gossip, confusion, intrusiveness, and flatness to the women as if they do not possess any serious, fruitful, and productive characteristics. This reinforcement and support of the traditional role of women and men is shown without treatment or remediation of the state of lack equalization of trade-offs between women's rights and men's rights.

Finally, it can be stated that children and females are more affected than males. The female imitates fashion movements, diet programs, sports, fitness, and clothes in the sense that she nurtures the imitation tendency in her behaviour as responsible for home and children. As for children, they are affected and imitate the periodic patterns that appear in animated cartoons. Therefore, television programs do not address the problem of equality but rather nurture, extend, and reinforce gender differences.

However, the Arabic TVs are more supportive of patriarchal domination, humiliating the women and wasting their human, national, and cultural rights. An example of this is the Egyptian TV that shows documentary about the southern region (Saidity) society where a woman is killed if she loves a man or becomes his friend because it is considered dishonour and shame to the family. As for the Jordanian soap operas, they present Bedouin stories portraying women as if they were a commodity in the market subject to buying and selling. . However, the Gulf soap operas display violent behaviour against women and their oppression within the family on how they are harnessed to serve children and obey their husbands. The Syrian series also portrays women as the exceptionally low-grade gender in the society showing her as a housewife who knows nothing but cooking, gossip, adulteration, and her submission to her cousin or her husband. In the sense that all these TVs support the choice of men over women. In their entertainment programs, they appear as a complementary link to the upbringing of the current generation. In most TVs, the daily activities of the head of state are displayed, expressing his role as being the father of society that must be obeyed by everyone without exception, as if he were the ruler of all its members. Therefore, it is a media outlet that reinforces gender stereotypes in Arab society while using women to polish the ruler's image in school, art, poetry, and soap operas.

The Arab magazines specialized in Arab women follow the same line as the TVs. It can be seen that the magazine Saidity of Saudi Arabia, Zahrat Al Khaleej of the Emirates, the Lebanese Alshabaka, and the Lebanese Fairouz magazines do not offer any remedies, treatments, or proposals for the issue of gender equality or the demand for

74

women's rights in the Patriarchal authority or Arab culture, or the religion brokers who distorted Islamic teachings to serve their interests and disputes. These magazines do not discuss the sexual promiscuity among students in universities and colleges where gender segregation is still practiced in the Gulf countries. Though they are specialised in women's affairs, they do not demand women's rights to choose their life partner, the abolition of guardianship over them, the freedom to express their views and ideas, nor their representation in municipal councils. They failed to address the issue of marrying underaged girls, defending women against domestic violence, or women's freedom of employment in government departments and elsewhere, focusing on trivial and shallow issues. For example, the Lebanese magazine (Fairouz) presents news of Arab and foreign actresses and singers, advertising for toiletries, costumes, fashion trends, the relationship of men with women, and investigations of antiques and perfumes. As for the magazine (Al Shabaka) also deals with news of Arab singers and actresses, Alshabaka stars, a section on entertainment, and photo news aboutLebanese society. The same situation. With the Emirati "Zahrat Al Khaleej," which is dealing with the news of Arab and foreign TV and movie stars and advertising perfumes, bags, shoes, fashion, and home furniture as if it is suitable for soft-class women of high incomes, talking about women's fashion and home decor, and comments on films of Arab series.

An evolution in the concept of Arab femininity

Traditionally, strength and braveness were man characteristics, while weakness and inferiority were women's characteristics. Now, the concept of courage has changed and is no longer limited to men as many women proved they are brave, bold, and strong. Therefore, the use of the manhood word to describe the woman's braveness and praise her is not valid anymore though it may detract her from her femininity. (Mona Abdel Nasser) 25 years old Administrative Assistant thinks that manhood is not the monopoly of a man who owns a moustache and well-built muscles. A divorced woman who is able to face the outside world without the need of a man (who acts as her lawyer), and a woman who seeks her livelihood, able to raise her children and resilient to attacks of the society and its views against her; equals a million men. Nada Ibo, 40 years, fine artist and poet, says: attitudes are the ones who positioned the women in this place. When the manhood qualities of generosity, selflessness, containment, and embrace in today's youth diminished and equality became a requirement for both sexes, the woman came with her worth, knowledge, and culture to prove this saying. The woman did not want to be a man and did not want to rob the man of his qualities, nor to compete with him, but he was the one who gave up his manhood so that she takes his place and bear the full responsibility, as she equals to thousand men. A woman who travels to receive education and works in sensitive and important positions such as a pilot or trainee pilot, and whoever works after the death of her husband to support her family, all of them equals a thousand men. [Saidity Magazine No. 1924 dated 20-1-2018]

Female professions for Saudi women

If there are professions that need specialization, fast professions like makeup artists, photographers, models, marketers, and promoters for a specific product, have emerged and adopted by women. They became fashionable, and many women were able to break into it without specialization and sometimes without experience. Many women have proven themselves on the scene, and some of them have taken it as a source of livelihood only without developing themselves. For example, (Fadwa Al-Sayed) who completed her studies until the high school stage, said," I entered the field of advertising 6 years ago and began to search for self-employment that is not stable but is the best for me as work is not routine. I am paid for the day I work. I have been advertising for a specific product, whether it is food, electrical appliances, or products for hair and skin care, at the expense of the advertising agency. I sometimes gain 200 riyals as for today and 180 riyals at other times. The best thing about this work; it is variable, renewed, and not fixed, and the worst of it; is that it is not continuous, sometimes I work for a week, and I stay for a month not working, but this work does not require academic specialization or specific experience, and at the same time I can be knowledge to increase job opportunities". [Saidity Magazine No. 1920 dated 23-12-2017]

In order to fulfil one of the Saudi women's rights (in their conservative and traditional society) to drive a car in 2018, 24 steps were taken that paved the way for Saudi women to drive cars. So how long the requirements will be for other wasted rights such as the marriage of underaged, guardianship, changing the stereotypical view of Saudi women, and entering the world of cinema, singing arts, musical and mixed education in schools and universities, and choosing a life partner before them and many others.

CHAPTER 3: GENDER AND SEXUAL IDENTITIES

INITIATION
A. THE EXCITING CHANGE OF TRADITIONAL GENDER IDENTITY IN THE WESTERN WORLD
B. SEXUAL IDENTITY
C. HERMAPHRODITISM AND TRANSGENDER

CHAPTER 3

GENDER AND SEXUAL IDENTITIES

INITIATION

Gender identity is determined by the role they play when any of them occupies a specific social position because such a position includes conditions and requirements that must be performed and fulfilled by the occupier. The social culture usually predetermines these requirements. Manhood and femininity are determined by society's culture of the man's social position as father, brother, son, or of the female as a wife, mother, sister, or daughter. Therefore, the behaviours of each social position are predetermined by behavioural expectations as a requirement for their occupancy. For example, the female's identity requires her to be, in the traditionally conservative society, subservience to the man, emotional, shy in front of him, tender sense and patient with the man's injustice, as well as accepts his domination over her. She is trained not oppose his words and orders, abide by and respect the elderly, and not interrupt him during the talk. These are unwritten expectations that her mother and father raised her with from childhood. These are the conditions for the girls' and eastern woman's roles, which give her the feminine identity. The identity of the eastern man, however, is determined through his exercise of the conditions and requirements of his masculine roles that his family establishes on him, such as being bold without shyness, strong and violent, defending himself, independent in his opinion, defending his honour, his sister, and his mother, and respecting the elderly but not being courteous at the expense of truth. The positional role determines the gender identity and not the other way around.

There is no harm in presenting a summary of (Wakley 1972) theory which she has established to know how the social upbringing is manifested in modern industrial societies through the determination of the characteristics of the identity and behaviour of girls and boys from an early age. This summary consisted of four methods by which the gender roles are established and take its place: -

1. The child's self-concept is crystallized through the interactions and interests that the mother makes when buying special girls' clothes for her daughter, and she is interested in styling her hair and buying special toys for her. And encouraging her to practice what is expected of her when she grows up, such as buying kitchen tools in the form of small toys, garnishing tools, and a model of the sewing machine, while she buys for her son toys in which the requirements of strength and boldness are expressed in them such as a rifle, sword, and plane.

2. The second aspect of social upbringing is uttering special words that reinforce gender identity, such as you are a naughty boy, and you are a good girl, or you are a goblin boy, and you are a passionate and sensitive girl, and so on.

3. The mother is more interested in the appearance and elegance of her daughter than her son, such as her hairstyle, cleanliness, fingernails, and the model of her dress, than her child in this regard.

4. The mother encourages her daughter to perform the tasks of housekeeping in cleaning and arranging and taking care of helping her in other household affairs without encouraging her son to perform the same in cleaning and arranging.

All of these methods motivate and push the girl to imitate adult women. In contrast, the boy is motivated to imitate his father in not bearing the housekeeping responsibilities because his mother did not raise him on that. [Vankrieken and etal. 2004. P. 317)

In other words, the mother enhances the gender distinction in her children as she implants the culture of her society in their upbringing. Through that, the features of the gender identity are determined by which the mother implements the standards of her culture. The influence of the media in cinema and television in the upbringing of the gender role has aggravated the situation through the movies and series that show the masculinity of men and their relationship to the femininity of the women and the struggle of her roles. They display stories about the traditional methods of raising the mother and the conservative father of their male and female children that reinforce and sometimes oppose nurturing gender roles. In other words, the mother enhances the gender distinction of her daughter and son by influencing the culture of her society, , the features of the gender identity are determined by which the mother implements the standards of her culture. We do not forget the influence of the media in cinema and television in the upbringing of the gender role through films and series that show the masculinity of men and their relationship to the femininity of the girl and the struggle of her roles and provide stories about the traditional methods of raising the mother and the conservative father of their male and female children that reinforce and sometimes oppose the methods of nurturing gender roles.

A. THE EXCITING CHANGE OF TRADITIONAL GENDER IDENTITY IN THE WESTERN WORLD

The gender pattern in the Western social structure does not remain static and frozen over time. There are influential global and technical events that have acted in various aspects of social, political, and economic life in the Western and Eastern world, such as the collapse of the socialist block and the demise of many political systems and economic blocks. On the other side, the information technology revolution, new communication means, computers and satellite channels, the spread of democracy, and free market economy, have affected the evolution of various gender characteristics.

All this has triggered the change of many social and economic standards and values that created the need for competencies and skills with precise scientific and technical specializations, regardless of skin colour, race, gender, nationality, religion, religious sect, and social class, to promote the changing global events and keep the pace with the free economy, democratic politics, and respect for human rights. Such changes required abandoning or waiving the sexual differentiation between men and women, especially those with high experience, know-how, and skill in humanitarian work and community service without considering fanaticism and partial and individual bias, but rather adopting the movement of continuous scientific and technical progress in change and development based on free competition and the acquisition of the best and fittest. In the face of these events, women emerged to occupy major and essential fields in the Western world, such as the position of prime minister, as happened in New Zealand, which she won as the youngest prime minister in the world through her gigantic achievements for her people and (Angela Merkel) who won the position of German chancellor after fierce election battles. For the fourth time, she was able to successfully walk the boat of the European Union despite the euro crisis. Theresa May was the Prime Minister of Britain who saved her country by strengthening its economy after the UK exit from the European Union, and Christine Lagarde emerged in France, who took over the position of General Manager of the International Monetary Fund for a second term. Away from the official position, (Melinda Gates) has made a qualitative leap in the lives of women in the Western and Eastern world by expanding educational opportunities and bringing information technology to various parts of the world and other women. These new facts were able to bring about a change in the old traditional gender identity so that the modern woman assumes a high-level position on the global level in the Western worlds, which will take its course to other paths and processes not only on the political track but on the economic, educational, social, artistic, sports and literary tracks. All this showed the gender identity as a new identity that does not coincide directly with the sexual identity, but rather inversely with it in order to effect a change as happened in gender.

Promising modern woman accomplished persistent and impressive works which revealed her success in Western society. She has acquired a unique professional role in a vertically upward direction movement rather than inherited a traditional or horizontal expanded social movement. She managed to master the social, media, political, artistic, and sports stature based on the acquired role of intense objective competition and wading in more than one professional, political, and social activity. Her role is recognized and witnessed by the financial and political crises, just as (Angela Merkel, Theresa May, and Margaret Thatcher) who obtained recognition of their courage and their overcoming of the male element, so they saved their countries from severe financial and political crises and brought their countries to safety.

They draw an incredibly positive image about the women and prove that they have the skills and possess professional, cognitive, and administrative capabilities and qualifications in leading civilized and advanced societies of global influence and with full free competition at all levels. The engagement in such an endeavour revealed these women's outstanding and promising ability and their real determination. They emphasized without hesitation and without daydreams or mirages, but by rational strategic planning and common sense. On top of that, these qualifications did not distract these women from their human and emotional feelings in their assistance to women and families.

The femininity here has surpassed her biological sex. She changed the concept of weakness, shyness, and reliance on men in making decisions and not taking responsibility outside the home and being satisfied with taking care of a small number of children within her family. Now she has become strong in her competition with the men and bold in making long-term international, regional, and societal decisions, receiving the responsibility to live and the well-being of an exceptionally large society in terms of its population size and heavy international weight. On the other hand, there is a free and intense competition made by some of the stars of high art in acting, drawing, and fashion shows.

They were attested by international professional organizations that awarded them high-level prizes for their artistic and scientific performance, such as (Emma Stone and Rose McFeon, and Lubina Hamid). (Melinda Gates) on the other hand, has been able to promote healthcare and reduce poverty. Such a task was not easy to undertake unless she had solid determination and long-term humanitarian planning, showing that women did not remain in the kitchen and at home but invaded into major global spaces to help the women of the world in the latest technological innovations. As the woman climbs onto the ladder of fame and visual media, she faces full defamation and scandals concerning her past, family background, and biography. It is surprising as she does not deny her past and customary or religious culture, and she is not ashamed of it.

On the contrary, she admits her past and announces it without feeling shame or disgrace. This is due to her high confidence in herself and her ability to continue with her creative resolve, as did (Lubina Hamid) Zanzibari Muslim, and (Megan Markel), who faced the media campaigns that wanted to undermine them. But both (Markel and Hamid) remained respectful of their deep black roots in a white society that practiced hidden racism like Britain.

Therefore, the modern Western female seems more anchored, daring, and arrogant in her climbing struggle on the modern gender ladder rather than remaining confined to the constraints of the biological scale. This is in turn, builds solid rules for changing the traditional perceptions and conservative judgments inherited by the old gender and changing the balance of the equation that prevailed between men and women in the last century.

There is no question of women's knowledge and fame in managing the family budge. Still, the current modern woman excelled in managing the budget of the International Monetary Fund, which was received by (Christine Lagarde) the French lawyer and politician entrusted with the management of the Ministry of Economic Affairs in France, which has emerged as the best finance minister in the eurozone. This task and responsibility were not obtained by her husband, son, or lover but positioned by the influential people of the contemporary capitalist Western world after they recognised her as the most capable in the world. This means that the modern female is different, and her newness was obtained by competency and merit rather than by heredity. This tremendous task illustrates the tremendous gender shift that the modern woman has made in the Western world.

At the same time, the modern woman is able to compete with men for positions that he used to occupy and monopolize. It is a distinguished leadership that surpassed the leadership of men in non-traditional societies of heavy weight in the global, economic, and political levels. Moreover, the modern Western woman has become more daring and bolder about what is happening to her in terms of exploitation and extortion by men, such as harassment and rape. The story of Rose McFeon means a lot as she was subject to sexual harassment and abuse by one of the Hollywood producers, but she did not stay silent. She and many other movie stars who have been subject to similar abuse disclosed him to the British and the American police and wrapped him with disgrace and shame. Previously, the woman was shy, and feared the man and the imperative social controls for such a discloser. But now, her self-confidence has strengthened because of her success in performing her work.

On the other hand, there are other cases of disclosing the female's experience of drug addiction and associated abuse and risks. Women involved in such a dilemma, have voluntarily educated young girls about the dangers of addiction, warning them to fall into such a trap. This is, in fact, what is performed by the parents, but these women became row models in community engagement and upbringing. This public disclosure about the drugs was done before the public opinion by (Adwoa Aboah) who won the modelling award, was praised by the press, and given her the title of queen of catwalks.

The point in presenting these cases is to affirm that modern Western women have become more mature in their work outside the home, especially in famous international institutions such as fashion and cinemas, which cannot be successful without high and specialized qualifications and competencies that make them overcome the obstacles that were placed before them by society or the exploited man. The female did not remain submissive, obedient, subservient, broken, and withdrawn. Rather, she became a woman who made a rational mental decision, a planned visionary, and a distinguished achievement that surpassed the privilege of men. She made her way through her efforts, intelligence, and subtlety without the help of her father, husband, lover, or brother, and this tells us that it is a gesture to promote a new gender in Western society that surpasses the second side of the gender (the man). In this aspect, she built a new role for the female that differs from the one attributed to her by the man. Through her efforts; she succeeded in fields that she had no experience in but walked in with her determination.

It is important to mention that modern Western women have been s accused of racial discrimination against people of color. Such discrimination was not clear before as it was unavailable to women in the twentieth century. This is right because they were oppressed, suppressed, and deprived of will by the man who used his influence and power to differentiate sexuality. On the female level, the written media praised the critical tendency that was rejected by (Rashida Jones), the Artist of Humanitarian Attitudes, and then the challenge style that Ashley Graham introduced in order to change the stereotypical view of beauty and elegance. This challenge does not come from a submissive, obedient, subservient female. It comes from a female revolting against a calcified reality of preferences and unfairness to the rights of women, especially against the empowered, expressing a deaf cry against the stereotypes to remove obstruction used by men in the fashion world. Here, the modern Western woman revealed her strength against the monotony prevailing in the world of beauty and elegance.

In conclusion, it can be said that the modern woman in modern gender has the following personality traits: -

1. The challenge to stereotypes in the world of elegance, beauty, and agility.
2. The critical tendency rejects discrimination and ethnic and humanitarian intolerance.
3. Publicly disclosing to the public opinion, the sexual harassment and rape committed by the man.
4. Free competition in political elections.
5. Wise leadership in managing financial and international crises.
6. Upgrading information technology education.
7. Withstand in the confrontation of media campaigns against women.
8. Carrying political responsibility in managing ministries and succeeding in them.

Individual Models of a New Gender Identity

To highlight the achieved step change of the new gender direction, 15 modern women of the Western world who achieved remarkable success during 2017 are presented here. They have proven that a woman with solid determination can accomplish huge success and turn dreams into reality. Yes, it is the time of the woman who always sees hope in whatever she is doing and strives to achieve it as with the following women: -

1. Zaha Hadid…. The most powerful female engineer in the world

The Iraqi-British architect Zaha Hadid was described as the most powerful engineer in the world. She saw that the field of architecture is not restricted to men only, as she made Arab and international achievements. She was chosen as the fourth most powerful woman in the world in 2010. She Born in Baghdad in 1950 and died in Miami in 2016. She graduated in 1977 from the Architectural Association in London. She worked in 1987 as a lecturer at the Faculty of Architecture, and a visiting professor at several universities in Europe and America, including Harvard, Chicago, Hamburg, Ohio, Colombia, New York, and Yale. She received many prestigious awards, medals, and honorary titles in architecture, and was one of the first women to win the Pritzker Prize in Architecture in 2004, which is equivalent in value to the Nobel Prize in Engineering; The Stirling Prize on two occasions; She was awarded the Order of the British Empire and the Imperial Order of Japan in 2012. She won the Royal Gold Medal at the RIBA Prize for Engineering Arts in 2016, becoming the first woman to receive it. She has implemented 950 projects in 44 countries. The projects of the fire station in Germany in 1993, the building of the Museum of Italian Art in Rome 2009 and the American Museum in Cincinnati, Abu Dhabi Bridge, and the London Marine Sports Centre, which was dedicated to the 2012 Olympic Games, the Underground Station in Strasbourg, the Cultural Centre in Azerbaijan, the Scientific Centre in Wellsburg, the Steamship Station in Salina, and the

Ski Centre Innsbruck and Heydar Aliyev Cultural Centre in Baku in 2013 are some of the prominent projects for Zaha Hadid.

2. Angela Merkel.... Winning the fourth time

The year 2017 saw (Angela Merkel) 63 years old, win the position of Germany's chancellor for the fourth time after a fierce election battle that ended in her favour. Thus, she kept her political position and also her famous title (Iron Woman) as she is still ranked first in Forbes magazine's list of the most powerful women in the world in the year in 2017. Merkel entered the field of politics when she was 35 years old to occupy the post of Minister of Women and Youth and Minister of the Environment. In 2005 she won the position of German Chancellor to be the first woman to hold this position in the history of modern Germany since 1871. She succeeded in marching the European Union despite the protracted euro crisis and the Brexit earthquake.

3. Theresa May ... the strongest woman

She is the second woman to hold the post of Prime Minister in Britain after (Margaret Thatcher) and has been placed by Forbes magazine in second place in the list of the most powerful women for the year 2017. She took power last year at an exceedingly difficult time after Britain decided to exit the European Union and after David Cameron announced his desire to step down from his position. Here (Theresa May) appeared as the saviour of Britain and took the helm with the courage to lead the world's most powerful economies to safety. The media linked her and (Margaret Thatcher) because of her strictness, but she always tries to distance herself from this comparison by saying, "I am not Margaret Thatcher," despite my conviction that this woman was distinguished. Still, I do not like how they try to find similarities between us.

4. Emma Stone.... Oscar Best Actress

The star (Emma Stone) achieved remarkable success in 2017 by winning the Best Actress award in Oscar awards. The award appreciates her effort for her role in the musical film (Lala Land). This young star (28 years old) achieved another milestone when Magazine Forbes placed her on the list of highest-paid stars. In the same year, she won the Golden Club Award, the British BAFTA Award, and the Actors League Award. This victory was not easy, as four big stars competed for it, namely (Isabel Hubert) for Elle and (Ruth Nega) for Loving and (Meryl Streep) for Florence Foster Jenkins.

5. Rose McFeon.... Woman of the Year

In 2017, many media nominated the star (Rose McFeon, 44 years) for the Woman of the Year award after she raised a serious case that was folded up to this time and revealed several tweets on Twitter about the sexual harassment scandals that Hollywood stars are exposed to, accusing the famous Hollywood producer (Harvey Weinstein) of raping her. This accusation was a wake-up call that awakened the rest of the stars and encouraged them to reveal their experiences with him. Police in the United States and Britain began investigating the accusations against this producer, including allegations of sexual abuse dating back to 2004 and the 1980s.

6. Melinda Gates ... Personality of the Year

She is the wife of the billionaire (Bill Gates), the owner of Microsoft, the largest software company in the world. She works alongside him in a charitable foundation named after the Bill and Melinda Gates Foundation, actively empowering women to make qualitative changes in their lives by expanding and strengthening health care and reducing poverty. Melinda won the (Sheikh Mohammed bin

Rashid to Maktoum) award for knowledge and the title of Person of the Year in 2005 and the (Prince of Asturias) Award for International Cooperation. In 2017, she entered into addressing the lack of information in the field of technology among women and was selected by Forbes magazine as one of the most powerful women in 2017.

7. Adwoa Aboah.... Model of the year

The British model (Adwoa Aboah) won the (Model of the Year) award among the British Fashion Awards. The press called her the (Queen of Catwalk). Although she is 25 years old, she has worked with the most famous international fashion houses and has appeared on the cover of Vogue more than one time. She became the most sought-after model in 2017. On the social level, she is one of the activists in society who started her experience with drug addiction since she was 13 years old. Still, she overcame her suffering and turned into the most wanted model. Hello, Magazine placed her on the list of the most successful women in 2017, and she is working now on educating young girls about the dangers of addiction.

8. Lobina Hamid ... The heroine artist

The Turner Prize for the Arts for 2017 went to a British African American Muslim (Lobina Hamid) professor of contemporary art at the University of Central Lancashire. Thus (Lobina), 63, became the oldest artist to win this award and the first black British woman to win it. The artist, who has her origins in Zanzibar, has been creating large paintings, pure African colors, and bright spaces. She addresses the issue of racism towards black people, the issue of slavery, slavery, colonialism, and the dispossession of rights and dignity. The Daily Telegraph newspaper described her as the heroine that reflects the art of black in Britain.

9. Megan Markel ... Challenged the media.

Her name was the most requested in the search engine (Google) during 2017, and the frequency of search for the advertisement increased. She and Prince Harry got engaged on November 28 last. Many have bet on the impossibility of this marriage for many reasons, including that she is three years older than him and that she is a divorced woman who has played an inappropriate role in one of her TV shows, she is the daughter of a woman of colour and is not suitable for Prince Harry. Some newspapers went to undermine the relationship and reached the point of racism and focused on her black mother. Still, this woman withstood the media campaigns and did not care She confirmed in a television interview after the engagement that she deeply respects her roots and finds no intersection between her social situation and her love for Prince Harry.

10. Christine Lagarde.... Best Minister

A French lawyer and politician born in Paris in 1956, she assumed the position of Director-General of the International Monetary Fund in 2011, to be the first woman to hold this position. She was previously appointed as Minister of Finance by the French President (Nicolas Sarkozy) in June 2007 and is considered (Lagarde) the first woman she holds the position of Minister of Economic Affairs in the Group of Eight. The Financial Times described her as the best finance minister in the eurozone. In 2009, she was ranked 17th in the list of the most influential women in the world by Forbes magazine. In 2017 she returned to occupy a position in the list of the most powerful women in the world, according to the magazine. In 2018 she was re-selected to run the International Monetary Fund for a second term of 5 years.

11. Rashida Jones.... Artist of Humanitarian Attitudes

In 2017, the 41-year-old American star (Rashida Jones) took a decisive stance that was praised by the media. She left the movie Toy story 4 to declare her rejection of how Pixar animation studios deal with people of colour and how they practice racism towards them and do not give them an equal creative imposition with eggs. She also criticized the way they dealt with women and emphasized that only one out of every ten films produced by this studio gives a woman the opportunity to direct. The press praised this bold position and nominated her for the award of the artist with humanitarian attitudes for the year 2017.

12. Ashley Graham.... Changed concepts of elegance.

She got the title of Model of the Year despite her extra weight. From here begins the challenge that this woman entered to change the stereotypical view of beauty and elegance and encourage millions of women around the world to accept their bodies as they are. She has called on fashion makers to adopt the principle of diversity and difference in women's bodies and not stick to specific measurements and leave overweight women in a state of sadness and anxiety. This stocky model has appeared on the covers of famous magazines such as Elle Glamor Vogue and has succeeded in bringing the 26-inch size to the New York Fashion Show Fall / Winter 2017. She is on Forbes's list of women who have made positive changes in the world.

13. Yu Xiuhua.... Cerebral palsy did not stop her dreams.

The Chinese (Yu Xiuhua) was born on a small farm in Handian, China, and she was complaining of cerebral palsy, yet she lived a quiet life and worked in agriculture. After she finished work, she began writing poetry despite her ceaseless tremor. She remained so for 41 years until a year came 2014 when she sent one of her poems to one of the sober Chinese magazines, and it had a loud impact on readers, as it was republished repeatedly. By 2015 two books of her poetry were published, and her best-selling writing became the vice president of the Association of Literary and Artistic Circles. She began organizing seminars in China, America, and some European countries. 2017 witnessed the release of a documentary film about her, titled (Still Tomorrow).

14. Serena Williams... and a new title

American tennis player (Serena Williams) crowned the Australian Open in 2017 at the expense of her older sister (Vones), to run out of the record in the number of times winning the title of this tournament. (Serena Williams), 36, is the best female tennis player and one of the most prominent athletes in the world. After the tournament, she released a heavy surprise when she confirmed that she was playing in this tournament while pregnant with her first child. No one noticed that because she was in the second month of pregnancy and indicated that she would leave training during the remainder of the months of this year to see her daughter (Alexis Olympia) and would continue to participate in 2018.

15. Elif Shafak.... Continues to harvest successes.

The Turkish novelist (Elif Shafak) continues to reap successes after her novels this year topped the list of best-selling books in Turkey. She has been translated into more than 30 languages around the world. More than 750,000 copies of her novels have been sold, and she won the ALEF Prize in France. She was nominated for the Dublin Prize. The literary world has a wide Arab audience and follows her works, especially her famous novel, The Forty Rules of Love. Shafak won many literary prizes, including the Rumi

Award for the best literary work in Turkey. Her third novel, The Deep Look, won the Turkish Writers Union Award, while her fourth novel, Qasr al-Barghout (the palace of a flea), achieved the highest sales rates in Turkey.

16. Jacinda Ardern.... the youngest woman to lead a country.

Jacinda Ardern, 37, became the youngest woman to lead a country in the world after assuming the duties of prime minister in her country. She focused on higher education, decriminalizing abortion, reducing immigration rates, and lifting children out of poverty. According to Radio New Zealand, she plans to call a referendum on legalizing marijuana within three years of taking office. (Ardern) is the youngest Prime Minister of New Zealand for 150 years and the third woman to hold the position. She joined the British Labour Party at the age of 17 and worked in Tony Blair's office and entered Parliament in 2008. [Saidity Magazine No. 1921 dated 12-30-2017]

B. SEXUAL IDENTITY

The sociology of gender is not satisfied with defending women's rights, demanding their equality with men, and reviewing the path of their feminist movement through history and societies. It is rather extended to address the biological cases that deviated from the biological, social, and cultural nature as it happens to males and females in modern society and how to deal with them by portraying their suffering as a result of such an interaction. This is because they represent a social problem that expresses the social role of the individuals and their psychosocial suffering, as it happens to the bisexual person who wants to be of the opposite sex but is faced with the desire of others who want to treat him as a heterosexual individual plus his uneasiness and concern about the gender of his birth.

Many psychological diseases are associated with the genetic defect that occurs to those who want to give up their sex, whether by external change or a transforming surgical operation. These diseases are mainly attributed to biological factors such as, genetic makeup, which makes him hate his sex and the disturbance in the hormones that the fetus is exposed to before birth. This means that the sexual identity reflects the conformity of the biological sex (male or female) with the gender behaviour of the biological gender so that the features of this identity appear in the period of adolescence or the sexual puberty period. In this aspect, many societies and cultures despise in the sense of mocking and criticizing the heterosexual sexual behaviour of the gender, which in turn affects the personality of the bearers of this dual identity due to the criticism they are subject to by the people around them in the family, school and neighbourhood. Therefore, it leaves them feeling the inferiority, unease, and anxiety that is crystallized deep inside them. All this makes them avert their sex with a burning desire to belong to the other sex. It is, in fact, a pathological condition that expresses those who want their biological sex to be removed from them so that they can manifest the other sex (male or female). It is therefore, a self-dissonance with their sex that occurs and is accompanied by constant anxiety and anguish because they want to be in the opposite sex in behaviour, dress, logic, speech, adornment, hobbies, imagination, and temperament.

There is no harm in saying that sexual identity and its problems reflect social elimination or social exclusion for those who suffer disturbance. Such an exclusion is represented by isolating them from society, averting them, and not contacting or interacting with them after being stigmatized socially. Such stigmatism is often associated with the removal of confidence and social consideration from them because their behaviour is not identical to their biological sex. They are being called bisexual or tomboy, so social disdain and collective exclusion take place, which makes his social status shaky, his social role debilitating, and a lonely and withdrawn personality. In fact, this problem was not known in the past because it expresses a sharp dichotomy between body and soul, behaviour and thinking, self-perception and social exclusion, and a contradiction between his psychological feeling and the nature of his biological body. Meaning, if he is completely masculine, his psychological feeling is completely opposite to his masculinity and the same situation with the female. This disconnection, stigma, and social ostracism may lead to suicide if the suffering of the owner of the troubled identity continues for a long period of time.

In brief, gender identity disorder is an expression of a mental illness of a certain sex in another sexual body, like a man in a woman's body or a woman's mind in a man's body. Sexual identity concerns the conformity of the biological body with the senses and the mind of its kind, such as the body of a man with masculine mind and senses, and the same for the woman where her femininity conforms to her senses and mind. As for her illness, it involves the body of a man inhabited by the mind and female senses, or the body of a woman in which a male mind and senses are trapped. It can be said that this case which is defined by the sexual identity, is contrary to social provisions and people's perception of this schizophrenia. It generates a social rejection of the sufferer due to the divergence of biological sex from the sociocultural role attributed to him according to the sex he was born with. As for the symptoms of sexual identity disorder, they include the following features: -

1. Extreme and permanent identification with the opposite sex.
2. Repeatedly expressing a desire to belong to the opposite sex.
3. Preference for the clothing and roles of the opposite sex.
4. Strong desire to participate in entertainment and games of the opposite sex.
5. There is a clear preference to play with and behave like mates of the opposite sex.
6. Desire to live and be treated as if he were of the opposite sex.
7. Convinced that he possesses the feelings and emotions that are characteristic of the opposite sex.
8. Appears uncomfortable with his sex.
9. Feeling incompatible with the sexual identity attributed to him.
10. His thinking that the sex he was born into was not good.
11. His preference for isolation and alienation from members of his sex leads him to a lack of self-respect, which leads to a feeling of hostility towards the family and the school.

On the whole, sexual identity disorder represents an individual psychological and social problem at present that requires studying from modern science such as gender sociology in order to inform its students about the latest social and psychological problems of the new generation.

Finally, we refer to gender identity disorder related to intersexuality, which we will discuss in more detail in the next chapter.

1 – GENDER DYSPHORIA

It is an internal conflict that involves annoyance, dissatisfaction, anxiety, and discomfort with the male or female body. It may interfere with the daily behaviour and habits with this disorder, such as his behaviour in school, work, or during social activities. Gender identity disorder (dysphoria) is the feeling of anxiety and distress caused by a mismatch between biological sex and gender identity. This disorder is sometimes known as "gender paradox " or "transgenderism."

Biological sex is determined at birth according to the genitals, and gender identity is a person's sense of their sex away from their biological make-up. Biological sex and gender identity are often the same for most people, but this is not the case for everyone. For example, the body may be the body of a man, but a person identifies himself as a woman, while others may not feel that they are male or female.

Mismatch between sex and gender identity can lead to painful and uncomfortable feelings called gender discomfort. Such discomfort is a recognized medical condition and may sometimes be treated, but not a mental illness. Some people with gender identity disorder have a strong and persistent desire to live according to their gender identity rather than their biological sex. These people are called transgender people.

Signs of Gender Dysphoria: The first signs of gender dysphoria can appear at a young age. For example, a child may refuse to dress as typical boys or girls or be averse to participating in games and activities typical of boys or girls. In most cases, this type of behaviour is just part of other signs that will appear in the future when they get older and into adolescence. Still, the signs are apparent for those who suffer from a gender imbalance from childhood until adulthood.

Adults with this social distress can feel trapped inside a body that does not match their gender identity. They may feel uneasy about aligning with societal expectations that they are living according to their biological sex rather than the gender they feel they belong to. They may also have a strong desire to change or get rid of physical signs of their biological sex, such as facial hair or breasts.

It is important to consult a doctor if a child is thought to have a sexual disorder. If needed, the doctor can refer the child to a gender identity specialist for a personal assessment and provide any support they need.

Gender Dysphoria Diagnose: Usually, gender dysphoria is diagnosed with in-depth evaluation by two or more professionals. This may require several sessions at different stages that last for a few months and include discussions with family members or friends.

The evaluation identifies any defects in gender identity and needs, which can include:

- An apparent mismatch between biological sex and gender identity
- There is a strong desire to change special physical properties due to any mismatch.
- How to deal with any difficulties in the event of a potential incompatibility
- How feelings and behaviours develop over time
- What kind of support is needed from others, such as friends and family?

The evaluation may also include a more general evaluation of physical and mental health.

Treating Gender Dysphoria Discomfort: If the results of the evaluation indicate that the child has a defect in his / her gender identity, professional doctors and psychologists will work to come up with an individualized treatment plan. This includes any psychological support the patient may need. The treatment aims to help reduce or eliminate the painful feelings a person experiences due to a mismatch between biological sex and gender identity. Here, the nature of suffering differs from one person to another. For some people, they can live as their preferred gender. For others, it could mean taking hormones or having surgery to alter their physical appearance.

Causes of Gender Dysphoria: The development of gender identity is complex, and the possible differences that cause a mismatch between biological sex and gender identity to vary. Sometimes, hormones disrupt the improper development of biological sex on the brain and genitals, causing differences between them. The reason may be:

- Additional hormones possibly as a result of taking medications.
- Androgen insensitivity syndrome: sexual dysfunction due to the failure of hormones to work properly in the womb.
- Congenital adrenal hyperplasia. [https://ellearabia. com]

2 - GENDER IDENTITY DISORDER

An abbreviation is known as (GID) which is the medical terminology of dysphoria. It is a diagnosis that doctors, psychologists, and physiologists give to people who are uncomfortable or anxious about the sex they were born with. It was considered a psychological classification, and then the diagnosis was removed from the list of mental and psychological diseases. But all sources, whether old or recent, recognized that the causes are biological, such as the genetic makeup of the human being or the brain structure related to the hormonal effects on the brain in the period of embryogenesis (prenatal). This diagnosis describes the problems related to hatred and discomfort with the body. The mind of the sufferer is charged with changing the body or correcting the physical sex to match the sexual identity. It is a diagnostic classification that does not generally apply to "sexually corrected" or "transgender people."

The diagnosis of gender identity disorder as described in available psychiatry literature: It is a defect in which a person is born, and they attribute its cause to the environment or education. But with medical progress, it became clear that there are so-called (gender lines) or (sexual lines) in the brain responsible for defining and feeling the brain about the sex to which it belongs, which is called sexual identity. Scientists have concluded that these lines are different in these patients so that a person feels from birth that he belongs to the opposite sex to his anatomical sex.

It turns out that this difference is due to a disturbance in (hormones) that the foetus is exposed to "before" birth, which affects its genes, and thus affects the sexual lines in the brain. Hence the tragedy of the disorder of sexual/gender identity begins. Symptoms begin to appear from birth, and since the behaviour of the male infant differs from the female, the infant follows the behaviour of the opposite sex, then increases. The symptoms become clear during early childhood. The male child, for example, who is less than 3 years old, feels that he is a female and behaves like a female child in various aspects of his life, from the style of play to the way of urinating.

Harry Benjamin was an endocrinologist who specialized in sex reassignment issues. He was one of the first to open clinics specializing in the reassignment of the sexes of people of both sexes.

The diagnosis: Childhood gender identity disorder is usually described as "present from birth" and is considered "clinical." It is not similar to gender identity disorder that appears during adolescence or adulthood. At a time when many cultures denounce heterosexual behaviour, they negatively affect people who suffer from it and those close to them. In many cases, there is a feeling of discomfort that stems from this person's body being "wrong" or different.

Gender identity disorder is characterized by a severe aversion to the actual gender of a person, with a desire to belong to the opposite sex. There is a permanent preoccupation with clothing or activities of the opposite sex with a rejection of the actual sex, and this disorder is more common in boys than in girls.

Manifestation of Female Sexual Disorders: Constant and continuing stress about being a girl with a desire to become a boy, playing rough games, owning guns, avoiding playing dolls, and refusing to urinate in a sitting position. Some of them pretend or imagine that a male organ will appear to her and that she will not grow breasts like her girls' peers. They do not care about female roles, and they make male friends.

Manifestation of Male Sexual Disorders: Constant stress about being a boy and a desire to become a girl, wearing dresses, playing with brides, refusing to play with boys, paying attention to what girls wear in terms of underwear or outerwear or accessories, and paying attention to fashion and what the fashion houses offer, and some of them imagine that he will become a woman and his masculine genital disappears, and female genital organs will appear to him to be able to become pregnant. They suffer from social rejection and exclusion to a greater degree than girls with troubled sexual identities. The diagnosis of gender identity disorder requires the presence of a disorder in the natural sense of masculinity or femininity. However, there are no organic reasons for that, and that male childish behaviour among girls or female behaviour among boys is not sufficient.

Transgender people: There are many children who are born with visible birth defects, so their parents rush to plastic surgeons to realize these defects. But there are other types of birth defects that are not recognized by society and approaching them in order to try to fix them is considered a religious taboo, including birth defects in the genitals or the so-called (intersex), or people with gender identity disorder, where some need psychological treatment and others need surgical intervention for immediate gender correction. The suffering of these people lies in the fact that there is a message recorded in the brain that determines their true gender. In the past, determining the sex of a new-born was done from the shape of his genitals only. But with the development of science, society discovered that such a criterion for determining sex was not sufficient to determine the identity of the new-born, as there are hormones and their proportions and the glands responsible for their secretion. Hence, scientists added a new standard for determining the sex of the child. These are genes, hormones, and the places and times of their secretion. They discovered females with internal testicles in their womb, males with a womb, females without a womb or ovaries, and much more. After many years passed, it was discovered that there are full-fledged feminine females and all the previous criteria prove that they are female. Still, they carry a male chromosome, as is the case for males, and after a while, they discovered that there

105

are cases carrying a non-male and non-female chromosome. Still, studies returned to prove that transgender people carry the combination of the sex mind, which they turned to because the chemical structure of the brain differs from male to female. And there are many researchers interested in these cases of correcting sex (transgender).

Scientific Explanation of This Disease: When the foetus is in the eighth week of pregnancy, certain hormones begin to communicate, and the message begins in the brain and then moves to the gonad, where in the beginning, before the eighth week of pregnancy, the gonads are not classified. At this stage, the foetus has the ability to be female or male, but this is not classified. When the eighth week of pregnancy passes, the brain sends certain hormones to the gonads, either male or female gonads, which will convert to the female or male reproductive system. The message is sent from the brain to the bottom to say: Do your work and then go back to the top; sometimes the message does not return to the top or back up partially, so a biological defect happens due to non-return or partial return of the response message which represents the onset of the sex disturbance.

Scientific Aspect: From a scientific point of view, the disease of gender or sexual identity disorder means the sexual transition from male to female or the opposite. This type of disease and the possibility of sexual reassignment were not known in the past, but doctors today believe; it is a real disease recognized in reputable medical encyclopaedias. The British Encyclopaedia also mentioned the disease of transgender as (a disorder in the sexual identity that makes the sufferer believes to be of the opposite sex). The male, for example, is born with full male genitalia, and he is therefore not hermaphroditic. Still, he identifies himself with women from an early age and behaves as one of them. He looks forward to establishing relationships with males as they are the opposite sex while not homosexual. Therefore, homosexual societies in America refuse the affiliation of transgender people because most of them do not want to practice homosexual sex. He is not afflicted with sexual perversion that pushes the man to wear women's clothes or the opposite as a matter of imitation. Rather, he desires a complete conversion to the opposite sex, which is a desire that cannot be avoided because (Transsexual) disease is an actual disease as well. . As the doctors say, afflicted people swear it is not a satanic whim. As mentioned in the British Encyclopaedia: (This disease continues for many years, and most of the life, with the risk of developing depression and leading to suicide). It begins at an early stage before puberty as it has nothing to do with sexual desires and continues until surgery though it does not completely end with it. One of those infected with this disease says (he has no choice in this disease, rather it is a calamity that befell his head). The disease causes serious mental illnesses. Various studies of the symptoms of this disease have revealed that psychological diseases are associated with it. The patient withdraws and retreats to endure his terrible torments for fear of revealing his truth. Psychological treatment of this disease does not help, as Dr. Saeed Abdel-Azim says, especially since most of these cases are not discovered until at a late stage after puberty. The patient himself does not admit that he is psychologically ill. Rather, the idea of converting to the opposite sex becomes urgent for him, controlling all his thoughts and pushing him to resort to surgeons.

An extensive investigation on this issue conducted by Osama Al-Rahimi in Cairo and published in Al-Shorouk Magazine (Issue 329 dated 7/27/1998) shows that the transgender disease is a severe dichotomy between the soul and the body, so the male is fully masculine in terms of the visible genital organs, but his psychological feeling is completely opposite to that, as he feels that he is a female, just as the female is completely feminine in terms of her visible genital organs. Still, she feels that she is a male. . Suppose psychological treatment cannot end the schizophrenia. In that case, sexual transformation by surgery becomes a must with the aim of re adaptation between the soul and the body, which is the basis of mental and physical health as per doctors and scientists.

Difference Between Correction And Conversion: There is a big difference between the terms; correction and conversion, as: (sexual correction) is a term that applies to those who suffer from congenital mutilation of the genital organs, such as; if there are two reproductive systems at the same time, one a male and the other a female, or there is a hidden genital organ need to appear, or the person's chromosomes are male, while his external appearance is female or vice versa. This condition is pathological and results in a disorder in the personality of the sick person that goes beyond being a mere psychological disorder. A congenital deformity affects the personality, which needs surgery to correct the dominant sex on the other. On the contrary, in cases of (transgender), there is no congenital defect, but the issue is a behavioural or psychological state that afflicts the individual for various reasons. It could be environmental, educational, erotic, etc., where these cases do not need to correct the gender or an identity. Still, it needs psychological treatment and brain washing from contamination attached to it. Sex change, in this case, is called (sexual transformation) because it is the result of only self-desire and is not based on legitimate justifications according to medical controls.

Family Role in Transformation and Correction: The family has a great role in treating the imbalance related to offspring (male or female) through understanding the issue from a specialized medical point of view and behaviour. It is a grave mistake to attribute the defect in some people in their gender and the presence of disturbance in their formation as if it is a trivial imitation of the opposite sex, or as if it is due to a curse and expulsion from the mercy of God. This is absolutely right because the sick person suffering such a disorder did not seek it out of his own will, nor with longing from him, but it is his bad luck, and he will be lucky if the problem is addressed from the beginning. It needs the parents to have a conscious understanding of recognizing the issue and exerting medical reasons for examining it and resolving it without being affected by social emotion or blaming anyone for it. This is true because in eastern society, in particular, most parents are covering it up or rejecting it, hoping that it will correct itself as the child grows. Some parents may resort to punishing their new-born, and the disease worsens, and even if the father were able to bury this new-born, he would have done, but he resorted to beating and threatening. Others threw the patient to the police departments to fix its defect. Some even went further in depriving him or expelling him from the country. The issue of correction or transfer is according to the opinion of the medical specialists, and after examination and consideration, appropriate action can be taken regarding such pathological cases. Operations can be performed, and official papers related to the person can be changed to end the problem before it is aggravated, and the parents then do not know how to solve it.

Reasons: There are no specific causes for gender identity disorder as they are auxiliary or predisposing factors: biological factors such as abnormalities and sexual bisexuality.

The sixth edition of the International Statistical Classification of Diseases and Health-Related Problems showed different diagnoses of gender identity disorder, including transgender, heterosexual imitation, and childhood sexual identity disorder. Other gender identity disorders are not identified.

Arguing: Many people with gender identity disorder do not consider their mixed sexual feelings and behaviours a disorder. People who suffer from gender identity disorder always ask what "normal" gender identity or "normal" sexual role should be. There is one argument that sexual characteristics are social and have nothing to do with biological sex. This perspective shows that other cultures, especially the historical ones, were evaluating the sexual roles that presently suggest homosexuality and transsexual change is normal behaviour. Some people see sex change as a way to deconstruct the sexes. But not all Tran's people want to deconstruct sex.

Problems and Obstacles: The problem is that many religious scholars, particularly in Muslim countries, do not know specifically the nature of the disease of sexual or gender identity disorder, and sometimes they confuse it with homosexuality or the deviation of sexual and moral behaviour in general. This is the responsibility of psychiatrists to explain to them the nature of this disease and its repercussions so that the fatwa issued by them is clear. This was evident in the fatwa of Sheikh Faisal Mawlawi, as he had read, heard, and knew a lot about illness. Therefore, his fatwa was specific and estimated for the difficulty of the suffering of the sick and also compatible with the fundamentals of religion.

The treatment of gender identity disorders must be multi-faceted or multidimensional, and therefore it includes: -

1. Distinguishing the patient's condition by a psychiatrist to know if it is just a behavioural condition or a real problem of sexual identity and does the patient view himself as a male or female?

2. When the condition is diagnosed, it is treated accordingly. If it is a behavioural problem, he is treated behaviourally. Suppose it is like (schizophrenia) associated with that. In that case, the patient imagines he is a female, and vice versa; he can be treated with drugs and many cases that resemble the disorder.

3. Studies have shown that it is not possible to change the sexual identity of a person, whether a child or an adult and if some of them were changed, that means their conditions were not more than behavioural cases.

4. Suppose the diagnose has proven that the case is a gender identity disorder contrary to the biological sex, and psychological treatment did not change the feel for 3-6 months during which the patient lives in the role of different sex. In that case, they undergo hormonal treatment and then surgical treatment to correct the sex.

5. Finally, there are many controversies about the disease (gender identity disorder) due to the difference of concepts among some doctors. Some believe that it is just a behavioural phenomenon, while others the issue and put every person likening the opposite sex under the disorder's name. Therefore, knowledge and studies about this phenomenon must be considered more seriously, especially in the eastern societies, to avoid converting the patients of this disease into victims of the society.

Youngest Known Case of Gender Identity Disorder (GID): Various British media have taken an interest in the case of this boy called Zachary Avery, who is now 5 years old. He has blonde braids and wears a short purple skirt; he has now been living as a girl for more than a year after he first refused to live as a boy when he was three years old. Instead, he chose to wear pink dresses and have ribbons in his long blonde hair - because he suffers from the disorder known as GID.

The British newspaper The Daily Telegraph indicated in this regard that the elementary school he goes to in Essex has changed the children's toilets into ones that can be gendered in support of Zachary since his condition was officially diagnosed last year. Zachary is one of the youngest children in Britain to be diagnosed with a gender identity disorder, meaning that he feels like a girl trapped inside a boy's body.

Mother Teresa Avery, 32, said that Zachary was a "normal" little child but suddenly decided at the end of 2010 that he wanted to live as a girl. And that from her time, he began to tend to everything related to young girls and began wearing girls' clothes. This worried his parents, especially about his behaviour, which is why they took him to the doctors.

After a number of consultations, he was formally diagnosed with a gender identity disorder by national health professionals, making Zachary one of the youngest children with this disorder in the United Kingdom. The specialists explained that this disorder is a conflict between the actual physical sex of a person and the gender that the person, whether male or female, sees that he or she suits him.

Mother says: "The specialists have told us that although Zachary has the body of a boy, his brain tells him that he is a girl. At school, his classmates deal with him well, and the

112

school itself handles it wonderfully, and it gives Zachary all the support." She continued by saying, "I do not deny that I would love for my son to go back to where he was in the beginning, but I want him to be happy. And if that is the path that he would like to take, and if that is what will make him happy, then so be it. To him is my full support. "

For its part, a spokeswoman for the Tavistock Clinic in London refused to comment on a specific case, saying only that there are only 7 children under the age of five who were diagnosed with this disorder last year, and Zachary became one of the youngest sufferers.

Reaction of Eastern Societies to Gender Identity Disorder: The sufferers of GID in the eastern society, particularly in Muslim society, are no different from those of the western society half-century ago. The confusion and misunderstanding of the cause of this disease make it difficult to be handled and accepted socially. The religious quotes and their deep roots in, society complicated the issue by mixing the concept of gender identity disorder, a real disease, with the psychological behaviour of homosexuality as it referred to. Recently a Kuwaiti cleric (Daham Al-Qahtan) broke the silence and issued a declaration for the permissibility of transferring sex from male to female or vice versa if he/she suffers from TRANS-SEX. He is the first cleric in Kuwait and perhaps in the eastern countries decrees such permissibility of conducting this type of sexual transformation operation. His call was categorically rejected by large segments of the society, especially those belonging to religious groups. In his advisory opinion, the cleric Rashid Al-Alimi asserts that it is a grave mistake to view those affected by GID disease as imitating the opposite sex "because the sufferers did not seek this matter out of their own free will, nor with longing from them." He emphasised that the process of sexual transformation is only permissible for people with TRANS-SEX disease, and this does not include imitating the opposite sex for reasons that are not normal and not related to this disease. This declaration would support the efforts made by some of those affected by transgender people. Yes, as their focus is the law prohibiting imitating the opposite sex, which was enacted by conservatives and other representatives in the National Assembly in 2007. The objective of the complaint is to amend the law or to put in place an executive regulation that can specify the limits of imitating the opposite sex. He acknowledges that he agreed with the process of sexual transformation. It takes place according to the opinion of the medical people after a medical and psychological examination and through appropriate protocol regarding such pathological conditions. He indicated that society's values shall not be sacrificed by copying the practice of other societies as each society has its own values in terms of cultural and religious boundaries. The sufferers of GID confirmed that they are not homosexual and do not want to practice adultery or lesbianism. They emphasized that they are real patients in a state of schizophrenia between the body that follows a specific gender and the mind that deals and belongs since childhood to another gender different to the features of their bodies. Therefore, their imitation of the other sex cannot be considered a malicious need in thinking, or a malicious instinct aimed at practicing fornication or lesbianism. This is exactly the interpretation that Al-Alimi adopted, considering the conversion to the opposite sex acceptable religiously. According to scientific opinions, it protects a person from the risk of self-killing, which is the inevitable end for those affected by this disease.

Diagnostic Rules for Gender Identity Disorder According to the American Classification of Psychiatric Diseases:

1. There is a strong and enduring tendency to identify (self-identification) with the heterosexual sex, not just a desire due to a better social position for the opposite sex. In adolescents and adults, the disorder appears with symptoms such as recognition of the desire to be of the opposite sex, act often as a member of the opposite sex, or the desire to be treated by others as a member of the opposite sex, or the complete conviction that he/she belongs to the opposite sex and feels his/her feelings and interacts in his own way.

2. Permanent distress and dissatisfaction with his/her feeling of inadequacy of the social role dictated by his anatomical sex. In adolescents and adults, this appears with symptoms such as Preoccupation with getting rid of sexual characteristics and members of the body that belong to the rejected sex, so he/she requests, for example, hormone therapy to change the tone of the voice, and perhaps he/she dreams of surgery to change those organs so that he resembles members of the opposite sex, and some of them believe that he was born wrongly with this gender.

3. This disorder should not be diagnosed in cases of intersexuality, that is, the actual biological overlap between the sexes, not just psychological.

4. The disturbance must not be accompanied by defects and discomfort in social, functional, or other aspects of behaviour. [https://ar.wikipedia.org]

3 - GENDER IDENTITY DISORDER IN ADOLESCENTS

From time to time, we hear about a young man who turned into a girl after an operation. This news is usually accompanied by media inflations and a variety of exciting opinions.

We also find around us some males who are young children that their hair is long, and we can hardly distinguish that they are males by their appearance or behaviour.

From a medical and psychological point of view, there is a psycho-behavioural disorder called "gender identity disorder," whereby the patient becomes dissatisfied with his/her natural sexual identity with which he/she was born. He/she tries to be assimilated continuously and in multiple ways in the form of characteristics and behaviours of the opposite sex. This disorder is generally rare and not common, and it affects males several times more than females.

This disorder usually begins at an early age, from the age of two to four years, when the male child tends to play with female games such as dolls (Barbie, Fella, etc.) and pay attention to the appearance of his hair and clothes in a manner similar to females through hairdos, ribbons, and so on, in addition to his imitation of female movements, various styles, and behaviours. In the case of the female child who suffers from this disorder, we find that she tends to rough physical games and speculation, playing with male games such as guns, swords, etc., and appearing masculine in form, behaviour, and interests.

In adulthood, adolescence, and youth, the turmoil continues for a large proportion, and their suffering increases within the family and in society. Some of them resort to hormonal drugs to affect their body and appearance in

116

proportion to the shape of the opposite sex. Some also resort to requesting a change of sex surgically. Homosexual fantasies, as well as same-sex sexual practices, are generally more common in this category.

The Reasons: The causes of this disorder are still not clear or precisely defined. The old theories talked about a hormonal imbalance. Still, recent studies have proven that there is no disturbance in the level of male or female hormones, respectively, as each one has his/her hormone levels normal. . However, one of the theories attributed the disorder to the isolation of the child from his peers of similar age and same-sex, which leads to a lack of representation of the characteristics and behaviours appropriate to the sex of the child.

Learning theories stress that gender identity disorder results from a misrepresentation of the corresponding gender or a contradiction and inconsistency in encouraging the correct assimilation of the corresponding gender. It seems that the parents and the home environment have an important role in the development of the child's view of himself and the representation of his natural sexual identity properly. Parents can encourage sexual behaviour that does not correspond to the child's gender. For example, when a male child plays with a doll or wears a female's dress or shoes, then finds positive laughs and smiles of those around him, such behaviour becomes desirable, which he will try to repeat until normalisation level.

On top of the above and in particular, in the eastern societies, there are many explanations for the wrong behaviour of the parents, including some of the inherited and strange popular beliefs related to issues of envy. The parents, for example, resort to lengthening the hair of the beautiful male child to show him in a feminine look to avoid envy!!!

A mother can contribute to her male son's turmoil through her own relationship with him. She encourages him to be like her instead of resembling his father through a satisfying merging relationship with him. This occurs due to marital and family conflicts and the formation of axes and fronts within the family.

The separation of the father from the family also plays in cases of frequent travel, separation, or other reasons; a negative role in being represented by his male children. Likewise, in the event that the father's personality is weak or disturbed, and his professional or social failure. Of course, the natural basis for the growth and development of a healthy sexual identity is the representation of sexually compatible models starting from the name to the look, appearance, behaviours, interests, and general characteristics.

The truth is that children's maturation and growth processes pass through several stages, and they continue into adolescence and beyond. The individual's view of him/herself and his/her evaluation of it is undergoing multiple developments, changes, anxiety, and contradictions, and the educational and social upbringing conditions play a major role in reaching a healthy enough degree of self-confidence, body, and status, and with the appropriate appreciation for it, in proportion to masculinity or femininity.

Treatment: For children, it is based on controlling, preventing, and punishing the disturbing behaviour. And also, to stop clearly and resolutely encouraging disruptive behaviour by everyone in his environment. The method of reward and repeated encouragement benefits the natural behaviour proportional to gender and gradually according to the details of each case.

It is necessary to pay attention to conflicts within the family and the psychological and practical problems of the mother. Family sessions are useful to alleviate family problems and direct efforts in a positive and constructive manner. In adult cases, psychological and behavioural therapy is useful in modifying an individual's view of himself and adopting his natural sexual identity. The remedial effort represents a kind of gradual re-learning. A male therapist is recommended in the case of a young man who suffers from the disorder, which contributes to his adoption of the positive and understanding image of the same-sex therapist, which facilitates reshaping the natural sexual identity. In the case of the young female, female therapy is recommended to facilitate the re-assimilation.

In a number of severe cases, surgery can be performed. Initial studies have found the surgery to be a successful treatment, with enthusiasm, propaganda, and misconceptions. But after the increase in the number of cases treated surgically through a sex change, it became clear that there are significant psychological and social problems. These included an increase in suicides and depression in transgender patients. And also, the increase in addictive problems, problems of divorce, prostitution, and others. Some of them were unable to adapt to their new body and requested that it be returned to its previous position. This is, of course, unrealistic after the removal of the external male sexual organs and the surgical formation of female-like physical organs.

Finally, there is no doubt that prevention is always better than cure. And severe cases of sexual identity disorder are not easy to treat and deal with. There are various other instances of lack of self-confidence from a sexual point of view, which are widespread and should be distinguished from a gender identity disorder. And in it, the young man is not confident in his masculinity, that he is not attractive to the opposite sex, that he is not beautiful or short in stature or any other inferiority complex related to sexual matters. The same applies to the girl, who feels that she is not beautiful or obese and is unpopular. This is linked to the normal and natural anxiety that usually increases in adolescence.

It may occur to a young man or woman that he or she is a homosexual if he/she is attached to and loves someone of his gender or if he/she has unacceptable personal fantasies. All of this is understandable and normal and needs more medical sexual education, amending some misconceptions about himself and his behaviour, building self-confidence, and positive development of personal skills and abilities in various fields.

It must be emphasized that the aforementioned feelings of anxiety and the accompanying thoughts about self-confidence in terms of sexual, do not indicate a pathological disorder in sexual identity and do not lead to dissatisfaction with the body and the desire to convert to the opposite sex. The anxiety here is relative and does not extend to the essence of sexual identity. And in some cases, people who have "borderline personality disorder," which is characterized by changing identity, interests, and activities from time to time. These cases may appear to have been suffering from "gender identity disorder" for swhile. Still, they retract their behaviours and return to their normal gender identity. Also, some "homosexual" persons of both sexes may show desires to change their features and their physical, sexual identity, thinking that they will become more acceptable to the same sex. Usually, these desires subside from time to time.

120

It is worth mentioning that modern society has witnessed changes in its traditional composition, male and female behaviour patterns, and the roles associated with each gender. Of course, there are similar rights and duties of the two genders, which must be affirmed. There are also changes in shape and clothing that have become common and acceptable, such as unisex short hair, jeans, sports shoes, and others. However, it does not mean ignoring the differences and points between them or leaving them vague or confused in the educational or social field. These include the natural gender identity and the sexual and formal differences between women and men that cannot be changed.

It must be emphasized that the male and the female each carry within themselves mixed characteristics, roles, and hormones, but in proportions that increase according to the anatomical sex that each carry. These deep aspects must be reconciled and integrated.

Finally, self-confidence from the sexual point of view is related to the qualities of the body, intelligence, and the entirety of skills, personal, moral, intellectual, and social characteristics, and so on. This trust must be continuously developed and maintained, and sexual and psychological awareness must be increased, which contributes to more psychological and social health.

The following are a number of general educational, psychological advice.

1. Confirming the child's belonging to his gender by likening him to a father, brother, maternal uncle, or other male. As well as for the girl and her mother and other females. In the event of the great similarity in the face, skin, eyes, or anything else. Between a male and his mother or sister, differences between them must be found and emphasized. And also looking for points of

similarity with the father and the rest of the males in form, body, and behaviour. The same applies to the girl who is physically similar to her male brother or father.

2. Moving away from encouraging anything that distorts the representation of the natural sexual identity. Especially in childhood, such as excessive hair lengthening for males and excessive hair shortening for females.

3. Encouraging the child's assimilation to the behaviour consistent with his sex continuously. There is nothing wrong with exploring, experimenting, and getting to know the opposite sex, its behaviours, style, and games within the framework of a love of knowledge and broadening perceptions. Attention must be paid to the seriousness of such behaviours and the need to control them and stay away from them in the event of their recurrence and continuation.

4. The participation of the child or girl in selecting toys, gifts, and clothes. And pay attention to its connotations and links to the appropriate sexual identity.

5. Emphasizing that the child mixes with his peers and learns from them. The mixing between the sexes does not mean mixing and distorting the sexual identity, but rather the similarity in rights and duties and useful learning about the other. [http://www.almostshar.com]

C. **HERMAPHRODITISM AND TRANSGENDER**

This topic is closely related to the Gender/Sexual Identity Disorder that was covered in the previous section. It is worth mentioning that the sociology of gender is modern science that deals with gender's social difficulties resulting from biological problems, which could lead to a gender identity disorder, and its subsequent effects on the roles of the sufferers within their societies. It is not concerned with the biological base and their medical treatment; instead, it covers the dissonances, paradoxes, and dissociation between the present identity and the stereotypical image of male and female gender identity. It also investigates the reflection of such disconnect in terms of psychological and social problems such as anxiety, continuous distress, stability, and a sense of inferiority of the sufferer.

Hermaphroditism refers to intersexuality and concerns a person who has physical characteristics that are not clearly masculine or feminine, and it is not limited to the visible sexual characteristics such as the genitals, but characteristics within the body such as hereditary elements and hormones. Intersexuality is of four types: feminine intersexuality, masculine, real and complex. The symptoms of intersexuality are the resembling of the opposite sex and imitation in terms of wearing clothes, imitation of the voice, or walking, then aversion and disgust of his/her genitals. People with hermaphroditism have a strong desire to own the genitals of the opposite sex and to get rid of their genitals.

Very briefly, hermaphroditism is considered as an innate violation of sexual development in which the external genital organs have signs of both female and male gender. Besides the feeling of inferiority and shame with advancing age, the health of the hermaphroditism's sufferer degrades and appears in the form of a feeling the loneliness and isolation from social life and society, depression, a tendency to suicide and open hostility to others. The hermaphroditism in the eastern societies creates and is associated with a lot of family problems by or between the parents, such as the divorce, exchange of blame in having a child of dual sex, preventing the child from going to school to avoid embarrassment, or continuous conflict because of him.

Transgender, which refers to the individual's knowledge of his gender, whether he is male or female, is not his or her true gender or the gender of his or her newborn or born into it. Some of them feel psychologically that they belong to the other sex completely or partially, but they do not want their body or gender to change to Another gender, this category is known as genderqueer, and there are other groups who feel gender identity disorder called gender identity disorder, and they completely reject their body in which they were born and seek to change it into another gender from man to woman or vice versa, and this type is called trans-sexual in the sense of crossing to the other sex.

As for the effeminate and transgender in a male society, as is the case in eastern societies, his situation is thorny because the society lives a traditional setup focused on masculinity and femininity and not what is in between. It glorifies virility, strength, boldness, roughness, and glorifies femininity, tenderness, timidity, shame and modesty, and does not mix between them.

It is a dividing boundary, so the effeminate and transgender people are met with ridicule, alienation, ostracisation and social stigmatisation, which hinders their lives and let them feel the alienation and social isolation that led them to leave society or to commit suicide. All doors are closed Infront of them, and their career progress is aborted. They cannot work in commercial, administrative, or political businesses that require direct interaction with the individuals in charge because of their reputation and low consideration by eastern societies, which ask their members to live in the spirit of their biological body. It can be said that eastern societies lack awareness and education about disturbances in sexual identity and human rights for transgender people who are not officially or socially sponsored.

1. Intersexuality

There is no specific definition for intertextuality, but in general, it can be explained as; the case of a person who was born with middle sex (intersex) between what is considered a standardised criterion of masculinity and femininity. And he/she is, therefore, different from any of them. The differences from the usual norms of the male and female sexes may be organic, chromosomal, differences in the secondary sexual characteristics or other differences that are known or unknown. And cannot be conclusively identified as male or female according to medically, legally, or socially accepted criteria. Medicine has adopted this term during the last century, referring to any person who is not classified as male or female.

Common Misconceptions: Intersex does not necessarily mean ambiguity or confusion in the external sexual organs, nor does it necessarily indicate the presence of two male and female organs at the same time, though the latter is one of the multiple types of INTERSEX cases. It is not like as many thinks that the affected person wants to undergo sexual correction surgically, as the damages may outweigh the gains. It is also not in the interest of the newborn to force corrective surgical intervention to determine his/her sex early (in their infancy), contrary to what the common people and some doctors believe, as this person may acknowledge his belonging to the opposite sex upon reaching his/her adulthood, opposite to what doctors specified (or the choice of the parents). Therefore, the psychological and physical consequences on this person will be catastrophic because it will create another artificial hermaphroditism of increased symptoms and complications.

Controversy Due to Misuse of Description Terms: Many are on purpose disgracing the intersex by describing them as bisexual, bisexual, transsexual, and transvestite in a pejorative and insulting manner. The word of intersex and its derivatives carried the disadvantages, regardless of its meaning in the past, so the blame here falls on the community that distorts the words and changes them to obscene meanings, not blaming the language. In old Arabic literature, the effeminate was described as the one who softened his words and broke in his gait, and he was praised like a woman. That was in his creation wherein most conditions he has no sexual desire in women, and the women are not attracted to him [https://ar.wikipedia.org].

2. Hermaphroditism, its Types, and the Third Sex

It is a group of cases in which there is a contradiction between the external and internal genital organs (testicles and ovaries). The old term for intersexuality is known as hermaphroditism, and this name came as a result of combining the names of the Greek god and goddess with each other, "Hormuz and Aphrodite". Hermes is the goddess of the male sex, and Aphrodite is the goddess of female sexuality, love, and beauty. This condition is now called Disorders of Sexual Development (DSD).

The Reasons

Hermaphroditism can be divided into four categories:
1) feminine hermaphroditism.
2) masculine hermaphroditism.
3) true hermaphroditism (true hermaphroditism).
4) complex or unspecified hermaphroditism.

They are detailed below, but in most cases and despite modern diagnostic methods, the cause of hermaphroditism (intersexuality)cannot be determined.

I. **Feminine Hermaphroditism:** This is a noticeably clear medical problem as the person, in this case, has the woman/s chromosomes and well-developed ovaries of a woman, but the external genitalia is masculine. Medically it seems that the mechanism in such a manifestation has happened during pregnancy. Here the fetus is often female, but she was exposed to excessive amounts of male hormones before birth (during the pregnancy). Due to such an excessive hormone, the labia majora of the female vagina fused together, and the clitoris enlarges to resemble a male penis. Typically, the uterus and fallopian tubes of this person are normal. This condition is also called "virilisation" or "female pseudo-femininity". pseudo-hermaphroditism. And this very type occurs due to several reasons, namely:

- Genetically or congenital adrenal hyperplasia: It is the most common cause of increased production of male hormones (androgens)
- Prescribing and giving male hormones such as testosterone to the mother during pregnancy.
- Male hormone-producing tumours in the expectant mother, especially ovarian tumours.
- Aromatase enzyme deficiency: This cannot be noticed until adulthood.

Aromatase: It is an enzyme that converts male hormones into female hormones. The increase in aromatase activity leads to the accumulation of large amounts of Aromatase: It is an enzyme that converts male hormones into female hormones. The increase in aromatase activity leads to the accumulation of large amounts of oestrogen (the female hormone), while the deficiency of the enzyme leads to female hermaphroditism.

Since this condition may not be noticed until adulthood, children (of the feminine chromosome XX) who have grown as females may begin to develop male characteristics. (the female hormone), while the deficiency of the enzyme leads to female hermaphroditism.

II.   **Feminine Hermaphroditism**: Here, a person has male chromosomes, but the external genitalia are unclear, or they may be clearly female. Internally, the testicles may be normal, deformed, or absent. This condition is also called "under- virilisation" or "pseudo-hermaphroditism".

The formation of the male external genitalia requires a balance between female hormones and male hormones, and for this reason, this requires the presence of male hormones in an adequate amount and with normal function.

The reasons that lead to this type of hermaphroditism are:

- Problems with the testicles: The testicles naturally produce the male hormones, and if you do not do them, this will lead to the occurrence of this type of intersexuality. There are several reasons that lead to the failure of the testicles to function, including Gonadal dysgenesis.

- Disturbance in the formation of testosterone (the male hormone): Testosterone is formed during several stages, and each stage requires a different enzyme. The deficiency of any of these enzymes can lead to the formation of insufficient amounts of testosterone, leading to the development of various forms of this hermaphroditism. Congenital hyperplasia of the adrenal gland may also be under this type of cause.

- Problems with the metabolism of testosterone: Some people have normal testes and sufficient amounts of testosterone, but they are intersex, so how did this happen? This happens in two cases:

a) Deficiency of the enzyme "5 alpha-reductase", which converts testosterone into dihydrotestosterone (DHT). Therefore, deficiency of this enzyme will prevent this

128

necessary and important transformation from benefiting from testosterone.

The deficiency of this enzyme has at least five patterns, so some children have male genitalia, and some have female genitalia, and there is a division that has male and female reproductive organs. The transformation of the external genitalia into masculine organs usually occurs at puberty.

b) Androgen insensitivity syndrome, which is the most common cause that leads to male-hermaphroditism. Here the hormones are normal, but the problem is at the level of the receptors as they do not work properly. There are more than 150 forms of this syndrome, given that there are more than 150 defects that cause this syndrome.

III. **Hermaphroditism True Gonadal (True Hermaphroditism):** In this case, the person possesses ovarian tissue and testicular tissue at the same time, where the two tissues exist in one gland (the same gonad) or what is called the ovotestis, or the person has one ovary and one testicle. A person may have XX or XY chromosomes, or both. The external genitalia may be vague, and it may be female or male. This condition is called "True Hermaphroditism," and in most cases of this type of hermaphroditism are of unknown cause, although some animal studies have shown a role for agricultural pesticides in their occurrence.

IV. **Complex or Indeterminate Hermaphroditism:** Some chromosomal disorders may cause disturbances in sexual development, and these disorders include:

1) Turner syndrome (XO-45): In this case, the patient has only one X chromosome, and the second is absent.

2) Klinefelter syndrome (XXY-47) and trisomy syndrome (XXX-47): In both cases, we have an extra sex chromosome; Either X or Y.

The previous disorders do not appear as hermaphroditism, but they are associated with disturbances in the level of sex hormones, sexual development, and the number of sex chromosomes.

Symptoms

The appearance of symptoms here depends on the condition causing hermaphroditism:

- Ambiguous genitals at birth
- Small penis
- An enlarged clitoris
- Undescended testicles (which may turn into ovaries) in males
- Groin masses that may turn into testicles in females
- Hypospadias (hypospadias), where the opening of the urethra, in this case, is below the penis in males, and in females, the opening of the urethra may be open within the vagina
- Strange and unusual genitals
- Ionic disturbances
- Delayed or no puberty
- Unexpected changes in puberty

Treatment

The prevailing opinion in the past was that it is better to determine the sex as soon as possible, considering the external genitalia rather than the chromosomes, and to inform the parents so that they do not have any confusion or ambiguity in their minds about the sex of the child. Urgent surgery is often performed, in which the ovarian or testis tissue is removed from the opposite sex (i.e., the ovary is removed from the male, and the testicle is removed from the female).

In general, they considered reproducing female genitals easier than manufacturing male genitals, so if the correct choice is not entirely clear, the child is often programmed to be a girl. Recently, the opinion of many experts has changed, as many of them are motivated to delay corrective surgery as long as the child is in good health in order to take the child's opinion in determining his sex.

In the end, it must be noted that intersexuality is a complex issue, and its treatment is accompanied by short and long-term consequences. The best treatment, therefore, depends on several factors, including the specific cause that led to hermaphroditism. [drjaderjeb.blogspot.com]

3. **Effects of Hermaphroditism on The Family (Eastern Society)**

The problem of hermaphroditism has a congenital nature, as we are facing one of these cases when a baby girl with female chromosomes is born, and then a benign tumour appears that secretes male hormones that then control the projection of some organs (penis, beard), and vice versa. The solution to these problems is assigned to surgeon par excellence to share the responsibility with the family to avoid the pain from the ruthless society.

Based on the above, the medical definition of a hermaphrodite is the presence of confusion in a newborn that represents this situation between the external male and female genital organs, as he has a vagina, a penis and two testicles. After the birth of the "hermaphrodite", problems begin to arise between the spouses. The father wants to give him a male name, and the mother wants to give him a female name. The dispute between them is resolved by registering it in the debtor case as agreed upon. However, the arrival of

131

the hermaphrodite to the stage of adulthood and the clarification of his tendencies and orientations pose a new problem, which is Name change if needed. For eastern society, these problems require that special names be chosen for the hermaphrodite that can be launched simultaneously on the male and the female, such as the name "Aman" (means Safe in English), according to the suggestion of Dr Abbasi. The suffering in the eastern society is not limited to the changing of the name, but extends to the schooling, as many families force their children, who suffer from this congenital problem, to stop studying because of their actions because when approaching puberty, the bisexual sometimes plays with the males the ball and at other times he wears girls' clothes, puts makeup on his face, and is treated as if he is a girl. At this stage, the gender of the bisexual woman should be determined, whether he is male or female, and surgery to correct the sex must be performed.

In most cases, these problems lead to divorce and the collapse of the family. Four cases were cited in this respect:

The first case: When a hermaphrodite is born, each of the spouses begins to blame the other party for the birth of a child with deformities, and it can be asserted that 90 per cent of men blame their wives when they are given a hermaphrodite.

The second case: The mother resorts to secrecy, so she does not inform the father that the newborn is a hermaphrodite, and when the matter is discovered, they enter into a continuous struggle.

The third case: When the surgical operation is performed, the mother insists that the hermaphrodite shall be female, while the father clings to his desire to be a male, and they enter into an endless struggle.

132

The fourth case: When the transsexual process takes place in childhood and during puberty, it shows a tendency towards the opposite sex, and the suffering thereof leads to suicide. The blame for the party will be on who made the decision to determine the sex during childhood.

Suggested Solutions

At birth, medical analyses and DNA studies can be done to find out whether the hermaphrodite tendencies towards male or female. If the chromosomes are of the type (X), then the orientation is towards the female. However, if on her growth the breasts are absent and she has no menstruation, drugs can be prescribed, and she can be treated. If the chromosomes are of type (XY), then the orientation is towards the male.

In the two previous cases, Dr Abdullah Abbasi stated that the surgery could be performed at an early age, but the big problem that scientists have confused about is when the chromosomes are of the type (XXY). In this case, the surgery should be delayed until the stage of puberty, and then an agreement can be reached between the specialists and the concerned people. In the light of the results of the medical analyses, then the process of determining the sex can be decided.

(Abbasi) confirms that after the recent surgery, "the concerned person or concerned should undergo psychological treatment to overcome all the effects, and the sooner these problems are resolved at an early stage, the better and more appropriate."

It seems the name is still one of the important issues that need to be regulated. For example, the artist "Noor" still bears the name of Nour al-Din even though she has defined her gender and preferences of being a woman. Therefore, various educational sessions were organised by a national media meeting in which fathers and hermaphrodites take part. Doctors and surgeons also attend these sessions to explain the cases and the required treatment. There are full-fledged cases in Rabat (Morocco) that want to undergo an operation to correct the sex. and according to a medical source, urgent calls were announced for the need for officials in the health sector to pay attention to this issue and to organise awareness campaigns aimed at encouraging parents to correct the sex of their children. The calls focused on the children who suffer from this congenital problem and need surgery during childhood to avoid the negative repercussions in the youth stage.

Frequent visits to the hospital are included in the category of those who come to remove the congenital growths, such as a woman with testicles that have no function or a man with a small hole between the exit and the genitals. However, the hospital rejects those who want to change their sex without being linked to birth defects. [https://www.maghress.com]

4. Transgender in the Middle East

Contrary to what is thought, the Middle East is full of celebrities who have undergone sex reassignment surgeries. Sexual terms, societal dictates, and controversial prohibitions are not sharp and clear in Middle Eastern countries. No real action was taken to ban the conduct of sex reassignment surgeries, and there is no harsh dispute against the gay and lesbian communities. Although there are many laws that in its general frame restrict homosexuality, it is rarely that Middle Eastern countries punish homosexuals, lesbians, or transgender persons, as required by these laws.

According to United Nations estimates, homosexuality (and certainly transgender) is prohibited according to the laws of 78 countries, and in seven of them, it is customary for those convicted of having same-sex sexual relations to be executed (data are correct for 2014). Middle Eastern countries that by-law prohibit the establishment of same-sex relations and in which homosexual minorities are persecuted are Algeria, Egypt, Libya, Morocco, South Sudan, Tunisia, Iran, Kuwait, Lebanon, Oman, Qatar, Saudi Arabia, Syria, the United Arab Emirates and Yemen. Penalties prescribed by law in these countries range from fines to years of imprisonment, flogging, and in exceptional cases, the death penalty and stoning.

The Iranian case, however, is unique, as, during the era of Shah Muhammad Reza Pahlavi, it was possible to find news coverage of gay marriage. Although homosexuality was never accepted by society in the 1970s, it was possible to find places of entertainment in Iran that were used as places for gay gatherings. However, since the Islamic Revolution in 1979, it has become impossible. But in order to preserve social order and the marriage framework between a man and a woman, homosexuals who desired to fulfil their love for their partner were forced several times to undergo a sex reassignment process against their will.

Perhaps surprisingly, Iran is the country with the largest number of sex reassignment surgeries after Thailand. Most of them, by the way, have at least partial support from the government.

The most famous female singer in Turkey, Bulant Ersoy, is transgender. Ersoy, who was born in 1952, started his career as an actor and singer in the 1970s. In 1980 she underwent sex reassignment surgery in London and, in 1988, was awarded a Pink ID (a card given to women). However, there is a huge gap between Turkish society's treatment of the great singer Bulant, the rest of the transgender and the gay community. In 2015 the first beauty queen contest was held for transgender people in Turkey, but most of them work in prostitution because they are not accepted into normal jobs and are forced to support themselves from sexual services. In fact, in April 2014, a well-known Turkish transgender woman was murdered due to hatred against the gay community.

The famous Moroccan dancer, Nour, had fought for years to change her gender on the ID card from male to female. Nour Talbi was born as Noureddine in Agadir and raised in Casablanca. She was a young athlete who won medals in hurdles but has since loved dancing and has appeared at family events. When she was eighteen years old, she left Morocco, underwent sex reassignment surgery in 2004, and then returned to her country as a woman. Today Nour is considered the number 1 dancer in Morocco. She teaches belly dancing in the United States and other countries and appears at prestigious parties of the aristocracy. She even attended the wedding of the daughter of Russian President Vladimir Putin.

The gay community in Israel enjoys relative freedom in the public sphere. Indeed, legislation has been strengthened in recent years to achieve equality in their legal and economic status with the rest of the population, especially in establishing family units. Transgender people are also gaining more and more recognition in Israeli society, but the road to equal rights is still long. Although the law does not prohibit the establishment of same-sex sexual relations, Israeli society, in general, continues to view them unfavourably.

Sex reassignment surgeries have not been performed in Israel for nearly three years because there are no surgeons in Israel who are specialised in these surgeries, and many are forced to perform them abroad, especially in Thailand. New regulations stipulated by law have recently been established by the Israeli Ministry of Health that gender reassignment operations from women to men are performed abroad and are financed by the state. Male-to-woman sex reassignment operations are carried out in Israel by American experts who are specially invited to Israel and are also partially funded by the state after receiving approval from the medical and psychological admission committees. [https://www.al-masdar.net]

5. Transformation and Sexual Identity from the Psychological Point of View

Dr Muhammad Adel Al-Hadidi, a professor of psychiatry at Mansoura University - Egypt, stated that gender identity disorder is, in fact, a psychological disorder that has psychological causes, not organic, as a person is born 100% naturally sexually and has primary and secondary sexual organs, but with the beginning of the age of 3 years it appears on the child are some of the signs that parents should pay attention to, and not go overboard with them.

In exclusive statements to Al-Youm Al-Sabea magazine, Al-Hadidi explained that these signs begin with noticing that the male child tends to the opposite sex and prefers to play with girls 'games. Adolescence shows some feminine signs in behaviour and appearance, and we find that his friends are of the opposite sex, and with the passage of time, this person suffers from religious and social pressures, and the family begins to prevent him from playing with girls, and he has a strong feeling of discomfort and loss of self-consistency.

He explains that the male child looks around and finds his father, who is an example and a role model, to follow his steps. In the event of his father's absence due to death, divorce, or travel, he begins to search for the role that he is assuming and does not find around him the supposed male form, especially when he lives with the mother alone or between his sister's girls, so he is merging with them and feeling as if he is one of them. Also, he is emotionally close and sympathises with his mother because of the cruelty and violence of his father, which leads to his hatred for the father. Internally, however, he becomes averse to the male sex because of the image that his father left to him, so he tends to the opposite sex and follows their example in form and behaviour.

In some families that give birth to females only, we find that the mother and father deal with the girl as males and buy her boys 'clothes and shorten her hair like them and call her a name suitable for boys and girls such as: (Rida, jihad, charity, Islam, etc.), and if she tries to deal with femininity and enjoy her femininity, they denounce and blame her. And with the passage of time, it becomes established within the girl that she is a boy, not a girl, and she acts like them. When signs of femininity begin to appear on her, society and the family around her begin to pressure her and direct her to deal as a female after they have implanted that masculine feeling within her, and here the conflict begins, and the crisis flares up inside her.

Al-Hadidi commented that the treatment of such cases needs a long treatment because it is basically a psychological illness that started in the early years of childhood, and its causes are psychological and not organic. Therefore, intensive psychological treatment is required for at least a year for these cases to correct perceptions about gender and treat the psychological conflicts that he/she suffered during that period. The objective is to compensate for the parental side that was absent or it was present in a deformed manner. 70% of cases often respond to the treatment, while 30% of them insist on switching to the opposite sex. In this case, it was found that the best route is to resort to hormonal therapy to psychologically compensate and to give him/her the opportunity to experiment in a trial period the living in the state of the opposite sex. Therefore, he lives the female life if he is a male or vice versa for a period ranging from 6 months continuously to a full year. Many of them, once they live with this new state, come out of the experience, hating the transition, and are satisfied with their lives after discovering their mistake and returning to complete behavioural therapy. Or they make their decision to continue hormonal therapy and perform the sexual transformation process, which is the last step.

Al-Hadidi asserted that many of those insisting on sexual transform (transgender) perform exaggerated operations, then become depressed and feel that they are unhappy in this sex and end their lives with suicide. Therefore, before carrying out such operations, it is advisable that he/she has already passed all the required treatment stages for a period of not less than a year and that he/she sits with two psychologists, a specialised surgeon and a legal official to implement a complete protocol. And they make sure that it does not respond to treatment.

He pointed out that these operations are not common in Egypt, so many people resort to doing them abroad, and we cannot determine the exact proportions because many of these surgeries are done in secrecy, and the rates declared in Egypt are much less than the reality.

He explained that hormonal treatment is dangerous and has health damages and causes fertility problems in a female who takes male hormones as a result of stopping the menstrual cycle, and with its prolonged use, it causes a person to have strokes, bleeding and tumours, so he needs long medical follow-up.

Al-Hadidi pointed out that the disorder of sexual identity is completely different from the cases of the third or intersexual sex that are born with male and female organs. In this case, the sex is determined by performing a surgical operation after taking the person's opinion and making sure of his desire and inner sense of himself and the ability to have sexual intercourse later. He may have a more efficient, effective, and capable organ. Then the ineffective organ is removed based on desire and ability.

Al-Hadidi stressed the need to take the decision after the age of legal maturity in order to be responsible for himself and his decisions, with the exception of certain cases such as the undescended testicle that needs rapid surgery in early childhood to remove it from the abdomen into the scrotum; otherwise, it will cause cancer. (https://www.youm7.com)

CHAPTER 4: THE FEMININE POSITIONING OF THE IN-MARITAL CONJUGATION

INITIATION
A. SOCIAL INFLUENCES ON THE FEMININE POSITION IN MARITAL
B. DIVORCE ON THE BASIS OF GENDER
C. SINGLE-PARENT FAMILIES

CHAPTER 4

THE FEMININE POSITIONING OF THE IN-MARITAL CONJUGATION

INITIATION

The construction of the family cell begins with the choice of a spouse. The feminine and masculine represent the family's nuclei, and since they are related to their families, their bond is decided and directed in the traditional, conservative, rural, feudal, class, sectarian, and ethnic societies by their families, particularly in the eastern societies. This is because their conjunction expresses the relative (blood-kinship) intermarriage and social kinship and preserving the ownership of the two families, their wealth, and their names. In other words, the choice of the spouse is on their behalf, as romantic love does not exist with them, but it crystallises after marriage, and if differences arise between them, their families mediate between them and resolve the difference in most cases. Therefore, this marriage continues and is longer than the heterogeneous marriage, where it has differences in the income, social position, and profession of the two spouses.

Accordingly, the heterogeneous pairing is affected by the age of the spouses, their place of work, their beauty attractiveness, marital pressures, or the marital gap, which is manifested according to the society developmental stage. In the process of choosing the partner, the positioning of the feminine could go up or down in the barometric scale of society. In traditional, feudal, and conservative societies, the barometer scale is usually down and is rising following the influences of age, workplace, aesthetic appeal, stressful conditions on marriage, and the gap between marriage and non-marriage.

A. SOCIAL INFLUENCES ON THE FEMININE POSITION IN MARITAL UNION

1. The Influence of Extended Family and Kinship

Whereas the eastern traditional, conservative, feudal, and rural societies include solid kinship relations, respect for lineage, neighbourhood, extended family, and the tribe, the individual is not free or independent in it but is subject to the patriarchal-male authority of the head of the family. The pairing in these societies is in most cases organised by their parents without passing through romantic love and mutual affection between the two spouses because the conjugation was between two families and two lineages through the marriage of their children. Therefore, the position of the feminine woman in the conjugal barometer is inferior and is dominated by male authority. This is a fact because the wife helps her husband in animal bringing up and in extracting their products to sell them in the city market.

2. The Influential Place of Study and Work

In contrast to the above-mentioned societies, there are urban, industrial, capitalist, information, and advanced technical societies where the education is of the mixed type between the sexes in school, college, or university. In these societies, the women also work in factories, shopping centres, government departments and companies with men under one roof whose sites provide good opportunities to see each other and develop emotional and romantic bonds between women and men, which facilitates the choice of a marriage partner. This environment provides them with a platform to meet, have dialogue and exchange ideas with each other while they are at the age of searching for their independent and ambitious personal identity. Therefore, such a platform in finding a suitable partner replaces relatives in the process of conjugation without having a background of knowledge, kinship or culture between them. Here, romantic love emerges in this marriage that was not arranged and coordinated by the family or relatives, but rather the university campus that created a state of chance for them, so there was an equal harmony between them, and they are from the level of one culture and an equal scientific stage. It is free from compulsion, coercion, and family pressures on the female. It represents a new opening to the personality of the contemporary female after she was subdued and pressured by her family and the patriarchal power to make her decisions about her future and her future life. However, this does not mean that the family of the young man and the young woman do not interfere or have no opinion in this pairing, but rather have a secondary and formal opinion in most cases. This conjunction is called (assertive mating), which means harmonious in its though, temperament, hobby, aspirations, culture, mate choice and affiliation class is more than its difference. Demographic characteristics such as age, race, class, and religion are among the primary elements that clarify the mate selection process. They seem ineffective with emotional attachment and romantic passion because they are not connected to emotional feelings. In fact, are variables that predict partner choice and family stability more than an idea that expresses romantic love, that they are not considered influential and helpful in deciding with whom or who will we love or fall in love with him? Because romantic love is narrated in the university market or workplace that brings the two partners together and is not crystallised for it.

144

As mentioned before, the homogeneous marriage represents a basic criterion for a tuned relationship between the two spouses, with no connection to romantic passion. This is exactly what a wise woman is looking for to marry a mate who enjoys a high economic and social status that has nothing to do with homogeneity. This tendency is motivated by the rise of the movement towards the top to financially guarantee her future life. It allows her to live with an educated and cultured partner who has a source of livelihood that satisfies her modern needs, and here the female is able to combine her vision of the family and work in her marriage. However, it highlights the disparity between her and her peer at the level of age, race, and attraction, all of which is evident in the marriage contrary to the so-called heterogeneous marriage.

Due to the weakness of kinship ties in the urban and industrial society and the prevalence of anonymity in the social relations due to the large size of the society and the diversity of its groups and classes, the process of choosing a life partner by the parents has been ended and has not been used anymore. Instead, the urban standards emanating from the population components (demographic) requires a skilful and civilised woman to look for a partner who can achieve comfortable livelihood at an urban material level that satisfies her civilised and renewed needs in order to continue her upward mobility on the social hierarchy. This is a pioneering gender shift that works to free herself from (relatively) patriarchal power, her financial independence, and her freedom to make personal and family decisions.

3. **Age Influencer**

Age is considered a variable influencing the pairing of the two spouses, as it is noticed that they are coupled within several years, varying between them, and if there is a difference or disparity, then the male is older than the female. This is due to what the traditional expectations of gender dictated that he be a source of livelihood and owner a rewarding professional skill to be able to support his family. This is the main reason why he delayed his marriage longer than the female. This means that the woman does not delay her marriage in order to obtain a pioneering professional skill and a high income in order to finance her family. This is what she learned from her upbringing in practicing family roles.

But since 1950, there has been a gradual increase in marriage for both sexes (in American society) with the knowledge that feminine women now represent more than half among university students and half of the workforce, and that traditional gender roles have also changed since 1890 and are close to men (see Figure 1) as there were marriages representing the young woman who was married to an elderly man much older than her.

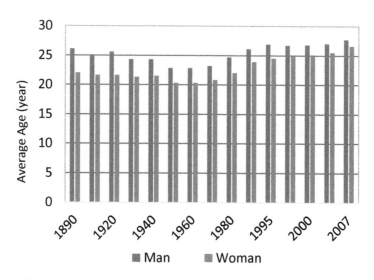

Figure 1: The average age of first marriage by gender in American society

The chart in (Figure 1) shows the ages of husbands higher than those of wives for more than a century as if it had become a permanent gender rule in most societies. It is worth noting in this context that a divorced woman and a widow does not have a chance in a homogeneous marriage because it requires a divorced or widowed man. Therefore, her chances of marrying a different (heterogeneous) are much more. In the light of this situation, a trend has emerged in American society where a young man marries a woman older than him by an average of seven years. Since there is temperamental, cultural, or religious homogeneity between the spouses, the age difference does not matter here. But this case highlighted the possibility of elderly women marrying for the second time as such possibility was very slim before due to the availability of many young females that are more attractive to a young man. It also released the feminine (divorced or widowed) from the domination of her family over her, and even released the man from the control of his family upon his marriage to a woman who is older than him, divorced, or a widow. This is a new image of the feminine gender in her liberation from the constraints of the patriarchal power in her marriage after her divorce or the death of her husband, and the man's acceptance to marry her despite her old age.

4. **Attractiveness**

The attractiveness factor has an effective influence in urban, industrial, and capitalist societies more than ethnic, cultural, and religious homogeneity due to the influence of the media (television, cinema, magazines) that display the latest trends in fashions, accessories, grace and elegance for women and men. This influence appeared about three decades ago and is increasing around the Globe. It led the man to place a high value on the attractiveness of the shape of the partner to be married with, then her grace, elegance, and taste, which led to his falling into love faster than the woman. The feminine, on the other hand, does not focus on the man's agility and the attractiveness of his beauty as much as the man does. Therefore, she places a high value on the loyalty and sincerity, continuity, and sustainability of relationship with him, his financial independence, and his ability to earn a good livelihood. In the sense that she is preoccupied and attracted to the capable, competent, and stable man more than a good-looking man of beautiful shape and outside beauty features such as his weight and the beauty of his face. And this is the criteria of the feminine to enter the orbit of romantic love with the man, unlike him, who enters the orbit of romantic love with her through her body weight, her grace, and her elegance. This is the fundamental difference in the attractiveness of the two partners when choosing a life partner in this era.

5. Influencing Marital Pressures

Age plays an influential role in the marriage of the two partners because it determines the available numbers of men for women and the number of women available to marry a man. Suppose the numbers among them are not equal in their ages, then (pressured marriage takes place) because it implies that there is a limited number for one sex that is not proportional to another number. It is known and known that men marry women several years younger than them. But after World War II, birth rates increased rapidly, so there were more women who gave birth in 1950 and more men who were born in 1940. And in 1980, a shortage appeared in the number of people eligible to marry men, which in turn revealed a decline in the birth rate in In 1960 and 1970, men were in their mid-twenties, which faced a shortage of women.

148

Pressured marriage does not deal with a woman who is unwilling to marry a man who is not compatible with her. Usually, heterogeneous marriage comes out of pressure from those who are outside the marriage market, such as women with high educational qualifications or high income and great wealth, while men are of low academic achievement or low economic status; both of these types remain outside the scope of marriage. As for single women, their number increased due to the increase in the number of widows, and there is a case that the woman decides, which is her preference not to marry (as a bachelor) who left the marriage train and remain without marriage because she is economically secured, so she does not need to marry a man left in the bachelors market and if the woman is very successful in her work outside the house, for she is accurate and delicate in choosing her husband, so she does not accept a pressured marriage. It seems that the financial independence of a woman and her culture is a strong fortress not to regress in a pressured marriage. But the spinster in most of the eastern societies accepts pressured marriage even if she has a good financial income or a high academic achievement. As a female, she wants to marry even from a younger man than her, in terms of age, culture and experience, because her social culture pushes her in this direction.

Spinsterhood is a term used to describe a girl who has passed the marriage age recognised in every country. However, the rise in the marriage dowry in the eastern societies has led to a high rate of female spinsterhood. This rise is due to the traditional cultural standards for expressing the status of the partner's family. The rate of spinsterhood for the year 2016 in Tunisia was about 69% after the rate was much lower in recent years. The higher rate of spinsterhood is mainly attributed to the high expenses of marriage required by the customs and traditions that make the young man evade the marriage. The report issued by the National Office for Family and Human Urbanism in Tunisia revealed that the number of single women has increased to more than 2.25 million women out of about 5.0 million females in Tunisia compared to about 990 thousand buffers in 1994. The spinsterhood reached its highest rates among females of fertile age. Al Aqsa (25 - 34 years old). [arabic.sputnik.com]

6. **The Marriage Gap**

This gap occurs when there is a high rate of unlawful sexual intercourse outside the normal marital relationship compared to a low rate of legal marriage. The gap has started in American society during the fifties and increases year after year. It seems that the increased consistency in the practice of adultery (illegal sexual intercourse) acted as compensation for the continuous decline in the rate of proper legal marriage. Parallel to that, it was also noticed that there is a decline in the rate of divorce as per US official statistics (see Figure 2). Unmarried and married women were and are participating in this gap and its widening mode, as there are a lot of women who are committed to and enjoy sexual relationships without legal marriage. Even in the low rate of divorce, the divorced woman has a very slim chance to marry a second time, while a divorced man has a better chance of marrying for the second time. Women who postpone their marriage or marry a second time may not choose to marry again permanently. In addition, life expectancy increased as women outlived men. Widows found themselves without a partner for several decades after the death of their husbands, and for the first time in American history, there were a large number of women who lived without a husband (see Figure 3).

From the evidence and statistics, it can be said that the marriage gap is related to the economic gap. The poor are less inclined to marry than the rich, so they remain or prefer to be without marriage. Therefore, the marriage gap is an indication of the combined effect of the social and economic class. The poor men and women are economically pressured and do not think about marriage, especially the poor woman with children who does not tend to marry again. On top of that, the sexual perversions of gays and lesbians widen the marriage gap. In the end, the marriage represents an emotional and economic bond of family and social benefit for women and men.

Finally, we say that social developments have caused a change in the influences that bring together the two partners, thus removing the influence of the extended family and kinship in the union of the two partners at the present time and replacing them with the influences that we mentioned in this section. At the same time, cases appeared that were not prevalent in traditional, conservative, and rural societies, such as the marriage market, which included: -

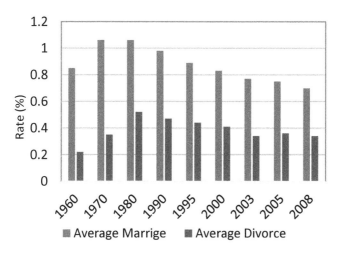

Figure 2: The rate of marriage and divorce in America for the period 1960 -2008
151

1. Feminine women with high educational qualifications
2. Feminine women with high income and great wealth.
3. Widows
4. Maidens
5. Divorced
6. The surplus number of women due to the reduced number of men as many disappeared by the many wars, then a phenomenon of marriage strikes due to:
a. The existence of illegal sexual intercourse between a man and a woman.
b. The high rate of poverty with the presence of children with the wife.
c. Divorced and living with her children.
d. Immersion in study, scientific research, and work.
e. Women's high income and economic independence.

Figure 3: Marriage position by gender in 2007 in United States of America

B. **DIVORCE ON THE BASIS OF GENDER**

Divorce has a profound social, psychological, and economic impact on the separated partners and on their children because it creates sequential troubles and hardships for them. But these difficulties diminish and increase when the divorced people represent the old gender roles (which reflect biological differences, i.e. the dominance of the male over the female) than those who represent the modern gender roles (i.e. they are different with biological differences) as featured by the economic and professional independence of the woman. This type of partner divorce is rapid, but it does require a quick post-divorce financial settlement. Modern gender roles with children are less protective of her divorce and have a painful emotional toll on motherhood and opposition to a woman's well-being. While the husbands who seek divorce have arranged their situation in the association with a second partner, they hasten their divorce and settle their accounts with their divorced wife. Age has an important and vital role in making a divorce decision for a married woman, as the more she takes her decision to divorce at an early age, her ability to rebuild her life anew is much better than if she had taken it at her old age. If her decision to divorce was for the first time, then it would be quicker and easier. Needless to say, a woman often initiates divorce before her husband embarks on it. As for married women in the prime of her life, she filed for divorce more than older men, and we see that the rate of divorce is high among women less than 40 years of age. As for older women, when they file for divorce, they often face strong and continuous psychological trauma until a new partner comes to marry them, and married women who are under the age of 40, their divorce prompts them to develop new ideas to improve their long-term living situation.

153

Not only does age play and influence the decision-making of divorce, but the wife's work outside the home, as it happens in most of the urban, industrial, and capitalist society, which means that women have become owners of financial income that is independent of their husband's income. Most of their income is spent on their own material possessions such as clothes, toiletries, and transportation, more than they spend on family needs. In view of this, the husband may feel that his marriage had become a threat to him and a challenge to his income. Also, some of them had wives with higher incomes than theirs, which added an extra source of trouble for her and her husband and children. This is right as the wife's income gives her the authority and the power to shape the family decision-making process on expenses and daily life. The husband traditional authority, therefore, will be shaken and threatened over the decisions of his family. In conclusion, it seems that the wife's work and income freed he and made her more inclined to separate from her husband and divorce from him than her mother and grandmother were thinking about divorce. It is a problem that does not reflect the generational gap; rather, the wife has become a pillar in building the family because:

1. She has a financial guarantee that is independent of her husband.
2. She felt free in her own expenses.
3. Her work is outside the home.
4. She shared with her husband in making family decisions.
5. She is no longer subordinate and subordinate to her husband, who was the head of the family, but rather the legislator and enforcer in her family.

No harm in pointing out that divorce is no longer, legally, a difficult process, but rather an easy formality in ending the bond of marriage, especially divorce marked (without a misdemeanour or guilt) in which neither partner blames the other for sin or misdemeanour any of them committed. The wife who is deceived or insulted by her husband, or the elderly husband who hopes to remarry a young wife, or two young partners who married legally at an early age and without rational thinking and face marriage obstacles that push them to divorce. This type of divorce is common and widespread in American families today. It is called legally and socially as (none-felony divorce) from the wife or the husband. [Lindsey. 2011. P. 227]

But divorce faces major financial problems when there are children because they need care or/and custody. The divorced wife often bears the care and custody of her children after the divorce, and the situation is more difficult if she works outside the home, and the wages for her work are low that cannot pay the costs of nurseries or care for their health. The divorce makes a divorced woman's financial situation worse because she has one source of livelihood that is not enough to pay for the costs of caring for her children. These are additional burdens that fall on the shoulders of a divorced woman who is the victim of unequal rights with men to social and health security in developed countries.

But divorce faces major financial problems when there are children because they need care or/and custody. The divorced wife often bears the care and custody of her children after the divorce, and the situation is more difficult if she works outside the home, and the wages for her work are low that cannot pay the costs of nurseries or care for their health. The divorce makes a divorced woman's financial situation worse because she has one source of livelihood that is not enough to pay for the costs of caring for her children. These are additional burdens that fall on the shoulders of a divorced woman who is the victim of unequal rights with men to social and health security in developed countries.

Mrs. (Flora or Mama Flora) did not expect that after several years her restaurant would become special for divorce events and that the cake of her restaurant would be dedicated to the celebration parties of the divorce and migration of husbands. She became very well-known, and her idea turned to be very profitable. It started when a Bahraini woman in her thirties has requested a special cake for her divorce party, writing on it "I'M SINGLE AGAIN". She receives a lot of congratulatory messages through social media to the applicant of the divorce featured by an image of the divorce cake. She says, "From the comments on the image of the divorce were: "the misfortunes of some are benefits of others", "it seems she who asked for divorce", "this is the best cake in my life", "congratulations to being single" and "sitting alone by your own".

This event expresses the great change that has occurred in the traditional role of Arab women, especially among the current generation that does not want to succumb to rigid restrictions in the era of openness to the outside world. It also indicates the material and social independence of Bahraini women and their high self-confidence when they openly celebrate divorce in a conservative country like Bahrain, and the news is spreading on social media. It motivated many gulf females to follow her suit, as well as to be an unfamiliar expression in the eastern society, especially in the Arabic Gulf society. It expresses the women freedom from rigid controls inherited from earlier generations that do not reflect the requirements of the new era influenced by foreign cultures. The publicity of divorce in a Gulf society, which we consider a high gender mutation that does not reflect the old traditional gender who used to reflect the subordination of women to men in all his interactions and relations with her.

C. **SINGLE - PARENT FAMILIES**

Among the negative family phenomena with social problems in our contemporary world in urban, industrial, and capitalist societies is the transformation of the family from the extended to the nuclear and then to the mono-parent (single-parent) that includes the mother only with the children, and this is a deterioration rather than development in the family structure and lack in the family upbringing. It is a burden on the role of one of the parents leads to making the family (lame) during its institutional function, due to: -

1. The parents are separated from each other.
2. The parents' divorce.
3. Or the death of one of them.
4. Or studying one of them.
5. Or artificial insemination of the mother.

All of this affects the gender negatively as a mother or a daughter who did not grow up in her natural cell of traditional conservative values to enrich her first cell (the family) but jumped into the civilised and industrialist society, which made her lose many important pillars. Often the wife or grandmother bears these burdens in upbringing the children differently from what she used to. And such an effect is manifested within the emotions and feelings of the children and drives them towards deviation in their behaviour and thinking. This is true, and it is one of the faults of the technical age, which is inconsistent with the nature of the human and the nature of family members.

Some examples are given here to clarify single-parent families that include their children who are under the age of 18. They are as follows: In 1950, 7% of all American families were defective by one of the parents (father or mother). Currently, more than 40% of all American single-parent families have children under the age of 18 with them. (See Figure No. 4). More than half of American children live in poverty with one of their parents, and the single-parent family headed by the mother has outnumbered those supported by the father by four to one. Also, half of America's children of African descent live in families supported by the mother and sometimes the grandmother. As well as official American statistics today indicate that two-third of the children of America who are under the age of 18 years live in a single-parent family headed by a woman who is not of the parents [Lindsey. 2011. P. 231]. The media usually focuses on the rate of unmarried mothers in single-parent families, which makes people often forget that single parents include divorced women, women who chose motherhood over marriage, women with financial ambition who adopt children, usually girls, instead of having children from legal marriage, or those who choose children through artificial insemination and surrogacy. In all these cases, the woman has a child or children outside the legal frame of marriage or without building a family.

The decline in the rate of marriage increased the rate of illegal sexual intercourse, which in turn increased the rate of single-parent families. It seems that the high birth rate from unmarried women did not compensate for the decrease in births from married women. Besides the above-mentioned facts, it was noted that grandmothers are the breadwinners in the family of half of African American families. Also, it is evident that the number of unmarried poor single women who have children is increasing continuously. And that half of single fathers are divorced, and the second half has never been married. And half of the divorced single mothers are in a better financial position than the mothers who have never been married in terms of their financial income and owning a home of their own. As for the children of divorced women who live with their fathers, their income is one third a third higher than the children who live with their mother. Finally, the poverty rate of all single-parent families is on the rise despite the deepening of the economic recession.

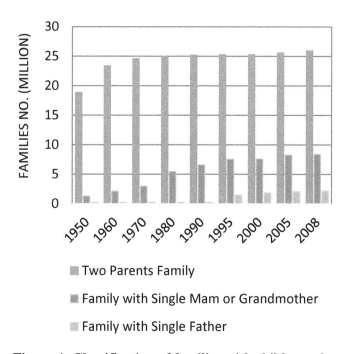

Figure 4: Classification of families with children who are under the age of 18 in American society.

1. Single-Parent Family Headed by Mother

Single-parent families (in American society) supported and cared for by the mother or grandmother have been exacerbated and spread. The father is absent due to divorce, death, separation, illegal sexual intercourse, or because of a woman's love for motherhood more than marriage. This type of family often has an exceptionally low income and lives in a low level of poverty. Even if there is joint support or care with her divorced husband, their financial situation remains weak and low due to the continuous increase in the standard of living and the diversity of children's living needs in health, food and clothing.

The financial scarcity causes psychological and emotional diseases in the single mother, especially teenage mothers who do not have average education, and the situation is worse for the African American family in which the mother is not educated. Finally, we say that a single mother who supports her children suffers from financial, psychological, and social problems that do not encourage her to get out of her acute living crisis.

2. Single-Parent Family Headed by Father

This type of American family is where the father is the breadwinner and the household provider, as there are 15% of all single-parent families headed by a man, and 4% of the children live with their father only. This type of family is on the rise in American society. As for the problems of the caring father, they are less than the problems of the caring mother, especially when the fathers who were before the divorce do housekeeping, but after the divorce, the children help their father, especially the girl, and there are no financial problems that this family faces as the family of a divorced and single mother faces because the man's wages are in work is higher than the wages for her work. Therefore, he does not need outside help for his family's expenses, not even in managing his house. Note that the father in his care of his children makes his relationship with them stronger and stronger and makes his family unit more solidarity and sympathy.

CHAPTER 5: THE POWERS OF TOTAL FEMININE ENSLAVEMENT

INITIATION

A. THE FIRST TOTALITARIAN POWER OF SLAVERY: RELIGION

B. THE SECOND TOTALITARIAN POWER OF SLAVERY: SOCIAL CULTURE

C. THE THIRD TOTAL SLAVERY FORCE: THE GOVERNMENT

CHAPTER 5
THE POWERS OF TOTAL FEMININE
ENSLAVEMENT

INITIATION

The term slavery means a fraudulent and unjust possession of female by a male who humiliates and insults her humanity in the name of the forces of religion, culture, and government. Under the effect of these forces, the female is considered possessive of the male. She is not allowed to participate or share with him an equal relationship. The man has interpreted and adapted the teachings of religion, standards and values of social culture, and government laws to serve his interests, satisfy his instincts, raise his social status, and inflate his influence and wealth. At the same time, these forces have lowered the status of the female and pushed her to be completely under male control. They weakened the female and facilitated the usurpation of her human, aesthetic, reproductive, professional, and sexual rights. Therefore, slavery led to the weakening of her morals to become submissive.

Accordingly, there are three enslaving forces with a holistic dimension and have an effective and strong influence on the feminine, which the man (forcibly) considers as legitimate, in the form of customary or legal status, with inherited historical roots in the societal land. They were implanted by men who held high positions, power, influence, and wealth that made them a preferred class over women. This unjust arrangement is not subject to discussion and debate from the feminine or from a sympathetic side with her. This differentiation is practiced and taught in the small cell (family) and the larger institutions and organisations such as the school, university, and workplace. However, the questions that are put before these forces, which are responsible for the coordination of the main social structure, are: If the heaven teachings are exercised, is it correct for the Creator to create an impure and despised creation like the woman full of sins and shame whom they accused her of. And what about the children she gives birth to? Will they be like her, unclean, degenerate, and despised creatures? Is this reasonable? If so, how does a man allow himself to live with a diabolical being and fatal sedition of sinful origin and with an unwanted catastrophe? He has sex with her and she gives birth to children who carry his name? This claim is nothing more than a fabrication and falsification of religious truths to exclude women from religion to make the religion masculine and restricted to men only. Certainly, this was not accepted by the Just Creator because his message is for both sexes without differentiating them as he supposed to be a symbol of divine justice and equality among his worshipers. Accordingly, this interpretation and its attribution to religion is not correct and it lacks credibility because it distorted the image of God, even if it was issued by politicised men who abused religion to cover up their true intentions to enslave women and usurp their rights while leaving a slight margin for her to continue serving them without objection.

The second totalitarian power of woman slavery is the social culture whose standards, traditions, values, norms and all its customary controls were also set by the men. In eastern society, this power is manifested by various actions. In the past, the father killed his infant daughter to avoid bringing shame to the family when she grows and becomes a mature woman. Up to the present, in various eastern societies, the girls are subject to circumcision and ironing of their breasts to eliminate their natural lust and sexual desire. Moreover, they forced the girls to marry while they were minors to get rid of them as soon as possible to be the responsibility of their husbands. The family, particularly the father and the brothers, exaggerate the female dowry as if she is for sale. The question which is imposed here and clearly reveal the unjust utilisation of this power is: If the woman represents the chastity and honour under the pretext of protecting her and fear for her from the man, so why the man insists and affirms her humiliation, and making her inferior to him rather than equal? A lot of these behaviours have disappeared under the pressure of the women movements and humanitarian organisations.

The third power of slavery is represented by the government and its legal system. It has a holistic dimension and is practised in official institutions which have sound logic and rational mentality, but when it comes to women, the behaviour is no different from the first and second powers represented by religion and the social culture. It is in direct response to what the men of religions and social culture do in a harmonious and homogeneous manner by not giving the woman the professional positions that match her competency. Although these institutions employ a competent woman with high academic and professional qualifications and vast experience that equal or better than the man, they isolate her in trivial professional positions and deny her receiving fair wages equal to those of men of similar competency to her. Just because she is a female, even if she is of the same race, family, or nationality to which the man belongs, still intolerance and discrimination are exercised against her, regardless of whether the society is advanced, developed, or underdeveloped. This ill attitude against her is based on the claim that she has many vacations and absences during work, and her achievement is minimal to an accomplished man!!!

In a nutshell, the official organisations created two jobs, the first is professional, and the second is for women employment!! Is this not considered slavery rape of her? She is a citizen! Why did they treat her as a second- or third-class citizen? Are a male citizen rights different from the rights of a female citizen? Were they not the owners of leadership and sovereign positions with high qualifications? Why then did they not think about gender equality? Sure, there is underestimation and disregard for women coming from cultural backgrounds that prevailed and then no longer coincide with the spirit of the age? Doesn't this constitute a developmental handicap? And the crippled half of society is not participating in the construction process? Didn't this mean government-official, legitimate male masculinity?

And when the man needed her in office and engineering work, her domestic, reproductive, and caring work for children inside the house was kept as it is, which doubles her troubles, concerns, and duties inside or outside the home. Neither the government nor the official companies compensate the woman financially when she is required to take care of her children, pregnancy, and childbirth. In fact, there are many departments and companies that dismiss the mother if her maternal leave is repeated, and this is a usurpation of her legitimate professional rights. For this, the woman was transformed into a commodity to be bought and sold in the commercial market, but most of her administrative work was part-time, not full-time, and with low wages, which expressed intolerance and prejudice against her, and the man put her in such a situation to control her outside the home just like inside.

It is appropriate to point out that the men of all heavenly religions considered the woman the root of evil in the world and the one responsible for the first human sin. They claim that she is the reason for Adam to be kicked out of paradise. So, why do the clerics continue to accuse women and measure their position for unattended crime on an old backward scale? They charged her for a crime that she did not commit, and there was no connection between her and Eve. Is this just because she was a female. This is crude and unjust thinking that does not indicate enlightenment. Rather, it is a male excuse wrapped in a religious cover that intended to humiliate women and to force them to submit, though all prophets of God born by women, and they married to women and had daughters. Didn't these prophets know the act of Eve? Is it correct and reasonable for the prophets to marry from the first and impure sin? Why do the clerics not view women through their participation in building the family and society and raising their children? Did God not honour her from among his servants? Why would a man marry a creature inferior to him? Wasn't this talk tucked in on religion and distorted talk of religions? It is not the word of the Lord that does not favour human beings and does not diminish the rights of women. It is the man who used this event that Eve performed as an excuse to make women serve him and submit to his commands, desires, and authority.

Therefore, the man's concern about femininity and his fear of her does not justify his handling of her arrogantly. He looks at her with love and passion exploiting her beauty and sex skills to satisfy his masculine instincts. Once he fully satisfies his desire, he goes back and deals with her in an overly slavery way and domineering manner. If she tries to use his masculine strength to serve her interests or object to such bad treatment, she will be faced with insult, violence, and in some cases, even murder. With all this, he does not find anyone from his family and community opposing him because his masculine stature allows him to humiliate the feminine and considers it legitimate and supported by values and customs. Was not this multi-strength slavery to keep her isolated within the original mother's culture of traditional household activities rather than allowing her to crystallise a common culture with him in engineering, medicine, pharmacy, philosophy, law, and administration.

There has been the rape of feminine rights by clerics, culture, and the government, all of whom have used violence against her by appropriating her legitimate rights to life as a human being. They treated her in an oppressive and unjust style, imposing on her their domination by coercion while relying on her in the family, work and wages, as she represents more than half of society. She was the major victim in society and the first sacrifice for the individual and the family.

A. THE FIRST TOTALITARIAN POWER OF SLAVERY: RELIGION
1. Jewish Teaching

These teachings usurped many of the human and social rights of the feminine, making her status inferior to the status of a man. She is considered an impure creature that must be avoided. In fact, whatever the reason, it is injustice and oppression for her because she did not commit a sin or any act that violated any statutory, customary or religious law other than she has born as a female, whom God created. Instead of appreciating and respecting what God has created and thanking his bounty for her birth, it looks as if it is rebellious against God will. The Creator does not create an impure or hateful person; rather, the clerics wanted evil,

167

contempt, and disrespect for her. This contempt is not accepted, Lord, because he created man and woman without any differentiating. But the teachings of the clergy emphasised the usurpation of her human and social rights, despite her being their sacred and ethnicity. These men see the woman as the basis of sin and the basis of every calamity. And because of her, death entered the world. Thus God punished her with a three-dimensional punishment: childbirth with pain and suffering and longing for a man who has been given supremacy over her. They also forbade the menstruating from coming close to her husband for a period of seven days, and her impurity is contaminating and spoiling anything that she sits on, plus they are considered unclean after childbirth for seven days in the case of the birth of a male child, and she must remain thirty-three additional days without touching anything sacred. They restricted her freedom and made her subject to the man without any entitlement to divorce her husband. This is what makes her submissive, and she has no right to update freely inside her home.

Submissive women are the minor daughter, wife, and widow married to the brother of the deceased. As for the independent women, they are the freed and divorced daughter and the ordinary widow. In order to dive deeper into the rape of women rights according to Jewish teachings, the following study is presented: It is necessary to talk about the Jewish woman in the Jewish religious heritage, starting from the Torah, as it is the source of the judgments and laws of the Jews. The study here deals with the biblical text circulating independently of the proposition that it is true or false, whether from a historical or religious point of view. Also, citing texts from the Talmud would clearly clarify the position and status of this woman in the ancient eras of the

Jewish religion, a position that was, in large part, subject to the concept of the Jewish rabbis and their interpretations.

The Torah begins talking about women for the first time, as Philip Haddad sees it through the novel "Creation." As we read the following: "Then the Lord God caused Adam to fall asleep, and he fell asleep, so he took one of his ribs and filled its place with flesh. And the Lord God built the rib that he took from Adam a woman and brought her to Adam. So Adam said: This is now a bone from my bones, and flesh from my flesh, this is called a woman because she is taken from a man. "

The Jewish doctrine saw in these verses a justification for attacking the woman, accusing her of being unkempt and of that lower and marginal status compared to men because she was created only from Adam's rib.

And this proposition that Eve - a woman was created from Adam's rib was approved by many thinkers, such as Alexander Ross, who believed that "Eve was created from Adam's left side, and this rib was the weaker side. Therefore, women were described as weak and inferior." Perhaps the most prominent example of a woman's inferiority is what comes in the daily prayer that a man recites when he says: "Blessed are you, Lord, for you did not make me a pagan, nor a woman, or ignorant." While the woman says in this prayer: "Blessed are you, O Lord, who created me according to your will."

In fact, describing a woman with this characteristic (weakness) is more evident through chapter three of Genesis, where the Torah holds the woman responsible, but rather the sin of eating from the tree. God created Adam and Eve and made them live in Heaven, and He permitted them to eat its fruits except for the tree in the middle of Heaven, from which eating would lead to the advancement of thinking and the emergence of the covers of ignorance. That is why God forbade them from eating it, saying: "... did you eat (the speech addressed to Adam) from the tree that I commanded you not to eat from?" Adam replied, "The woman you created with me is the one who gave me from the tree, and I ate." The punishment of the Lord for Eve - because she was the one who seduced Adam - by addressing her: "The greater the burden of your pregnancy, the pain you give birth to children, and to your foot your longing will be while it prevails over me." Thus, God punished Eve with a three-dimensional punishment.

The Torah - according to this chapter - considers the woman a vulnerable race capable of seduction. In the book of Leviticus, we find that a menstruating woman is forbidden to her husband for seven days. Its uncleanliness contaminates and spoils the things on which it sits. Also, a man becomes unclean as soon as he touches her or holds the bed on which she sat. This impurity is removed from a man with the onset of evening, just as a man who has intercourse with an unclean woman becomes unclean for seven days as well. Also, in Leviticus, a woman is unclean after childbirth for seven days if a male child is born. And she must remain thirty-three additional days without touching anything sacred or entering holy places throughout this period. In the case of the birth of a female, the woman remains unclean for fourteen days, then sixty-six additional days, which means eighty days in this previous case. Thus, "the childbearing age - as you see (Susan Niditch)) is a testimony to the impurity of a woman. This impurity is associated with the psychological and physical states that a woman passes through during pregnancy and childbirth. On this basis, the woman becomes a source of danger, strength, and impurity every month. And it corrupts everything, making the

170

religious connection between man and God impossible. That is why, from a priestly point of view, women remain without value in most aspects of religious life. After all, these are the cultures that make women who are capable of childbearing unqualified and inactive in the religious field".

The Jewish Woman in the Talmud: Viewing the chapters of the Mishnah, as an important part of the Talmud, suggests that there is a difference in the perception of women by talking about some independent women and others submissive. This division was indicated by (Judith. R. Wegner) by saying: "On the aspect related to the status of individuals, the Mishnah divides women into two contradictory parts: one subordinate and the other independent. There is no doubt that the division of women into these two parts is based on their social position, the rights and duties that they entail, and the systems of purity. In this regard, Jacob Neusner pointed out that "the social vision of Judaism Mishnaic includes issues of gender, social structure, wealth, and private dealings, as well as the social caste system.

Thus, the submissive women are the minor girl, the wife, and the widow married to the brother of the deceased. As for the independent women, they are the freed girl, the divorced woman, and the ordinary widow. In order for this division to be clear, some Mishnah texts are included here that justify the duality of this image: submission and independence, or rather the negative and positive image that the Mishna drew about women.

About the positive aspects, women enjoy, like men, independence in conducting their engagement or appointing a representative: "The man addresses himself or his representative, and the woman addresses herself or her envoy." If the husband decides to divorce his wife because of doubts about her fornication, then the Mishnah dictates the existence of two evidence or two witnesses as per Rabbi Eliezer. The Mishnah's text here gives a woman her moral value when it recognizes this right for her during the marriage. And even if the divorce is concluded, the woman can claim compensation for it or for widowhood. Also, the woman is acting on behalf of her husband in selling his goods or appointed as the manager of a shop or appointed her as a will overseer. He has the right to take her oath whenever he wants.

But with regards to the negative image of the submissive woman, it can be found find that the deceased husband's brother inherits the sexual position of his brother's widow, who cannot marry according to her desire: the eldest brother is forced to marry his brother's widow, and if he refused, he offered her marriage to all the brothers in succession. If they refuse, the offer is returned to the eldest, and he will be told: You must do an obligation, either take off the shoes or marry your brother's widow. In this regard, Baskin believes that "the personality of this widow is a sacrifice to her socio-sexual function. Therefore, the Mishnah system absolutely links the social identity of the woman to the possession of her sexuality."

Women are also opposed in the religious field by scholars, as they are forbidden to study the Torah. (Rabbi Eliezer) says, "Whoever teaches his daughter the Torah, it is as if he taught her prostitution." Depriving a woman of studying the Torah means depriving her of the symbolic capital that would gain her power and material and moral benefit in terms of knowledge of religion and its matters. Because the Torah legislates the duties and rights of women, studying it gives women knowledge of their rights. However, the Rabbis are depriving her of that so that she will not benefit from this negative freedom whenever she thinks about divorce or discord. But the scholars of the Talmud did not think about the positive aspect of a woman's education and mastery, which would make her contribute alongside the man to the supremacy of the divine law, spreading it and using it to bring benefit to the individual, family, and society.

In addition to this image that makes the woman free and submissive, another issue can be mentioned, which is that the Mishnah law does not authorise the wife to divorce her husband while authorising the husband to divorce her whenever he wants. This is to make the woman, in general, a subordinate element who is not even allowed to speak freely inside her home or to enjoy a portion of this freedom in the street. So why such a law is enforced on the woman only rather than on the man also. In the Kitbot class, a woman is divorced if she goes out with a bare head, is spun on the street, or speaks to a man. However, (Rabi Tarfoun) added, "And so she will be divorced if her voice is high, and neighbours heard her while she is speaking inside her home. [https://religmag.wordpress.com].

2. Christian Teachings

The monotheistic religions dealt with the feminine through Eve, who was seduced by Satan and caused her to descend with Adam from Heaven. Accordingly, the hatred of the Christian sects towards women appeared, so they usurped her presence and her participation with the man in building the family and society and everything she does in social life. They described her with the ugliest descriptions and the worst stigmas, such as their saying on gender, it is contrary to nature and the divine instinct and that she threatens the future of children, and that the woman is the origin of sin, the tool of Satan, an inevitable evil, a natural seduction, a

173

desirable disaster, a domestic danger, deadly sedition, an evil on it, and other harmful and bad epithets.

The Roman Catholic doctrine reinforces the preference of the male over the feminine in all social institutions, as it allows the man to dominate the housewife and invoke social, economic and sexual restrictions, and the rest of the patterns of living in the humiliation of the feminine at the same time, the feminine of the woman requires her to glorify the role of motherhood and bear the misery and cruelty of her husband and not to complain but to be silent She is silent about what the man is doing towards her. These feminine attributes are now prevalent among all Latina females in their behaviour and thinking, but these religious requirements are not mentioned for males in Latin America because they are transcendent and domineering over their status and social role. For more information on the usurpation of feminine rights from the Christian religion, we mention the following studies:

The attack was launched by Pope Francis on (the gender theory) while speaking to a gathering of Catholics in the Republic of Georgia. He considered it as part of a (totalitarian war) on the institution of marriage and the family. His speech has provoked a state of divergent reactions in the Western media, especially considering what is the Pope is known for being lenient with the issue of homosexuality, compared to his predecessors. The Pope had stated that the gender theory violates the laws of nature and the divine nature, and it threatens the future of children. He called for the necessity of sound awareness in schools so that the theory of sexual transformation is not the basis of education, as this will have severe consequences for future generations and for the continuation of human reproduction in this universe. And Francis considered that teaching of the theory of transsexuality to children is ideological colonialism and that this theory has turned into a dangerous doctrine that disintegrates the concept of male and female, which is also inconsistent with the church's concept of men, women and the family. These statements prompted a question about the truth of the church's stance on women and family issues, considering its contradiction with previous statements by Christian clerics?

The church has been and still is a party in a state of public debate about a number of sensitive social issues related to the ideology of the feminist movement, towards the issues of same-sex marriage, gender change, abortion, non-traditional family forms, artificial insemination, and contraception. In order to understand the contradictions of the church and the turmoil in its positions on these issues, it is necessary to shed light on the historical position of the church on issues of marriage and the family.

The Church and Women in the Age of the Fathers: The early Christian church fathers saw the woman as the root of sin and the tool of Satan. That is why she was treated with severe humiliation, and priests and religious scholars view her as if she was (a necessary evil, natural seduction, a desirable disaster, a domestic danger, fatal sedition, and evil with paint).

Priests of the church believe that because of Eve, humans lost the Garden of Eden, so it is Satan's beloved tool with which he leads men to Hell. And (Thomas Aquinas) had in some respects given her a status lower than that of a slave, as he says: "The woman is subject to the man due to the weakness of her nature, and the man is the principle and end of the woman, just as God is the principle and end of everything, and he imposed submission on women pursuant to the law of nature, but the slave it is not so, and children must love their fathers more than they love their mothers. "

And (Paul the Apostle) says: "I do not allow a woman to teach and not rule over a man, but rather be in silence, because Adam was created first then Eve, and Adam was not deceived, but the woman was deceived, and she got into transgression."

And since, in their view, women are bad and despicable, the Bible was directed towards the induction of monasticism and left the marriage to escape from the bondage of Satan (the woman). (Paul) said: "It is good for a man not to touch a woman." And he says: "I say to the unmarried and to the widows: It is good for them if they remain as I am, but if they do not control themselves, then let them marry because marriage is better than to burn with passion." And to humiliate her, she is commanded to remain silent, says (Paul). Also: "Let your women remain silent in the churches because they are not permitted to speak."

Those (holy!) Teachings in the Christian world have borne disrespect and contempt for the female like what (John, nicknamed the Mouth of Gold) said: "The woman is a family danger and a pictorial misfortune."

In fact, the woman, in their view, is not a human being! Therefore, she does not deserve humanity, as (Pope Eno Sensius VIII) declared in (1484 AD), "The human being and the woman seem stubborn opposites!"

In the fifth century AD, the Macon Council met to discuss whether the woman was a soul or a body without a soul. Finally, the churchmen gathered and decided that the woman was devoid of the surviving soul - from the torment of Hell - except for the mother of Christ, peace be upon him.

The Church and Women in the Middle Ages: In the Middle Ages, the status of women worsened so much in

Christian societies that until the first half of the nineteenth century, the husband had the right to sell his wife just as animals were sold according to the law.

A French bishop wrote in the twelfth century: "All women, without exception, are prostitutes, and like Eve the cause of all evil in the world!" Father (Gregory Tomarchus) said: "I searched for chastity among them, but I did not find any chastity!" And (Tertullian) said: "You women, the entrance to Satan, you who picked from that forbidden tree ... you who deceived Adam ... Even the death of the Son of God is due to your heinous deed!"

This view is not specific to Catholics or Orthodox, but even the so-called Protestant reformers could not break from the Bible's stain on women of contempt, degradation, and persecution, for this is Martin Luther (the inspiration for Protestants) says: "If women are tired, or even die, it does not matter, let them all He dies in the process of childbirth, for they were created for that!" This syndrome (the curse of the female sex) is transmitted in the books of both the Old and New Testaments!

In the year (1500 AD), a social council was formed in Britain to torture women! That council invented new ugly means for this pathological sadism, and thousands of women were burned to death with a crime that they were the daughters of Eve! The males (not the men) enjoyed pouring boiling oil over their miserable, naked bodies!

In the era of Henry VIII, King of England, the English Parliament issued a resolution prohibiting women from reading the New Testament because they were unclean beings!

Women were not counted within the citizenship according to English law, and they had no right to property at all! This unjust law was in effect until the middle of the

177

nineteenth century! (That is, they are numbered from the category of animals, not humans! Or from the category of slaves who are not free!).

In 1567 AD, a decision was issued by the Scottish Parliament that woman should not be granted any authority over any of the things.

As for the French law, Article (217) stipulates the following: "A married woman - even if their marriage is based on the separation between her ownership and that of her husband - is not permissible for her to donate or transfer her property, nor to lease, nor to own with or without compensation without participating her husband' in the contract or his written consent to it.

This ecclesiastical view of women pushed women in Christian societies to rebel against the authority of the church and created a state of conflict between the clergy and women, and the alienation of women from Christian teachings, which was reflected in the relationship of women with the church in the era of the Renaissance and Enlightenment. [http://www.lahaonline.com]

When the Christian West speaks especially about women, their rights, and the status they have reached, it seems to you that women have really become equal to men in everything, and who follows the living reality in Europe and America and carefully examines the files before the courts, he will be dazzled by the huge number of cases that discuss the subject of sexual harassment and rape and the material exploitation of women.

Women as seen by Christian eyes (from the texts of the holy book): Paul considered women to be inferior to men. He said: "Let your women be silent in the churches because they are not permitted to speak. Rather, they commanded them to submit to obedience, so the law

178

commands, so if they want to learn something to ask their men at home because it is shameful for a woman to speak in the church." [1st Paul's Letter to Corinthians 14:34]

He also wrote: "I do not allow the woman to know nor to usurp authority - from the man - and not to gain control. He (means Adam) is the one who subjugated, but the woman was subjugated, and she fell into disobedience." [1 Timothy 2: 12-14].

The woman is not the glory of God: Paul said in his first letter to Corinth (11: 7): "The man should not cover his head, as the image of God and His glory. The woman is the glory of the man. The man was not taken from the woman, but the woman was created for the man."

The woman without the man: Paul said in his first letter to Cornish (11: 3 - 9): "I want you to know that the head of every man is the Christ. As for the head of the woman is the man, and the head of Christ is God ... Every woman who prays or prophesies with her head uncovered shame her head because she and the shaved woman is the same thing. If a woman is not covered, let her hair be cut ... The man is not from the woman, but the woman from the man because the man was not created for the woman but the woman for the man...

Paul invites women to wear the veil: Here are texts that confirm the inferior view of women in the Bible. A divorced woman does not marry!!

It came in the Gospel of Matthew (5: 27-32). And before the one who divorced his wife, give her a letter of divorce. As for me, I tell you: He who divorces his wife except for the reason of adultery makes her commit fornication, and whoever marries a divorced woman commits adultery.

Reality has proven the impossibility of dispensing with divorce, as evidenced by the fact that Christian countries

179

have enacted laws that allow divorce, so is it in the interest of a divorced woman not to marry?!! Where is absolute humanity? Where is the natural right to life? Why do you live, shunned, hungry, eager for marriage, and cannot?

The provisions of menstruating women in the Bible: Book of Leviticus (15: 19) says: "19 If a woman gets her period, she stays for sevenfold days in her unclean menstrual blood, and anyone who touches her becomes unclean until evening. 20 Everything she sleeps on or sits on while she is menstruating shall be unclean. 21 Whoever touches her bed shall wash his clothes and bathe in water and be unclean. 22 Whoever touches anything she sits on, he washes his clothes, bathes in water and be unclean until the evening. 23 And who touches something found on the bed or on the place she is sitting on shall be unclean until evening. 24 And if a man has sex with her, he becomes unclean if something of her impurity got on him, then he shall be unclean for seven days. And every bed on which he sleeps becomes unclean. "

The strangest thing is that, to get rid of her impurity, she must go to the priest with two pigeon chicks!!

The writer of Leviticus (15:29) says: "On the eighth day she takes two doves or two pigeon chicks for herself and brings them to the priest to the door of the tent of meeting. This is a huge embarrassment to the woman as she goes to the priest with two pigeons in her hand. Everyone who sees her will know that she is on the days of her menstrual period and how embarrassed she will be while the people look at her with their poisoned gaze. No reasonable human thinks that any woman who has an iota of shyness will be happy to be put in such a critical situation, God unless the Bible wants to strip her respected feminine shyness.

The amazing thing is that because of the menstruation that was created by God (as the formation and creation of the

180

female), the woman is considered as the sinner, and she must purify herself from her sin!!! So, a woman is unclean during the menstrual period of seven days and rejected by others, then her impurity period continues for another week, i.e., half a month, and for half her productive life, she is unclean and forbidden!

The provisions of sexual intercourse with a woman: The Book of Leviticus (15:18) says: "18 If a man has sexual intercourse with his wife, they both bathe in water, and they will be unclean until the evening."

The wisdom behind the pain of childbirth: In the Book of Genesis (3:16), the Lord said to Eve when she seduced Adam: "Then He said to the woman: I will multiply the pains of your labour, and you will give birth to children with pains. Your longing will be on your husband, and he is ruling over you."

The woman silence: Paul said in his first letter to the Corinthians (14: 34): "the women should keep silent in the churches. For they are not permitted to speak but should be in submission, as the law also says." 35: "If they want to inquire about something, they should ask their own husbands at home, for it is disgraceful for a woman to speak in the church."

The man alone is the teacher, and he is the one who understands, and he is the one who has to speak. As for the servant, his wife, she does only what her husband dictates to her, and she only knows what he has done, and her husband understands.... We ask whether the church adhered to these teachings. We find women talking and singing loudly in the churches, so why does the church violate Paul's teachings and allow women to speak and sing in the church?

The female impurity double of the impurity male in the bible: The writer of Leviticus (12: 1-5) says: "If a woman conceives and gives birth to a male, she shall be unclean for seven days. Then she shall reside thirty-three in the blood of her purification. And if a female gives birth, she shall be unclean for two weeks.... Then she stays of sixty-six days in her blood to be purified. "

Inheritance is for males only in the Bible: Deuteronomy writer says (21: 15 17): "15 If a man has two wives, and he loves one but not the other, and both bear him sons, but the firstborn is the son of the wife he does not love, 16 when he wills his property to his sons, he must not give the rights of the firstborn to the son of the wife he loves in preference to his actual firstborn, the son of the wife he does not love. 17 He must acknowledge the son of his unloved wife as the firstborn by giving him a double share of all he has. That son is the first sign of his father's strength. The right of the firstborn belongs to him.

In the Bible, a female does not inherit except when there are no males: According to the Book Numbers (27: 1-11): The daughters of Zelophehad came forward too and stood before Moses, Eleazar the priest, the leaders, and the whole assembly at the entrance to the tent of meeting and said, "Our father died in the wilderness. He was not among Korah's followers, who banded together against the Lord, but he died for his own sin and left no sons. 4 Why should our father's name disappear from his clan because he had no son? Give us property among our father's relatives." 5 So Moses brought their case before the Lord, 6 and the Lord said to him, 7 "What Zelophehad's daughters are saying is right. You must certainly give them property as an inheritance among their father's relatives and give their father's inheritance to them. 8 "Say to the Israelites, 'If a man dies and leaves no son, give his inheritance to his daughter. 9 If he has no daughter, give his inheritance to his brothers. 10 If he has no brothers, give his inheritance to his father's brothers. 11 If his father had no brothers, give his inheritance to the nearest relative in his clan, that he may possess it. This is to have the force of law for the Israelites, as the Lord commanded Moses."

The Bible gives a man the right to sell his daughter: The Lord said in the Book of Exodus (21: 7): "When a man sells his daughter as a slave, she shall not go out as the male slaves do."

The Bible requires a woman to marry her husband's brother if her husband dies: (Deuteronomy 25: 5 - 10): 5 If brothers are living together and one of them dies without a son, his widow must not marry outside the family. Her husband's brother shall take her and marry her and fulfil the duty of a brother-in-law to her. 6 The first son she bears shall carry on the name of the dead brother so that his name will not be blotted out from Israel. 7 However, if a man does not want to marry his brother's wife, she shall go to the elders at the town gate and say, "My husband's brother refuses to carry on his brother's name in Israel. He will not fulfil the duty of a brother-in-law to me." 8 Then the elders of his town shall summon him and talk to him. If he persists in saying, "I do not want to marry her," 9 his brother's widows shall go up to him in the presence of the elders, take off one of his sandals, spit in his face and say, "This is what is done to the man who will not build up his brother's family line." 10 That man's line shall be known in Israel as The Family of the Unsandaled.

The woman who has given birth in the Bible is wrong, and she must atone to repent for what she did not commit: (Leviticus 12: 1-8) (1 The Lord said to Moses, 2 "Say to the Israelites: 'A woman who becomes pregnant and gives birth to a son will be ceremonially unclean for seven days, just as she is unclean during her monthly period. 3 On the eighth day, the boy is to be circumcised. 4 Then, the woman must wait thirty-three days to be purified from her bleeding. She must not touch anything sacred or go to the sanctuary until the days of her purification are over. 5 If she gives birth to a daughter for two weeks, the woman will be unclean, as during her period. Then she must wait sixty-six days to be purified from her bleeding. 6 " 'When the days of her purification for a son or daughter are over, she is to bring to the priest at the entrance to the tent of meeting a year-old lamb for a burnt offering and a young pigeon or a dove for a sin offering. [1] 7 He shall offer them before the Lord to make atonement for her, and then she will be ceremonially clean from her flow of blood. "These are the regulations for the woman who gives birth to a boy or a girl. 8 But if she cannot afford a lamb, she is to bring two doves or two young pigeons, one for a burnt offering and the other for a sin offering. In this way, the priest will make atonement for her, and she will be clean."

punishments for women on the pages of the Bible:

- Cut off the woman's hand: (11 "If two men fight together, and the wife of one draw near to rescue her husband from the hand of the one attacking him and puts out her hand and seizes him by the genitals, 12 then you shall cut off her hand; your eye shall not pity her.) (Deuteronomy 25: 11-12)
- Burning a woman with fire: (9 And the daughter of any priest, if she profanes herself by playing the whore, she

184

profanities her father: she shall be burnt with fire (Leviticus 21: 9). All this is filled the holy book and insulted women!! [http://www.m.ahewar.org].

3. Islamic Teachings

In Islam, like other religions, the practice is usually different from what is given in the holy book of Islam (Quran). The difference between Islam, Christianity and Judaism is that the Quran has been conserved while Gospel and Torah were not conserved from the original divine but rewritten by clerics after prophets Jesus and Moses by many years and translated into various languages. They had, therefore, been subject to various alterations, additions, cancellations, and adjustments to suit the clerics' desires and match the social circumstances away from the divine provisions. For Islam, However, the deviation source came from different routes. Despite the conservation of the Quran, its interpretation had come in different versions depending on the level of understanding from one cleric to another as per the time and the social circumstances. Therefore, the Islamic teaching reflects the social customary in most of its topics rather than what God stated in the Holy Quran. Such customary became holy traditions by the clerics and considered as part of Islam religion provisions to be by time red lines that cannot be changed, ignored, or overridden. Accordingly, the misinterpretation of the Quran will not be used in the context of this book, but rather the translated manuscript of the Quran verses will be presented and explained.

Going through the text of the Quran, the rights of the women were reserved and had not been raped by the Islamic religion, but all evidence shows that the actual practice is conducted away from Quran teaching. In such teaching Quran commands man to deal with her in kindness and forbade him from marrying her compulsively and consuming her money.

In the event of her disobedience, the man is obligated to treat her with a gentle and compassionate gradation, beginning with light advice and then abandoning her in the bed, after which the ultimate stage comes by advising her harshly. God has permitted the husband to separate from his wife. Islam has forbidden the infanticide of daughters and considered the women as the companions of men. That is, they are like men in destiny and stature, and it never detracts from them because they are women. He recommended the good treatment of the mother, and he had mercy on her in several cases, such as allowing her not to pray and fast during menstruation, and spending on her by her husband and bequeathed for her by her husband, that is, he made her an inheritance from her husband, her brothers, her children, and her father, and required a dowry for her and it is forbidden to divorce her while she is menstruating, and other prohibitions. To expand and deepen the position of women in Islam, the following study is presented:

Islam and women: Islam addresses men and women alike and treats them in an almost equal manner, and Islamic law in general aims at a distinct goal of protection, and legislation provides women with accurate definitions of their rights and takes a keen interest in guaranteeing them.

Quran instated women's inheritance from the left wealth after the death of her father, brothers, sisters, and relatives in noticeably clear verses as women had no share in inheritance in the pre-Islamic era.

Undoubtedly, Islam enjoins the husband good treatment of his wife, and it has permitted the husband to separate from his wife through a divorce in Islam is not a preferred option, so He Almighty said: O' believers! It is not permissible for you to inherit women against their will or mistreat them to make them return some of the dowries as a ransom for divorce— unless they are found guilty of adultery. Treat them fairly. If you happen to dislike them, you may hate something which Allah turns into a great blessing (Al-Nisa '(19)):

Before the advent of Islam, some Arab fathers used to infanticide their female daughters, and when Islam came, it urged the prohibition of infanticide the girls, then Almighty said: Al- Takwir: 8-9 "And if the alive buried baby girl asked: by which guilt she was killed?" God commanded that the women and orphans must be treated with justice, and it is forbidden to treat slave women and orphans with injustice in what Quran instated: (... Do not force your slave-girls into prostitution for your own worldly gains while they wish to remain chaste. And if someone coerces them, then after such coercion, Allah is certainly All-Forgiving, Most Merciful ˈto themˈ.) And so to ensure the safety of women risks in her character, and lethality of society if you follow this path that Lord and Prophet forbade.

Islam and the mother: Islam have honoured the woman being a mother and recommended that the sons and daughters treat in good treatment of parents, especially the mother. Quran featured this in portraying eloquent and miraculous in more than one place. He said to God: Al-Isra 23 (And your Lord has decreed that you worship not except Him, and to parents, good treatment. Whether one or both reach old age [while] with you, say not to them [so much as], "uff,"1 and do not repel them but speak to them a noble word.).

The Almighty said in the second position: Al-Ankabut 8 (We have commanded people to honour their parents. But if they urge you to associate with Me what you have no knowledge of, then do not obey them. To Me, you will all return, and then I will inform you of what you used to do).

And the Almighty said in the third place: Lukman 14 (And We have enjoined upon man [care] for his parents. His mother carried him, [increasing her] in weakness upon weakness, and his weaning is in two years. Be grateful to your parents; and to Me is the [final] destination)

He says in the last position Al-Haqf 15 ("And We have enjoined upon man, to his parents, good treatment. His mother carried him with hardship and gave birth to him with hardship, and his gestation and weaning [period] are thirty months. [He grows] until, when he reaches maturity and reaches [the age of] forty years, he says, "My Lord, enable me1 to be grateful for Your favour which You have bestowed upon me and upon my parents and to work the righteousness of which You will approve and make righteous for me my offspring. Indeed, I have repented to You, and indeed, I am of the Muslims.").

Islam and the wife: Among the things that may be mentioned in this place is what the Messenger of God - may God bless him and grant him peace - recommended in the farewell pilgrimage, as he commanded women, and said: (Fear God in women, for you have taken them with the trust of God and have permitted them to leave them with the word of God).

Islam has made her a sister to the man in all his conditions and actions, she participates with him in raising children, works to serve them, and stabilizes their home, and with the stability of the house for the spouses, he produces a good house according to the Prophet's guidance, this house contributes to building society, so it can be said that it is half of society, but more half of it, the woman is the mother, the wife, the daughter, and the sister.

188

Islam and the child female: When Prophet Mohammed came, he honoured the child girl, made her rights and duties on her, and forbid the issue of infanticide of girls that was widespread in the pre-Islamic era. Since Quran was revealed, it included all provisions about the rights of women in the inheritance to become a fact that is practiced in the current Islamic contemporary societies.

On the authority of Aisha (Prophet's wife), she said: (A woman with two daughters entered her and asked, but she found nothing with me but dates, so I gave it to her, so she divided it between her two daughters and did not eat it, then she got up and went out, so when the Prophet came in I told him what happened, he said: (whoever has given daughters they would be his cover from the fire of hell) a covering from the fire).

Islam and the widow: The Messenger of God has raised the destiny of the one who takes care of the affairs of the widow to the degree that no one can imagine, and among the best that can be mentioned here is the saying of the Prophet: (The one who seeks over the widow and the poor is like the one who strives in the path of God.). What virtue and any greatness are these? This is nothing but an honour and preservation of women, for she is like the jewel in Islam, where he defends her with all strength and courage.

4. The Position of Women Between Judaism, Christianity, and Islam

As a conclusion to this section, the status of women is compared between the three monotheistic religions to point out the differences and similarities between them in this regard.

I. **The Status of Women in Judaism:** The status of women in Judaism is an evil position, and the evidence for that is:

a. Judaism considers the woman the root of evil in the world, or she is the one responsible for the first human sin, because - according to them - she is the reason for Adam, peace be upon him, left paradise, and we see that clearly in the Torah: And she said to the woman: Indeed, God said: Do not eat from all the trees of paradise? Then the woman said to the serpent: Of the fruits of the trees of paradise we will eat. As for the fruit of the tree in the middle of paradise, God said: Do not eat from it or touch it, lest you die. Rather, God knows that on the day you eat it, your eyes will open, and you will be like God, knowing good and bad ... So, I took some of its fruit and ate and gave its man also with it and he ate ... So, the Lord God said to the serpent: Because you did this cursed you from all the beasts, and from all wild beasts ... And he said to the woman, "The more the burden of your pregnancy, the more pain you give birth to children, and your longing will be to your feet, and he will prevail over you" (Genesis 3: 1--16).

b. Women in Judaism are bought and sold: "And if a man sells his daughter to a slave woman, she does not go out as slaves come out" (Exodus 21: 7).

c. T - The Jewess believes that the uncleanness of the birth of a female is twice the uncleanness of the birth of a male: "If a woman conceives and gives birth to a male, she shall be unclean for seven days ... Then she shall reside thirty-three days in the blood of her purification ... and if a female gives birth, she shall be unclean for two weeks ... Then she shall reside sixty-six days in the blood of her purification "(Leviticus 12: 1-5).

d. The woman in the Old Testament: "And I discovered as bitterer than death the woman whose heart is snares and nets, whose hands are chains. One who is pleasing to God will escape from her, but the sinner will be captured by her." (Ecclesiastes7:26). The status of women in Judaism can be summarized by stating what (William Barclay) said: "The standing of a woman was officially exceptionally low. Teaching a woman, the God law was like keeping a pearl to a pig.

e. Judaism has not seen equality between men and women since ancient times, and it is worth mentioning the phrase in its origin, "Gender inequalities found in the Torah suggest that women were subordinate to men during biblical times."

II. **The Status of Women in Christianity:** It was found That (Paul)

a. Believed that Eve was the one who sinned first, then she seduced Adam, so he escaped after her and sinned again (1 Timothy 2: 12-14).

b. He commanded all who served him - men and women to greet each other with holy kisses! (Romans 16: 1--16), (1 Corinthians 16:20), (2 Corinthians 12:13).

The one who looks at Christian Europe finds it looking at women as filthy, so that (Udo Al-Kalni) in the twelfth century AD mentioned that embracing a woman means embracing a bag of rubbish. It is worth mentioning the phrase, as mentioned in the encyclopedia: A point of interest is that the exhortations to chastity are addressed to men only; the man is regarded as the victim, the woman as the temptress – women are never warned against men or against the general seductions of society.

Adrian Thatcher expresses the church's view of women, saying: "The Western world has done a lot in the last century

191

to surpass its contempt for women, but this contempt remains constant in the Church" (The Savage Text, The use, and Abuse of the Bible. 108. 2008. Wiley-Blackwell. So, Christianity has not historically been on the side of women. Women were often worthless or weightless, and they held a bad position in society. This has been inherent in Christianity from the earliest years - after Christ and his Apostles - to the present day. Christianity has not been incredibly supportive of women historically speaking. Much of the time, women have been denigrated and forced into second-class status. This was true right from the earliest years of Christianity and has continued down through today.

The husband - in modern Europe - had the right to sell his wife, and the price of the wife was fixed to six daughters, and this law was in effect in England until 1805 AD. (Henry VIII) forbade English women to read the Bible, and until 1850 AD, the women of England were not numbered in any census, and until 1882 AD, they had no personal rights or the right to private property. In the fifth century AD, the Macon Council met to discuss the question of whether a woman is just a body without a soul. After researching the council, the council decided: It is devoid of the soul that will escape from the torment of hell. In 1958, the French held a conference in which they decided that she was "a human being created to serve men only." After the French Revolution and to this day, a married woman is not allowed to conduct financial behaviour except with the permission of her husband, and a woman's wage for her work remains today less than that of a man, and she loses her name and freedom as soon as she gets married, and until the nineteenth century, she was also deprived of education.

III.   **The Status of Women in Islam:** The position of women in Islam is completely in contradiction to what Judaism and Christianity say about bearing women the burden of the first sin and the misery resulting from it. Quran explicitly defines the responsibility of Adam, for that, even if his wife shared with him. Disobedience is by eating from the forbidden tree. Roger Garaudy (the French thinker) said: "The Quran - from the theological point of view - does not define between a man and a woman a relationship of metaphysical subordination. The Quran does not carry the first women's responsibility for sin "after that responded he and his wife, temptation of the devil, in the hope of a mole and the king does not wear, the Almighty said: Taha 115-121 (And indeed, we once made a covenant with Adam, but he forgot, and ˹so˺ We did not find determination in him. And ˹remember˺ when We said to the angels, "Prostrate before Adam," so they all did—but not Iblîs, who refused ˹arrogantly. So, we cautioned, "O Adam! This is surely an enemy to you and to your wife. So do not let him drive you both out of paradise, for you ˹O Adam˺ would then suffer ˹hardship. Here it is guaranteed that you will never go hungry or unclothed, nor will you ˹ever˺ suffer from thirst or ˹the sun's˺ heat."1 But Satan whispered to him, saying, "O Adam! Shall I show you the Tree of Immortality and a kingdom that does not fade away?" So, they both ate from the tree and then their nakedness was exposed to them, prompting them to cover themselves with leaves from paradise. So, Adam disobeyed his Lord, and ˹so˺ lost his way).

Islam does not view men and women as an alternative to the other, but rather sees that they complement each other, and this follows the principle of the distribution of work required by divine wisdom, whereby the woman compensates for the deficiencies in the man and the man provides what the woman lacks. Likewise, there is no preference between men and women in remuneration, as God Almighty has indicated that the effort of one who does a righteous deed, male or female, will not be wasted. He said: Al-Baqarah 228: (Divorced women must wait for three monthly cycles ˹before they can re-marry˺. It is not lawful for them to conceal what Allah has created in their wombs if they ˹truly˺ believe in Allah and the Last Day. And their husbands reserve the right to take them back within that period if they desire reconciliation. Women have rights similar to those of men equitably, although men have a degree ˹of responsibility˺ above them). And Allah is Almighty, All-Wise. He said: Al-Imran 195 ("So their Lord responded to them: "I will never deny any of you—male or female, the reward of your deeds. Both are equal in reward. Those who migrated or were expelled from their home and were persecuted for My sake and fought and ˹some˺ were martyred; I will certainly forgive their sins and admit them into Gardens under which rivers flow, as a reward from Allah. And with Allah is the finest reward"). And the Almighty said: Al-Nisa 124 (And whoever does righteous deeds, male or female, while he is a believer, those will enter Heaven and not oppress). And addresses men and women alike, and treat them in a manner almost equal, the Almighty said: Al-Rum 21 (And one of His signs is that He created for you spouses from among yourselves so that you may find comfort in them. And He has placed between you compassion and mercy. Surely in this are signs for people who reflect.). The verse indicates that the woman was created from the same man, that is, from the gender of the man.

Islamic law, in general, aims at the distinct purpose of protecting society. The legislation provides women with precise definitions of their rights and expresses keen interest in guaranteeing them. The Quran and the Sunnah encourage women to be treated with justice, kindness, and compassion, as well as guaranteeing them the right to private property and inheritance. German Orientalist Hunke Sigrid says: "Men and women in Islam enjoy the same rights in terms of quality, and if these rights are not the same in all fields, therefore the Muslim woman must be free from foreign influence ... She should not take The European, American, or Russian woman as an example to follow, or to be guided by a doctrinal thought regardless of its source, because this is new empowerment for the intruder thinking that leads to the loss of the elements of her personality, but rather she must adhere to the true guidance of Islam. (Laura Veccia Vaglieri - Italian writer), One of the well-known academic orientalism - of Islam being fair to women, she says: "If a woman has attained - from the social point of view in Europe - a high position - then her legal position - at least - was until very a few years ago - and it is still in some countries less independence compared to the Muslim woman in the Islamic world. The Muslim woman enjoys the right of inheritance like her brothers, even in a smaller proportion, and she has the right not to give birth to anyone except with her free consent, and her right not to be mistreated by her husband, and she also has the right to obtain a dowry from the husband, and she can provide for her even if she is wealthy in origin, and she has the right - if she is legally qualified - to manage her personal property. The Quran mentions veneration and reverence as examples of women who have perfected their obedience to God. He said: Al-Tahrim 11-12 (And Allah presents an example of those who believed: the wife of Pharaoh, when she said, "My Lord, build for me near You a house in Paradise and save me from Pharaoh and his deeds and save me from the wrongdoing people." And [the example of] Mary, the daughter of 'Imrān, who guarded her chastity, so We blew into [her garment] through Our angel [i.e., Gabriel], and she believed in the words of her Lord and His scriptures and was of the devoutly obedient.)

As for Islam's view of women as deficient in reason and religion, this is not a defamation of women. Rather, the intention of the deficiency of the mind is that the affection of women is stronger because they govern emotion over the mind, and the problem of choosing opinions is when it relies on passion and emotion. As for the deficiency in the religion, the meaning is that she is exempt from things from which the man is never exempt. The man is not exempt from prayer, and it is exempted from it in monthly periods, and the man is not exempt from fasting, while it is also exempted for several days a month. This is an appreciation from God Almighty for her mission and nature, and there is no shortage of her, verifying what Almighty says: Al-Nisa 32 (And do not wish for that by which Allah has made some of you exceed others. For men is a share of what they have earned, and for women is a share of what they have earned. And ask Allah of His bounty. Indeed, Allah is ever, of all things, Knowing.). Therefore, the intention of Islam is not to stigmatize a woman with a defect but rather to describe her nature. Rather, Islam has charted for a woman a path in the middle that corresponds to her nature and fits with her physical makeup and the jobs that the Creator created for her (bearing in mind that the principle is that a woman does not go out of her house except if she needs or is needed by society, but if she needs it, society guarantees her need. Nevertheless, if she goes out, she is subject to a fundamental rule that is: Necessities allow prohibitions, and necessity is assessed by its value. This is in addition to the utilization of women in what is good for her by nature while adhering to the controls the legitimacy defined by Islam, on top of which is not to mix with men.

5. China Confucianism Teachings

An earthly, non-heavenly religion that views women with an inferior view and considers them stupid, with a naive, limited, and weak mentality and does not have any wisdom or jealousy. Therefore, man despises her because she has no occupation other than seducing innocent men. She does not have the right to inherit the family inheritance from owning finances, and when she goes to her husband's house, she is under his authority to serve him under his authority without discussing with him or any of his relatives, which is an extension to the prevention of her discussion with her father, brother, uncle, and uncle, but rather she must be submissive and obey him and implement what he is ordered to do. Rather, even the mother of her husband exercises full and complete control over her mal with the use of beating by her to her son's wife, and in special cases, the husband's mother can sell a wife where she is if she disobeys her orders or runs away from her husband's house.

6. Laws of Manu Hinduism

a. It made the woman totally dependent on the man.
b. Prohibition of a widow remarriage after the death of her husband.
c. Demonstrate her status and place her below that of a man.
d. Expelling her from society or burning her if she commits adultery.

B. THE SECOND TOTALITARIAN POWER OF SLAVERY: SOCIAL CULTURE

1. Masculine (Patriarchal) Authority

The patriarchal authority of the is not limited to the authority of the father as it is believed, but rather with all its forms (the other, son, uncle, the head of the tribe and the clan, the leader, the chief, the headmaster of the school and the institution, the minister, and the general manager) and every male occupies a leadership-administrative position responsible for a group of individuals and not the father in the family alone. This is just a preliminary notice, and then there is a secondary mention that male power is included and attached to authoritarianism, domination, conspiracy, control, tyranny, oppression, coercion, and forcing the rights of the feminine that may be his wife, daughter, sister, employee, or student. This means he is responsible for her, either family or professionally. More precisely, patriarchy does not have a biological-sexual difference, physical strength, or intelligence, but rather a cultural, historical, and social industry that makes him an epic hero, a warrior knight, a priest, a chivalric man, a merchant and a high-ranking shrine.

There is no doubt, then, from saying that the patriarchal authority includes male domination over the female. This domination prevailed in Eastern and Western civilisations alike. No one rejected it, and no one discussed it or asked about it. It was taken with certainty without change or alteration. It continued into the modern era as if it were challenging social, technological and globalisation changes. It remained constant, and this is something that attracts attention. Why has the male power not changed in the family, the factory, the market, the trade, the company, and all the fields of working and family life? The male is the one who dominates the family.

The gradual development of the male authority can be classified into three historical and societal stages as follows:

The First Stage: It began in the period between 1000 - 800 BC, during which the Greek and Roman empire arose, in which the male was featured with heroic epics that required courage, valour, physical strength, loyalty and honesty, and this was the beginning of the emergence of the patriarchal (male) authority.

After the fall of the two empires, the male was subjected to spiritual monasticism, which imprinted the character of the Christian religion that emerged between 1000 - 900 BC, which required combating illegal sexual practices, anti-femininity, and homosexuality, with an emphasis on the strict patriarchal system.

Then, in the twelfth century, the male was imprinted with chivalry, heroism, and magnanimity, which also required strength, audacity, the service of ancestors and the wives of the lords, while in the sixteenth century - in the European Renaissance, the male was marked by rationality and self-discovery. In the eighteenth century, the male was normalised with the bourgeoisie, the search for high status and success in commerce.

This first stage emphasised courage, strength and boldness, which were associated with religiosity and respect for ancestors of the male. It began in 1000 BC and ended with the end of the eighteenth century.

The components and enhancements of male power in this historical period are:
1. Heroic and equestrian epics.
2. The agricultural sector.
3. The ascetic hostage.

4. Loyalty and sacrifice for the sake of the ancestor (grandfather).
5. The teachings of the Christian religion.
6. Trade.

The Second Stage: The Western societies continued to develop under the momentum of the European Renaissance to assume power over the world during this stage, while it prevailed in the traditional, conservative, agricultural and pastoral Eastern societies the tradition of extended family, the clan, and the tribe based on the system of sheikhdom, tribalism, and the kinship link. The concept of homeland and citizenship, however, was not crystallised in it because of the domination of the Ottoman Empire over the region, after which Britain, France and Italy took control of it. Therefore, the definition of citizenship was a generic rather than intrinsic concept. Male authority is nothing but a reflection of the authority of the tribe, and since the community in the Eastern societies is pastoral and agricultural, early female marriage is prevalent, and polygamy is existing imposed by the unity of labour on the land, which means (the family) a productive unit.

Male power is embodied in the male domination of the female, enslavement of her, and her psychological and social oppression, thus obliterating her personality, diminishing her importance, and degrading her position in the family and social standing. It is multi-faceted authoritarianism, but its source was not physical strength but rather a social culture.

As for the components and enhancements of male authority at this stage, they are:
1. Agriculture.
2. The inherited social culture.
3. Wars, revolutions, and political coups.
4. Government and educational education.

5. The extended family and the clan and tribal system.
6. Ignorance and illiteracy.
7. Sports.

The Third Stage: which started from the beginning of the nineteenth century until the twentieth century, the patriarchal power prevailed in Western and American society, in which industry, industrialisation, and the diversity of scientific specialisations that required physical endurance, serious and hard work, sharp intelligence and material wealth, all pushed the male to gain access to it and excel in it, in addition to wars. And sports. All of them supported and strengthened the masculinity of the man and did not deal with female femininity; for example, the American society took the male power until the emergence of the individual value that was committed to masculinity due to the occurrence of absolute and indefinite job opportunities that allowed the man to enter the fields of industry, politics and commerce, and everything that he aspires to more than women all of this led to The increase in the independence of men and the expansion of industrialisation and the diversity of specialisations supported by the material success achieved by the man. The male authority of the American man was supported by the industrialisation movement that required physical endurance, hard work and perseverance with a high level of intelligence and the availability of material wealth. All of this led to the domination and dominance of the male over the American female, which did not come from the standards and values of traditional culture (because it is not present in the material and capitalist American society) while it is happening in eastern societies (Chinese, Indian and Arab) and has not been strengthened by the religion (Judaism and Christianity) and we do not forget the wars that Contributed to strengthening and strengthening the patriarchal authority in American society (World War II, the Vietnam War, Afghanistan and Iraq), as well as supporting sports in strengthening the man's muscles and masculinity.

Recruiting to engage in the military for the purpose of waging war takes place with males and not females because wars crystallise the nation's glory and promote manliness, courage, and courage in facing the enemy and defeating them, so wars build courage and boldness, defy difficulties and fight enemies, which the nation is proud of. This is the pinnacle of masculinity that saves the country from enemies, occupation, and acute crises.

Whereas women are not recruited to join the army because they do not possess these physical characteristics to endure hardship and struggle, but rather are skilled in nursing and service work and be companions of arms and not bearers of weapons. Then there is the male-nourishing sport, whether through competition or physical fitness. It is more like the military in terms of building the body. Therefore, we find the father in American society encouraging his son and not his daughter to exercise.

The constituents and reinforcements of male power (the Patriarchs) in the western industrial society are: -

1. Industrial work depends on the body's endurance of hard and serious work.
2. Trade depends on the continuous movement and coexistence with the movement of goods in the market and knowledge of cash liquidity.
3. Availability of financial and material wealth.
4. Individual independence and self-reliance.
5. Doing individual and association sports (differential).
6. Wars that require valour, courage, redemption, and sacrifice.

These constituents and reinforcements have supported the permanence and survival of male power in human society throughout the ages. Civilisations and urbanisation have challenged all kinds of social changes and the transition from one stage to another. The power of the man remained in the family, the school, the factory, the government, religious, artistic and military institutions, as political power changed from traditional to capitalism and socialism, commercial and economic power while the male power remained unchanged. What is the secret in that? In fact, the secret lies in the absence of a vibrant and active feminist organisation that works seriously in defence of women's rights, and the failure to occupy the feminine position of a sovereign and high leadership in society and does not possess material and financial wealth and did not raise her level of education and fight illiteracy then and did not weaken the position of men in systemic and constructive activities. Due to the perpetual occurrence of wars that seek men and not women, religion and social culture are still supportive of men, who use them to support their interests against femininity.

The elite of saying this authority is a traditional calcified in the mentality of the man granted to him by the inherited social culture and the clerics intruding on religion, feudalists and ruling men, so the male used it as a pretext for the enslavement of women and the dispossession of her personality, freedom, thinking and human nature that was derived from nature because she was the first to settle on the earth and discovered agriculture and domesticated animals And because the principle of fertility on the land is the same as the principle of fertility for her, her authority in society was a natural right for her.

However, with the development of the city-state, the control of state rights, the emergence of new regulations on sexual life, the development of the property system, and the spread of agriculture, the man exploited these developments to serve his needs and interests, to sacrifice the master of society through female slavery and usurpation of her natural and personal rights as oppression, injustice, and aggression, so he turned her into his victim in the name of religion and social culture.

In the table (1), the historical types of male roles in the first stage are shown with their main characteristics. This table shows the stages of the development of the male roles throughout the history in mankind societies, which were influenced by the historical eras of the sources that reflect each stage and present specific models that express the spirit of the era in which he lives. He has never been submissive or obedient to the woman, but throughout, he confirms his strength, masculinity, chivalry, and boldness. The historical, religious, military, and scientific events are what strengthened the male role in society and made him dominant, distinguished, and superior to the female. In a sense, his masculinity was made by serial and varied events in the forming of the characteristics of his masculinity, which were featured by valour, boldness, courage, denial of selfishness, sacrifice, chivalry, rationality, and preoccupation with worldly affairs to obtain a high status, excluding the female in her interaction with the events that he went through to be unique to him alone to surpass the female.

In his study on male patriarchal domination in society and power, Ibrahim Al-Haidari describes the position of the father in the Arab society as part of the eastern society compared with the western society.

Patriarchal system the term Patriarchy, Patriarchate, in its origins goes back to the Greek language and means "the rule of the father", that is, his domination and control over the family so that the decision is in the hands of the male "patriarch" as the head of the house and the head of the tribe. The term was also used in a religious sense, as "Saint Pater" was called "Our Father" in the later Orthodox Church.

The patriarchal-patriarchal system constitutes a distinct social and psychological structure rooted in the collective memory that characterises the family, tribe, authority and society in the Arab world and forms a hierarchical family based on authoritarianism and irrational submission that contradicts the values of modernity, civil society and respect for human rights resulting from historical, social and economic conditions and conditions and through a series One of the historical stages and the interconnected social and economic formations between them, where each stage is linked to a stage that precedes it until it reaches the stage of the modern patriarchal system, which is a specific type of social and economic organisation prior to capitalism that differs in its social, economic, and cultural structures from that of the patriarchal Arab system, which has taken a distinct type. As a traditional society, it corresponds to a modern society that is characterised by scientific and technical progress, whose characteristics are its ability to resist change to its original structure from the middle age until now and its ability to continue to preserve its traditional values such as belonging to the tribe, sect and region, and its connection to the desert environment that produced a patriarchal system that dominated the region Arabia has many centuries and still is. [http://iraqieconomists.net]

Finally, it became the fact that the male power is the oldest, most powerful, and hardest social force that challenged and continue to challenge all kinds of scientific, technological, cultural, social, political and religious changes. It remained the dominant and transcendent role over the female in all capitalists, socialist, feudal, conservative, rural and traditional societies as if it were a huge social hierarchy that was not affected by global or regional events.

2. Her Infanticide (The Girl Infanticide)

It is a form of violence against female babies after their birth, and even female circumcision or abandonment of them is considered a violent act against females, and this is what was followed in ancient civilisations such as Arabs in the pre-Islamic era before the advent of Islam, which prohibited and forbade the infanticide of girls.

At the present time, some large countries known for their advancement practice infanticide of girls from children (new-borns) with the aim or intention of controlling population growth in order not to increase, but to make the equation close between males and females. It is both an illegal and inhuman act. China, for example, practices this killing because its demographic policy requires the delivery of one newborn, and what is more than that is the death of the newborn girl. Likewise, India adopts a policy of infertility women after the birth of their third child. Knowing the masculinity of the child brings financial income to the family.

It is worth noting that the World Health Organization (WHO) has identified patterns of abuse of newborns, which has become widespread among poor, low-income, and limited countries. A global conference was held in Beijing in 1995 on child abuse such as infanticide, female genital mutilation, and abandonment, considering it a violent crime against women. The countries that infanticide girls after childbirth at the present time are India, China, Inuit and North America. [Thomsen. 2007. P. 27)

By the act of God or the powers of the universe, it was found that male and female numbers are balanced and almost equal throughout the globe, although the existing boundaries were found by the human being to divide the globe into countries and territories.

Since the inception of creation, the female has been subjected to various types of discrimination, contempt, and denial of her right to life, and if one wants to be neutral and fair with the monotheistic religions, it can be stated that apart from Islam, the female rights had not been reserved until Islam came to protect and support her, prohibiting all forms of negligence towards her, criminalising all kinds of harm directed towards her, preventing harm to her. It assigned for her and the male their own roles in this life in proportion to her nature and composition, and all roles are indispensable to each other, with exquisite harmony, wonderful complementarity, and uniquely unique harmony.

No.	Model Type	Source	The Main Characteristics of The Male Role
1	Epic Male - Heroic	The heroic epics of the Greek and Roman empires between 1000 and 800 BC	Brave, bold, and valiant behaviour, based on physical strength, loyalty, and honesty, is the beginning of masculine authority.
2	Male of the monastic - spiritual	Teaching the teachings of Christ, the early church monks, and the ascetic monastic traditions between 1000 - 900 BC.	Selflessness, strict restrictions on sexual activities against femininity and anti-sodomy attitudes with a strict and powerful pathological regime.

3	Male of the equestrian championship	The time of feudalism, a symbol of chivalry, chivalry, and its honour in the twelfth century, with social order.	Self-sacrifice, valour, boldness, boldness, physical strength, the honour of serving the wife of the Lord or the woman of feudal royal power, and the service of the ancestor (grandfather).
4	Male of the Renaissance	Sixteenth Century and Social Formation.	Rationality, Intellectual Efforts, and Self-Discoveries.
5	Male bourgeoisie from the middle class of merchants, urbanites, and those with material and capitalist interests.	The eighteenth century and the social system.	Success in commerce and the high worldly position, the one who is responsible for worldly affairs and being preoccupied with it and expert in life and people.

Table (1): Types of male roles historically (*Ref. Gender Roles. 2011. P. 242***)**

Despite progress, civilisation, urbanisation, human rights charters, international population conferences, women's defence bodies and pregnant and childcare associations, the infanticide of girls today is at its highest activity and application. If the two largest countries in the world, namely China and India, are taken as examples of such a practice, there is a lot of evidence on crimes against the female baby. The one-child family policy in China refers to the preference of spouses for a male rather than a female, and it is known to all circles that the girls born in the streets of Beijing and other cities of China are to be thrown in order to have a child born in the next pregnancy, but in India, the argument is that the girl is costly in raising her, so the sex of the fetus is determined using ultrasound technology, to be followed by abortion as it is female, and although doctors are forbidden and held accountable if they have performed an abortion, the Indian authorities are not serious about implementing such regulation to stop them. The result was what was published by the British medical journal "The Lancet" in its June 4, 2011 issue of Indian doctors from India and Canada that between three and six million girls had aborted in only the last decade and twelve million people from 1980 until last year. Even with the continuing abortion of girls over the years, the imbalance in the percentage of girls compared to boys increases. It is known that some Indian states have begun to complain about the scarcity of girls 'numbers, and who knows in the future that conflicts and wars will arise between the children of the same country and between countries and some of them not for the sake of expansion and wealth, but for the sake of the seizure of women, this is what the human hand has presented.

3. Her Circumcision

It is the usurpation of her right in her body, which represents the biological right with which she was created. It is taken away from her without her desire, but rather the desire of her social, cultural norms that violates her sexual feelings. Besides the violation of her sexual and physical rights, she is assaulted savagely by unjust standards and values of social culture. Therefore, the social culture invaded the girl while she was a child. She was not the victim of the man, but the standards of honour and chastity are estimated through her circumcision. It is an inhuman, religious, or medical standard, but just a wild, barbaric standard that does not place any respect on human beings.

Female circumcision or female genital mutilation (according to terminologies of international organisations such as the World Health Organization) means amputation or removal of part of the female genitalia, incomplete removal, or partial amputation for cultural, religious, or other reasons. The United Nations declared on February 6 an international day that rejects Female circumcision. It was noticed that immigrants to the Western world from Asia and Africa were practising this habit that led to the death of some circumcised girls. Accordingly, legislate laws were issued that criminalise and prohibit this habit and consider it a crime against the girl child, childhood, and human rights laws.

At the same time, scientific researchers paid attention to it in their medical, health, psychological and social seminars and conferences, as well as modern social movements such as the human rights movement, the women's liberation movement, and the sociology of women in order to study them, explain their risks, and defend women and emancipate them from old inherited value standards that do not reflect the characteristics of medical and psychological development. Female circumcision and the modification of the Female Genital Mutilation, which is symbolised by FGM, has become controversial and debates among societies of the Western world, so it has become a topic that disgusts them, and they defend the health and rights of the minor girl in the developing, conservative and backward world in order to enlighten the world about the danger of the primitive cultural habits that do not fit with the modern, technical and scientific man.

As for its types of female circumcision, they are the following: -

1. Ritual circumcision involves perforating the lobe of the clitoral hood so that blood can pass through while the sexual sensation of the clitoral is eliminated.
2. Social custom circumcision refers to the removal of the clitoris or the part within the labia in the vulvas of the minor girl so that her lust and the sexual arousal will not happen on rubbing this part for sexual enjoyment that she may be immersed in when she grows up.
3. Clitoridectomy or clitorectomy is the surgical removal of the clitoris. It is rarely used as a therapeutic medical procedure, such as when cancer has developed in or spread to the clitoris. It is often performed on intersex newborns. Commonly, non-medical removal of the clitoris is performed during female genital mutilation (FGM).
4. Excision of all parts of the labia and the clitoris opening a hole or a small opening for urination and menstruation (this circumcision is practised in Egypt and Sudan).
5. Amputation of part of the clitoris, not the total excision of it.
6. Cut the labia fabric.
7. Amputation of the clitoris and open an opening that connects the vagina to the anus (this circumcision is practised by the Aborigines tribes in Australia).

Areas of Prevalence of Female Circumcision in the World: Before explaining the areas of the spread of circumcision in the world, it is important to know the statistics of this problem. As per the estimations of the World Health Organization (WHO), there are 6,000 girls in the world who are circumcised every day from the ages of 4 to 12 years or among newborns (immediately after birth), and sometimes circumcision is done In the months before marriage or after the first birth. Most of these cases take place in East and West Africa, the Arabian Peninsula, and by some immigrants to Europe, America, Canada, Australia, and New Zealand.

In general, circumcision is done before reaching the age of sexual puberty because they believe that the older a girl has grown, her clitoris becomes large and grows, and since it is the source of sexual irritation, its amputation is safer and more comfortable for her and the parents to avoid her sexual deviation which is shameful to the family. And since circumcision represents one of the pillars of marriage requirements, it is considered right to do it while their daughter is young so as not to resist or reject, let alone the less pain. This is their belief and their shallow health and cultural knowledge. They do not realise that such practices mean a violation of a female's physical rights and distort the nature of the human body. They neglect its effects, such as bloody bleeding that leads to the death of a circumcised girl due to the lack of ingenuity of the woman who performs the circumcision process and to acute infections resulting from lack of sterilisation. The tools used in the amputation with the use of animal dung powder to stop the bleeding resulting from cutting the vulvar artery or the clitoral artery that leads to difficulty urinating or when urinating the girl feels severe pain in the urinary tract. Then there is the psychological trauma that accompanies her life and fear of marriage because it reminds her of the pain and aches that she went through during and after the operation. Also, the occurrence of AIDS (deficiency in immunity) with the loss of her sense of sexual pleasure and the weakness of the strength of her sexual energy with the smallness of her genitals and the pain associated with the menstrual cycle (menstruation).

Amnesty International has estimated that more than 130 million women worldwide are affected by the amputation of parts of their reproductive system, as well as the entry of 2 million females annually into the total. In 1995, the European Council in its various bodies condemned female circumcision and considered it as violence and torture for women, a violation of their right to equality and an attack on the integrity of their body, and in 1992 the World Health Organization confirmed its refusal to undergo medical circumcision of any kind at a conference in the Netherlands.

No harm in presenting the article written by the researcher (Azza Baydoun), who said on this subject: In some Arab countries, the woman's sexual organs are violated, in particular her clitoris, which is the most important part of her sexual organs when it is completely or partially amputated, in what has become known as "circumcision" or female genital mutilation. Circumcision is an infringement on small female genital organs from countries where acceptance is obtained, and it obtains a position in her body that has not been resolved. Yet the debate about its importance during the process of sexual intercourse and her sexual arousal, as if the excitement is not needed for sexual satisfaction, which is the attainment of orgasm (peak orgasm). That amputation is presented in popular beliefs as a protector from diseases of the eye and skin, as well as diarrhoea, infections, malnutrition, slow growth, and some beliefs, refer to circumcision resistance to poisoning (snakes and scorpions), which, in the opinion of his "supporters", is necessary for the cleanliness of the vulva and secures immunity against gonorrhoea. It expels evil spirits and protects the mother and child from diseases that fall prey to her in the first forty days after birth. But the most common belief is that circumcision confers a female "purity" by reducing the intensity of her sexual desire. The strongest argument in support of the necessity of performing circumcision remains that the man (husband) favours a female who has been circumcised as his sexual partner.

Feminists see circumcision as a sexual process that has similar symbolism in all patriarchal social systems that succeed in producing the same result, suppressing the sexuality of women. In the Victorian-social culture, for example, in which the "scientific" discourse prevailed in the late nineteenth century until the feminist revolution in its second wave was formulated, female sexuality in a manner that presumes a definitive suppression of clitoral sensations in favour of vaginal sexual sensations. And this suppression assumed a necessary condition for the success of the realisation of femininity in the female (i.e., heterosexuality, the incorporation of the characteristics of receptivity, narcissism, and masochism into her psychological structure, and secondly, the desire for motherhood). However, the Freudian theory of femininity that prevailed in the medical and psychological sciences until not so long ago and which had no effect on the understanding of female gender identity. Most of the women were classified according to this theory as 'gang bites' or 'tomboys' women because they were unable to suppress feelings that have an explicit physical source which is the clitoris but are "wrong". Feminist researchers interpret this transgression - symbolic or actual - as the clitoris is an organ that has no function in the sexual satisfaction of a man, so it was considered an excess organ and without a role in the reproductive process. Therefore, the lust feelings that the clitoris provokes should be suppressed or depressed so that it is not an obstacle to accepting the female with her supposed sexual negativity, as a condition necessary to achieve her heterosexual femininity and to accept the implications of her motherhood.

4. Ironing of Her Breasts

It is a rape like the circumcision of a girl and the annihilation of her femininity. This rape is conducted by ironing the breast of the girl before her sexual puberty to kill all sexual sensations associated with this part of the female body. It is a real assault on her dignity and her right to psychological stability.

Four million girls have been subject to breast ironing for fear of harassment and rape. It is a social custom practised by African societies such as Cameroon, Nigeria, Togo, Guinea, Ivory Coast and South Africa, which represents the harshest and fiercest brutal habit exercised on the physical femininity that represents the sign of sexual maturity for the African girl in the twenty-first century practised by civilised, traditional, culturally, and primitive societies. Society has not taken the position of punishing the customary and statutory officer of the young perpetrator who commits sexual harassment and rape of the girl. Rather (the authoritarian and prejudiced society towards the male side) goes to the girl to torture her and embrace her femininity while she is at the beginning of her adult development not to protect her, but to torture her physically, psychologically, and sexually. This is another case that expresses the male discrimination of society against the female (the same was seen in the crime of murder, a washing of shame, female genital mutilation, temporary marriage, minor's marriage, domestic violence, surrogacy, exploitation of their resources and the attachment of their presence to his existence).

All these social practices that the society legalised and made them customary controls at the expense of femininity, personality, dignity, conscience, and affection the female to satisfy the instincts of the male. Was this not arbitrariness, avoidance and unjust by society? It is the numerical half; its

215

resource and it's financed by human reproduction? Wasn't this tyranny forced by him on his productive, active, and vital half? Did he not turn her into his legitimate victim? Did he not realise that and need it? Did he not think about his revenge on her in the coming eras when she breaks all his controls and restrictions that he imposed on her? And her liberation and independence from him to do what she likes as an act of revenge on him. Has this not happened in the stage of the individual's downsizing of society at the present time in the capitalist, democratic, industrial, urban, and informational society?

Many articles were written on this topic; for example, Rose Al-Youssef magazine recorded this case and described it as the nightmare of the black continent, in which it came as follows: Girls have lived in a number of African countries since the age of eight in a nightmare. They are not like other girls of their young ages who dream of femininity and the prominence of its features on their bodies. Such signs of puberty for the girls of Cameroon, Nigeria, Togo, Guinea, Ivory Coast and South Africa represent life punishment as these signs must be obliterated to protect them from rape and harassment. Breast ironing is a tradition like female circumcision that has been inherited for hundreds of years in several African countries with the aim of preserving female honour. Their excuse is that it protects the girl herself from sexual desires according to inherited beliefs. It is carried out with the welcome of the parents, where the mother or a relative put inflamed iron skewers on the breast of the girl aged from 8 to 12 years to obscure the features of femininity and hide and prevent her breast from growing when she reaches puberty. And the beginning of the appearance of signs of femininity on her, or this habit is carried out by placing pieces of hot stones to obliterate the breasts. In some

216

places, they are satisfied with putting a piece of cloth and tightening it over the breasts to prevent the growth of the child's breasts.

According to the American newspaper The Daily Beast, the custom was used in the past to increase breast milk supply. With the increase in cases of harassment and rape, it began to be used to protect girls from male harassment and rape. And now, it has increased its spread to protect girls from terrorist organisations such as Boko Haram in Cameroon.

The United Nations report "breast ironing" mentioned that (3.8) million women around the world subjected to breast ironing, which was confirmed by local media in Cameroon, indicating that 50% of girls undergo (breast ironing) on a daily basis for a period of more than three months. Girls from wealthy families wear wide belts that compress the breasts and prevent breast growth. (Grace Chamy) A sixteen-year-old girl from Akum town in Nigeria was one of the cases that were exposed to breast ironing. She says that when she reached adulthood at the age of 9, her mother began to torture her to protect her. Where the mother gets up every morning at seven o'clock and takes one of the stone pestles that are used for grinding food and works on heating them on charcoal, then puts them on her breasts until she flattens the chest with the body.

Georgette Ari Nako of the National Network of Aunties Associations that Care for Sex Education for Cameroonians says that many women feel anxious when their daughters reach the age of 8 or 9 and think that this precocious puberty will attract boys to them and may fall into early pregnancy. When mothers flat the breasts of their daughters, they are forced to conceal them, thinking that they are thus controlling the effect of their daughters 'femininity on men, and then on their desire for sex, which is not correct, as they regularly receive single mothers who have had their breasts ironed.

5. Rituals of Adolescence Age for the Girl in Nibal

It is a ceremonial ritual celebrating the female's reaching puberty announcing to the members of the local community to know that the female (so-and-so) has reached puberty in a bride's wedding to her groom in a traditional - rural society. It is a ceremony (Barha Gufa) for an ancient ritual in the Nabwar community, one of the ethnic groups in Nepal whose language, lifestyle, culture, traditions, and rituals differ from other ethnic groups, which is the marriage of the sun.

First, the girl's family consults with a priest about the date of the celebration for their daughter, and the date is set accordingly. In a 12-day celebration in which girls between the ages of 17 and 13 are kept in a dark room, away from the rays of the sun and any contact from males, even from the closest people to them, such as their parents and brothers, and on the last day girls symbolically marry from the sun as they reach the age of puberty and celebrate this occasion with their friends and family in a traditional party. On the first day, the girl is placed in a dark room called (the cave or the hollow) away from the sunlight and remains in this state for 11 days. Two dolls, white and black, made of cotton or a piece of cloth, are placed in a dark room. The white one symbolizes a good ghost, while the black doll symbolizes a bad ghost. Once she puts it down, the girl has to give part of her meal to the doll herself before she takes it. According to their belief, if she does not do so, the bad ghost will scare her at night.

During her isolation, the girl is not allowed to clean herself or eat salty food, especially in the first five days, and her mother takes care of her and tells her about the reasons for her separation from everyone, the rituals that will take place and the changes that will occur to her body in the coming days after which she is given a natural product called Kaoo (a formula made of flour roasted, dried orange peel, sandalwood and other herbs) and asks her to put it on her face so that after the sixth day, her female relatives and friends come to visit with them carrying a variety of delicious foods.

On the twelfth day, the wedding ceremony with the sun takes place on this day. The girl should wake up before sunrise, take a shower, prepare for the ceremony, and wear the traditional wedding dress with red sarees and heavy gold jewellery like a real bride.

The priest performs the complex marriage ceremony where a piece of cloth is kept covering her face, or her eyes are covered throughout the marriage ceremony, after which he allows the girl to show her face to see the reflection of the sun in the water. The girl closes her eyes while her mother raises the piece of cloth until the sunlight touches it will protect her from evil.

Finally, after the marriage ceremony ends, the family organizes a party with relatives and friends to mark their daughter's reaching puberty. [Zahrat Al Khaleej Magazine No. 2046 dated 9/6/2018]

6. She Became Spinster Because of the High Dowry

This issue is very much related to Eastern society, where its marriage requirements are different from those of Western societies. For the time being, men in the eastern societies have a reluctance to marry because of the girl's family's demand for a dowry, and it is often associated with material demands. Such demands include complete furniture for the house with a private car and other incapacitating requests that do not coincide with the possibility of the beginning marriage, then men get an aversion to marriage or a strike on it, which negatively affects delay or failure The girl's marriage and here the girl lost her right to choose her life partner (due to the apparent consumption demands and the false ostentation of the high status and high-level consideration of the girl's family). It is correlating directly to the high standard of living and cultural awareness of the rising generation, and the rapid material changes that outpaced the movement of cultural and moral changes, so the spinsterhood of girls was one of the aspects of cultural usurpation of their rights in the Eastern society and in particular the Arab community opposite to the Western society which has not got such requirements.

There are several negative effects left by cultural traditions on the formation of the first cell (family) in society that is not immune to the pressures and harassment of outdated norms, values, and traditions in the formation of this cell consisting in the beginning from young man and woman. The problem does not lie in the young man and woman, but in the family of the young woman asking for a high dowry, furniture for an elegant and modern house, lavish wedding party, gold jewellery and clothes of the latest fashion before embarking on marriage in order to show off and fake consumption in front of people, relatives, and acquaintances of the girl. These requirements represent a huge financial burden on the young man that he cannot provide for the family. It seems that the family does not look at the emotional relationship or the desire of the young man and the young woman to marry, but rather to the material matters and the impression of the neighbours about the value of their daughter and her position in the local community. All of them are financially harassing the young man, so it will later reflect negatively on his relationship with his wife and her family and cause problems between the two families (the family of the young man and the young woman). This is social hypocrisy and is nothing but apparent consumption to give a misleading and exaggerated image of the family of the young woman to be married.

They are irrational and unrealistic demands and do not express the strength of the relationship between them. It is hypocritical demands that do not cater for the interest of the husband or wife and has no function in the family system. It is only to reinforce and support the tyranny of society in exercising its family controls with the belief of the young woman's family that the more demands, the better the impression they leave to the people around them. These are the costs of marriage, such as clothes, jewellery, furniture, a house, a car and a honeymoon whenever they give a brilliant, bragging picture of their daughter in front of the local community. All this is in response to the requirements of the outdated social standards in the costs of marriage and give an exaggerated picture of their daughter's standing, without giving serious importance to their daughter's relationship with her husband after marriage and paying attention to the demands of the newlyweds. In the face of this excessive exaggeration in the costs of marriage in eastern societies, they caused the reluctance of young men (males) to marry and led to the increase of spinsters. Such an environment also leads to slipping into the abysses of moral perversions and misdemeanours on both sides, such as sex with prostitutes (for the young man) and travelling abroad to enjoy away from the customary regulations of society.

As for the girl, she may slip into perverted behaviour such as lesbianism, hidden sexual relations, or psychological and neurological diseases, all because of the apparent consumption of marriage imposed by traditions and customs that have been finished by the time that the girl's family required, believing that this raises her position among the applicants for her marriage, which results in the opposition against her. Specifically, its effects are reflected in the tensions and quarrels among family members that are not explicitly announced, but rather that their real cause is "the girl's spinsterhood" and "the young man's reluctance to marry." It is an incorrect pathological condition whose effects are borne by society due to the outdated standards and traditions of social culture that are not in line with the spirit of the age and the material cost of living. The defect is in the traditions of society, and its reform must begin with changing the sterile and outdated standards of marriage and not through financial aid from the government or group marriage and the like.

Many young people suffer from the problem of high dowries, and this problem is one of the serious problems that prevent many who wish to marry, establishing a family, having children, and building society with the aim of preserving humans from conflict and repression.

7. Marry Her When She is a Minor

It is the ugliest form of rape against a girl who is under the age of majority (less than 18 years of age), who has no experience of family and marital life and is deprived of will by the male authority (the Patriarchs), in the sense that her rights as a person and as a woman and as a citizen in a country where there is a constitution and a law under which these rights are not taken. She is forced to enter marital life without taking her opinion on choosing a life partner, but her family is acting on her behalf, and the government does not reject such a marriage, and this is the seizure of her legitimate rights by oppression and injustice imposed by her social culture and the aggression of her feelings and emotions. This does not happen in Western society - the civilized and the developed).

Australian Cases: The negative model of women's rights will be addressed from the angle of the marriage of an Arab man to an Arab girl under the age of eighteen years who practices in the Australian continent from Arab families that have immigrated to her in this regard. Director of Immigrant Women's Health Services, Dr Iman Sharoubim, in Australia, said, "Underage marriage is widespread in Sydney, and an awareness-raising process must be carried out as new immigrants are ignorant of Australian law. The numbers by the Australian Bureau of Statistics indicate that there are 604 illegal marriages of underage girls aged between 14 and 17 years, born in Australia, and 63 cases of illegal marriages of minors born outside Australia.

The Minister (Gaurd) confirmed that the parents of a minor girl who marries must be brought to trial, and it is worth noting that the legal age for marriage in Australia is 18 years, and in special cases approved by the judge is 16 years old. The Minister of Social Services (Brogaward) admitted that underage marriage is widespread and that there are many marriages in this category. It is illegal and unregistered, and the department is aware of these cases, especially in the areas of southwestern Sydney, western Sydney, and Blue Mountain. And that the law must take its course when it is discovered that girls have the right to enjoy their childhood and not be deprived of innocent life. A leading health advisor in the field of health warned that hundreds are sent outside Australia at the age of 11 years to marry. This marriage, in fact, followed the Arab culture imported with the immigrants to Australia and did not submit to the laws of the immigrant country. Their excuse in the marriage of minor girls can be due to the following reasons:

i. The fear that the girl would be immersed in the liberal culture, individual freedom, personal and financial independence, and Western upbringing in her relations with the opposite sex.

ii. Fearing for the family's reputation and for social confusion over the honour and behaviour of members of the immigrant family.

iii. Getting rid of the responsibility entrusted of parents to pursue their daughters in a Western life that does not resemble their family upbringing in the family preimmigration original society.

iv. To preserve the unity and solidarity of the family and not to be drawn into the temptations of the girls 'youthful life.

In view of this thinking, the parents are inclined to forbid their minor girls from enjoying their childhood and depriving them of innocent life. In equal upbringing, however, the girl enjoys the freedom of friendship and sexual relations with the opposite sex or staying up outside the house and drinking alcohol and drug use and the Like.

That is, the control of a man (father or son) over an Arab girl in the diaspora with the immigrant family is doubled over her, not only because of Arab cultural norms and religious teachings, but also by getting rid of their family responsibility in raising their daughters according to the Western pattern and preserving the status of the father and mother in the family by controlling (the Patriarch) over Girls in particular, and their goal is not to break the laws of the country of immigration. This is from the viewpoint of the parents of the immigrant family, but it differs from the point of view of gender, which rejects such a marriage because it

224

does not represent equality between men and women in terms of age, but rather the male exploitation of the female.

Saudi Arabia Cases: There is no harm for the presentation of what Maliha Ahmed Shihab, the Saudi writer, recorded in her book, "The Saudi Woman, a Voice and an Image," about the state of the marriage of minors in Saudi society, which she said represented "the infanticide of childhood" in which she mentioned the following:

We had hardly breathed a sigh of relief after the salvation of the girl Onaizah when we were surprised by the girl of Al Thuqba, so the matter began as a setback, but in reality, it is an indication that the matter is not merely an exception that came as a result of difficult circumstances that the victim's father is going through and he had no way out except by sacrificing those who are powerless, so the exit came in the form of a girl jumping in the dress of her childhood, but it is more like a fierce culture that runs a segment of society. We thought that it was just an exception in the fabric of society, but we were surprised that our estimate of the size of this segment was wrong. In fact, it is not important to its size and the extent to which society adopts it. Enough to shake the human conscience and make us in its direct confrontation with our humanity. One case is sufficient for an entire society to degrade in the eyes of the outside. The fact is that this society trades in young women and violates their rights. This is exactly what confirms the story that my friend who is studying abroad mentioned to me. Her American colleague was interested in Islam and overly impressed with its teachings and its legislation to the extent that she asked my friend to give her lessons in Islam until that day came when I read a report on the CNN news site covering the story of the girl of Al-Thuqba. As a result, her view of Islam changed, and she stopped completely. What about his learning, saying: "How can I learn a religion that permits the rape of children?"

Yes, it is rape, and this is what scientific studies describe. Here is what Dr Subaihi said, which was published by Al Arabiya Net, where he said in describing marriage to young girls as rape. He added: "The experience of the first night of a minor girl who does not understand the meaning of sex will be a very ugly situation, and it a rape. It is known that children who are raped suffer from deep psychological illnesses when they know the meaning of that experience and live its bitterness. Beyond that was what was revealed by the scientific studies, which confirmed that those who marry minor are originally homosexual and uses the minor as compensation. As it is known, a homosexual person does not want adults, but rather searches for children boy under the age of 18, and therefore he takes a minor girl because her body looks like the young boy to avoid the social blame and the legal punishment which reaches the death penalty in Saudi Arabia, while he satisfies his ill sexual desires with the minor girl who her body looks like a boy.

There is another image provided by (Maliha Ahmed Shihab) on this example of women's rights violations, titled "Who Permits Child Infanticide," in which she said: "I would like to thank the premarital medical examination centre in the city of Jeddah (Saudi Arabia) for the medical staff performing their humanitarian duty concurrently with their professional duty. We thank them for their attempt to save two daughters (the eldest did not exceed ten and the youngest of five years) from a crime their mother sought to commit against them by marrying them to two of her relatives' men. As reported in the press that the committee (showed the mother the seriousness of this and the harm of her marrying her two daughters at this age, the mother accepted advice and promised to wait and not rush to the decision to marry.)

The news included other cases about the marriage of minors, such as the brother who sought to marry his ten-year-old sister to his 40 years old friend married of two women.

The mother promised only to wait, not to back down, and this means that the crime project is still possible. Or the brother who did not receive any attempt to persuade him to back down because the man in Arab culture does not retrieve from his promise even by mistake. Therefore, it is certain that the childhood of his ten-year-old sister was raped in the ugliest form.

Who is responsible for what happens to our little ones? Do not say, the family, this means that we are ignoring we live under the shadow of a state governed by laws and legislation based on Islamic law that preserved the rights of animals, so what about humans?

This door must be closed forever, as this crime is not accepted by religion, logic, or conscience. The marriage of minor girls is a death of the human conscience, child trafficking, and an obscene violation of innocence. It is a departure from the highest values of the Islamic religion that are based on preserving and protecting the human soul and protecting it from any future suffering for minors. According to published laws, no violation or exploitation of the minor girl's rights shall be exercised by her guardian. And if the legislator finds the guardianship does not protect the minor, it must be withdrawn from him to a person more qualified to carry out the duties of guardianship, but usually, this does not happen. The guardian has absolute authority, and since the minor girl does not have awareness about her rights or to demand her protection coupled with the absence of institutions to monitor the fate of the minor, her exploitation and childhood trafficking will continue.

Child marriage is an urgent human condition that cannot be postponed or delayed. It cannot wait for the clergy to become aware of the gravity of this crime to issue a fatwa that it is not permissible. The Ministry of Social Affairs must do its role and issue laws that prevent child rape from taking place under the noble cover of marriage.

Finally, (Maliha Shihab) ended her remarks on the violation of Saudi women's rights with an article entitled "Good morning, Human Rights Commission," in which she stated: "A society does not interact with what happens to its members with all their segments, and it is an apathetic society (to a minimum of description) and lives in a pre-hibernation state," which is the other face of death. I was afraid that our society had gone through this situation while I was seeing the news of the marriage of an eight-year-old girl circulating in the newspapers without hearing that natural echo that would have had when publishing such news.

Yes, I was afraid for my community is that it has reached this level of indecision, which makes us lose confidence that we are like other human beings who if one of them dared to marry a child he would be thrown into prison, this is a recent report by Human Rights Watch that puts us among the five Islamic countries that execute Young perpetrators, the public denounces the humanity of executing young people, and if they are perpetrators, how about those who did not commit a crime or sin? Which was published in Al-Watan newspaper under the title (A popular national campaign to prevent the marriage of children) announces the efforts of the association for the Defence of Women's Rights in Saudi Arabia, under establishment (in preparing a petition to be submitted to the Human Rights Commission on the anniversary of the National Day to demand an end to the phenomenon of child marriage). These efforts are not only in raising the voice of protest and rejecting what is being committed as a crime against our young girls. Scattered words of rejection will not do anything without embarking on positive action to express the true size of the tragedy of those who are powerless. This association exerts positive efforts because of its sense of the necessity to do so, and this feeling is not surplus to need as much as it is related to the dictates of the human sense of its members who Without it, they would feel that they were anything but a human being. When the body becomes ill, nothing indicates its life except the feeling of pain and what the association is doing is an indication that we are alive and that there is a defect that needs to be fixed. All I hope is that the Human Rights Commission will consider the petition that the association will raise and assume the full role in putting an end to what is called child trafficking and should put in place a program to pump the blood of humanity into the veins of a society".

Swaziland Case: The King of Swaziland has 13 wives, and his celebrations are greeted by virgins! There is a spot in the black continent which is a beautiful land with imaginary scenes. It is surrounded by South Africa on three sides and Mozambique on the east, which is Swaziland, which no one stood at its social customs except stunned because of its annual celebration, which is rich material for all international news agencies. So, what is in the mind of the 20 thousand girls who meet in front of the king of the country! Swaziland is still a country far from the global progressive movement in which elderly princes marry non-adult children under the pretext of national traditions and culture.

"Mswati" is the only son of his mother (Anthony), also known as "Angusikati Latvula", and she was the youngest wife of the king. He is also one of the sons of King Subuza II. He had 70 wives and 210 children, and upon his death, he had 1000 grandchildren. Where his mother took over the throne until he completed his studies in Britain, then he would return and take over the affairs of the country.

Royal decree: Official figures indicate that one in four citizens suffers from HIV in that kingdom, and the bad numbers are among pregnant women, which a study showed that 41% of them were infected with the disease, and for this reason, a third of the country's children became orphans here. The king took his position in the year 2001 and tried to limit the spread of AIDS. He called for the practice of the ritual (ancient chastity) known as (amchwashwa), which prevents women under the age of 18 from having sex. However, the Swaziland police applied the law on the risk of wearing very short skirts and low-waist pants because it facilitates rape - where the woman who is raped is considered as it is in these clothes that she is responsible. The ban did not include the traditional clothes that young women wear in the annual celebrations that take place in September every year, during which girls whose number exceeds 20 thousand dances, and it is assumed that they are almost naked in front of the king to choose them as his wife.

Amy Similin, 15 years old, one of the girls dancing at the party, says: "My mother tries to support me after my father died of AIDS, but we get our food from the World Food Program. I want to live in a palace, as rainwater leaks from the roof of the mud hut where she lives." Napselli Dlamini, 13, is interested in the king having other women, so all she wants is to drive a Mercedes.

A female tradition: From the king's point of view, the traditional "omlanga red" dance is an expression of femininity and virginity, but women's groups in the country see that his love for polygamy is inflicted with fate in the countries that suffer from the highest rates of HIV infection in the world. Despite the development the world is witnessing, the king - whose fortune is estimated by Forbes magazine at $ 200 million - insists on staying in his traditional clothes made of leopard and black skins and being a husband to 13 women, all of this while two-thirds of its population live below the poverty line and 40% of them suffer from unemployment. In addition to government decisions to reduce the spending, they reached to turn off streetlights and close schools, even prisoners' food was reduced!

$ 360 million: The 13 queens of Swaziland spend their luxurious annual vacation as they roam in a plane bought for them at the cost of $ 360 million, all of this in addition to the cost of the trip itself, where they spend two weeks in Asia and then tour the Pacific and Indian oceans. A British newspaper reported that the entourage alone included 100 individuals who served the queens on their tour In Japan, Australia, the Pacific and Indian oceans, the number exceeded this number when they travelled the previous year to the United States, Europe and the Middle East, and the royal vacation trip is usually very secret!

Bride's Runaway: The secrecy was not able to conceal the news of those trying to escape from marrying the king. When a young man, "Tensualo Ngobeni," asked for asylum, the latter sought asylum in Britain. Ngobini comments, "I refuse to be his fourteenth wife." King Mswati is allowed to choose a new wife every year after the dance, but he decided and chose Miss Ngobeni when she was fifteen years old after seeing her in the palace of his fourth wife. The girl says, "I was terrified when he started calling me at school and asking me if I wanted to be part of his royal family. Ngobini did not think that she would be inside a palace surrounded by guards, and she could not go anywhere - except after the king's approval - except to go to America once a year for shopping, regardless of the expenses, so she left her boarding school with the help of her aunt and fled to Britain to be with her mother who moved to Birmingham before five years this date to escape a similar marriage. "No one would dare to refuse the king's request or to refuse to obey his orders, so she preferred to flee."

Betrayal of wife: The escape of "Ngobeni" sparked criticism, and a series of scandals appeared on the surface. According to the British newspaper "The Telegraph", the king dismissed his Minister of Justice after he claimed that he had a relationship with Queen Nottando Diopi (the twelfth wife), who won the Miss Teen Contest at the age of six. Ten, but it seems that this girl is tired of royal life and protocols and waiting for her in the long line, and it was said that she disguised herself as a soldier to be able to pass the security guards in the palace and leave it. At that time, Minister Ndomiso placed the queen under house arrest for all her ruses, but she was able - and she in her prison - access to a South African newspaper to complain about her husband, the king, who keeps her imprisoned forever in her private palace.

In thousands: Every year in April, the king celebrates his birthday. Usually, the leaders of traditional tribes in the region of "Achiciloni" organize celebrations this month, and they may also be assigned to provide livestock to him. On that day, the Minister of Interior (Prince Jokkuma) said his sentence: "They are fully aware of the desired role of them as they will receive the king on this memorable day. "

The government may allocate five million rands from its budget ($ 652 thousand) to revive the ceremony. Although the banned opposition party has been calling for in the last two years to cancel the celebrations and allocate the money to be spent to grant progress to poor students, Christmas customs and the allocation of a mansion for each wife remain.

8. The Crime of Honour (Washing of Shame)

It is violent behaviour that does not accept and contest. In most Eastern societies, the feminine is an open sacrifice in identification and identification with the standards and values of the inherited cultural traditions. Such traditions do not adhere to the rules of positive written law, and the perpetrator is a member of the (feminine) sacrifice, and she may be the victim of rumours, doubts, or false gossip against her from those who are predisposed to her. Then, the victim and the sacrifice together have lost their right to life and their right to defend themselves and their honour because of the contempt for women by their social culture and the supremacy of the male status of men. This crime is often committed in secret to preserve family status.

It is one of the forms of rape of a woman's right not to respect her presence in the family or her right to express her desire, her personal interest, and her right to live as a human being. It is an inherited cultural usurpation carried out by the living on behalf of the dead who did not conform to the spirit of the age.

This practice is used by the traditional, rural, feudal, folkloric, conservative, sectarian, and ethnic society to reinforce its customary controls, and the individual remains under his sovereignty, authority, and upbringing. It sacrifices the souls of its members in order to satisfy their need to exist and remain immortal and eternally in control of the individual. Honour crime or honour killing committed by a man in the family against a female, a crime carried out in secret and not reported by the police. This is the man: the husband, brother, father, or son. As for the female, she is the human sacrifice that the family offers to the surrounding community in response to its desires to control the behaviour of women according to what was decided by this surrounding. At the same time, carrying a clear message from the killer and his family that reads, "I have removed the reasons for your refusal, so accept us again." As for the reasons for their perpetrators, they are based on convictions based on suspicions and rumours and whispers of neighbours and friends about the victim's behaviour, unfair distress, and confusion of people, that it is just intuition, obsession, suspicion, doubt, fear of people's speech and concern for the family's reputation without rational support. He said: (High honour is not spared from harm until blood is shed on its sides) and that (a woman's honour is like a matchstick that burns once). Then the rule of rural norms and values that are the product of a culture of contempt for women and violence against them. There are also other reasons for the female victimization that is practised in a male society that possesses a male culture based on the authority of the man (the Patriarchy) such as: -

i.   The girl's refusal to marry the family chosen man.
ii.   The girl escaping with the person she loves.
iii. A woman's betrayal of her husband.
iv.   Victim of rape.
v.   Homosexuals, both females and males.

These are examples of tyrannical practices carried out by society towards its members (the perpetrator and the victim), and we do not forget cell phones as a mechanism to blackmail the victim and make her slide into the abysses of the honour crime. As for the countries where honour crime is more frequent, they are Syria, Iraq, Turkey, Pakistan, Lebanon, Jordan, Palestine, Egypt, Saudi Arabia, and Yemen.

Egypt Cases: In recent times, marital infidelity crimes have multiplied and usually ends with the killing of the lover at the hands of the husband in revenge for his honour and revenge for his dignity, and the last of these crimes was witnessed by the Talbiyah area where a worker returned to his apartment, and he was surprised by his wife's lover hiding in the balcony of the apartment, and a quarrel broke out between them ending with the fall of the lover from the balcony And his departure from life when the husband was arrested for involvement in the killing of the lover, and the wife was arrested for adultery.

The Umraniye (Cairo - Egypt) area also witnessed a barber murdering his wife's lover by stabbing him after they were caught in a situation that violated his honour in his apartment. He then surrendered to the Umraniye Police Department and in the governorate of Kafr El-Sheikh. The barber killed his wife's lover after they were caught in a breach in the bedroom after he returned to the marital apartment, where he chased him. He stabbed him with a kitchen knife, killing him on the spot, and proceeded to kill his wife, wounding her with several wounds.

Although husbands are involved in committing murder crimes, their punishment does not amount to death or life imprisonment, as stipulated in the law in murder crimes, as the legislator reduced the penalty for these crimes to become one year to 3 years.

Dr Ahmed Al-Ganzouri, a professor of law at the Faculty of Law, Ain Shams University, told Al-Youm Al-Sabea newspaper that Article 237 of the Penal Code states: "Whoever surprises his wife in the case of her fornication and kills her immediately, and whoever commits adultery with her, shall be punished with imprisonment instead of the penalties prescribed in the two articles. 234 and 236, "explaining that if the husband caught his wife with her lover, he benefits from a reduction in the penalty, as his punishment may reach imprisonment from one to 3 years, and this article is the only one that provides a reduced sentence for a crime of murder.

Al-Ganzouri added that the wife's betrayal of her husband with her lover is considered confirmed if they are present together in the marital apartment with some manifestations indicating their illegal relationship, even if they are not caught in a breach of the state of in flagrante delicto. He confirmed' that if the husband caught his wife in an immoral position with her lover and they were kept in custody and the security services were informed, the punishment for the wife and her lover is fornication, and her punishment is imprisonment for 3 years. The husband has the right to reconcile and waive even if a final judgment is issued in the case. However, the husband is not entitled to file a suit for adultery against his wife if he has previously been caught red-handed who betrays her, and a case for adultery was filed against him, or a report on the incident is filed as long as the matter is legally proven.

For his part, Dr Muhammad Abu Talib, a professor of law at Ain Shams University, said: if a husband caught his wife with her lover in a breach of honour, he has the right to keep them in custody while others testify against them. If her husband kills her along with whoever commits adultery to

236

her is punished with a misdemeanour, not a felony. Abu Talib added that proving the crime of adultery is difficult to achieve, as Islamic Sharia law stipulates the testimony of 4 men and that they see them fully connected in sexual intercourse, such as the pen in the inkwell, but there are some indications that there is a relationship that proves betrayal, such as the existence of correspondence between the wife and her lover, and otherwise all murder cases are considered a felony of premeditated murder, and he shall be sentenced to life imprisonment with hard labour or the death penalty.

And there are honour killings: the son kills his wife after he saw her in bed with his father, he killed his sister after she danced in the joy of her uncle. He waited 24 years for his cousin to be killed, who had befriended his mother. It is not a stranger to these types of crimes known as honour crimes. It is where the male kills the female who has a relationship, whether at the family or marital level, due to doubts about her behaviour. It is natural for the male of this society that the largest percentage of the perpetrators of these crimes are males. A study conducted by the National Centre for Social and Criminal Research in 2006 revealed that 29% of the murders committed in Egypt at the time were due to "honour" and that 70% of these crimes were committed by husbands against their wives and 20% were committed by siblings against their sisters, while fathers committed 7%. Only of these crimes are against their daughters, while the remaining 3% of honour crimes are committed by sons against their mothers. The most dangerous thing in the study is the assertion that 70% of honour crimes did not take place in a state of 'in flagrante delicto'. Rather, whether the husband, father or brother was committed relied on rumours and the whispers of neighbours and friends about the victim's behaviour. The study indicated that in 60% of these, the crimes confirmed the perpetrator's mistrust of the victim and not more than suspicion though she was above suspicion. In this regard, we will deal with five honour crimes that express various segments of society.

1. He kills his cousin after he sees him having sex with his mother. The story begins when the killer was 11 years old, he saw his mother on the bed with his 22-year-old cousin, and since then, the child dreams that he will grow up quickly in order to avenge his honour. Because his cousin (the victim) was imprisoned for 8 years on charges of attempted murder, He could not kill him until the right moment, which was delayed by 24 years to kill him has as per the killer statement. He lured his cousin to the Island of Gold in Giza under the pretext of packing a new apartment. He was confined in an isolated place and then stabbed many times, and in every stab, he healed his hate until he left a lifeless corpse and fled. The defendant Muhammad Abdeen, 35, said in his confession to Sherif Siddiq, First Prosecutor of the Accident Prosecution Office in South Giza, "I washed my disgrace after 24 years, so how much I longed and dreamed of being stronger to kill him." The most famous of what is known as honour killings, what is the excuse on which the killer relied to carry out his act.

2. Just intuition, obsessions, and suspicion blinds him until he kills his wife. The husband directed several stabs at his wife in the chest, but this did not cure the fire of the killer. He caught his victim, who was blinded by the stabbing - perhaps - or the horror of the shock, and then he slaughtered her until people met her at the entrance to the building with all her clothes with multiple stab wounds in her chest and slaughtered from her neck. Al-Muntazah Second Police Department received a notification that the body of a woman was found at the entrance of property number 7, Street 9,

238

from Street 45 in the Asafra district. The police moved to the scene of the accident, and it became clear that the corpse of the so-called "Hala F.A.", 24 years old, is the wife of the real estate guard at issue, from Kom Hamada in Al-Buhaira Governorate, and with investigations and searches, officers of the Department's Investigation Unit were able to arrest the perpetrator of the incident, the husband of the victim named Adel KhA, 31 years old, real estate guard. During the investigations, the accused confessed that the incident had been committed due to his suspicion of her behaviour, and with his guidance, the tool used in the crime, "knife," was seized. The Public Prosecution Office was notified, and the body was transferred to the ambulance mortuary.

3. He kills his sister for dancing at the wedding party of her cousin, and what is the joys except for dancing, singing and greetings. It is a natural thing that happens in joy, especially if it is the wedding of her cousin. All of this may be seen by some as normal and usual, but this worker did not see it like this when his sister, who barely reached the age of fifteenth, danced in the joy of their cousin. He went to her room at night wrapped the scarf around her neck until it turned between his hands into a lifeless corpse. His name is Ahmed, 26, a worker behind the commission of the crime, and he killed her after she was tricked and strangled with a scarf. He wrapped it around her neck, leaving her dead body, in order to discipline her for dancing at the wedding of their cousin. Then he lei to their father and his brothers that he was surprised by a dead body lying in bed. The security services managed to arrest him, and the Qena Centre Prosecutor, under the supervision of Muhammad al-Yamani, the Public Prosecutor, decided to imprison him for 4 days pending investigations for premeditated murder.

4. A father kills his daughter after her pregnancy, and the mother is covering up for the crime. The girl, at the age of 18 years old, her mother complained about her health asked her to go to the doctor to surprise the mother with her daughter being pregnant in the forbidden. She tells the father, who is a 50-year-old farmer. The father takes her to the farms close to the village, kills her and disposes of her body by throwing it into the Nile. He tells the mother to report the disappearance of the daughter, and the mother does report so that his matter is not revealed. Major General Hassan Seif, Director of Minya Security, received a notification from Brigadier General Essam Jamal, the warden of Mallawi Center, from some fishermen that the body of a girl was found lying in the Nile River, and information was received by the Centre's Investigations Unit stating that the body was of a girl named "A.A.", 18 years old, and reported her absence since October 22, her mother, Sharbat S. The accused father is arrested, and in his confrontation, he confessed to committing the incident, and that he committed the killing of his daughter out of honour. Record No. 7189 of the administrative centre of Mallawi was released on the incident.

5. The son kills his wife after he sees her in bed with his father. Karim, a young man who loved his wife, Manal, married her when she was 21 years old, after he fought for her, and stood in the face of his father who did not agree to marry and was the strongest opponent at the beginning, the father stipulated that the two spouses live with him at home. The wife objects at the beginning but agrees at the end. Karim spends most of the time at work outside the house, reassuring that the wife sits with his father, who is now treating her well and treating him well. Karim saw that the conditions had gotten better, but he was surprised by a

240

situation that was a spark of suspicion when he saw the father put his hand on his wife in a way that raised his suspicion, jealousy, and doubts. He starts to sit longer in the house while looking for a new house to move to with his wife. The wife argues that she does not want his father of old, which pushes him to search further. All this was under suspicion until the fateful day came. The husband came back from work early, he heard strange sounds come out of his bedroom, opened the door, and he was in shock. The father and wife are in bed naked. He lost control of himself. He brought the knife and stabbed his father, who had raised him and then betrayed him and the girl he loved and married. But the crime has a clear end after a year and two months in prison, which is the term of the trial. The court decides to acquit Karim, the one who killed two for love and honour. The question here is this a manhood or madness?

Jordan Cases: Jordanian women are still being killed from time to time in all its forms in the context of what are described as honour killings, which are often the result of (convictions) based on suspicion only. Many girls or women are in the midst of this phenomenon that dominates the culture of the peripheral regions. They remain circulating between love, traditions and poverty that forces many young people to abstain from the idea of marriage because of unemployment or the absence of work opportunities and the high cost of living. It is noteworthy that some of these crimes that are committed against women have other despicable goals that may be related to inheritance or the delay of the dowry so that in the end, the woman falls into the knife of the people closest to her, which is imbued with the culture of shame prevalent in society.

According to local statistics, Jordan witnesses about 14 crimes per year in the name of (honour), but during the first third of the year 2016, 12 murders occurred against women and girls.

According to a statement by the Jordanian (Solidarity Institute for Women) Association (Solidarity), five crimes were committed by firing bullets, 4 by stabbing with a sharp object, 2 by burning and one by severe beating leading to death. The figures show that the husbands committed three crimes, the relatives committed two crimes, while the brother and uncle committed a crime for each of them.

Solidarity revealed that, during January, the body of a migrant worker was found burnt in a Sahab street, with burns in the upper part. In addition, the body of a 60-year-old woman was found in the Umm Al-Basatin area, who was stabbed four times in the Al-Ras area, and it was found that the perpetrator was a juvenile from one of her second-degree relatives, and the body of a charred girl was found in Wadi Shuaib in the Salt Governorate, lying on the side of a spring Water, and in the Al-Ghuwayriyah area in Zarqa Governorate, a daughter, upon her return from school, has found her mother (in her thirties) was killed in her house.

In February, a man in his sixties shot his wife in her fifties and then committed suicide inside their home in Hay Nazzal in Amman. The husband was suffering from psychological disorders, and his wife had cancer. A 17-year-old girl died after being shot in the chest in Ramtha, and in the Rujm al-Shami area near Sahab, a husband in his fifties killed his forty-year-old wife, wounding his three children, then committed suicide.

In April, a 60-year-old woman was stabbed to death with a sharp object at the hands of one of her relatives in the Seventh Circle area in Amman. In the Ruwaished area of northern Badia, the body of a dead young woman was found with a gunshot. A 16-year-old girl was severely beaten,

242

which led to her death at the hands of her brother in the area of a house of Ras, north of the city of Irbid, while a forty-year-old Syrian husband stabbed his thirty years old wife with a knife inside their home in the Rusaifa area. A 19-year-old university student was stabbed by a knife by her uncle, who was 23 years old, on the campus of the University of Science and Technology in Irbid.

Solidarity in the statement renewed its demand for government and parliamentary bodies, civil society institutions, decision-makers, clerics, and tribal leaders to intensify efforts to prevent the commission of (honour) crimes in particular, and to kill women and girls in general, and to ensure that the perpetrators do not go unpunished by taking administrative measures. And legal and legislative amendments when necessary.

The washing away of shame may lead to a serious challenge to the community, just as a young Jordanian man fired 5 bullets at his 24-year-old sister in the presence of hundreds of passers-by. He placed her on the main square witnessing heavy traffic in the town, and the attempts of a number of mediators did not succeed in stopping him from washing his shame with his hands.

According to a study prepared by the National Council for Family Affairs in Jordan, 42 per cent of honour victims are single women, 42 per cent are married, while the rest are divided between widows and divorced women. 56 per cent of the perpetrators were married, and 56 per cent of them were workers, which indicates their low educational level. The tools for committing the crime were the use of firearms or sharp tools.

The study entitled (Mitigating Excuses in Honour Murders: Legal, Judicial, Social and Religious Dimensions) indicated that 69 per cent of (honour) crimes were committed by a brother.

Many of the perpetrators of such crimes benefit from the "mitigating excuse" stipulated in the Jordanian Penal Code to escape execution or imprisonment for long years, like imprisonment, in this case, does not exceed a few years.

Article (98) of the Penal Code stipulates that "the perpetrator of the crime who committed the crime in a state of great anger shall benefit from a mitigating excuse, resulting from an unjust and dangerous act of the victim." The Jordanian government twice failed to cancel this article due to the Parliament's rejection backed by religious and tribal forces.

The study showed that 56 per cent of the victims were in the age group 18-28, indicating that 45 per cent of the perpetrators were in the same age group.

Sheikh Ahmed Grace, who works in the Jordanian Ministry of Endowments, attributed this type of crime to the absence of the family's role in education in morals and ideals, in addition to the absence of the teachings of the true Islamic religion from the members of these families.

Grace revealed that many of these crimes that are committed under the pretext of honour are, in fact, for the sake of monopolizing the inheritance, for example, or not paying the back (dowry) stipulated in the marriage contract by the husband who is considering divorcing his wife. Article 98 of the law encourages the commission of this type of crime because it gave everyone a mitigating excuse under the pretext that the perpetrator was in anger state.

He explained that whoever commits honour crimes is a criminal, but he uses the pretext of honour, and sometimes for many purposes other than honour.

Pakistan Case: A few years ago, the Pakistani authorities began a campaign against the rampant honour killings in this country, but its results so far seem very modest. Despite severe punishments, the men of this Islamic state continue to insist that "shame be erased with blood."

On July 15, 2016, Wasim Azim, 25, killed his sister, Fawzia, known in Internet circles as Candle Baloch - a blogger and model, and on that day, the wretched woman visited her parents' home in Multan, Pakistan, and during that her brother gave her a sleeping pill, and then he strangled her with his bare hands. After his arrest, the young man proudly said that he did not regret what he had done because it had "brought shame to our family."

The murder of the girl, dubbed "Kim Kardashian of Pakistan" in her country, sparked strong reactions in the local media, which prompted Parliament to tighten penalties for these crimes, but the situation has not changed - within less than a year, 280 crimes of this type were recorded. But that is not a simple matter because most of these crimes are carried out in secret and are not reported to the police.

This girl tried to rebel against backwardness and oppression in her own way, and after forcibly marrying one of the villagers. She fled his home and worked at first as a ticket cutter on a bus, but later she rode the Internet and opened her own blog in which she published her photos as a model. It brought her a million followers, but that did not intercede for her and her brother, who killed her asphyxiation and washing of shame.

Iraq Cases: Since the Arab society is dominated by a male culture that despises and nourishes women, the consideration and reputation of the family are attributed to the honour of its females.

On the morning of a fall in 2016, amid piles of waste in the (Al-Sada) area on the outskirts of Al-Zafaraniya in Baghdad, the police found the body of (F, S), a twenty-year-old girl, hit by bullets in her head and neck. After the body of the victim was handed over by the police to the (forensic medicine), her family brought her out with a death certificate confirming that she had suffered a sudden heart attack, which concealed the features of the crime.

The victim's sister, who is 33 years old, who lives in a tiny house in the middle of Zafaraniya, a suburb southeast of the capital Baghdad, initially refused to talk about the details of the story for fear of physical liquidation, but she accepted that after she was assured that her identity would not be revealed. My cousins were the ones who killed my 22-year-old sister in collusion with my father. After discovering her relationship with an unknown young man, "says the victim's sister adjusting her black headscarf, wiping her pale face, adding that her sister tried to escape. But her father locked her in a room in the house for two days, during which her cousins agreed to kill her.

"I intervened to prevent them, but they also threatened to kill me. Faced with my insistence, my uncle's eldest son struck my head and I fainted. When I woke up, I did not see my sister at home, and I did not know her fate until two days later, as my father told me to kill her and throw her body in an unknown place."

Her voice suddenly shuddered, and tears filled her eyes, "Four days after the accident, our policeman neighbour came to tell my father that my sister's body had been found in the Al-Sada area and delivered to the forensic medicine, so he hurried to go there to complete the burial procedures, fearing the scandal and uncovering the circumstances of the crime."

Meanwhile, the victim's sister went to the policeman's house and told him that the perpetrators were the father and the cousins, but the latter refused to intervene, fearing tribal prosecutions and the crime developing into a dispute between two clans.

Two days later, the father succeeded in obtaining a false death certificate confirming that the cause of death was the victim of a heart attack). Although the victim's sister refused to give the investigation clerk a copy of the death certificate, fearing that her case would be discovered and subjected to punishment, she agreed to give him the address of the policeman who told the family that the body had been found. The policeman admitted that his neighbour did kill his daughter "to wash his shame," and that the story is known to most of the people of the area.

The policeman commented on how the father was able to obtain a death certificate for his daughter, the victim, without being exposed to the legal issue. "Falsifying death certificates has become a very normal matter if money is paid for that. And what my neighbour did is try to avoid scandal and accountability."

Pointing a few papers in front of him and placing his finger on the place of the stamp and signature, he added, "In many cases of honour killing, forensic officials do not record in the victim's death certificate that she was shot or burned, which are the most common causes of death in such cases, due to the sensitivity of the issue that may expose the family's reputation, as well as fear of a tribal reaction."

No official statistics: FS's story is one of the dozens of similar stories of honour crimes committed against women in Baghdad, whose bodies are dumped on the outskirts of the capital, and their deaths are recorded on the basis of "normal death" or killed by unknown persons, in the forensic medicine departments. At a time when the police are afraid to open real investigations into the matter, for fear of tribal persecution in a country where tribal power is rising in defiance of state institutions.

Official institutions, whether the Ministry of the Interior, the Ministry of Health, or the authorities concerned with defending the rights of women, refuse to provide any numbers of women and girls, victims of violence, without citing convincing reasons, only to indicate that the security and political conditions are not appropriate.

In the absence of any official statistics regarding the number of women who are subject to murder or violent incidents, the author of the investigation monitored what was published by local agencies about the unidentified bodies of women that were found from October 6, 2015, to 9/21/2016, citing security sources on The Ministry of Interior, the number of corpses reached 52, ranging in age from 20 to 35 years.

And this number is exceedingly small because most of the killing incidents do not reach the media, according to lawyer Zayer Hassan, indicating that "the numbers of women victims of violence are very large, and they are on the rise, amid the conditions of violence in the country and the economic crisis, despite the insistence of government agencies "to hide it."

Hassan warns that this is linked with the rise in the power of the clans and the imposition of their customs and will, in light of the submission of government and parliament officials to them, by virtue of their need for its role in garnering the electoral votes.

Forged death certificates: On a visit to the main hospital in the Zafaraniya area, a nurse, who refused to reveal her identity, told the investigative writer that in July

2016, the hospital received a completely burnt body of a girl. Her family told the hospital that she had committed suicide, "but many hospital staff learned from the victim's relatives that her husband and her brothers were the ones who burned her after discovering her relationship with someone. " The results of the forensic medicine department proved at the beginning that the victim had not committed suicide, but after that, the parents forced the department's employees to change the cause of death in the certificate to read "suicide by burning".

The nurse recounted several other incidents, including the arrival of the police to the hospital in June 2016, a girl who was bleeding badly as a result of being shot by unknown gunmen before she died of the injury. "It turned out that the police found her lying in the dirt hills surrounding the area of Sadat al-Zafaraniya, and then her family came to the hospital and informed the responsible authorities that she was kidnapped by an unknown gang. But the victim's mother whispered to me, crying silently, that her uncles killed her, without mentioning any details. "

The investigation clerk was able to obtain the victim's mother's phone and contact her, but she refused to speak on the phone and told him that she would call him later to set a meeting so that she could tell him in detail the story of her murdered daughter, but one day later, a man who identified himself as a relative of the victim's mother called him, and he threatened to kill him as he promised to pursue him if he called again.

An old man from the people of Al-Zaafaraniya told the author of the investigation another story, saying that his relative "killed his daughter by burning and threw her body in a dumpsite on the outskirts of the city because she ran away from the house with someone she loved." Her body was left there for three days, and then "we, his cousins, buried her, after we obtained a death certificate for her, confirming that she died due to a gas bottle explosion while she was in the kitchen." He adds, "At the beginning, the forensic medicine and the police were not convinced of this, so we paid them an amount of 800 dollars, and we obtained a basic death certificate proving that she died as a result of being burned."

Al-Zafaraniya (corpse dump). Al-Zafaraniya is among the administrative units of the Karrada municipality in Baghdad, and the majority of its inhabitants were residents of the capital. After April 2003, many residents of the southern and western governorates of Iraq in which the tribal influence was evident have moved to the region until it became subject to the domination of tribal customs. Also, (after June 2014 incidents, hundreds of displaced families from the governorates of Anbar, Nineveh and Salah al-Din settled in it), according to what Abu Ali, one of the region's notables, stated.

And "the dam or the two dams", as it is known to the people of Zafaraniya, is a hillside surrounding the outskirts of the city. Military barracks, installations, and factories were built near these hills. However, following the entry of the American forces into Iraq, these sites turned into random shelters, shantytowns, garbage dumps and heavy water sites, especially as they were far from the police's sight.

The investigative reporter visited the Zafaraniya area and moved between shantytowns, and there he met boys who were collecting empty soft drinks cans.

Bilal, a 14-year-old, said, "From time to time we see at nightfall or at dawn, cars come to the area to throw Bodies. One night we heard gunshots, and in the morning, we

250

discovered the body of a young woman who had been shot in the head. "

Abu Muhammad, the owner of a wheelbarrow, collects plastic and metal bottles daily from the garbage dump adjacent to the Rasheed camp dam in the same area, and constantly finds the bodies of women, so that he became a person known to the police in the case of reporting the bodies. I found many of them and informed the police. Some were covered with a piece of cloth or a sleeping mattress. "

He added, "It is no longer shocking to me. I avoid knowing the details, but we know that the identity of the bodies of women is usually unknown, and most of them are killed in shame."

The police are afraid: Although the police are aware of the issue of killing women and dumping their bodies in dams and garbage dumps. They are afraid to open investigations into the matter, as Ali Luqman, an officer with the rank of the first lieutenant, in charge of the emergency police patrols (the only body responsible for bringing the bodies to forensic medicine), says: "Al-Zaafaraniya is a region dominated by tribal influence, and therefore the police are afraid to conduct any investigations, or to search for the identity of the perpetrator of crimes against women, for fear of the reaction of the tribes to which the perpetrators belong."

Luqman believes that the tribal and geographical nature makes Sadat al-Zafaraniya the most common area in Baghdad where the bodies of women were found shot dead, stabbed, or burned with fire. The security official explains that the rate of finding the bodies on a daily basis in the capital, Baghdad ranges between 8 to 10, the majority of which are women, "but their identity cannot be identified either because there is no document that indicates them or because they were subjected to mutilation."

251

A policeman confirms that fact, who refused to reveal his identity. "The conflicts and settling scores between armed parties usually target men, but we note that a large number of the bodies that we find belong to women."

Another policeman at Al-Zafaraniya Police Station said, speaking of their procedures, "The investigation officer opens a file to find out the circumstances of the crime as soon as the body is found, and if a person files a complaint against a person and accuses him of standing behind it, the investigation officer issues an arrest warrant against the accused, but if it does not submit for any complaint, the case is registered against unknown persons, which is what usually happens."

Al-Zafaraniya is not the only area where the bodies of women are found, but there are other areas in Baghdad, such as Hay al-Nasr, al-Salam, Hay al-Amin, Tariq neighbourhood, Sabaa al-Bour, al-Husayniyyah, al-Shaab, Hay al-Jihad, and Hay al-Amil, according to Officer Mahmoud Majdy of the Rescue Police.

Officer Magdy added, "The police force cannot remove bodies in inflamed areas that are beyond government control, and in which terrorist groups usually multiply, despite the presence of reports by citizens of the presence of corpses."

The author of the investigation visited most of these areas to reveal the general characteristics that distinguish them, which are the poverty in which most of the population lives, in addition to the control of the clan system, where the law is not invoked.

Forensic medicine denies: The Director-General of the Forensic Medicine Department in Iraq, Zaid Ali Abbas, denies that death certificates have been tampered with or subjected to tribal pressure to forge them. He says: "The rumours that talk about tampering with death certificates of unidentified bodies are incorrect because forensic medicine has no right to diagnose the type of crime in the death certificate. Rather, its primary function is to diagnose the scientific and medical causes of death. "

He explains that "the forensic report is submitted to the judge, and the latter approves it to diagnose the crime just as the investigator file at the scene of the accident and the eyewitness testimony is approved," noting that the forensic report is "a cycle of episodes that reveal the causes of crimes and prove the sexual assault and fingerprint of the suspect." But he did not deny while "forensic medicine receives one or two corpses in one day, and sometimes it is for women who have been killed under the name (washing of shame)."

The position of the General Director of the Forensic Medicine Department contradicts what was announced by the semi-official Al-Iraqiya TV on the night of February 11, 2017, on its screen, in which it reported that an armed group had threatened the doctors of Baghdad Health Department hospitals to force them to issue false death certificates.

Absence of public prosecution: The former member of the High Commission for Human Rights in Iraq, Bushra Al-Obaidi, confirmed that she had received 10 reports of fraud in the death certificates, but they were not written because the informants were afraid of tribal and legal prosecutions, expressing her regret that the fact-finding team at the commission did not fulfil its duty in this regard.

Al-Obaidi clarifies that recording the killings of women on the basis of suicide or any other reason that conceals the effects of the crime is contrary to the Criminal Procedure Law, noting that the judicial authorities "bear responsibility for such fraud."

And I was surprised that the (public prosecutor) did not move to activate the prosecutions of the perpetrators responsible for killing women, even if no complaints were lodged in this regard, especially since (murders, crimes of modesty, and crimes of severe harm do not need a complaint to move them, so even if the victim's family waives, the right remains. The perpetrator's file must be fully submitted to the court.)

Al-Obeidi explained that "finding the bodies of women in remote areas is due to the fact that these are areas controlled by the clans where ignorance prevails. They are also far from the eyes of the police force, while in the city the murderers are afraid of throwing corpses, fearing the law and the role of civil society organizations and activists in the field of human rights".

Human Rights Commission: Regarding the role of the Human Rights Commission in uncovering fraud in death certificates regarding honour crimes, Al-Obaidi says that the majority of the commission's members are not independent and are affiliated with parties. None of us moved it, and this is in addition to the members 'lack of awareness of human rights."

The investigation clerk tried to obtain an official response from the commission's fact-finding team about the reasons for not investigating complaints that reached the commission, but it was rejected under the pretext that he did not submit a license for that. However, a member of the team, who requested anonymity, explained to him that "dozens of complaints. They arrive at the office and there they deliberately not move to search them under the pretext that there is no financial funding to cover work expenses, "refusing to mention the names of the political parties or parties that impose their control on the commission.

254

Hana Adwar, President of the Al-Amal Association, one of the associations that defend women's rights, explained that there are demands submitted to Parliament by a group of organizations to legislate a law against domestic violence "with the aim of tightening penalties for honour crimes." Adwar expressed regret at the existence of what she described as "attempts to obstruct the passage of the law by the political parties in power."

Law Enforcement: Professor of Sociology at the University of Baghdad, Khaled Hantoush, believes that honour killings have existed since ancient times in Iraq, "and they are the product of a culture that despises women and practices violence against them."

He explains that urban life in Baghdad today "suffers from the influence of rural norms and values greatly, as a result of the frequent displacement operations to the capital, as these norms entered and penetrated all areas of life until they threatened everything civil and civilized in it."

Hantoush, therefore, calls for the activation of legal procedures in crimes of washing shame "especially that the victim's family is main accused in the case of inferring her identity, in addition to monitoring the work of forensic medicine and its role in examining identity and the manner of murder and following up on those who reported the disappearance of one of his relatives and linking the matter to the bodies of the murdered. ".

Lawyer Raouf Muhammad Nuri, in addition to another aspect of the crimes related to the killing of women, warns, "A person who commits murder under the name of washing of shame will be tried according to the Iraqi Penal Code No. 111 issued in 1969 in Article 409 which states that (he shall be punished with imprisonment for a period not exceeding three years Whoever surprises his wife or one of his female relatives in the event of her being caught in adultery or being in the same bed with her partner, then killing them immediately or killing one of them or assaulting them or one of them in an assault that led to death or permanent disability, and it is not permissible to use the right of legal defence against anyone who benefits from this excuse or Aggravating circumstances are applied against him).

He added, "This article gives the right to a man and not a woman to kill, despite their equal rights and duties in the Iraqi constitution."

Amidst the conditions of war, and in light of the rise of clan power, the weak rule of law and judiciary, neglect of governmental institutions, the inability of organizations concerned with women's issues, and the absence of the role of the public prosecutor and the Commission for Human Rights, the crimes of femicide and its registration as ordinary deaths will escalate. And their victims will turn into mere stories in the funeral councils while the perpetrators become heroes in their clans.

There is no harm in saying that the main cause of honour killing overrides all the reasons that were mentioned. They are the traditions, customs and laws of the inherited social culture that nourish the masculinity of the man, which is the focus of the male (patriarchal) system, which drives it (husband, brother, father, son) to the killing of a female as a human sacrifice for the traditions of the Balinese culture.

But there are hidden reasons for marital infidelity, virgin love, or romantic relationships, which are the emotional deprivation that Arab culture forbids to the female and permits to the male. This cultural bias makes the Arab woman do what her brother does in love with his sweetheart or her father in love with her mother, especially when she hears Arab songs charged with the passionate love of the lover and watches movies and TV series, as well as her strict upbringing against the opposite sex. All this makes her a prisoner of male power and the male culture that allows women to be violent, despised, and considered a creature of the third degree in the human race. This sexual distinction is present in Arab laws that do not defend them as they defend the rights of men, such as Iraq, Jordan, and the rest of the Arab countries.

In recent years, there has been a remarkable growth in the field of combating violence against women and in a report presented by the Council of Europe that more than 5,000 thousand women and girls are killed every year in the world in the name of honour. The rate of honour crimes in Jordan annually ranges between 12 and 14 crimes, while Syria is the fifth in the world in honour crimes, and in the Kurdistan region of Iraq, 27 women were killed on the background of honour killings within four months! Refusal to obey family orders, and even some victims were killed because they were "raped" as punishment. The penalties vary between being slaughtered with a knife or shot, or thrown from a towering, or by poison, or by burying her alive, or even forcing the girl to kill herself in order to record the case as a suicide. And it may be less than that, as happened in Canada, in a horrific crime in which the 17-year-old girl (Aqsa Berweyz) died at the hands of her father on the pretext of her refusal to wear the veil! All these cases are considered sins by the murderers!! Or was suspicion? How not? And the report of the director of the Zeinhom morgue in Egypt has a number that is extremely injustice and ugliness. He says that 80% of the honour killings are completely innocent and virgins. This strongly indicates the absence of law and customary arbitration in crimes devoid of humanity and must be announced as crimes without honour!! How not? And the history since eternity has nourished this archaic legacy and determines the perception of woman according to the orientations of local cultures with an unimaginable outcome, starting with: The high honour is not spared from harm until blood is spilled on its sides. And the honour of a woman is like a matchstick, which only burns once.

Woman's Suppression in Saudi Arabia: There are several indications of the seriousness of the situation in the Kingdom of Saudi Arabia.

The role of the mobile phone: The phenomenon of urbanization has increased in the Kingdom over the past years, and with it, there has been progress in the social structure, especially with regard to the roles of women and their dealings with modern communication tools, such as the Internet and mobile phone, and unfortunately there is a use of the latest advancements and global civic high technologies; to exploit women, and to return us to the days of slaves. It stands against any modernization affecting the human being and his freedom! In a report by Al-Quds newspaper, May 17, 2008, quoted from the British Independent, that one of the reasons for the spread of honour crimes in Iraq is the spread of mobile phones that contain sexual images that sometimes constitute a form of proof for the husband, brother or father and push them to carry out an honour killing. The same thing that the blackmailer in Saudi Arabia does, when the girls who are subjected to extortion agree that he threatens them with her image, which she sent to him via mobile. What increased the frequency of this matter was the lack of the necessary protection for them? This provided a fertile environment for the sexual blackmail of the girl, threatening her to publish her pictures and expose them to her family!

258

The role of blackmailing girls: Daily newspapers are not without news of extortion, which alerts that there are consequences for this phenomenon, which are represented by honour crimes of "washing the shame" that parents inflict on the blackmailed girl! The head of the District Court in Al-Ahsa Governorate, Sheikh Abdul Latif Al-Khatib, revealed that drug cases occupy the first place in the cases that the court witnesses continuously, while cases of extortion via the Internet came in second place, the first judgment was issued against a young man who blackmailed a girl, threatening her to publish her pictures through the Internet, indicating that the young man was fined 500 thousand riyals or a one-year sentence. Blackmail also comes through hacking of the computers, as Muhammad al-Minshawi's master's thesis on "Internet Crimes" concluded. It is the first thesis on regional and local levels to discuss this topic, in which the researcher concluded the following: that the breach crimes are the first (33.33%) their personal devices were hacked, (15.1%) they hacked E-mail, sending viruses, followed by the hacking of personal websites such as singles.

The role of violence: There are high rates of exposure of women to violence. Through a field study of a hospital in Riyadh that one hospital in Riyadh receives a case of violence against women every 5 days, and 25% of the victims are pregnant. The average years of abuse and assault were more than 7 years, and 25% of the victims of violence. They were pregnant, which indicates a new release of the violent psychopathic personality of men in society.

The role of emotional deprivation: In a study by Colonel Dr Muhammad Al-Saif, Professor of Research Methods and Social Studies - King Fahd Security College entitled (Emotional deprivation in the Saudi family and its relationship to female crimes in 1424 AH), he revealed the existence of a relationship between community culture and family emotional deprivation. He conducted this research in women's prisons and girls 'care institutions in the Kingdom (228) Saudi women. The applied study concluded that Saudi women who are sentenced to prison for committing criminal acts such as sexual acts, assault, and consuming alcohol and drugs often do not seek the criminal act to gain material benefits or to satisfy the sexual instinct. Most of them are looking for feelings of love, tenderness, and intimate relationships, because of the wife's feeling of emotional deprivation in her relationships with the husband and the girl's feeling of emotional turmoil in her relationships with her parents and siblings. The study concluded that the problem of family emotional deprivation is causally related to the culture of parents, siblings and husbands and strongly influences the woman's tendency to Saudi society is about to practice forbidden criminal acts, which will make her vulnerable to being a victim of "honour."

It is natural that she falls into the arms of the man she meets first and who shows her a little respect, treats her with tenderness, and makes her feel her existence and her being without being sure about the sincerity of his feelings and the correctness of what he says and what he does!!

The role of moral crimes: 90 ethical cases were registered in girls 'care homes this year, according to the annual official statistical report issued by the Ministry of Social Affairs. The report indicated that the number of girls who have been terminated and discharged from institutions in nursing homes in the Kingdom after the end of their sentences is about 927 cases, 11 of them were transferred to other care institutions, and 26 girls were returned to their families.

After the girl left the care institution, we find her family waiting for her to be punished, as happened recently, when a young man shot his two sisters in front of the girls 'care home after they were involved in an ethical case. The two girls were deposited in the girls' care home, and the father came to receive them. As they left the house, the brother shot them with a pistol he was carrying, and they died instantly.

The role of divorce: Society adopts a view of suspicion and suspicion on the divorced woman, and parents tighten their control over her and put red lines on any gesture, and if we know that divorce cases are on the rise, in a published statistic, "Saudi courts record between 25-35 cases daily. Divorce, that is, an average of 16,000 cases per year compared to 66,000 marriages / Al-Youm newspaper, number 11128. What confirms the pressures that divorced women face came in: "A study: 42% of Saudi divorced women suffer from personal maladjustment and the percentage of those who are not socially adapted reached 32 %. The percentage of those who are not adapted to families is 30%, which are merely proportions, and they do not record a majority. In any case, they are still significant. The PhD degree study prepared by the researcher in family sociology (Amal Al-Fraih) pointed out that divorced woman, in general, suffers from some basic problems. They include social tolerance for raising children and society's view of the divorced woman and the consequent excessive parental control, including what is also economical, such as bearing the responsibility of spending on the children if the ex-husband does not assume this responsibility, and the payment of various bills such as electricity, water, and housing.

The role of escaping from the home: The psychologist at the Ministry of Social Affairs confirms the Committee for

Protection (Moudi Al-Zahrani) that many girls have reached care homes fleeing their families, and she says about one of the girls: Her husband used to treat her violently, and her family refused to help her and abandoned her. Because of the abuse, she escaped to her friend, who threw her between the clutches of perverted relationships. After three months, she was arrested and taken to a care home. Her husband divorced her, and she was deprived of her children.

The role of the tribe: the most prominent examples in Saudi Arabia for the control of the tribe are the issues of the lineage that have surfaced recently, including Fatima, free from parentage, who was a victim of arbitrary social norms, and who was sentenced to live alone in harsh conditions like imprisonment in one of the social welfare homes in the Eastern Province. She was denied re-birth. Her family (her husband and two children) made her live in a state of frustration and despair that prompted her to try to put an end to her life!! The head of clerics of the Kingdom, Al-Sheikh, appealed to parents not to put their children in the swamps of tribal racism and despicable conflicts that are based on nervousness that Islam forbids, noting that in Islam there is no difference between an Arab or a non-Arab except with piety.

Honour crimes are based on the system of tribal values. Recently, the tribe's discourse has spread in the absence of a clear sense of reason, logic, and religious constants and the presence of the structure of tribal leaders. The meeting attributes the spread of honour killings in Jordan to the tribal character that characterizes Jordan.

Parents abandoning the imprisoned girl after the end of her sentence: Sabiha Al-Bu Ali, a social worker at the Ministry of Social Affairs, explained that the parents' refusal to accept their daughter if her sentence ends or the girl herself refuses to return to her family is due to the ignorance of both parties. And the social culture is based on fear of the scandal, and the girl refuses to return to threatening her family to kill her or kill her child if she had given birth, and sometimes she returns to the streets or prison after threatening her with death.

Lack of clarity in the concept of concealment among many: Many people have a misunderstanding about concealment in Islam teachings and its intention. This is because of the misunderstanding of the authentic statement of Prophet Mohammed that he said: "A Muslim conceals Muslim in this life, God conceals him on the Day of Resurrection." Narrated by Muslim. For religion, concealment meant that a Muslim does not expose the privacy of another Muslim, which could expose him and his honour to be unnecessary. However, they use this intention as an excuse to conceal a crime. On the contrary, if a Muslim knows about a crime or a plan to commit a crime, he shall inform the official authority to punish the criminal or at least stop him from committing his crime.

In a statement to the commission for the Promotion of Virtue and the Prevention of Vice that 393 thousand cases dealt with the commission by covering up those involved in it, representing 94% of the total number of incidents, which reflects the keenness of the commission's men to cover up according to Sharia evidence and regulations.

This statement comes after deaths following chases between the authority and people in illegal seclusion, which sparked controversy in public opinion: Tabuk police investigated with a patrol of the authority the impact of a chase between them, and a young man accompanied by a girl who was burned to death after colliding with a truck. Madinah police are investigating two members of the commission because they caused the killing of two young men and two girls after their pursuit. The death of a girl affected by her wounds and the injury of the young man (who was accompanying him) with wounds and fractures after their car capsized while they were trying to escape, and the chase lasted for about an hour, as the Authority men suspected that the two young men and the girl were involved in illegal seclusion inside a car.

In a positive step for the Promotion of Virtue Commission in Makkah, after the arrest of a young man and a girl in seclusion. The commission managed to marry the young man to the girl while taking care of the dowry, and one of the staff of the commission ensured that they would provide subsistence for a full month. Their marriage was held inside the commission's centre, and then the young man took his wife home and unfortunately the media did not convey to us incidents similar to this wonderful initiative, in reconciling between two young people with halal instead leaving them prey to falling into the forbidden or ending in prison and nursing home for girls! hopping that the authority will adopt this initiative in coordination with charitable institutions and help young people to get married in order to reconcile them

An increase in the number of murders in the media: What happens in local newspapers is that they report the killers' news without mentioning the killer's goals behind his crime and whether the crime was out of honour. It is not possible for educators, writers, jurists, and lecturers, to denounce and condemn the murder of so-called "dishonour" or "honour crimes" and expose those behind them and nourish this tribal culture and outdated social norms. Also, it needs the legal umbrella that guarantees women rights or even helps in forming committees to defend and protect them from violence and murder and to establish homes to receive women who are subject to violence by male members of the family or women accused of sexual practices and at risk of murder. No one asks for precise details but rather general statistics that do not affect the victims and guarantee their privacy.

Examples of some of these crimes are:

- A young Saudi man shot his 18-year-old sister by firing squad at home, leaving her as a lifeless body, and he escaped.
- A citizen in his thirties shot his wife with a pistol to his death immediately, in their home.
- A young man fired 3 shots at his divorced sister yesterday, one of which landed in her stomach and two in her hand.
- A citizen kills his wife in front of her children and then tries to commit suicide with the same murder weapon, but his injury was not fatal, as he was transferred to the hospital for treatment
- A citizen deliberately killed his wife, running over her by his car several times until her death, as he caused parts of her body to be scattered in front of her parents' house after he brought her back from the school where she works.
- A Saudi man kills his wife and her infant by drowning them in the bathtub.
- And a Saudi citizen killed his 25-year-old, pregnant wife, stabbing her in the face and neck with a sharp bale.
- The police opened an investigation into the case of a girl who was found dead in her room in her parents' home late. The girl was left to the home of her husband, who distributed the invitations to his wedding, which was scheduled for the evening.

The Ministry of Interior Affairs issued a statement regarding the execution of the death sentence for retribution against one of the perpetrators for killing his wife by severely beating her because of a family problem between them, which led to her death.

Previous cases represent dangerous indicators in a society that has a real struggle with honour crime, which is based on the principle of taking suspicion, fear of people's words, and concern for reputation without rational support. It is shameful to deny it or justify it! It is not a disregard for the values of honour and chastity or a view of personal freedom without the framework of values and morals!

But it is wrong that the only criterion is the criterion of honour! In a country that raises the banner of "There is no god but God" and ruled by Sharia law that codified punishments for such crimes, stressed issues related to the waste of human blood and confiscated the powers of the ruler to apply the rulings, which leads to chaos. The true honour does not lie in the shedding of blood and the application of the law of the jungle. Rather, with the honour of the word and honesty, and to stop the honour of the Muslims and throw away the innocent women who are deceived or who have been deceived... which ignites the spark of shame and ends with a tragic end.

Therefore, the Arab inherited cultural traditions bear the consequences of the honour crime, which gives the exaggeration in the Arab man's fear of people's words, their confusion, the whispers of neighbours and friends, and suspicions, especially since the Arab community glorifies and praises its masculine culture and kinship relations, whether in urban or rural cities. It is worth mentioning in this context that honour crime is more frequent in urban cities and Arab capitals than in their countryside. This type of

266

crime is less in capitalist and material western societies due to the prevalence of anonymous relationships between individuals and ethnic and class diversity, plus the individual's enjoyment of his personal freedom in his relationships, expressions, and ideas.

There is no harm in pointing out that conservative eastern and traditional societies focus on and adhere to customary controls and asks their members to abide by them and identify with them. If he does that, they give him a high social consideration and respect him and consider him to be among the notables of society.

This is the dictatorship of society over the individual. Meaning that he is bound by the restrictions of his society, even if the matter requires him to kill his sister, mother, aunt, or the daughters of his relatives. That is, society pushes the individual towards crime to protect its controls only. The individual with him is nothing more than being servile and obedient slave who executes his traditional orders, and his subservience increases if he is illiterate, ignorant, uneducated, and unaware of his social status. It is noticed that this practice takes place in cities more than in the countryside, and it is carried out by men against women.

The tyranny of society, therefore, becoming attached to the individual through: -

1. Shocking him socially and psychologically by isolating him from his family, his tribe, and his community.
2. By stripping him of his role, status, and social consideration.
3. His shameful stains throughout his life and with his family members.
4. Turning it into a bad example to be used by the people.

5. People talk about his lack of identification with the law of his society and the preservation of his honour in gatherings.
6. Punishing a woman with murder if rumours and gossip about her honour and behaviour are reported.
7. If she is not murdered, then her fate is ostracism and social deprivation.
8. No man will marry her if she is not killed.
9. Because of these punishments, it slips into vice, at the impulse of her society, which does not care about the value of the human being, but rather cares about not violating its rules. Therefore, it is a "tyrant" in punishing the individuals who do not obey it and rewarding the individuals who obey its controls because such society exists for itself and not for its members. [Al-Omar 2019. p. s. 194 - 218)].

9. Cubic Violence Against the Indian Wife

Violence amounts to murder (the husband kills his wife) or her suicide because of the persecution of the husband or his mother. This type of rape of women's rights is of three types, which are:

1. Not allowing her to defend herself in not being equal in not paying her dowry to the husband.
2. To usurp her right as a wife and mother in the family.
3. She did not take her right as a human being, as a wife, and as a mother to children in the Indian family. Rather, she was treated as if she was a worker and mother in the family and had no marital or maternal rights.

To expand on this type of violence against women, we offer the following:

This is the suicide of the wife or her murder by the husband due to her failure to pay the dowry to her husband in Indian society. It is the Indian culture and the building of

Indian society that determine all the social situations with which individuals interact. As long as the Indian family represents the nucleus of Indian society, this means that it includes all the standards of Indian culture. And the nature of the developmental stage through which the Indian society passes to direct and raise its members through it, regulate the relationship of its roles and determine the expectations of the wife's role towards the husband and towards the children and the husband's family, and the situation as well with the husband's role.

If violence occurs between roles, especially between the husband and his wife, then the first asked question revolves around the commitment and similarity of both partners to their role, which is the loyalty of each of them to the other. It means the sexual loyalty and fidelity away from infidelity and sexual relations outside the marital relationship, as well as compatibility and mood harmony between the two partners. In other words, if there is no harmony in the mood and sexual fidelity does not occur between the two partners, then the violent behaviour will inevitably take place, and this is confirmed by the standards of Indian culture from both partners. The family demands, however, also an emphasis on it to protect the Indian family unity. Any departure or deviation from this criterion is due to a severe and violent reaction from the other party in the family unit, and it often causes an explosion or agitation that expresses the deviation that triggered it or agitation. This means that if the partner or spouse does not adhere to them or conform to the requirements of their roles, then he or she becomes a victim after being violently assaulted, and this is confirmed by the systemic and constructive standards of Indian culture even though Indian law does not accept this aggression. Therefore, family disputes result from the incompatibility and harmony of the spouses in their moods, in addition to their inability to seriously reform their affairs related to their roles. And since the family is a means that transmits situations of deviation and violence when one of the partners does not fulfil the expectations of his/her roles (forced by social culture), this partner becomes a victim.

In some cases, the wife is a failure or is unable to conform to the mood of her husband and is unable to develop a fruitful marital relationship with her husband's mother or his family (and here, the wife becomes a victim). Therefore, any deviation from the pattern of family norms creates conflicts, tensions, abuse, violence, beatings, and torture. However, the family, as an institution that guarantees most of the friendly relations between the partners, is at the same time the biggest driver for most instances of discomfort and affection. The inconvenience between them will continue if any one of them or both want to cut the marital bond between them while they are in full hostility and rivalry. This situation is miserable and not without repeated violence that eliminates marital happiness between them, and one or both are the victims because of their intransigent stubbornness.

It is worth noting here that during the past few years (and during the eighth decade of the twentieth century), there has been a sharp increase in cases of violence within the Indian family. One of the most famous cases of violence that occurred during that period is the case of killing a young wife who did not fulfil her marriage dowry to her husband (which is usually an Indian woman who asks the wife to provide a dowry to her husband upon her marriage). And there are other cases that explained the wife's murder because of her betrayal of the marital sexual relationship. It happens between the two partners mainly due to the sexual incompatibility between the two partners. (Ram Ahuji) mentioned in his study in 1989 that there is one in every four marriage cases where the husband kills his wife (or she commits suicide) due to her failure to pay the dowry of her marriage to him in full. Not to mention beating and insulting, and here the wife turned into a victim because she could not adhere to the conditions of her marital role to pay the dowry to the husband. According to police reports that in New Delhi, there were 690 women killed in 1983, and 23 wives burned themselves while they were alive due to failure to fully pay her dowry to her husband, who persecuted, beat her and insulted her. It is considered as if the victim did not fulfil the requirements of her role as a wife towards her husband, as confirmed by the Indian value standards. Note that this violence and aggression against the wife is forbidden according to Indian law, but it is prevalent and accepted according to the standards of Indian culture and does not contradict its concepts or structural standards. Whether this violence comes from intentional, spontaneous, sadistic or pleasure in abuse, it leads to the demolition of the structure of the family unit because the victim and the perpetrator have roles in the composition of the family where the violence took place. In fact, domestic violence takes place in the family when the victim and the perpetrator are related for a period, interspersed with verbal quarrels, including criticism, lending, behavioural accountability, insult and denial of the other (neglect) or contempt. The other party feels that he is a fraud and a liar and has arguments and evidence confirming his claim and performance. All of this increases the tension between them and calls for the old conflicts and verbal quarrels to link it to the current one, which makes it take the form of a fight in which one or both are hurt, and sometimes one kills the other and goes to the victim of that accumulated conflict.

It cannot be said that the victim of the marital relationship in the Indian family is characterised by her submission three times simultaneously, namely:

1. Her husband's assault on her because of her failure to pay him the dowry is one of the criteria for the Indian family structure, so she accepts that without complaining to anyone.

2. Confirmation of cultural norms on the payment of the dowry by the wife to the husband, and if it is not within the right of the husband to demand it, he uses verbal or physical violence to take it from her. This means that the culture of Indian society does not oppose the use of aggressive - violent behaviour towards the wife who does not implement the requirements of her role that specified for her. This is another type of victim's abuse in addition to the husband's assault on her. The Indian culture did not do justice to the victim but rather supported the perpetrator in turning her into a victim.

3. Not to oppose Indian society in inflicting physical and verbal punishment on a wife who does not fulfil her promise and commitment to her husband regarding the dowry and the rest of the requirements and duties of her marital roles.

Therefore, the Indian wife is subject to three cases of violent and oppressive methods (from the husband, culture and society) and does not do justice to her right as a societal and cultural victim, hence my name of her as the cubic victim (it is permissible to simile and express).

This is another proof of the supremacy, domination, and tyranny of society over the individual, extending it and limiting it, and reducing the cycle in society through the use of traditions and standards of its inherited culture. It is clear that society is unfair to the roles of its members within the

Indian family. Although the Indian positive law does not recognise violence against women, the members of Indian society do, and their practice disables their positive law.

Since the husband and wife are Indian, why do Indian culture favour men against women? Why does the woman, who is half of society, despise those who give birth as members of it? The Indian wife's contribution to the costs of her family's marriage through the payment of her dowry to the husband, the Indian traditions must value that and not underestimate it and do not exaggerate its restrictions and controls on her to the extent that she prefers suicide to obey these restrictions. Then what is the position of Indian traditions on the killing of the wife by the husband when she does not pay her dowry? Why is the husband not stigmatised for this crime? Wasn't this prejudice against Indian women by her culture?

It was explained in this chapter the injustice and unfairness of the customary traditions inherited by the members of society, especially against women, who are the only offenders for the inhabitants of her society. Was this not one of the forms of tyranny in the right of women? Was this not a fanatic behaviour of a man against women in the same society? Didn't this practice help society expand against the individual? Didn't this situation terrify the woman and make her fearful and submissive to the oppressive and negligent traditions of society about her right and her existence? Doesn't a woman deserve to reject such practices in order to support the individual's curtailment of society's power in upbringing and social control? Does society not deserve to limit its influence and controls in order not to subjugate the individual? Didn't the tyrannical society resemble the method of foreign colonialism of poor and vulnerable societies? It has become clear that society's unfairness and fairness to the roles of its children is due to its inherited traditions that the dead put before their death to the living from the generations that come after them. Were these not these tyrannical practices compelling the individual by society, and we say that it is the dictatorship of society over the individual? [Al-Omar. 2019. p. s. 223 - 226)]

C. THE THIRD TOTAL SLAVERY FORCE: THE GOVERNMENT

This raping force is not committed by the individual, nor by the social culture, religion, globalisation, or the technical, technological industry, but by the government through bylaw setup and policies in the official organisations such as companies, factories, factories, and hospitals, which deprive the woman legitimate rights to work equally with the man. It includes the wages, forcibly and unjustly imposing their prejudiced and intolerant conditions against her under the pretext of unavailability of vacancies and a large number of employees. They look at her absence from work and her leave more than paying attention to her suffering during menstruation, childbirth, and maternity care. With all this, her performance of work and her merit in providing society with new members for it (children), bringing them up with a normal, non-deviant upbringing, is impressive. They use her suffering against her instead of helping her. Hence, they rape her work to not pay wages commensurate with her experience and competence expressing their intolerance against her and in preference to her role, its professional and social standing. They are biased towards the work of men, and the government establishments expressed themselves as a mirror reflecting the Patriarchy culture and the male power because she has no influence, money, or ruling power despite her formation of more than half of the population size. Was this not rape expressing its institutional-professional slavery?

Four main causes of official rapes are presented here, which are:

1. **Her work (paid of labour per gender division):** Regardless of the reason for a woman entering the paid labour market (whether by choice or due to economic necessity), she entered in unprecedentedly large numbers in the past. In 1940, about 30% of female workers in the United States were employed in the labour market. Nowadays their percentage is reaching 75% of currently employed women or those looking for a job. Actually, more than 45% of the working women are aged between 25 and 54, and there is a high share of women of all races, ages, and married women are working or looking for a job now more than ever. The share of men has decreased due to the continuous relocation and restructuring of plants and companies of the industrial sector or retirement.

These statistics of the United States on the women as a social force in the labour market reveal four facts that reflect the preference for men over them, namely:

a. Gender-segregated work.
b. Wage-based gender discrimination.
c. Gender bias, opportunities.
d. Spatially gender segregation.

In other words, women and men's work is separated from each other. They receive less remuneration than the men, and they have fewer job opportunities available to them. Based on these differences, it became natural that the position of the woman at a job is lower than those of men though both hold the same qualifications. Therefore, in spite of the increase in the percentage of female workers in the labour market, they suffer serious discrimination, and their occupational gender separation is a reality.

2. **Her wages (the wage gap):** In American society, most of the working women jobs are centred around operating computers, childcare, secretarial work, and clerical work in bureaucratic offices whose directors and bosses are men, and then there are other professions that women predominate, such as nursing, midwives, and organisations for official records. Few percentages of working women are in teaching and medical as doctors. Men work, however, is mainly in trade, law, manual labour such as blacksmithing, construction, mechanics, truck driving, and engineering. However, this gender segregation allows some women to work with men, albeit in limited and few numbers.

With reference to what was mentioned above, the work of the women was featured in gender studies as follows:

a. Pink Colour Occupation: This work requires elementary skill and a non-privileged position, such as simple clerical work, or receivers of customers' requests in restaurants, workers at the reception desk in hotels, doctor's assistants, or workers in social services departments. Their wages are typically low. It was called the Pink Works, after the pink colour cover, as the symbol of the girl, that covers the newborn in American society.

b. Contingent work: This type of work is conditional, unfixed and temporarily work for a limited or short period. Women resort to it because of its suitability with her conditions as wives or mothers. Men have extraordinarily little to do with such type of work as it does not add to their retirement and is not covered by social security. In 1995, there were 2 million women in this type of work.

In addition to this, racial and national discrimination continues in the gender segregation, where there is a high percentage and continues to be adhered to in the gender segregation to this day. At work, there are 21% of African American women, 17% of Hispanic origins, while 30% of white women are working. The opportunity of having a job in a specialised field for a specialised woman of African origin is extremely limited and less than the opportunities open to white women.

American sociologist (Elizabeth Higginbotham) 1994 found that most American women of African origin who are specialised work in the public sector as teachers at the government schools, employees of social security's offices, clerics, civil activists or as members of faculty in government colleges more than working in large companies, legal offices, or distinguished private universities. Both women of Hispanic or African origins more than white women work in service professions such as housemaids in private homes, and even this work has decreased in the last two decades. [Kendall. 2012. P. 79]

The disparity and inequality of what a man and a woman gain make it one of the best material documents that express the consequences of gender segregation at work and its subsequent outcome, regardless of their racial or national background. In 2006 the average earnings of full-time work for a man were $743 per week while it was $600 per week for a woman, which is 81% of the man wages. The wage gap is age-sensitive, as the older the worker is, the wider the gap is, and vice versa. Average wages received by women compared to men were recorded by their age category, which were: represent 95% for the category 20 -24 years, 88.2%

for 25 -34 years, 80% for 35 -54 years and 72.9% for 55 -64 years.

As for the entitlement to the wage, it depends on academic achievement, the duration of the training, the type of skill required in the event, and what are the environment and conditions of work. These are the benchmarks that control the equality of women's wages with men's wages as per Figure 1, showing the percentage of exploitation of men and women in American society for the year 2006.

3. **The glass ceiling and the glass stairs are self-propelled:** This is another type of woman rights rape by the government and official organisations. It concerns her professional experience, an assault on her scientific competence, and the unjust and oppressive robbing of her professional performance to dominate her with duress, violating her specialisation and her source of livelihood. In many companies her development and climbing the administrative ladder is very slow because of the obstruction of men. Whenever she got the opportunity to move forward, men opposed and impeded her progress as they did not want a woman to lead them and oversee their work. In addition to hindering the male administration for its progress, especially in major international institutions, this is what is known as the "glass ceiling" that includes invisible handicaps that are placed by the men of influential and effective sites in front of the women to prevent them from accessing top positions in major companies and organisations with a wide network of contacts.

The context requires fact clarification that there is a glass ceiling in 500 large companies in the world. In 2005, there were only 15.7% of women in high positions, eight of them were general managers, and 1% of women of colour were in administrative positions.

It is worth pointing out that women have reached higher positions in the service sector, such as banks, investment banking, publishing houses, retail trade companies, food service companies and entertainment institutions in sectors where they have a historical background. As for the wages of women in establishments and companies run by men, they are unjust and low, such as mining companies, oil refineries, brokerage companies and factories. As for the rest of the companies and institutions with a glass ceiling, women often leave their positions and jobs and open their own companies. The glass ceiling represents an invisible obstacle that women cannot overcome because outside the institution or company; they are working to ensure that women do not take over the position of general manager or head of an institution and have men under their responsibility.

Having said that, it is not difficult for women to enter the field of men work, but she faces rebellious men who do not allow her to raise up though her performance is extremely high; therefore, these men are acting to hinder her progress which looks as if the glass ceiling for the woman is fixed and cannot move up to accommodate her skills and competency. It is the opposite for a man who enters the field of women work such as nursing, primary education, libraries, or social service as he faces a rise in his positions to the top. This is like a self-moving glass ladder, which automatically raises him to higher levels in women's professions invisibly despite their desire to remain in their old positions of the lowest level.

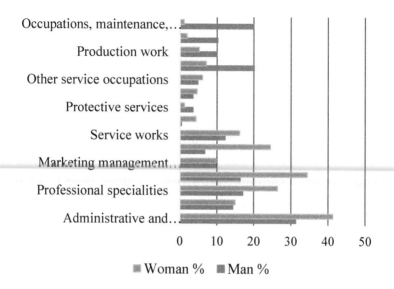

Figure 1: Employment rate of men and women in American society in 2006
(Ref: Social Problem. 2012. P. 78 Diana Kendall)

4. **Double Transformation:** Although there has been a major change in women's participation in the labour market and its power, the system of division of labour based on the sexual difference (male and female) remains the same in its essence without any appreciable difference. A woman who works full-time or part-time contributes to the family budget while keeping her work in managing her routine home, and this is a double burden for her because after she finishes her work outside the home, she handles all her household activities inside her home in preparing, food for the family, cleaning, dish and clothes washing, ironing, shopping, and taking care of the children. These are traditional duties of women, and they increase when she follows up children on their studies, take them to school, and take care of them if they are sick to take them to the doctor or hospital. In the eastern societies, this type of generation has been featured as

280

the sandwich generation that the mother prepares for her children and her husband as well as for the elderly if they are living together (grandfather or grandmother) before she goes to work. All this causes her to give up her right and her time to rest and enjoy free time and hours of rest and sleep.

As for the husband, his participation in domestic and family affairs after the end of his work outside the home is to repair some household furniture or lawn mowing in the garden, and this responsibility is less than the wife's efforts and responsibility. Therefore, the woman's effort was called the double effort that transformed and doubled her responsibility upon entering the work market outside the home. This is the new gender inequality in this contemporary world.

Whatever the social environment, modern or traditional, living in an industrial or agricultural society, educated or ignorant, women are crushed between two jaws. The first jaw represents the mentality of the patriarch man who is fanatical to himself and does not bear participation by another sex in his work or his responsibility because he wants to excel. He feels and enjoys his authority and supremacy over a creature that does not have power, influence, and money. The second jaw, however, is represented by the official institutions of men that he presides, leads, and practices his narcissistic tendency through his skill and competence that precedes the skill and quality of women.

Between these two jaws, the woman in the present world cannot alone break these two jaws rooted in the social, cultural, and religious land, but rather she needs redoubled efforts to avoid her grinding. She did not give up and succeeded in going out to work and obtaining her financial independence, yet she could not give up the essence of her natural duty related to her sexuality as a female. She still requires assuming the responsibility with her husband and her children, whom she bore them. These responsibilities are sex-oriented and outside the scope of the male sex, such as pregnancy, breastfeeding and childcare. Therefore, her responsibility becomes three times, at work, family, and at home. With all this, the wages for her work remained lower than the wages of the man, and she remained the target of sexual assault on her by the man. The obstacles in the eastern societies are expected to occur, mainly:

1. That the woman has not become accustomed to or not given the space and time openly for her to work outside the home away from her family, except in rare cases.

2. She faces difficulty in dealing with a man outside the home and therefore becomes overly cautious for fear of people's words and stigmatisation of negative stigmas and/or her fear of sexual harassment and the rape of the man while she is under his responsibility and control.

3. The family's upbringing is characterised by the distinction of housekeeping, preparing food for members of her family, and helping her mother. This is one of the factors that attract her to be in-home more than to be outside the home.

4. The spirit of competition at work outside the home weakens her enthusiasm for working outside the home.

5. People's view of women working outside the home in a conservative and traditional society that does not encourage girls to do so.

6. Her continued submission to the man inside and outside the home makes her hate working outside.

7. The existence of ethnic, religious, and national discrimination is one of the obstacles that do not push them to work seriously outside the home.

8. Upon her marriage and childbearing, her work becomes influential on her marital and maternal relationship, which doubles her problems at work outside the home and strengthens the man's fight against her at work.

9. Being subjected to extortion and exploitation of men during work makes her a weak factor in the labour market.

10. Her weakness lies in her femininity, maternity, and her lack of experience working outside the home, which makes her hit her head with the glass ceiling that prevents her from climbing to the top of the career hierarchy.

11. Whenever new fields of work appear, the woman takes the initiative to enter them according to her ability and skill, but the man remains a competitor for her because she is a woman (emotional and rational in her decisions and weak in the face of acute and hot events and this is one of the remnants of gender stereotyping)

12. Nevertheless, the development of women's competence and the rise in their morale in exercising power outside the home weakened the man's resistance to her work and her attributes of masculine epithets that do not reflect the spirit of the current era.

CHAPTER 6: THE POWERS OF SITUATIONAL AND SYLLABIC FEMININE ENSLAVEMENT

INITIATION
A. HER RAPE BY WAR
B. HER RAPE BY MAN - VIOLENCE AGAINST HER
C. HER RAPE BY GLOBALISATION SEXUAL INDUSTRY
D. HER RAPE BY ARTISTIC TECHNOLOGICAL INDUSTRY – PORNOGRAPHY
E. HER RAPE BY CRIMINAL GANGS

CHAPTER 6

THE POWERS OF SITUATIONAL AND SYLLABIC FEMININE ENSLAVEMENT

INITIATION

This chapter complements the previous one, but it differs in the type and the extent of its content in its temporal and human surroundings. It concerns the enslaving force, which is of another kind in its extent and influence, but it conforms to the same usurpation of feminine rights in their personal and public lives. It is situational and syllabic, which does not always occur, but rather according to the circumstances available to her by an individual or a criminal gang or the owners of the technology industry to sexually exploit her, and then the war soldiers invading her society. These enslaved forces are limited to the sexual rape of the woman and the trafficking of her body, not in her job at work, factory, company, or state departments, and it has nothing to do with the wage gap nor with the teachings of her religion or social culture.

The rapist here is the man himself to satisfy his sexual instinct from her, to trade her sex and her body, or to avenge her society by raping her. The victim here cannot give up her biological type (as a female), nor the man can avoid her because she represents a financial source that cannot be underestimated. For example, the war crystallised the mass rape carried out by the soldier or terrorist, in which thousands of innocent women are victimised in poor and ethnically diverse countries. In fact, this type of rape does not take place out of the soldier's sexual instinct, but rather in the spirit of revenge, contempt and humiliation of the group he is fighting with, because women represent the nation's honour and because they are not fighting and do not know violence and aggression. In 1945 during the second world war, up to 1.4 million women had been raped. In 1994, half a million women were raped around the world. It's more like the genocide of women. This rape is carried out by men taking advantage of the state of war. It is the greatest act of aggression in the name of war against the women because they are the honour of the supreme society.

It is a mass rape on top of the individual rape performed by the husband against his wife by attaching her existence to his existence or by seizing her earnings. This type of usurpation of a woman's right, while she is his partner, imposes control or terror on her to obey him, fulfils his sadistic pleasure by her, or prevent her from going outside. There is a usurper of her virginity from a male member of her family as if she is part of his property or to sexually assault her via his professional position in his office or outside. All these attacks express the desire to force her to give in and submit to his authority, his sick desires, thoughts, and orders unjustly and coercively. He takes advantage of his position as her husband or her employer. The question that comes to mind: Is there a man who loves to see a female oppressed, frightened, submissive and has no personality? And has no opinion or decision regarding her marital relationship or her household affairs and raising her children? If this prevails, then it means that the man is sick with sadism in making his wife a slave to serve him and satisfy his sexual desire only, and not emotional participation or a life partner who represents the housewife and the mother of the children.

The gang rape, on the other hand, is not part of the character of the warrior soldier as he does not fight for the sake of rape, but he fights another soldier like him. Although the women have no room in the war, the euphoria of victory makes the soldier take revenge on his enemy who defeated him, so he detracts from his honour by raping his women. And, it is not considered as manliness, courage, or strength, and such a rape will never be endorsed by the United Nations or the countries of the free world.

Then the woman is the enemy of herself as she entered the feminine enslavement through the investment of her body, particularly with luxury hotel companies, commercial airlines, exchange card companies, nightclubs, massage parlours, and slimming clinics. In this enslavement, no individuals or governments interfered with her body investing, so they turned prostitution from home to commercial agencies and companies. This transformation started a long time ago but was limited and increased vastly after the fall of the Berlin Wall and the collapse of totalitarian regimes of the twentieth century. This downfall and collapse had many damages to many women who were working in these systems and found themselves without work, so they became valuable targets for international criminal organisations to convert them into a sexual commodity for trafficking with no legal or geographical obstacles in front of them. The sexual trade became like a business subject to supply and demand presented for enjoyment and entertainment, and sexual tourism appeared to primarily serve the staff instead of serving customers in:

1. Organised and international criminal organisations.
2. Owners of bars and nightclubs.
3. Human smugglers.
4. Five-star hotel owners.
5. Owners of tourist cities.
6. Owners of airlines.

7. Employees of customs and border police departments (corrupt).

Accordingly, a group of merchants who invest in the feminine gender have emerged across the developed and capitalist world. They are not involved in sexual relations with women but with customers in all countries of the world during the tourist seasons and official holidays.

Besides these merchants, there are those who appeared in the era of advanced technology, personal freedom, and free expression to trade in pornographic and obscene images expressing pornographic art that has become widespread on the Internet, as well as industry related to the sexual process and artificial sexual organs, who used the female body in its external appearance, strength, and grace of her body as a profitable graphic material. This is the usurpation of the dignity of the female and her dispossession as a human being by converting her into an amusing commodity for men and depriving her of marriage, childbearing and forming a family. It is one of the contemporary forms of slavery in the era of advanced technology and the second globalisation.

Then there is another group of merchants that takes advantage of times of war, economic stagnation, economic sanction, and the spread of terrorism in the world. They take advantage of the insecurity to steal girls, smuggle them forcibly to other countries, rape them, and then sell them to gangs specialised in the white slave trade. This slavery is based on fully possessing the female and harnessing her investment, usurping her right to marry, procreate, form a family, eliminating her presence as a human being. Dependence of slavery on the kidnapping of the girl and then selling her to be a trafficked woman and collecting the costs of her travel and livelihood from her work as a prostitute.

This is a new model of slavery because it rapes her earnings even after investing her sexually.

The question that arises here: Why has the white slave trade and its investment inflated in this era? It may be, though, because of the facilities provided by globalisation, technological development, and the information and communication revolution? This is part of the answer; however, the real reason is the overthrow of the political regimes and great ideological camps that have existed for more than half a century and the subsequent collapses of the social structure. The society's stability and security offered by these regimes suddenly disappeared on their collapse, leaving the society suffering from severe fragmentation where their members and families became without work and had nothing to live on. The criminal networks found such disturbed environments very fertile for their crimes. They moved in and targeted women as the first soft and most expensive target, which outweighed the goal of smuggling weapons and drugs. They devoted hotel, aviation, tourism, and banking companies to their work in sex tourism. However, the questions which might be asked is where the national governments and what are their positions on this inhuman and immoral trade? Where are the border and customs controls? Where is the neutral media in revealing the dangers and shortcomings of this trade on women, including the spread of AIDS, the delinquency of youth, and the high rate of domestic and international crimes? Does the female gender overwhelm all of these? What is the position of the patriarchal male authority on it? What is the position of the clergy on it? It seems that they do not oppose it or stand against it, but rather encourage and nurture it!!!!

There is a fundamental difference between the merchants who invest in the feminine gender (in the powers of the feminine slavery of the feminine situation) and the men who exploited the totalitarian feminine. The politicised and intrusive people of politics and traditions have a strong backing and support that pushes them to exploit, supremacy and bullying the feminine, which is the religion for the clergy and the law for the intruders of politics and the traditional conservatives backed by The inherited social culture, while the sex industry merchants and professionals of law, religion and traditions, their enslavement is circumstantial and segmental, while the men who are the forces of totalitarian slavery have permanent and continuous exploitation that does not stop.

After this introduction, the various comprehensive situational and cross-sectional forces are explained, namely:

A. HER RAPE BY WAR

Gang rape against women: The mass rape of women whose country fell into an occupation, or a civil war was practised after the mid-twentieth century. It was not out of sexual or personal motivation but to terrorise them and dismantle their community. It happened in Somalia, Bosnia and Herzegovina and Kashmir, where about 60,000 women were raped in the period between 1992 – 1995. Bangladesh, Liberia and South Sudan women suffered various types of rapes, and in Uganda, 250,000 to 500,000 women were raped during 1994, the civil war in it, while in Rwanda where it was a mass genocide of women.

It is the collective violence in the form of gang rape without mentioning the psychological effects of rape survivors that require continuous medical and psychological treatment. Moreover, there is another type of violence against women in the form of their unpaid work (forced labour) and their affliction with AIDS. All this is considered

290

collective violence against women while they did not participate in the war and did not resist the military force. Rape was used in these countries as a weapon of war to break the essence of society psychologically, socially, politically, and militarily. According to United Nations statistics, there were approximately 19% of global violence led to death. In 2002 there were 301,000 deaths due to civil wars that occurred in poor countries with low economies, and between 60 and 70% of the deaths did not take part in the fighting, including women and children. [Thomson. 2007. P. 26]

The mass rape of German women in 1945 by Soviet forces triggered many international laws about such aggression against women and children. Women were easy prey for Soviet soldiers as a form of revenge. Germany was the scene of more than 1.4 million rapes known in human history. Between January and August 1945, Soviet soldiers did not hesitate to execute any woman who refused to bow to their demands. At the beginning of the year 1945, an overwhelming proportion of German men were recruited in the ranks of the German army to fight on various fronts. Therefore, the German cities were almost devoid of males while the females were abundantly present and coinciding with the advent of the Soviet army where German woman was their prey.

With the beginning of the Soviet army's intervention in East Prussia, German women lived on the impact of a terrifying nightmare. During that period, due to the rape crimes in East Prussia, the Soviet army gained a bad reputation that preceded it wherever it went. Accordingly, and based on numerous reports, many German women did not hesitate to commit suicide to avoid falling into the hands of Soviet soldiers through an incident like the one in the city of Damien.

Between January and August 1945, and over the course of eight months, at least two million German women were raped by Soviet soldiers. Moreover, according to numerous testimonies, some women were subjected to repeated rape, sometimes reaching seventy times. Between mid-April and late May 1945, the German capital Berlin alone witnessed more than a hundred thousand rapes, according to local hospital reports. In addition, the regions of East Prussia, Pomerania, and Silesia (German regions during the Second World War) were the scene of more than 1.4 A million rapes.

According to many reports, at least two million German women were raped during a period not exceeding eight months, and the ages of the women who were raped ranged from ten years (the youngest) to eighty years (the oldest). In addition to all this, no less than 200,000 women died. German life due to diseases and infections that followed repeated rapes. During the months following the end of World War II in the European arena, a large percentage of German women were forced to go to hospitals for abortions. Moreover, according to doctors' reports, abortions were performed daily and continuously in various German hospitals.

With the advent of August 1945, the rate of rape gradually decreased, and this came after the Soviet military leadership took strict measures against its soldiers accused of rape. Meanwhile, at the beginning of January 1948, the rape operations came to an end completely after the return of Soviet soldiers to their camps, and they left the residential areas. [https://www.alarabiya.net]

There are many examples of mass rape that took place in different parts of the world in this and last century. In all of them, they represent the spirit of revenge, contempt, and humiliation of the society through the rape of the women because they are the nation's honour and its high dignity, while physically they are the weakest, and they lack the training to carry a weapon to defend themselves against the usurper.

B. HER RAPE BY MAN - VIOLENCE AGAINST HER

The man raping her through Marital Violence: As a behaviour, the violence is related to the individual, except that its triggers are usually verbal or physical, and since it is this way, it does not happen spontaneously or automatically unless there is a response to stimuli that are not necessarily equal to it in force and direction. Therefore, the occurrence of violence requires a negative social relationship between two individuals, which is acquired rather than a legacy that can be learned from the family, school, society or sect. It is important to understand that the mind and the violence contradict each other. The more the individual uses his mind, the less violence and vice versa, while the emotion meets the violence and therefore, the more emotional the individual, the more violent he is when stimulated.

And when sex is associated with love for one of the two partners, they generate extreme negative reactions if this partner (who has an emotional or sexual relationship with another partner) faces a verbal attack from the partner that affects his feeling, beauty, loyalty, behaviour, morals, or ideas, causing injury to his feelings and excitement. It leads to violent, aggressive reactions that turn the partner into a victim. For example, if the husband knew that his wife had betrayed him emotionally or sexually, this would push him to commit a criminal act in revenge against her because the husband realised that his wife was not sincere, loyal and explicit in her emotions towards him, which is the greatest irritation and excitement for him, causing him to hate, hatred and a high resentment against her, so he turns her to a victim who pays the price for her misdemeanour. Women are vulnerable to domestic violence, which is practised on them either as rape by a strange assailant or coercion by their husbands, beatings, or persecution. The cause of domestic violence is the lack or weakness of compatibility between spouses in their marital life jealousy, or lack of love for each other, marital infidelity by one of the spouses, or the rough treatment of mothers-in-law, spouses, or both. These are the main reasons that cause the emergence of maladjustment between the spouses or one of them for married life. And it leads to severe tension between them, the failure of one or both to fulfil the periodic marital expectations, or the dispute over ownership and inheritance. The effect of these reasons increases if it is combined with emotional enthusiasm (stupidity), the abolition of the mind, the use of self-moods, the continuing pressures, and frustrations on the husband with the nature of his complaining character about everything (with or without reason) with his tendency to dominate and dominate his wife and she does not want that, which leads to the use of Verbal or physical violence, or both.

This violence takes place within the smallest and most important community cell in the social body (society), which is the family, i.e., the husband's mistreatment of his wife due to the unequal cultural, educational, age, aesthetic, ethical, personality, mood or mental levels. Note that this violent abuse occurs towards his wife with the intention of:

a. Trying to bully her.
b. Imposing his control over it.
c. He let her live-in fear and dread.
d. Imposing obedience and submission to it.

e. The narcissistic sadness in itself.

f. Extreme jealousy.

As for the violent methods of abuse, it takes some of the following actions:

1 - The threat	10 - pushing it towards convergence
2 - Anger	11 - Loss of self-confidence
3 - Restriction	12 - Sexual humiliation
4 - Compulsion	13 - Isolate from the family environment
5 - Prohibition	14 - Observing their actions and actions
6 - Expulsion	15 - Deprivation of thinking
7 - Beating	16 - Depriving her of expressing an opinion
8 - insulting and degrading the wife	17- Letting her feel the shyness
9 - Utilising her as a mean for his personal purposes	

Faced with this violent abuse, it takes one of the following actual responses:

1 - Submission	2- Sexual Abandonment
3 - Crying	4 - Beating
5 - Supplication	6 - Hate
7 - Resorting to parents	8 - Revenge
9 - The quarrelsome	10 - Resorting to justice

It is worth mentioning that this violence forces the mother, who is the wife, to reflect her suffering on the rest of the family and the community alike. If it happens, the

295

family will not be able to perform its formative functions, and the society will receive human elements which are sick in their behaviour (deviant, delinquent, or psychologically ill).

There is no harm in pointing out that this makes the wife's position in the interactive equation unbalanced or equal. She accepts - coerced - domination over her and controlling her behaviour and interference in her personal life, but it makes her suffer from these violent abuses throughout her marital life. It is a multifaceted rape (sexual, psychological, and social). However, it is legitimised by the Patriarchal social culture.

1. Her Existence Attached to the Existence of Male

This part concerning Saudi society which has a special arrangement for a woman as she cannot go out of her house unless a male from the family who is forbidden from marrying her called (Mahram) such as her son, brother, father, uncle, grandfather, father-in-law, is with her. This arrangement is considered as another raping of the rights of the Saudi girl to the freedom to travel, leave the house, and her follow up of her papers or approvals with the government departments, and shopping. He is the shadowed male who robbed her legal personality through oppression and injustice and imposed his narcissism on her. In other words, he attacks her in thought, behaviour, and expression, whose rights are supposed to be parallel to the male rights. Arab culture does not support what the Mahram person does towards a girl while she is the daughter of his society.

The Saudi writer and critic, Maliha Ahmed Al-Shehab, who has a weekly column in the Saudi Al-Watan newspaper, wrote in her 2010 book, "The Saudi Woman, a Voice and a Picture," about the phenomenon of Mahram, in which she said: "The Mahram is the only thing that gives Saudi women the status of being and the right to practice life and enjoy the joys of the world and be an effective member in building society. In the event that it is not there, this woman is an unnecessary extra, and in front of government institutions, she is treated as an entity that has no legal personality and, therefore, no transaction can be done for her. If she loses her male shadow (Mahram), she becomes non-existing, and she has no value. Therefore, she has no life requirements or existential necessities. In order for a woman to have the right to acknowledge her existence, she needs a male shadow in all stages of her life. No matter how old is she and what are her scientific achievements which supposed to be enough proof that she possesses a mind capable of thinking, recognising, and creativity, and she revealed a pure soul, nothing intercedes for her except for that shade, even if he was young and too short to cover her smallest fingertips.

This is not a mode of social thinking that can be tolerated. Rather, it is legislation and law upon which government institutions are based on their dealings with women, and it is a system that governs the movements of women, paralyses her movement, and prevents her from obtaining her most basic rights. Whoever enacted this law dealt with the fact that the Mahram person is available to every woman, and it is assumed (in good faith) that this person must be just. Therefore, the legislator assumed that Mahram would not extend his injustice to women under his protection. Accordingly, no specific legislation to protect the woman from the oppression of her Mahram was issued, and no procedure has specified to preserve the right of the woman if the Mahram exceeds the purpose of the legislation, and he has deprived her of her right. Also, the legislator did not put a solution for the woman who has no Mahram in her life. Therefore, it was found that a woman who does not have

297

a Mahram faces complication in all her life affairs, such as obtaining a passport and a status card or marriage as well as the right to study and employment. All these formalities are all rights and acquisitions that women can only obtain with the consent of a Mahram, and the lack of his availability leads to the suspension of the interests of women. It is certain that this is outside the objectives of the legislation, so we urgently need to reconsider some of the legislation related to women and work to modernise them in a way that eliminates the harm that prevents a woman from getting her rights in life."

Regarding her being prevented from driving a car in her country, she said: "The Saudi woman is the only one among the women of the world who is forbidden from driving a car. As soon as a government delegation leaves the homeland to a Western country, it faces the chronic embarrassing question: why are you denying and preventing a woman from driving a car? And when will you allow her to do so?

His Highness Prince Saud Al-Faisal replied on Channel 4 of the British TV when asked about women driving a car, saying, "For me personally, I think that they have the right to drive cars, but we are not the party that decides that. Families should decide that, and it should not be imposed by the government, and the government will not do it." The government does not force women to drive and does not prevent them. " [Al Shehab, 2010. p. 129)]

In recent times, the level of demand to grant women the right to drive a car has increased. These demands are announced and advanced by the group affected by the ban, mainly women, with the absence of direct support from the man who is also affected in one way or another. This man, and in particular the one who repeats in all his social conversations the necessity for women to be granted the

298

right to drive a car. He is the same man when he hears the women and their serious attempt to obtain this right, raising his voice in frustration to the women, saying astonishingly: Is the woman's greatest concern in our country is the driving of a car?

My sir, who is keen on women's rights, do you not know that women are insulted and humiliated because they are deprived of driving themselves ... Women die because they are prevented from driving ... Women are raped because the custom ruled that a woman does not drive a car ...Women disrupt their energies and remain confined in four walls of the suspicion of seclusion because there is nothing in front of her other than to meet her needs. And whoever is available for her to play with her obsessions, for every time she goes to the university accompanied by her Mahram, who is less than seven years old, she was wondering in a panic if this foreign driver decides to veer in the car to the path of crime, how can this little boy prevent him? She imagines herself divided between the resistance of this wolf and her desire to cuddle this child to her chest in order to stop him from crying, to dwell on his horror, and to remove fear from him. Her imagination will go to the psychological complexes that will afflict this child and will continue to accompany him throughout all his life. So, she ended up deciding not to go to university and stopping her education process. As for the dealing with her as a minor and she is temptation project, one got to understand that since Hammurabi, laws have been enacted to protect rights, control community movement, and prevent harm and abuse of others, except here in Saudi Arabia, as many laws and legislations impede the movement of society and facilitate the abuse of the rights of others, and appear as an umbrella for many of the human abuses and this is clearly evident (to the point that seen by the blind) in legislation related to women .... A single visit to any government department is enough to be shocked by the extent of the harm inflicted on women due to the legislation enacted for decades, and it has not been reconsidered in any attempt to update and develop it in line with the new social situation. Therefore, it became unable to meet the needs and evolving requirements of life, which was the cause of many types of human abuse shamefully. And I saw it with my own eyes when I went to the Passports Directorate in Dammam, and the first thing that received me was the sound of crying and screaming as if it were a sighing from a woman over the age of seventy, and he repeated insistently: I will not get out of here until you get my passports for me ... Her image was a mixture of bereavement, pain, confusion, and anger. Impotent Even that employee whom you seek help and you do not find an answer except Get out and bring your guardian to give us permission to renew your passport, the features of this employee were overflowing with sympathy for this old woman, and he wished that he would find in the tight law even a loophole he can through which he can help this woman to obtain her passport and saves her from the humiliation that her guardian will compromise on her, and he is nothing but her only son out of eight daughters.

What law is this that helps a child to disobey his mother!!! What is the law that grants the son the right to dominate and have full jurisdiction over whoever was the reason for his existence and who spared her life in his upbringing...!! What law deals with women as minors and legitimate sedition and sabotage even after they have reached old age...!!! This is a law that is enacted on the basis that women are deficient in reason and are the ones who are entrusted with the most difficult task of life, which is raising generations. [Meteor. 2010. p. s. 145 - 146)]

300

2. Exploiting Her Resources

This usurpation is another type of rape that concerns the confiscation of the wife's salary by the husband without any consideration to her rights and needs. She deserves this earning as it is from her work and efforts outside the home. He spends it on his needs without her consent which is a total assault on her professional and financial rights without giving her the right to build her family. This rape is not a cultural rape, but a personal and individualistic which is practised by men who are traditionally exercising male authority in all its details. It is obtained from her by threatening while legally it is her right. Although the woman held many positions and competed with the man in a lot of business, she is still subjected to oppression by her husband in appropriating her salary by force. Sometimes the husband threatens the wife, and unfortunately, some husbands have given themselves the right to dispose of their wives' rights without knowing the ruling.

It usually happens in eastern societies. The preacher Sheikh Muhammad Al-Majid spoke in detail from the religious point of view about this issue. He explained the ruling on taking the wife's salary by force and the ruling on her disposing of her salary without returning to the husband, and asking her for a special expense for her, as well as taking her from the husband's money without his knowledge and providing instructions to the husband not to take her money.

Ruling on taking the wife's salary by force and threats: In western societies, the wife and the husband agree on how to share and participate in the expense of the family as well as the right of each of them when the divorce. In eastern societies, however, the situation is different because the right of each of them in divorce is to follow the religious rules, which are different according to sect.

For example, the Muslim preacher Sheikh Muhammad Al-Majid says: It is not permissible to take the wife's salary by force and threat, whatever the reasons, based on the saying of Prophet Mohammed: "The money of Muslim is not permissible without his own acceptance". A wife who wants to give her husband or help him with part of her money has personal freedom to do so, but on the condition that it shall not be rape or coercion. He added: A woman's salary is her right, because she is the one who got it by her efforts, and sometimes she sacrifices her time and tries to reconcile her work and the house in order to maintain the home and work, and this costs her a lot of time and effort. It happens with many and because of the excessive sensitivity and the constant disagreements that disturb the peace between them. He said: There are men who prefer to marry an employee to exploit her and take her salary, and this is not permissible, of course."

3. Incest Practice Against Her

Incest is the most hated type of rape that is done by a male member of the girl's family, where the male member rapes her and sexually assaults her virginity. It is happening in the poor, rich, urban, or industrial family because of the man's control over her and his control over her personal life as if it is part of her material possessions. It is exercised between blood kinship where the male rapes, in most cases a minor girl, he attacks her femininity, dignity, innocence, and her future. The problem becomes complex when it involves a complete sexual relationship between two persons (male and female) who are related by a kinship that prevents and prohibits sexual relationship between them socially and religiously. It is more and more common among fathers, daughters, brothers, and sisters. It is a social problem produced by the blood kinship between males and females

302

so that the closer the blood kinship between them, the more the occurrence of the incident, and the more it diverged, the more it diminishes with them.

It is, therefore, the most disgraced taboo of all social taboos, in the present and in the past. Historically, this practice was quite common among ancient royal families, such as the pharaohs of ancient Egypt, to preserve blood purity in the ruling dynasty. Modern societies, however, have laws regarding incest or social restrictions on the marriages of close consanguinity. In certain societies, it is illegal. Consensual adult incest is seen by some as a crime without victims. Some cultures extend the incest taboo to relatives with no consanguinity, such as milk-siblings, stepsiblings, and adoptive siblings, albeit sometimes with less intensity. Third-degree relatives (such as half-aunt, half-nephew, first cousin) on average have 12.5% common genetic heritage, and sexual relations between them are viewed differently in various cultures, from being discouraged to being socially acceptable. Children of incestuous relationships have been regarded as illegitimate and are still so regarded in some societies today. In most cases, the parents did not have the option to marry to remove that status, as incestuous marriages were, and are, normally also prohibited.

In the past four decades, it was noticed that in the eastern societies, this rape has increased and exacerbated due to many social and economic problems such as youth unemployment, the low standard of living, and the overcrowding of housing with family members, with the increase in the number of widows and divorced women, plus the weakness of religious faith as moral deterrents. These causes represent short-term variables that afflict all societies the poor and overcrowded, such as Egypt and Morocco.

Incest was considered a social problem because it occurs within the family, violating the religious teachings and its customary controls, defiling its blood kinship, and it is leaving psychological effects on the victim. In most cases, these effects appear as difficult-to-treat psychological complexities as well as distorting the developmental process of the family and converting it into an unhealthy social cell that can raise a normal generation free from psychological disturbances within the fortified family relationship.

Incest can be categorised as part of contemporary social problems because it renews its characteristics in its exacerbation and spreads among social strata more than before utilising the internet tools. This is due to the high rate of change of modern society and its associated problems coupled with the weakness of religious faith as moral deterrents forced the abnormal behaviours to float on the surface and actually practised. These social problems are manifested especially in a family environment ready for them which can be aggravated by the use of drugs inside the home in a muffled and hidden atmosphere. Such an atmosphere encourages the practice of incest. It lies between a man who has influence and domination with a female who does not have influence or authority; therefore, it is between the strength of the authoritarian male and the weakness of the submissive female.

What was noticed about this problem is that men in the family are the ones who sexually assault the girl or woman, and it does not reach women's assault on men. That is right due to the difference in the upbringing of the male from the female. The male wants to prove his masculinity, and he is the initiator as he who attracts the other sex, while the woman who was brought up in submission to the male and used to admire his strength and financial independence will be obedient and submissive to him naturally.

In eastern societies, it seems that the main source of incest is the feeling of a father, brother, and uncle of his influence within the family, so he acts with the female members of his family as if they are part of his material property. There is no harm in indicating here that this sexual intercourse is practised in the utmost confidentiality and secrecy. It is not disclosed to anyone, not even to the security, judicial or religious authorities, for fear of scandal and defamation because it is a taboo that stigmatises its owner or practitioners with disgraceful and defective stains that spread quickly among people. It harms the reputation of the entire family and applies even after the death of its practitioners to their family.

It is not sanctioned by religious teaching and contrary to human nature, and it represents sexual perversion, behavioural deviation, moral degradation, religious debasement, and legal breach.

In western societies, where the living of the individual lives in freedom and is socially secured by law, incest is not more than discharging sexual instinct outside the social customs. In eastern society and on top of the natural sexual instinct, both the freedom the social security of the individual is lacking, which act as catalysts for incest behaviour. It was found that the following reasons could be the main reasons behind such behaviour:

1. Unemployment and low level of education for young men.
2. Financial poverty.
3. The absence of religious faith and moral value deterrents.
4. Late marriage age for girls.

305

5. The house is crowded with a large number of members of the same family.
6. Divorced and widowed women.
7. Feeling miserable and depressed.
8. Absence of sexual education in schools and universities.
9. The absence of laws, particularly in Egypt, provides for punishment for the adulterer.

Some studies that were conducted on this problem to confirm its contemporaneity classified it according to behavioural patterns. And the most common pattern is the father's relationship with his daughter, as it constitutes 75% of the reported cases. Other patterns are:

Adaptive Pattern:

It occurs between a brother and sister who sleep in the same bed or in the same room, and they physically get too close, especially in pre-puberty and adulthood.

Severe Disease Disorder Pattern:

In case one of the parties is psychopathic, consumes alcohol, or suffers from schizophrenia or any other psychotic disorder.

Children Adoration or Boys (Paedophilia) Pattern:

This pattern results from a disordered parental pattern where the boy watches his father doing this or knows that he is doing it and imitates him.

Marital-Relationship Disturbance Pattern:

Where the wife refuses the sexual relationship, then the husband searches for his sexual desires in the wrong place (in incest).

Family-Relationships Pathological Disorder Pattern:

It occurs when family relationships become torn in a way that does not give a sense of sanctity in any relationship among the family members.

It was found that a third of those who were subject to sexual assaults were under the age of nine years of age and that the most cases that had been observed were in the most crowded places, the poorest and the lowest in social levels, and this increase may be real due to physical contact in these crowded environments or because of the presence of These groups are under the microscope of social and research bodies more than the richer environments or higher social classes, in which incest may occur in silence and away from the monitoring of the legal and research authorities.

It is important to diagnose social, psychological, and biological factors that play roles in breaking the sexual taboo barrier so that this activity escapes and moves towards directions that are religiously or culturally unacceptable. Incest is clearly linked to alcohol and drug addiction, overpopulation, families isolated from society (or clearly internalised), and mentally disturbed or retarded people.

The initiative often comes from older males towards children (males or females), and from here, there is an overlap between incest and rape (sexual overtaking, which is against the victim's desire), although this does not preclude the presence of seduction from females or children sometimes.

Based on the victim's reaction and feelings resulting from the incest behaviour, three basic styles can be observed, which are:

The Angry Style: Where there are feelings of anger from the victim towards the perpetrator, and this occurs when the victim has been completely forced to do this without having any ability to choose, resist or reject, and hence the victim bears feelings of anger and the desire for revenge. Anger may spread towards all members of the perpetrator's sex. That is why she fails her relationship with her husband and is alienated from the sexual relationship and all that surrounds her. She suffers from a state of sexual frigidity that she may try to overcome or get out of it by engaging in multiple sexual relations. Or she learns that control over a man takes place by a sexual relationship with him to become a kind of robbing of his power and ability, and even control over him and his money. Studies have revealed that 37% of prostitutes were preys of incest which explains the relationship between this and that.

The Sad Style: In this case, the victim feels that she is responsible for what happened for the fact that she prepared herself for it or did not refuse it, or did not show the required resistance, or she tried to take advantage of this situation by obtaining gifts and money or by occupying a special place in the family by possessing the father or older brother. Here she feels guilty, and her aggression is directed towards herself. She may make attempts to harm herself, such as inflicting cuts or scratches in various places on her body, or she tries to commit suicide from time to time, or at least wishes to die, and she has a strong hatred for herself.

The Mixed Style: In this style, the reaction, and the feeling of the victim of incest is a mix of sadness with anger. It is difficult to predict the next move of the victim and the results; therefore, it is the most complex among the three types of styles.

Spread

This was more accurately demonstrated in the research conducted by the Rome-based Unicri Institute on crime victims and included 36 countries. It published a summary in the international report issued by the Institute in 1991, where interviews were conducted with women, each representing a family. Of the answers, 10% of the total sample were exposed to incest. Although this deserves scientific scrutiny, someone may say that the percentage may exceed that as many cases are reluctant to disclose what happened. This is true, and therefore it is necessary to be careful when deciding about ratios and figures related to an issue such as incest in various societies, and with this, the estimated ratios stay useful for approximating the relative size of the phenomenon to deal with it or to give it the attention it deserves.

Cofactors

Ethical Factors

Weakness of the moral system within the family, or in the language of psychology, the weakness of the superego (the conscience) of some or all of the family members. In addition to their habit of physical interaction in their daily dealings more than the usual, with the absence of boundaries and barriers between the sexes, the absence of privacy and the storming of closed rooms without permission. In these families, we find that there is a weakness in the parental authority of the father or the mother or both, and this leads to the collapse of the authority of control and linkage and the collapse of the prisoner law in general.

Economic Factors

Such as poverty and the accumulation of the family in one room or in a narrow space, which makes sexual relations between parents take place in the ears and sometimes in front of the sons and daughters, in addition to the widespread poverty deprivation of many basic needs that may be compensated sexually within the family. Poverty is accompanied by a state of unemployment, late marriage age, and a feeling of unhappiness and misery, which makes adherence to moral laws in the most vulnerable cases. A report of the Central Agency for Public Mobilization and Statistics - stated that 30% of families in Egypt reside in one room with an average number of seven members. It can be imagined what would happen between males and females in such an environment.

Psychological Factors

Suppose a family member suffers from a mental illness such as schizophrenia, mania, personality disorder, mental retardation, or an organic brain injury. The following subfactors are fuelling and enhancing the psychological disorder.

The media: the materials broadcast day and night that ignite sexual arousal in a society that suffers from deprivation on multiple levels.

Addiction: The abuse of alcohol and drugs is one of the strongest factors leading t;o incest, as these substances lead to a state of disturbance of consciousness and disturbance of the moral and ethical balance to the extent that it is easy to violate all prohibitions.

The Internet (in particular): The existence of porn sites under the use of minors and adults without clear boundaries causes the generation of a mental image of the girl's gender that differs from the normal behaviour.

Psychological and Social Implications

Two researchers, Adam, and Neil (1967), tried to study this matter from a purely biological point of view. They tracked the case of 18 children who were the offspring of an incestuous marriage and found that five of them had died, five others suffered from mental retardation, and one had a cleft in the lip and the roof of the throat, which is especially alarming. Compared with this, the birth defects in normal people are about 2%, and most of them are unnoticed defects.

Therefore, these researchers concluded that if incest was spread, it could lead to the end of human existence from its

310

foundations, and this may be part of the wisdom of religious prohibition, legal criminalisation and social stigmatisation.

The roles overlap and their turmoil, as mentioned above, with the resulting negative feelings that are destructive to all family relationships, such as jealousy, conflict, hatred, contempt, and anger. It could be imagined that a young girl who expects innocent love and pure gentle caress from the father, older brother, uncle, maternal uncle, or others, so when sexual practices occur, she faces an uncommon matter that afflicts her with fear, suspicion, confusion, and confusion. Doubt and hatred, and she is concerned about the perpetrator with contradictory feelings that make her tear from within, for, on the one hand, she loves him as a father, brother, maternal uncle or uncle, and this is an innate love that she grew up on, and on the other hand, she discovers, later or sooner, that he is doing something strange, embarrassing, or disgraceful, especially if he asks Including not disclosing what happened or threatening to hit her or kill her if she spoke. These feelings often develop into a state of depression, isolation, and aggression towards oneself and towards the other (the perpetrator and other men), and the victim may try to reduce her feelings of shame and shame by using drugs or indulging in sexual practices of his followers exaggerating revenge on herself and the perpetrator (by tarnishing his reputation especially if he is a father or an older brother).

Shaking of the Values: when the essence of the noble meanings of parenting, motherhood, and brotherhood, which form the sound human consciousness and the alive conscience, are diminished in the mind of the victim, she becomes emotionally and sexually disabled. She suffers difficulty in establishing normal emotional or sexual relationships where the memory of the abnormal relationship and its extensions continues to affect the perception of emotional and sexual stimuli. The victim (in particular) develops negative feelings (mostly) or contradictory (sometimes) towards emotional and sexual issues. Establishing a relationship with another man outside the taboo is a matter of doubts and difficulties. Or the two involved are given in to the forbidden relationship, and they become its prisoners, without thinking of alternative healthy relationships at all.

Adjustment Disorder: where the image of the relationship between the two people is disturbed and distorted, so it moves away from that relationship between brother and sister or between father and daughter and is replaced by relationships tinged with contradiction and volatility, leaving deep wounds in the soul. In addition, both parties involved find it difficult to establish normal marital relations with others due to the distortion of relationship models. Adjustment disorder is not limited to emotional or sexual relations only, but also a disorder that includes many aspects of the life of both parties.

Feelings of guilt, shame, and disgrace, which can lead to severe depression that may be a complication of the suicide attempt. Loss of virginity or pregnancy resulting in serious moral, social or legal problems. Often one or both parties subsequently become involved in communal sex, and the girl whose sanctity has been violated, for example, turns in most cases to prostitution.

Prevention

If prevention is important in all problems and diseases, then it is here of exceptional importance, as the occurrence of incest will leave traces that may be completely difficult to treat, so it becomes necessary to have the following preventive measures:

312

a) **Paying attention to vulnerable groups:** such as crowded, poor, and deprived places, especially in the case of overcrowding, psychologically disturbed people, or alcohol or drug addicts. Attention here means discovering the risk factors and working to treat them effectively.

b) **Satisfying Needs:** especially the basic needs of housing, food, clothing, and legitimate sexual needs, as those deprived of satisfying their needs (especially nationality) are sources of danger in the family and society. Accordingly, serious steps need to be taken to encourage marriage at all levels to reduce, as much as possible, the number of men and women who have been under the stress of deprivation for many years, as is the case now.

The statement issued by the Egyptian Central Agency for Public Mobilization and Statistics was shocking. It showed that nine million citizens, three and a half million of which were females, have passed the thirty-fifth without marrying. It can be imagined what could happen as a result of this abnormal situation due to the long time since they became adults without having the opportunity to deplete their sexual instinct in legitimate gratification by marriage. The problem is compounded as there are five million unemployed, deprived of marriage while exposed continuously to violent sexual stimuli at home, street, through the media, and at the same time, they lack the moral barrier that prevents them from crossing religious and moral boundaries.

c) **Observance of Public Morals Within the Family:** such as seeking permission before entering the rooms of the family girls, observing privacy in closed rooms, distinguishing between boys and girls in bed, and the mother or girls not appearing in revealing or lewd clothes that show the charms of her body in front of men and boys who are their Mahram, and adhering to a reasonable amount of

313

respectful dealing away from vulgarity and indulgence. Physical caresses between males and females in the family should also be avoided.

d) **Reducing the Factors of Excitement:** those who show off in homes or streets and from informational materials on satellite channels, channels or pornographic sites that raise instincts, reduce the barrier of modesty, and invade the boundaries of the prohibition.

The Treatment

a) **Disclosure:** The first and most important step in the treatment of incest is to encourage the victim to disclose through a reassuring therapeutic relationship supported by a psychiatrist, psychologist, or social worker. It has been found that disclosure of that relationship leads in most cases to its complete cessation because the person who is assaulted is deterred for fear of scandal or punishment, in addition to what the disclosure provides of protection measures for the victim at family, professional and legal levels. Despite the importance of disclosure, there are difficulties that prevent or delay its occurrence, including fear of punishment or scandal, or denial at the level of family members, and therefore the therapist must open the way and assist in this step without revealing to the victim things from his imaginations or personal expectations. And the matter may require (and often calls) presenting direct and gradual questions that reveal the extent of the relationship between the victim and the aggressor if there are suspicions or clues to that. The psychological problems that afflict the victim are exacerbated due to her inability to disclose this matter, so all thoughts and feelings inside her are silenced and shrink on herself, and from here the treatment is by giving her the opportunity to talk about everything inside her while supporting her and reassuring her during the restoration of those traumatic experiences and then trying to rebuild the psychological New after overcoming this crisis.

b) **Victim Protection:** Once the victim discloses the issue of incest or breach of honour, the therapist must create a safe environment for her to protect her from recurring sexual, physical, or psychological assaults. This can be done in cooperation with some normal family members. If this is not available, then it is through available government agencies. The matter may require isolating the victim in a safe place (nursing home or a health or social institution) until the family's conditions are examined, the defects in it are addressed, and the parents 'ability to protect their children is reviewed. In the event that these goals are impossible to achieve these goals, the victim needs to prepare a safe place of residence with a relative or with any governmental or charitable institution. In other cases, the perpetrator is isolated away from the family, especially when he fears that he will repeat his attacks on other members of the family or if he suffers from a disease that requires treatment. After ensuring the safety and security of the victim, we must try to find out if some other family members have been subjected to any harassment or sexual practices.

c) **Individual psychotherapy:** it is provided to the victim to heal the problems and wounds she suffered because of the sexual assaults that occurred. The treatment begins with catharsis, then clairvoyance, then the decision to change and then implementation, and all this takes place with the support of the therapist and in the presence of a healthy relationship in which the victim returns her vision for herself and then for others (especially adults) from a healthier perspective through which she modifies her distorted vision that was formed during her relationship with the aggressor. The therapist needs to help the victim express negative feelings such as anger, self-hatred, depression, guilt, and other accumulated feelings as a step to get rid of them or review them with a more positive vision. And many of the victims become unable to establish normal emotional or sexual relations later, due to the surrounding of painful memories or contradictory or forbidden feelings, and eventually, they reach a state of hatred of sexual relations, which leads to their repeated failure in marriage, and this all needs to be discussed and dealt with during Therapeutic sessions. The aggressor may also need such treatment, especially if he has a psychological disorder, personality disorder, or unsatisfied needs, or he is a victim of seduction on the part of the victim.

d) **Parents:** The condition of parents is assessed psychologically and socially by a specialised team in order to determine the extent of their ability to carry out their parental duties. In the event of a defect in this matter, they are subjected to a rehabilitation program in order to be able to carry out their duties towards their children, and in case this goal cannot be reached, a third-party caregiver for the children is selected so that they do not become victims of their parents' turmoil.

e) **Family Therapy:** Since incest leads to disruption of roles and relationships within the family, therefore it is necessary to restore the atmosphere of safety and tranquility, re-demarcate boundaries and arrange roles and relationships with healing the wounds that arose as a result of that forbidden relationship. This calls for repeated family therapy sessions in which the therapist helps family members to express their thoughts, feelings, struggles and difficulties to help them to re-adapt again on better levels. The therapist may need to play the role of the superego (the conscience) of this family, especially if the values are shaky, ambiguous, or weak in this family. This role continues until the value system grows within the family through their union with the therapist and his values. The healer here is a symbol of good parenting or responsible motherhood until one of the family members recovers and takes this role from the healer to protect the rest of the family from falling.

f) **Drug Treatment:** It is provided for cases with mental disorders such as anxiety, depression, addiction, schizophrenia, or mania. This treatment can be directed towards the victim or the aggressor, according to their needs. Considering the needs of family members and how to satisfy them in correct ways. The presence of family members who suffer from sexual deprivation for long periods and do not have sufficient relationships or activities to absorb their energy is considered a risk factor that could lead to sexual problems within the family. Therefore, the encouragement of marriage for unmarried family members or reforming the relationship between spouses who have been separated from each other for years. This is right as it has been observed such interrupted relation increases the likelihood that the sexually deprived husband of his wife will be involved in incest. Also, it is important to open horizons for successful and extended social relationships outside the family or direct energy towards practical successes or saturated hobbies. [https://ar.wikipedia.org]

Stories from Egypt (Eastern Society Examples):

Many stories about the incest phenomenon have been published, but the strangest one was when someone fell in love with his sister and practised immorality with her. They have enjoyed themselves in complete sexual relation with her full acceptance while he isolated himself at home to stay with her refusing to go out and deal with others. He was not satisfied with that but went to his father and asked to marry her, so the father shot him and surrendered himself to the police, which ruled him innocent.

The other one put sleeping tablets to his father in the juice, and after he slept, the son raped his father's beautiful wife.

The third one practised adultery with his daughter, and after arresting them in flagrante delicto, he explained that he was not accused, but he wanted to satisfy the desire of his spinster daughter instead of letting her satisfy her sexual desire with others and contaminating his reputation.

In one of the villages of Al-Santa Centre, a person practised immorality with his daughter-in-law, who was at the same time the daughter of his sister. After the matter became known, the resounding surprise came when the mother learned of these events, and she did not appear any astonished as she was also used to practising incest with him as her brother before her marriage.

The other example happened in Mahalla al-Kubra city after a young man proposed to a girl. After completing the sermon and during his visits to her family's home, he noticed the gazes of deprivation in the eyes of the mother of his bride. He played on the strings of the mother's femininity and flirted with her many times until she became unable to block him and fell into his clutches. She turned herself in, leaving behind her the customs and traditions of the people of the countryside and immersed in the forbidden pleasure. She continued in this manner until she became pregnant with a "thug" fetus in her guts. Even though it did not prevent her from completing the wedding of this traitorous young man on her deceived daughter, she tried to get rid of this fetus, but her fear of scandal did not help her until the fetus became nine months old. After the delivery process, everyone was surprised at what happened because her husband was dead.

She was pressured to find out the details of what happened, but the news came like a thunderbolt to everyone, especially the deceived daughter of her husband and mother. The daughter collapsed immediately, and she did not know what to do while she was four months pregnant.

Shedding light on this phenomenon that has spread in eastern societies is especially important to know what the reason for it is and what is behind the spread of that obscenity. Due to the severity of this phenomenon, the media began to search and find out the number of those who fell victim to this phenomenon and found that many cases hesitate to disclose what happened. Thus, it is difficult to know the size of the problem. Therefore, it is necessary to be careful when we talk about "incest" as it may be difficult to close this file when it is opened, and for sure, it has very risky consequences. However, the modest studies and inaccurate estimates remain useful for approximating the size of the phenomenon in a relative way to deal with it and give it the intention it deserves.

There are ethical factors represented in the weakness of the moral system within the family, or in psychology terms, the weakness of the superego in some or all family members. And in this family, we find some phenomena, including the habituation of its members, especially women who wear revealing or pornographic clothes in front of the rest of the family. In these families, we find that there is a weakness in the parental authority of the father or mother or both, and this leads to the collapse of the authority of control and binding and the collapse of the family law in general.

As for the opinion of religious scholars, they have expressed their strong dissatisfaction with this phenomenon, which threatens all religions with the danger posed to their children. They explained that the reason for the spread of this phenomenon is the lack of moral and religious awareness among many individuals, and this represents one of the greatest sins. The occurrence of this immorality begins through unintended light harassment and mockery between the girls and boys of the family. The matter develops to a looking at places of nakedness or friction coupled with the use of sexy words in the form of jokes. In the end, it leads to complete sexual practice and sins committed by a provoked person who cannot control his instincts. He becomes in a state that he cannot differentiate between a foreign woman and his mother or sister, as he's accustomed to watching nudity and immorality on television screens or the woman showing her nude body in front of her mahrams. This is a bigger calamity as many women believe that there are no limits to a woman's nakedness in front of her mahrams.

In Islam, the woman must know that all her body is considered naked, and she must not show it to her mahrams apart from the face, hair, neck, hand, arm, and feet to avoid any disobedience to God.

Regarding the view of the Christian religion, all laws and religions in all societies reject this bestial instinct, whose perpetrator only looks at his desires, and thus he resembles a foreign animal that has no mind. There is no difference between a Muslim and a Christian, as normal instinct rejects such actions.

4. Her Sexual Harassment

It is one of the forms of extortion, blackmailing, exploitation, and intimidation that is actioned by a man to a woman or the opposite in the workplace or in the street. It is exercised by who has the upper hand and the owner of power, influence, money, or attractiveness over the one who has not had these privileges. It is often costly, professionally, and financially because it ends with being fired from work or not being promoted or upgraded if the targeted refuses to respond to the harassment. Most of the time, it is done by the man towards the working woman under his official responsibility in the office, and it is rarely exercised by a woman towards a man if she has the authority.

In the developed world and in particular western societies, sexual harassment has reduced immensely during the last fifty years as the workplace is governed by strict policies and the street is controlled by laws that prevent such harassment. However, in the developing countries and, in the eastern societies, sexual harassment has increased in both the workplace and in the street as a greater number of women entered the job market, while there is a clear lack of policies and laws that prevent sexual harassment in both places. Moreover, these societies support the man through cultural beliefs and considerations or based on his distinct cultural background. Therefore, sexual harassment is very much expected from those who are prominent such as the occupants of religious, tribal, partisan, or security forces positions.

One of the characteristics of harassment is that it is not based on previous knowledge or the relationship between the harasser and the harassed, as it starts from a strange or sudden coincidence that is not planned or thought out. It was noticed that some of the women in the eastern societies like to hear soft emotional caresses passionate words from the harasser as an expression of his admiration for her beauty or her elegance which could lead to an innocent friendship that ends in a marital relationship.

Usually, the sexual harassment begins with the impudent initiative and the blatant audacity to achieve the goal of harassment, but it is not without subtle and skilful that involves insinuating and encoding the altruistic and attractive aspect of the external physical appearance (elegance, makeup, perfume or body movements when walking) coupled with sweet and romantic flowery phrases expressing false admiration (most of the time) and exaggerated and insincere fascination in order to reach his sexual goals. If he is unable to reach his goal in the official offices, the harassment turns into the infliction of administrative or financial penalties on the harassed side, such as delaying promotion, cutting a salary for several days, or moving her to a bad workplace. But there is no doubt that punishment is the last card that the harasser plays, despite his beginning with gentleness, tact, and verbal elegance.

Traditional Sexual Harassment: Sexual harassment includes but is not limited to the following:

- Letting her hear expressions of admiration and love.
- Touching her body, especially the erotic areas.
- Kissing her.
- Cuddling her.
- False Wooing to her.
- Artificial jealousy.
- Distressing or hurtful verbal harassment.

An example of sexual harassment prevalent in western society is the harassment of the waitress who works behind the bar or in a restaurant, where her work core is to serve the customer with kindness and softness in talking to him with friendliness and transparency and not to bother him or to talk to him with dryness or harsh in order to get tips and to win customers admiring her work style to secure her job continuity. This requirement makes her subject to many harassments and sexual harassment by customers who are frequent visitors to the restaurant or bar.

It is advisable to distinguish between the sincere desire to establish an honest social relationship and sexual

322

harassment, especially in Western society, which is dominated by anonymity among individuals due to its large size and the intertwining of its relational networks far from intimate-kinship connections that require the individual to start his relationship with the other with gentle words and courteous and sweet expressions in order to pave the way for marital relation which is not classified as sexual harassment. It is important to refer to the report published in the United Kingdom in 1985, which showed that there are 7/10 British female employees who have been subjected to sexual harassment in their workplaces and they have ended up taking sick leave from work or leaving their work permanently to get rid of the pressures and inconveniences or the sexual harassment they encounter at work. [Giddens. 1994. P. 188]

It can be said that it is a perverse behaviour, away from the friendly and honest relationship in animalistic instinct character, distorted the warm, honest behaviour, and affianced the high-level moral manners and corrupted people's confidence.

There is no escaping from the use of the state of harassment against women that occurs in the Egyptian street, which has become so usual that it has reached a state of social scourge after it represented behavioural deviations. The Saudi Al-Jazeera newspaper published in October 2007 stated: Harassment takes place daily, and all Egyptian women are exposed to it and before the eyes of security through ugly looks, sexual comments, and touches.

Harassment of women has become so commonplace on the Egyptian streets that observers consider it a social scourge that can impede the development process. The National Centre for Women's Rights defines harassment as (any inappropriate behaviour that has a sexual nature that harasses women and gives them a sense of insecurity) and the centre confirms that this phenomenon is described as a community cancer. Harassment takes place daily in public places and is not limited to a specific age group or social class. The Egyptian Centre for Women's Rights indicates that all Egyptian women are exposed to harassment, whether they are veiled or not.

"As soon as I go out to the street, I feel surrounded by erotic gazes," Rasha Shaaban, a twenty three year old woman who lives in Alexandria, said, adding: "I do not feel safe, and the problem is increasing day by day, and it has become so unbearable that I am thinking of leaving the country". According to the report of the National Centre for Criminal and Social Research, which is a state institution, crimes of a sexual nature are constantly increasing, and there are no official statistics about harassment, but two rape crimes occur every hour, according to a study of this centre, but 90% of the perpetrators of these crimes are unemployed and several factors stand behind. Besides the unemployment, the delay in the age of the marriage due to its high costs represent an important factor in the expansion of the sexual harassment phenomenon.

Most of them are Muslims, and Islam forbids sexual relations without marriage. Therefore, young people feel sexual repression as they cannot satisfy their sexual instinct. Engy Ghazlan, who is responsible for the campaign against harassment at the Egyptian Centre for Women's Rights, considers that men are emptying all their sexual repression and all their frustrations on women, whatever the causes of their frustrations. The Egyptian Centre for Women's Rights affirms that harassment is increasingly affecting economic development. Ghazlan says that there are women, and in particular young women stop going to work or university because of harassment, so how can development be achieved if there is no comprehensive mobilisation in society. She adds if the Ministry of Tourism wants to keep tourists, the security services should be stricter with people who harass women in the streets and confirm that if she goes to a country where she is not respected, she will never return to it.

This activist regret that the problem is not recognised by officials who deny the phenomenon, or at best, the government says yes, harassment occurs, but the media greatly exaggerate its size. According to the centre's study, only 12% of women who are subjected to harassment report to the police, which is evidence of a complete loss of confidence in the security services and in the judicial system. Egyptian bloggers said that last year, groups of youths harassed women on the second day of Eid in downtown Cairo in front of the police. One of those bloggers, Wael Abbas, who was present by chance when the incident occurred, said: They were aroused by the existing women whether they were veiled or not, and even the veiled women could not escape the harassment. The Ministry of Interior denied this information, confirming that it had not received any complaints. The Saudi Al-Jazeera Newspaper in October 2007, reported that "We note this important news that it includes several social issues that we can use to learn a lot about sexual harassment in one of the Arab societies, namely:

1. Although it is an annoying and offensive problem for women and girls, the security services are indifferent to it. They are not interested and do not admit its existence. This is shameful because it represents witnessing harassment in society in the streets and shops in front of people's eyes.

2. Because harassment affects the reputation and honour of the girl, she does not inform the police, security, or officials about what happened to her so that it does not turn into a scandal that will reflect negatively on her and her family. This is because the Arab community do not blame the harasser and considers the woman as the starter because she is wearing a short skirt or tight dress, and by moving her body in a sexy way, she ignites the young male energy which is polite, bold, and daring and behaves with virility, attractiveness and other qualities of which the young man is proud, and it is reinforced by the Arab community.

3. The lack of complete confidence in the security services and the judicial system when people look at such moral abuses because society, in general, does not see it as such.

4. Harassment is not restricted to a single age group, but more than that (among young people and others) and is not limited to street children but includes students, employees, military, and all social strata. It is socially acceptable among males more than females, reflecting its social standards of superior masculinity and dominance over femininity. Even on public morals, transparent behaviour, and anonymity in urban social relations.

5. Weak customary social controls within civil society and the lack of serious attention given by official controls.

6. Sexual harassment is a behaviour that is not appropriate for a civilised and modernised person because its goal is the sexual drive and not something else.

7. It gives the impression of the woman who is harassed by her feeling of insecurity when the young man harasses her and that she needs someone to protect her from her family or relatives when she goes out of her home.

8. Most of the harassers are unemployed or school dropouts.

9. There is a good reason for this collective behavioural deviation to delay the age of marriage among young people because of its high costs in society, which causes it to deplete its sexual energy through sexual harassment and engaging in other deviant practices.

10. And there is sexual repression, which is another motivation in pushing young people to deviate and harass the opposite sex.

11. Due to unemployment and late marriage age, the young man found that sexual harassment is the easiest way for him is to empty his sexual repression and his frustrations on the women he does not know, and he found many of them in the streets, shops, parks, train stations and parties.

Electronic Sexual Harassment:

In the previous part, the traditional sexual harassment model was shown in examples from Egyptian society, but electronic sexual harassment is a new type of harassment that is performed through the Internet. Examples from British society are considered in this part to demonstrate the exploitation and blackmail of the young British woman. It does not reflect the abuse of the owner of power and influence over her loss, but rather reflects a new case called (porn revenge) or pornographic revenge that involves a state of blackmail and exploitation in distorting the image of the opposite sex and assaulting it). In the sense that harassment represents aggression based on inequality between adolescents and not between the responsible and the dependent, it reflects the power of the male over the female. It is peer harassment, not an employee and worker harassment in the workplace.

327

The harassment of teenage girls over the Internet in London was revealed in a scientific study conducted by the British charity Child Net. It provoked great reactions in British society and caused a lot of confusion after the study concluded that about a third of teenage girls in the UK are subjected to sexual harassment through social networking sites and from teenage boys of the same age.

The study selected a sample of (1559) adolescent girls whose ages range from 13 to 17 years. It confirmed that 31% of them had been subjected to sexual harassment, which includes gossip about their behaviour and the pressures they are subject to to exchange shameful images with boys. Also, psychological abuse in the form of bullying through inappropriate comments on the regular pictures that they put on their pages and facing what is known as the painful and hurtful pornographic revenge. In comparison, 10% of them said that something had gone beyond all this and amounted to a threat of assault.

The study found that cases of sexual harassment usually occur on social media, especially via (WhatsApp) and (Snapchat). A Facebook official stated that the company takes this issue seriously and that it is currently training young people in secondary schools in England for the sake of support and helping teenagers who are experiencing online harassment.

Among the results of this study, 23% of adolescents witnessed the publication of inappropriate photos of adolescent girls without their consent. 8% of them admitted to doing this work. 53% try to ignore these matters, 56% find them very embarrassing, 49% are afraid of the parents' reaction and deny them access to the Internet, and 47% are worried about what things will reach in the future.

This is in terms of results, as for the healing of these wounds and psychological abuse expressed in painful and traumatic (revenge porn), the British government has prevented the exercising of (revenge porn) or what is known as upskirting, which is the sharing of her inappropriate pictures or videos to a third party without her consent. It has also pursued fake people who assume fake names to assault teenagers.

The government is reflecting at the present time the preparation of a new guideline explaining how schools deal with harassment and developing educational resources in schools in order to be able to prevent harassment of students via the Internet and the development of the application (Snapchat) to deal with the complaint within a period not exceeding a few hours. [Saidity Magazine1956 Issue 23/6/2018]

Although the British society is an urban, civilised, democratic and educated society, its teen girls have not got immunity to electronic sexual harassment in terms of (revenge porn) or (pornographic revenge) carried out by the male (perpetrator). As a preventive remedy for this emotional wound and the exposing of the reputation and dignity of the female, the British government has done the following:

1. Pursuing fake people who use fake names to assault teenage girls.
2. Developing educational resources in schools to be able to prevent online harassment of teenage girls.
3. Developing the (Sunny Chat) application to deal with complaints within a period not exceeding a few hours.
4. Preparing a new guide that explains how schools deal with harassment.

This is, in fact, a preventive and not curative treatment, but it does not equalise between the sexes because equality requires educating the adolescent males to not harass the female because their action is a weakening of high moral controls by exploitation and aggression via sexual harassment to blackmail, rape and persecute the weak element of the society.

C. HER RAPE BY GLOBALISATION - SEXUAL INDUSTRY

The most recent rape in the history of mankind is the cosmic rape (globalisation) that emerged at the beginning of the twenty-first century through the feminine sex industry that uses the female body and her sexual attraction as a biological-human commodity that is invested in modern luxury life by hotel and tourist companies, nightclubs, massage parlours, gambling and card companies Automated instant exchange in most of the rich and advanced industrially and urban areas of the world, transcending geographical boundaries and customs laws. These companies, their male owners, raped the feminine dignity and humanity and raped her desire to marry, her motherhood and the stability of her life, which in turn turned her into an enslaved slave to the owners of the hotel and tourist companies, nightclubs, gambling, and massage parlours, so they eradicated her from the social fabric to live alone in the conviction of vice, far from the family atmosphere, moral chastity and religion.

The observer and the monitor of the major developments that prevail in the human community in the civilised world find that one of the most widespread and interesting phenomena among civilised societies is (prostitution), which has been dealt with three decades ago in a new, modern, and organised way. Prostitution has become rapidly and freely spread, not hindered by legal barriers among the countries of the world. Its organisation attracts attention and not as it was half a century ago (criminal, stalked and secret), but has become widely and overwhelmingly practised, which has drawn the attention of workers in commercial markets who deal with their goods and commercial activities in a material way. To facilitate the transfer and exchange of their goods through service agencies that serve their activities such as (hotels, airlines, nightclubs, drinking bars, massage parlours, instant exchange card companies, and everything that the trader needs in his global trade).

It goes without saying that prostitution was carried out through individual interaction in brothels without the use of commercial agencies. But thirty years ago, that is, after the fall of the Berlin Wall and the totalitarian regimes in Eastern Europe, unemployment, poverty, migration, and individuals took refuge in these societies, prompting women to trade their bodies in order to obtain a living. As is the custom of merchants and criminal gangsters, they were exploited in order to trade them. Then they were used, as well as children, as a sexual commodity to be trafficked, especially after the disappearance of legal obstacles during the structural collapse (social construction) of the Europe eastern bloc when the sexual action became part of enjoyment and entertainment.

And when this happened considering globalisation, prostitution has become a sequential and interconnected process in its circles that moves between countries of the world, and every link supports the connecting link. A ring, therefore, was formed that represents the chain hotels with several branches in several cities of the world. The airline companies also formed a ring utilising their several outlets

331

in many capitals and cities of the world. A special ring has emerged for nightclubs with branches scattered in the Western world, as well as the presence of sex clubs providing their services in major and famous cities. In addition to that, there is a ring for massage parlours (massage), gaming halls, and companies for instant exchange cards that have economic interests from the introduction of the sex tourism industry.

Prostitution

So, prostitution has become an economic activity over the sexual activity that requires the services used in the trade of goods and commodities in the commercial markets bypassing the legal barriers that prohibit the practice of sex as a commodity. This is a new situation that appeared in the last quarter of the last century, so it is considered as one of the contemporary social problems. It is new because of its rapid automatic and technical subordination to global trade that transcends borders and restrictions and interacts with major events occurring in the countries of the world, such as civil, regional and international war, mass international migration, the collapse of political systems, and the displacement of thousands of owners of higher government positions who used to govern and manage their institutions.

Whereas sociologists represent the sensitive and poetic sensing of what is happening from the strangeness of matters and events in society, whether negative or positive, this case was monitored by the social researcher (Kathleen Barry) in 1991, who alerted scholars in sociology to this case which she called (The Informed Sex Industry). [Kendall. 2012. P. 13]

The following are the increasing reasons for prostitutes under other circumstances than the ones mentioned above, namely: -

a. Times during which a long war is far from the homes of the soldiers and their families.
b. Trade far from the merchants 'residence and livelihood that is, far from their families.
c. The presence of military barracks for soldiers.

Such additional variables attracted organised crime men to the slave market and the use of prostitutes as a sexual commodity to be invested, and we found this growth and demand for prostitutes during the Vietnam War and the wars of El Salvador and Bosnia that appeared on television screens of many bars that many pubs' owners forced Korean women to offer sex to American soldiers and all proceeds go to the owner of the bar.

It is evident that prostitution did not emerge as an industry and had nothing to do with commercial globalisation; rather, it existed centuries before that. It was introduced as an industry by the beneficiaries, such as smugglers (local and international), organised criminal groups, war and arms dealers, owners of bars and nightclubs, and military and commercial acts practised far from the prostitutes' homes. The instant electronic communication and the new World Trade Organization policies, which eliminated the borders and geographical restrictions as the main mechanism of globalisation, have greatly contributed to the conversion of prostitution into the commercial sex industry to serve the interests of merchants, smugglers, criminals, night club and five-star hotels owners, and regions tourism.

No harm in pointing out the negative effects of the globalised sex industry in causing the spread of the HIV virus (AIDS) to risky levels for those seeking sexual pleasure. In its initial outbreak, the Japanese health institutions have alerted the people about the involved risk and the deadly effect of the HIV virus, but they could not control it.

The negative impact of the globalised sex industry is not limited to what was mentioned, but there is the effect of the wide disparity between poor and rich regions. Women and children are usually trafficked from poor regions to be as a commercial commodity subject to sale and purchase in rich regions, such as Europe, the Middle East and North America, where the globalised sex industry is promoted to those who seek seeking sexual pleasure.

Some women working in the sex trade pin their hopes on establishing relationships with their clients in order to go out to other countries to live with a better standard of living. But their hopes are often evaporated, they become frustrated and disappointed in their endeavour, and their personal ambitions are not fulfilled.

So, the globalised sex industry has serious negative effects on the general society in which it resides, such as the deadly health impact (AIDS) and the widening of the economic gap between the rich and poor countries of the world. This means that it is a destructive industry that sacrifices health, morals and human of the human race to serve the interests of merchants and organised criminal groups. As the globalised sex industry is universal with complex social, health, political and cultural implications, it is considered as one of the long-term problems.

D. HER RAPE BY ARTISTIC TECHNOLOGICAL INDUSTRY – PORNOGRAPHY

This rape is manifested in displaying models of pornographic and obscene pictures of the girl while she is naked and in positions erotic to the male. It is used by artistic and photographic companies for financial gain by using the girl as material for their enrichment and fame. This commercial activity is respectless for the woman's dignity, femininity, humanity, decency, and life. Rather, she obtains material temptations or the use of violence and cruelty to force her to perform nudity and picture her while she has sex with a man. It is a cinematic, television and photographic industry popular in special markets. These films and pictures have negative repercussions on females, including: -

1. Provoking male sexual arousal.
2. Encouraging male violence against women.
3. Humiliating her humanely.
4. Demeaning her socially.
5. It takes away her civil rights.
6. An expression of her mistreatment as a human being.
7. Making her a factor encouraging moral decay and moral decline.
8. Emphasis on her obeisance and submission to the man and making her a tempting vessel for his sexual desire. Awareness

This is on the level of a woman, but at the level of a man, it motivates him to perform violent behaviour and assault against the woman and nurtures his sexual orientation and violence to her. Educated, respectable, and activist women in feminist movements reject this cheap and poignant art because it offends the status and role of women in society. And multiplies the troubles of gender-based feminist organisations in their demand for equality between women's and men's rights. This art also faces denouncing and reproaching from fanatical clerics of all religions.

In 2006 a study was conducted in Denmark on a sample of 100 young men and 100 young women of ages of 18-30 years to know the effect of pornography on them. The experimental group was shown pornographic pictures and films displaying rape, gender stereotyping, sexual differentiation, and violence. When comparing the viewing results of the experimental sample group with the control specimen, they found that the experimental group was affected by it emotionally and stood negatively against all violence. That is, it submitted to the support of the woman and emphasised that this image crystallises violence and aggression against the female sex. This is the goal of the United Nations' rejection of these films because they lead to violence and sexual aggression against the female. [Thomsen. 2007. P. 27)

This is unique rape and different from the rape of social culture and the individual rape; thus, it deserves more details.

When archaeologists during the Victorian era began to systematically search for ancient monuments in Bombing, they were shocked by what they found. Between the stucco drawings on gypsum and the beautiful works of art were distributed here and there, they found many drawings and sculptures that were sexually explicit, and their nature is shameful that disgusted the authorities. They, therefore, put them in secret museums and invented the name (pornographic art) based on the two Greek words, (Burnie and Gravos), which mean (writing about prostitutes) to classify these discoveries as scandalous. Today, the term pornography is defined as the depiction of sexual behaviour in books, photographs, statues, and movies in a manner that targets sexual arousal.

Pornography is widespread these days and seems to be acceptable in most modern societies. It was previously confined to the notorious cinemas and prostitution neighbourhoods, but now it is very prevalent in many societies. In the United States alone, pornography has generated more than ten billion dollars annually.

Some proponents of pornography encourage it as a way to restore a boring marital relationship to life. One writer says that it stimulates the imagination and provides instructions for sexual pleasure. Others claim that it encourages frankness and openness about sexual matters. [wol.Jw.org]

The Content of Pornography

It is a contemporary social problem in the modern era (the era of advanced technology, personal freedom, and free expression) involving sexual nudity and obscene images expressing pornography, consisting of two types of networks:

1. Network of contemplative thoughts that can be perceived and known. This network refers to the realism of the social situation expressing the problem. The materiality of this network depends on pornographic and obscene literature and art, expressing the behaviour and attitudes of individuals.

2. Network of the content of literary - moral with significance. This network represents the moral objection to the mechanism of literature and fictional art because it represents false imagery, unreal, that allows the individual to express what is forbidden and forbidden without engaging in forbidden and forbidden behaviour. This is the content of pornography.

337

Pornography became available and widespread among the people via the numerous numbers of websites on the Internet within reach of everyone, regardless of the educational level, class, ethnicity, or religion. It reached homes, offices, shops, and all arenas to allow seeing and watching blatant pornographic pictures and movies on PC, mobile phones as well as TV channels. Social media and its real-time chatting facilities have expanded the event to be more interactive in showing sexual scenes of different tempting positions and exchanging pornographic images such as nudeness and sexual positions. Such a tendency and trend towards this sex industry drives many venture capitalists to invest their money in this industry regardless of its undermining of moral and religious disciplines. The budget for this type of film industry was estimated at half-billion dollars per year, excluding the cost of pornographic magazines.

Social media networks promote nudity and pornography in the form of advertisements to industrial products related to the sexual process, such as oils, perfumes, sexual stimulants, and artificial sexual organs. Therefore, workers in this industry gain enormous financial wealth, especially for women who earn (50) % More than men. The woman's gain depends on her external appearance, attractiveness, beauty, and gracefulness of her body. As for men, their financial gain depends on their ability, sexual energy, and sexual performance. Nevertheless, they see themselves as exploited by this industry.

As for social analysts, they see the prosperity of this industry as the increase in demand for it by young people and adolescents who have a desire to watch every new technological innovation that addresses the issue of gender and lure investors towards this industry and continue to search for new technologies to produce newer innovations in order to continue their presence in the pornographic art market. In addition to the sexual practices provided by social media, it attracts the attention and desires of young people and adolescents more than what magazines and comic books offer.

It is worth mentioning the interest of government officials in America in this national industrial phenomenon, which relied on technological innovation to enter it on special and conservative activities that were prohibited. In the beginning, and specifically in the eighties of the twentieth century, I researched the relationship of pornography with sexual crimes and hostile and anti-social behaviours, and there was no definite and confirmed connection between them. But after the eighth decade of the same century, these authorities found a link between sexual crime and the exacerbation of male aggression towards females. They also discovered that pornography stimulates male lust for females as well as increases the tendency of young adolescents to engage in sexual relations with children. Then these authorities expressed their view that pornography represents a danger to community health. As for American sociologists, they do not agree with the statement that there is a link between pornography and violence and male domination of females because they believe that such control does not occur through an external influence. [Keenall. 2012. P. 142].

In addition, more than 80% of pornographic films display male control over females and their violent exploitation. Most of them display physical violence by men to women where half of the women were raped with real practice of physical violence. It is confirmed that pornography contributes to the aggressive behaviour of its viewers and at the same time did not raise a situation for censorship of watching pornographic films and purchasing their artificial resources.

It goes without saying that pornography is not seen in an overt manner, but rather secretly and in disguise, which makes the studying of its associated problem difficult. All factual field information on this problem is therefore scarce and limited and only obtained through the observation of the visitors at the shops selling sexual industrial products, magazines, movies, and steroids. Most of these frequent visitors are relatively educated white, married, and middle-class men between the ages of 25-65. At the same time, another study found that more educated young men are more likely than women to watch and enjoy porn movies due to the type of family upbringing for the gender role it has. Societies whose culture is (patriarchal - masculine) build their children on the masculinity and virility of a man and the femininity of a girl. That is, the man's control over women and her submission to him is one of the criteria of social culture. Such societies accept the viewing of sexual oracles that display a woman's submissiveness to the man sexually and her acceptance of all kinds of oppression and sexual violence. They value the man's sexual oppression and cruelty in his sex with her and the woman's subservience and submission to the cruelty of the man.

As for societies that do not consider the patriarchal culture, women do not yearn to watch erotic films out of respect for their dignity and femininity. Recently, however, women have shown a tendency towards acquiring sexual magazines and pornographic literature, but they are less revealing about their sexual relationship and their frankness with them. On the class level, pornography is more acceptable to poor boys than the rich due to their family upbringing, which lacks sexual education and the biological health of men and women.

Is Pornography Real Social Problem?

Despite many claims to justify the quality of modern life, it is a social problem at the individual, family, community, and security levels. It leads directly or indirectly to the man's rape of the woman and fuels violent behaviour during sexual intercourse. And since pornography is watched by young people secretly and not in public, then its viewers live in constant fear that their parents or friends will discover what they are doing. This fear does not only cause anxiety in the present but also prevents sexual pleasure in the future and when the mind of the young man or girl is contaminated with sexual images. It leads to vivid memories of these images or scenes that pop up at unwanted times that cannot be predicted or controlled. Moreover, the young man who filled his mind with pictures of beautiful and unrealistic girls, when connected in the future, will not appreciate the beauty of his wife, no matter how attractive she is, and he will not feel in his sexual relationship with her. Not only that, but women are seen as insatiable sexual objects, which leads to him becoming more hostile towards women. Finally, dealing with pornographic art makes young people desire to obtain these materials and images increases until they become addicted to them because of the sexual excitement provided by these materials and then increase their desire to obtain abnormal and strange materials that may last for several weeks, months or even years and may also continue after marriage.

The problem of cultural appropriation that fed by pornography on everything is sexual gives the impression as if the culture endorses and confirms everything that is perverted. In addition to its contribution to the degeneration of moral values and addiction to sex that led to sexual diseases and lack of respect for women in viewing them as a means of pleasure only, pornography represents a decline in the morality of men towards women.

This art emerged at the end of the last century and is still flourishing today. It is classified as a social problem because of the effect it leaves on its viewers who go to addiction to sex, afflicted by its diseases with total disrespect for women. Instead of viewing it as a temporary means of enjoyment, it occupies their lives and may crystallise marital problems between spouses. It may cause disagreement about the practices shown in sex movies and clips by sex professionals (prostitutes). The husband expects a similar practice from the wife, while a chaste wife has no experience in sexual diversity and does not know more than what she has learned from him about the sex, and hence it could generate distortion and confusion among its viewers.

This is on the individual level; as for the family level, it transforms the romantic, affection and emotional relationship between the spouses into a sexual goal that is devoid of feelings, admiration, love, and spiritual feeling between them. The addicted husband to pornography looks to the wife as a discharge to empty his sexual energy in her without any romantic feelings.

On the cultural level, when pornographic art nourishes social culture with its mechanical, not spiritual ways and innovations, then social culture is stripped of its elements that regulate the marital bond and the family upbringing of children. It dilutes or violates, and it loosens up and tends to affect marital and family ties. Pornography may enter an external factor in arousing lust sexuality among adolescents, and young men are driven to abnormal sexual relations, such as masturbation, homosexuality, incest, or rape. Therefore, pornography is a disintegrating factor for normal social life on the individual, family, and cultural levels. It is yet considered a short-term social problem because its size does not exceed the youth, investors, and prostitutes.

The beneficiaries of this art are investors in the artistic field and the sex industry, prostitutes and traffickers of women and children. It goes without saying, then, that it is a conditional problem confined to modern societies that have been caused by technological developments and faced with objections and complaints from intellectuals, officials, conservatives, and members of the advanced generation. This is because its effects are incompatible with the customary and situational social controls, and it is not welcomed as long as it produces pain for people and affects the health of society in its nourishment of sexual rape, incest, and violent behaviour at the same time. No one denies that this problem is one of the secretions of social change that has been nourished by technological innovations related to the advent of the Internet and modern cameras in light of the unknown relationships in modern society or the widening gap between the poor and the rich and the lack of upbringing of children based on healthy sexual education and the promotion of value standards for proper behaviour. All of this crystallises a social problem that pornography has produced.

E. HER RAPE BY CRIMINAL GANGS
I. Trafficking Her

It is a contemporary global crime that occurs during times of civil, regional, and global wars, the economic siege on a specific country, the global economic recession, the spread of terrorism, and the fall of political regimes. That is, when violent disturbances occur in which the official controls and national political governance are absent, they affect the coordination of the social structure and disintegrate them (such as the family, political, educational, administrative, financial, judicial and security systems) so that security, political, military, and customary chaos occurs. This non-standard and unstable situation is exploited by organized gangs and global mafias to take advantage of the lack of legal legitimacy and security control in stealing children, girls and women, smuggling them forcibly and forcibly to other countries and raping them and selling them to merchants and gangs specialized in the white slave trade. But this does not mean that this trade was not prevalent in history. Human rights were prevalent, but not at this density. According to the United Nations statistics in 2006, the number of traffickers ranged between 700 thousand to 2 million girls and women every year, and their profits of trade ranged between 5 to 7 billion dollars every year. In 2006, 50 thousand girls were deported to the United States and Western Europe. Also, 50,000 girls were forced into the sex trade. The percentage of trafficked women was 87%, and girls 54% [Thomsen. 2007. Pp. 27-28].

This crime means transforming a woman who is powerfully and financially weak and socially and politically oppressed by fraud or force and coercion into a human commodity of great long-term investment by exploiting her body in this investment or harnessing her for works contrary to her human value. Therefore, developed countries and humanitarian organizations that defend the rights of women have stood up to fighting this inhuman oppression and enslaved transformation because it does not represent the evolutionary stage through which the human being is going through at the present time. For example, women, girls, and children who are looking for a destination other than their country to live in but cannot reach it by legal means (legal immigration). They, unfortunately, fall into the hand of these gangs where they are subject to material and sexual exploitation, forcing them to work in activities that are humiliating for human value and strip their personalities independence and depriving them of their individual freedom. All of this turns them into submissive slaves and obedient to cruel persecution that has no human mercy. By capitalizing on the suffering of these poor women, these gangs obtain huge sums of money illegally by specialized merchants in the search for these social strata that appear quickly and clearly in poor (economically) or politically collapsed or militarily defeated societies (the losers in its war with a powerful state) or in which administrative, financial, and political corruption prevails or under economic besieged.

It is not surprising to say that these merchants do not operate in their trade alone, but rather have commercial links with organized criminal groups that help them carry out their trade and obtain large sums of money with exposure to few financial or judicial fines compared to the drugs' smuggling and arms trading. It is a popular business at the present time due to the collapse of many political, communist, and single-party regimes after the Cold War and regional wars in the Middle East. It was facilitated by the flourishing of globalization activities and the communication and transportation facilities that brought it above and beyond financial standards and their control of traditional and ethical standards, as well as the existence of tyrannical political regimes that use force, cruelty, and brutality in their dealings with their citizens.

All this attracted the ambitions of some outlaw traders, quick profit-seekers, escapees from legal liability, and dealers with local, regional, and international groups and gangs specializing in prostitution, sexual exploitation and the sex industry (pornography). Such gross work requires a system of division of labour implemented by several criminal groups (local, regional and international) that have experience in luring, kidnapping, smuggling, deportation and immigration laws and have a relationship with those with influence in the countries of origin and destination. A trade that has less harm to its workers but generates abundant money for a long period of time because merchants deal with children, girls, and women, and it is in constant demand, and it has (tourist) and seasonal demand in wealthy countries.

It is worth noting that women traffickers are recruiting and taking girls and women by force from Eastern European countries after the fall of the socialist camp, China, Thailand, Africa, New Zealand, and Australia. [Thomsen. 2007. P. 28]

It is worth pointing out that most of those interested in gender are educated women who are socially and humanly aware are defending the rights of women and girls, who live in such conditions and are subject to rape, sexual exploitation, and sex trafficking. These women relied on United Nations resolutions issued in 1945, which called for the protection of women's human rights. And proposed 20 mechanisms by which to raise the status of women and deal with them as a human being of equal value to men, and not to turn the woman into a victim that criminal gangs exploit, taking advantage of her weakness, poverty and want, to practice all kinds of violence (physical, sexual, verbal and living) against her. They reap huge sums of money from women's sexual exploitation in prostitution, which amounts to between 7 and 12 million dollars. This is one reason, among other reasons, for the proliferation of criminal gangs to trade in women as the risk of working in them is much less than trafficking in weapons and drugs. Also, the weakness and backwardness of the legal rules prevailing in most countries of the world encourage the gangs to proceed in their disgraced action. These laws do not punish and criminalize the traffickers and the suppliers of prostitutes to the prostitution markets.

All this prompted women's rights defenders to stand up to fight her trafficking, but there are two groups of these women: the first group accepted the woman's decision to choose her work in prostitution but condemned the trafficking of her sex, and the second group condemned the forced and imposition of the work of women in prostitution and considered it a brutal and barbaric act. So, this is the position of defenders of women's rights towards trafficking in her and her sexuality, and it supports United Nations resolutions in this regard and a supporter of civil laws in most countries of the world.

The trafficking in women is therefore linked to sexual exploitation, sex industry, prostitution, and other commercial sexual services. 700,000 thousand victims of women and girls fell in the hand of trafficking gangs in 2002 in Europe and Asia, and the proceeds of this trade ranged between 150 to 200 million euros. [Lehti and Aroma. 2002. P. 1]

II. Enslaving Her

Slavery stipulates the right to own property after trafficking in women, which includes investment and exploitation, and the ensuing oppression, violence and sexual exploitation in prostitution and the sex industry. Accordingly, the financial investment in prostitution and the sex industry takes place in the country of destination (the country of investment), and this is similar to the right to own property in slavery. Then slavery requires that trafficked women be forced to work in the destination country in difficult and dirty works against their will and desire.

It is worth noting that slavery involves the recruitment, transfer, harbouring and concealment of women, the practice of threat, force, oppression, and coercion with the compulsion to take wages from the person in control and extort them into forced labour or provide services by force.

Slavery requires ownership and control over the slaves because they are treated by their traffickers and dealers as commodities or merchandise owned by the trader. In addition, they are losing their legal personalities, and the merchant has lifelong ownership of the women who are trafficked as they are deprived of their personal, civil and human rights. They have no right to move from one place to another except with the order of the trader, and they strip them of their property if they own something. Not only that, but they are not entitled to purchase or own anything; even they cannot own their selves because they are mortgaged to the merchant.

Every crime has a victim or victims, and trafficking in women crime is no different, but the number of its victims is quite large, and all of them are of young ages who are financially weak and have no power to defend or save themselves. What is striking about the crime scene is the presence of advertisements in the source country through newspapers, magazines, and advertisements on the Internet and through brokers, often women or concealed or misleading agencies that offer employment opportunities in European Union countries such as maids, nannies or workers in nightclubs, models, strip dancers, tour guides, or hotel employees. Through these advertisements, prey of the crime is hunted and recruited from the start in prostitution, but even in this case, the merchants do not fulfil their promises. That is, they receive less than what they were agreed upon in the source country.

The Baltic States are practising personal conscription instead of relying on public announcements. In these countries, women are recruited through kidnapping, and this is what happened in Albania, Kosovo, and the other part reported that they sold their daughters to traffickers.

It is inevitable to say that when the victim is recruited, she is under control during her transfer to the country of destination or when she passes from countries before her arrival to the country of refuge (destination). However, through these stages (recruitment, deportation, and transportation), various types of violence against her are used. Torture, ill-treatment, rape, and sometimes even murder (this case occurs in particular in the Balkan countries in which the most hideous and harsh methods of violence were practised on victims inside and outside the Balkan countries where this practice became familiar).

Then there is another method that traders and brokers follow with the victim, which is forcing her to take drugs in order to be controlled easily without resistance and to be addicted and submissive to the brokers and dealers to supply her with drugs and resort to them in their residence to obtain drugs, which increases the debt that was recorded on them by the exploiter (the broker or the trader). This is right because some of the victims agree with the exploiter to pay them the travel costs and the fees for the recruitment, which they will pay it back when they get their wages in the future. This debt increases over time and with many merchants until they reach the stage of slavery.

Countries of recruitment	Countries of slavery (sexual and physical)
Moscow	Germany and Austria
Czech Republic	German and Austria
Ukraine	Germany and Austria
Slavia	Germany and Austria
Hungary	Germany and Austria
Middle East	Greece and Italy
North Africa	Spain and Italy
Turkey	Italy and Austria
South and Central America	Portugal and Spain
Iraq and Iran	Germany, Austria, Greece, and the Netherlands
Georgia	Germany, Austria, Sweden, and Norway
China	United States of America

This table was taken from the book New Crimes [Omar. 2011. p. 93].

One of the oddities of things is the emergence of the white slave trade as a profitable business in Georgia, in which the professional criminals and government employees in the highest and ruling positions in Georgia contributed to them. They called them the law thieves in Georgia. They represent large numbers and have a wide network of communications and transportation and have continuous relations with criminal organizations outside Georgia, especially Russia, Ukraine, and rich governments like the United States of America, as they worked in prostitution, and there are more people forced and exploited in menial jobs which were also victims of deception and filthy material temptations. [Glonti. 2004. Pp. 70 - 71]

It is worth mentioning the link between trafficking in women, sexual exploitation and prostitution, as more than 80% of the victims of this trafficking are from Southeast Europe. It has become a major area for trafficking in women and employing them as prostitutes, and up to 15% of them represent a source of performing other erotic and sexual services. As for their approximate ages, they are between 15-18 years old, and 10-30% of them are less than 18 years old. At the same time, there are ages above 18 for women, as well as children. In Sweden, which provided annual estimates of women who are trafficked into their countries, they are estimated at 500,000 thousand women for the purpose of sexual exploitation, where they are exported to European Union countries. According to recent estimates made by the United Nations, the total number of trafficking in women in the European Union countries amounted to 20,000 thousand. As for the United States 'estimates of this type of trafficking in the world, it reached 500,000 thousand female victims. The total of trafficking in women across the Balkans is 200,000, and according to estimates by the US Department of the Interior Affairs, the number it put forward was 700,000 victims. [Lehti et al. 2004. P. 115]

Finally, we present the Iraqi girl who was trafficked after her kidnapping (after the American occupation of Iraq in 2003) and the luring and seduction of her by women who used to work in prostitution. Usually, this girl is young in age and from a financially poor family looking for work in order to live. She lives in a structurally, ethically, and politically collapsed society. She was recruited after being kidnapped by brokers to Jordan and Syria in the form of

351

tourists or visitors. They raped her virginity and forced her to have sex while photographing her more than once and with more than one client so that she cannot think of returning if she wants as they are threatening her by handing over her videos to her family.

As for her enslavement, she is housed in a special building in Syria, where people are encouraged to approach her because she is protected by a personal guard, and the person who brought her to work with him provides what she needs. No one is allowed to reach her place of residence, leave with her, or ask her about anything related to her or the nature of her work. Then work in several nightclubs and present a program in each club, and the profits that she sometimes achieves per night amount to $ 500, except for the (tip), which is what the customer does or gives her from the sums while she performs the dance show, and if one of the customers wants to take a picture with her, he pays her $6.0. As for working in furnished apartments, the wages of every Iraqi girl who works as a prostitute range from 10 to 20 dollars an hour. Usually, the pimp broker orders her to achieve sexual and physical pleasure for the customers, and she must give the impression that she is happy and enjoying sex with them no matter how offensive, humiliating, or violent towards her. This means that she has been transformed into a human commodity that is financially invested in favour of the criminal gang and deprives her of the simplest requirements of normal life for the female, such as marriage and childbearing. Confiscating her sexual instinct for the benefit of clients, stripping her of maternal feelings, and amputating (cutting) her blood ties to her parents, brothers, and relatives. She became a soulless body that is used for sex trafficking for the benefit of the middleman and the female human gang. It has been embalmed socially, psychologically, and instinctively to make her a machine for illicit investment, and it is located between the two jaws, the first one represents the threat of death if she does not respond to the gang's orders, and the second represents the provision of sexual pleasure to customers regardless of their mood, personality, or shape. This is human slavery in the twenty-first century for women.

CHAPTER 7: THE THIRD TYPE OF GENDER

INITIATION

A. LACK OF CLARITY OF GENDER AND AMBIGUITY OF ITS KNOWLEDGE
B. SOCIAL TRENDS OF SEX
C. THE REALITY OF THE THIRD TYPE OF GENDER IN SOME SOCIETIES OF THE WORLD
D. EUNUCHS
E. EUNUCHS AND IMPROVISED ONES IN THE THREE DIVINE RELIGIONS
F. COMMENTARY AND FOLLOW-UP

CHAPTER 7
THE THIRD TYPE OF GENDER

A. <u>LACK OF CLARITY OF GENDER AND AMBIGUITY OF ITS KNOWLEDGE</u>

It comes from the physiological nature of the fetus, as there is a case of hermaphrodites in that one-third of the children who are born with female and male sexual organs or who do not have clarity in their genitals, such as the clitoris that resemble the penis of the male. It is a deviation in the rules of the duality of the shape and form of the fetus. It requires separating the sex into two different and distinct types that are not alike to have the biological transfer of an individual from one sex to another. It must be done before the child reaches three years old because, within this period, the child's gender identity is determined as he learns the behaviour of his gender and its difference from the other one, and from it, he begins to realize himself, his self-awareness settles so that he begins to act according to it. If the child has learned the behaviour of the girl and continues to repeat it through his interaction with his parents and brothers, then he will act spontaneously and smoothly with the behaviour of the girl.

Parents' acknowledgement of changing the genitals of their child is extremely embarrassing and controversial because the child has no opinion or decision to change his genitals, in addition to the fact that the after the performance of surgical operation for the change cannot be returned back to what it was. However, it can be performed after the child grows up and becomes more mature to decide for himself when to undergo the process of changing his genitals, especially since it needs hormonal treatments for the process to be completed successfully, and this is especially important

355

for the components of gender identity development (gender). [Spriggs, Merle and Julian, Savalescu. 2006. p. 25]

We now come to the distinction between the scientific terms for transsexuality. The transsexual person is different from the individual in whom the male and female characteristics overlap together (intersex). The transsexual is originally male or female but psychologically believes that he or she belongs to the opposite sex. If he is male and bears female characteristics, he feels that he is feminine, or if the individual is a female and bears masculine characteristics, then she feels that she is a tomboy and belongs to the masculinity. Whether the intersex is male or female, they feel that they are caught in a trap. It is necessary for him or her to undergo surgery to correct this body error in which he or she has fallen in so that his or her gender identity and biological sex are harmonious and conform. It is worth mentioning that a transsexual person is not considered a deviated or homosexual, and he or she does not incline to his or her own sex. But intersex represents another sexual type, and his typical love is for the opposite sex, Heterosexual, asking him for intimate affection on a realistic level.

In conclusion: there is the transsexual through surgery for the sexual organs, and there is the individual whose characteristics of female and male overlap at the same time (hermaphrodite), and there is the sexual pervert.

So, there are three types of gender: male and female, which is a normal condition, and transsexual through surgery to the genitals, and there are carriers of both male and female characteristics. It is necessary for the presence of harmony and congruence of male behaviour with the male gender and the similarity of female behaviour with the female gender so that the harmony motivates the behaviour of self-confidence expressing the gender and gender identity. For example, when his biological gender is male, and he bears feminine characteristics such as effeminacy, liquefaction, high pitched voice and sexy movements, his self-confidence is not expressive of his being male due to the lack of conformity and similarity of his expressive behaviour with his biological gender.

B. **SOCIAL TRENDS OF SEX**

These trends express sexual preference and inclination towards it. The tendency and the inclination towards the opposite sex are known as the Heterosexual nature, while the inclination towards the same sex features the Homosexual nature as it is prevalent in Western cultures. But such a tendency to sexual love is not decisive or determined by the biological sex (male or female). There are individuals who prefer both sexes in their sexual desires, and they are called Bisexual because they respond to both sexes in their sexual desire.

Suffice it to say that the lustful tendencies of individuals in satisfying their sexual instinct are the same, and they have the same ability to enjoy sexually, but there is a great variation in their satisfaction because it is subject to social upbringing and social interaction plus the consistency of gender identity with biological sex, particularly according to their upbringing on what is prevalent and dominant in gender roles.

In more detail, the individual's sexual desire is largely subject to the social influences that are practised on his interactions with others, his family and companionship upbringing, and the determinants of masculinity and femininity qualities by the culture of the society in the exercise of its role or its function. Therefore, the individual cannot escape from the social influence, whether he is in love with the opposite sex, his own sex, or both, he is subject to many social factors and not to his biological sex (female or male) only.

To give more attention to the subject of socialization and its gender formulations (male and female) in order to know why the homosexual individual prefers to have sexual relation with the same sex and in accordance with the standards of social culture regarding masculinity which is featured as the strength and muscles, and femininity which is featured as the soft and delicate. Therefore, gender symmetry is largely subject to changes that occur over time. In the sense that it is not fixed and stable, does not change and does not develop in its feminine or masculine characteristics. For example, in the mid-nineteenth century, the sexual trend in Western society was different from the present time. The masculine, muscular role was associated with his functional work, which included administrative work and education in primary schools, but this trend did not continue but rather changed, so that these jobs such as secretarial, primary education and clerical work, are now managed by the female, meaning that her gender role has become active in functions that were not within her scope two centuries ago. This is due to society's needs for her and not because of her compliment or favouritism and thanks to the scientific, cultural and media influences. The situation is the same in Arab society, as the Arab woman has become involved in judicial, scientific, educational, engineering, and medical work after it was a century ago restricted to men only. We are now witnessing the change in the gender trends taking place in Saudi society for women who were allowed to drive a car and take commercial, leadership, educational and medical positions after it was restricted to men only. In other words, the gender role of the Arab woman has evolved, and she has not maintained her old role confined to domestic affairs and raising children. It is good to point out that 10/10/2018 is a historic day in Saudi Arabia after King Salman bin Abdelaziz issued a royal order allowing the issuance of car driving licenses for women in Saudi Arabia and approving the application of the provisions of the traffic system and its executive regulations, including the issuance of driving licenses to males and females on all Both. This decision is much happier than women are men. (Madam) the magazine met with women to learn about their plans and what they had prepared to go on time. Will they drive the car as soon as the decision is implemented, or will they wait a while? Sarah and Yara Taher are two high school students who are eagerly awaiting this day. Indeed, it is an expected and historic day for Saudi women. God willing, she will be one of the first women to drive, and there is Lulu Al Yahya's husband. Fahd Al Yahya says there is no objection to my wife Lulu being one of the first female drivers. As for Amneh Abu Al-Hassan, she says, I am overly excited and excited to drive the car in Saudi Arabia, as well as to set off immediately, waiting for the zero hour impatiently. [Sayidaty Magazine No. 1938 dated 4/28/2018] This lofty order was issued by King Salman, under an official directive from the government, to allow Saudi women to drive a car. This means that official directives or culture can change and modify the characteristics of the gender.

So, there has been a change in the concept of delicate and soft femininity and the concept of masculine and rough masculinity in the field of jobs and work that is no longer limited to muscle, strength, and roughness, but rather to educational attainment, intelligence and accuracy in work. All of this led to a change in gender roles, whether in

Western or in Eastern culture, and if there is a difference between them, it will be in the degree rather than in kind.

In fact, the influences and differences that affect the human race also affect sexual trends. However, the differences between gender identity (male and female) and sexual trends were not clear, but rather blurred, because they represent procedural, which are field concepts like the intellectual, influence, class, prejudice and social consideration, rather than fixed theoretical concepts. It is general and comprehensive in most societies, such as the concept of construction, layout, role, status, family, and others. Transsexual is described as non-identical with traditional cultural determinants of gender roles, but they identify with homosexuals, i.e., see themselves as homosexual in their male or female counterparts.

However, the ancient historical situation of that was prevalent in the ancient Greek society during the Greek Empire, where the society accepted homosexuals and Heterosexuals, considering them as representatives of non-deviant natural relations. In the sense that they do not differentiate between the two types with the exception of some literary inductions. Not only that, but this society saw the preference of men for males or females due to the taste and desire of the Greek individual to enjoy a certain type over the other. The men were classified according to gender differentiation in their interaction with the opposite sex. A man who pursues a male for sexual enjoyment does not see himself as different from the other who pursues a girl and does not see himself as a sexual or social pervert. This situation was prevalent and common among them, not only that, but when a man wants to change his sexual pleasure from a boy to a girl after having spent an enjoyable time in

360

his love for him, it is a natural thing, and there is no deviation in it.

In fact, with regard to the Greek gender and its identity, it was present and prevalent, but the sexual trend did not exist at that time because many Greek males describe sexual differentiation as moving between gender roles in ways that are proportional to their sexual preference and their lifestyle at the time. Therefore, masculinity and femininity existed in Greek society, but sexual trends by social culture did not exist, and it does not differentiate between them because it sees equality between them, so it does not see any harm in changing the sexual pleasure of a man with a boy or with a girl because both are equal in their social status. What pleases a woman pleases a man, and what pleases the latter pleases the first. And there are no cultural and social divides between the biological sexes. This happens in the affluent, the civilized and the prosperous society, and this is what the Greek society was like during his empire. The situation is similar in contemporary Western capitalist societies, the affluent and civilized, which see sexual enjoyment with the same sex as individual pleasure and a mood and taste desire that is not opposed by material culture, so there is no place for masculinity and femininity in sexual relations in such societies. [Fouucault Michael. 1990. p. 221]

C. THE REALITY OF THE THIRD TYPE OF GENDER IN SOME SOCIETIES OF THE WORLD

Before explaining this type of gender, it is important to know the essential difference between a biologically transsexual and a socially transgendered person. The first is through surgery on the genitals, while the transgender is the one who acquires a social role that is different from his or her biological sex. This type of transgender is called "Third

Gender". Away from the Western society, which has many transgenders let take the Sultanate of Oman as an example on the Eastern society, where this type of transgendered person is featured as effeminate, and he is called (Khanith). Biologically he is a male who works as a prostitute and practices sodomy in addition to his work in domestic services. He bears a male name but wears distinctive clothes and has a special haircut. His clothes and haircut do not resemble the normal male or females in the Sultanate. The effeminate in the Sultanate is not a man because he cannot interact with women (sexually), and he is not a woman because his head is not veiled like an Omani woman.

Another example is from Tahiti, where the transgendered person is called (Tahiti Mahu). He is originally a young male boy who has adopted a female gender role since his early childhood and found a feminist work performed by women. His status is acquired rather than inherited, and he practices sodomy as sexual relations with those who are not Mahu, as he prefers sex with males and the Tahitian society accepts them as members of it.

There are many stories for the Indian third gender, but the most interesting one is of Lor Rama in the Hindus literature. It states that when Lord Rama was exiled from Ayodhya and his entire kingdom began to follow him into the forest. He told his disciples: "Men and women, please wipe your tears and go away." So, they left. Still, a group of people stayed behind, at the edge of the forest, because they were neither men nor women. They were hijras (the third type of gender), which in Urdu means something like eunuchs. Those people waited in the woods for 14 years until Lord Rama returned, which won them a special place in Hindu mythology. There is a bit of a mystery about the story's origin — scholars say it's not in the early versions of ancient Hindu texts — but in the past century, this folk tale about the hijras' loyalty has become an important piece of their identity. Hijras figure prominently in India's Muslim history as well, serving as the sexless watchdogs of Mughal harems. It is worth mentioning in this context that most of the hijras are, in reality, eunuchs who have had their testicles removed, but they are not gay homosexuals because they see themselves as females, so they prefer to have sex with men who they consider as the opposite sex. In general, they dress as women and represent an isolated subculture. Today hijras, which include transgender and intersex people, are hard to miss. Dressed in glittering saris, their faces heavily coated in cheap makeup, they sashay through crowded intersections knocking on car windows with the edge of a coin and offering blessings. They dance at temples. They crash fancy weddings and birth ceremonies, singing bawdy songs and leaving with fistfuls of rupees. Many Indians believe hijras have the power to bless or curse, and hijras trade-off this uneasy ambivalence. [The New York Times 17 February 2018]

In Indonesia, however, and in contrast to gender binarism, Bugis society recognizes five genders: Makkunrai, Oroané, Bissu, Calabai, and Calalai. The concept of five genders has been a key part of their culture for at least six centuries, according to Associate Professor of Social Sciences Sharyn Graham Davies of Auckland University of Technology in New Zealand, citing similar traditions in Thailand, Malaysia, India and Bangladesh. They are the most numerous of the three major ethnic groups of South Sulawesi, with about 3 million people. Most Bugis are Muslim, but many pre-Islamic rituals continue to be honoured in their culture, including the view that gender exists on a spectrum. Most Bugis converted from Animism to Islam in the early 17th century; small numbers of Bugis have converted to Christianity, but the influence of Islam is still very prominent in their society. Oroané is comparable to cisgender men, Makkunrai to cisgender women, Calalai to transmen, and Calabai to transwomen, while Bissu is androgynous or intersex and revered shamans or community priests. In daily social life, the Bissu, the Calabai, and the Calalai may enter the dwelling places and the villages of both men and women. According to the Bugis gender system, Calabai is generally assigned male at birth but take on the role of heterosexual females. Their fashions and gender expression are distinctly feminine but do not match that of "typical" cisgender women. Calalai is assigned female at birth but takes on the roles of heterosexual males. They dress and present themselves as men, hold masculine jobs and typically live with female partners to adopt children. It is worth noting that there is no expression for gender in the Bugis language. For Bugis, gender is understood by their different perceptions about sex on a biological and mental level, as these perceptions are especially important for understanding the culture and freedom of all boogies. [Gender in Bugis society - Wikipedia, the free encyclopaedia]

And if we move back by two centuries of time to know the reality of gender about the Native Americans, we find that the role of (Berdaches) is present and familiar to them that does not express the traditional gender roles. In their tribe, there is the mediator who mediates between man and woman and between the real and the spiritual world, acting outside the terms and limits of traditional gender roles and possessing two types of souls. It is worth mentioning, in this context, that each of the Hijras, the hermaphrodite, the Mahu, and the Berdache, and the three types of the Bugi

364

gender, are roles associated with approbation, contentment, and pride more than sarcasm, contempt, insolence and immorality. All of them represent intersex (male and female bisexuals) that they are transgender despite their violation of the foundations of gender bisexuality, but they clearly demonstrate the power of the influence of social culture on gender identity and biological sexual orientations. [Lindsey. 2011. Pp. 35-36]

For the sake of enrichment and expansion, examples and historical, social images will be presented to highlight the groups that prevailed and then perished in the societies of the ancient world, such as (eunuchs). This type of the third gender was common in the Assyrian Empire around 850 until 622 BC as well as in China, ancient Greece and Rome Byzantium, the Ottoman Empire (Turkey), India and South Asia, with the presence of a religious and artistic castration for singers. "Eunuchs" or "the Eunuched" are a category of men without offspring, either because they were born without reproductive organs or disabled members, or who were subjected to a deliberate castration process to disrupt their sexual energy in order to work inside the palaces of sultans, merchants, and statesmen.

In the deliberate castration process, a eunuch's testicles are removed early in his life and who is used as a servant or slave in order to make him safer than the officials of the royal court to be the permission of the ruler, sultan, or caliph, enjoying high confidence and less desire to establish a dynasty and be a harem guard.

This is just an introduction to the eunuch as another model of the third sex and the third gender, where he is a male, whose genitals have been removed to perform female duties, who exercises non-masculine roles and who is not stigmatized or despised by the ruling elite and the affluent

365

class, so he is a social class product. My control of boys who do not decide to castrate them, but rather trade them. It is a moral and inhuman crime against poor boys to convert them to the third gender, especially in the great empires and the powerful and rich governments. They are exploitative practices of weak human elements that cannot defend themselves and do not represent an economic, military, and political weight.

D. THE EUNUCHS

Eunuchs or Scoptes is a secret sect that spread in the Russian Empire. They are famous for their practice of castration of men and the extirpation of women in accordance with their teachings against eroticism. The sect arose as an extension of the sect known as the "People of God", to which it was first referred to in the late 18th century. Eunuchs were persecuted by the imperial government and then by the Soviet Union and had a significant growth before fading into obscurity in the mid-20th century.

Eunuchs is a plural form of the plural "eunuch", and the origin of the word in Russian is "skopets", meaning "eunuch man". As the name indicates, the primary feature of the sect is castration. They believe that after Adam and Eve were expelled from the Garden of Eden, they had the remaining half of the forbidden fruit that was implanted into their bodies, making up both testicles and breasts. Therefore, when these sexual organs are removed, the eunuch then returns to a state of serenity and purity before the original sin. The eunuchs believe that when they do this, they will fully repay Christ, according to what is mentioned in the Gospel of Matthew 12:19 and 8:18, 9.

There are two types of castration: a smaller castration and a larger castration (i.e., partial castration and full

366

castration). For men, a smaller seal means only the testicles are removed, while in a larger seal, both the testicles and penis are removed. The men who did the greater seal used cow horns when urinating. Castration is performed using starting means such as a razor, and no anaesthetics are used during the procedure.

The first castration of a female dates back to 1815. The breasts are usually removed, and according to the 1911 Encyclopaedia, some accounts indicate that the vaginal labia are removed, making the procedure a form of female circumcision.

Eunuchs believe that the main evil in this world is (physical beauty, human sexual behaviour, sexual desire, etc.) which in turn prevents humans from communicating with God. The path to perfection begins with the eradication of cause and then the liberation of the soul. Castration ensures that none of the sins caused by sexual desire can be committed.

Castration History: Eunuchs were first discovered by the Russian civil authorities in 1771 in the Oryol region. A Russian peasant named Andrei Ivanov was convicted of persuading thirteen peasants to castrate themselves. He was assisted by another peasant named Kondraty Silivanov. An investigation was conducted following these events. Ivanov was arrested and sent to Siberia. Silivanov escaped but was captured in 1775.

The doctrine of eunuchs spread with Silivanov's flight from Siberia and his claim to be reincarnated in the person of the late Peter III of Russia. Silivanov also claimed to be "the king of kings and the god of the gods" and declared that his mission was to deliver believers through the process of castration.

For eighteen years, Silivanov lived in St. Petersburg, in the house of one of his disciples, and received double loyalty as Christ and the Tsar. In 1797, he was arrested again on the orders of Tsar Pavel I and placed in a lunatic hospital. He was released under the rule of Alexander I but was soon arrested again in 1820, but this time he was deposited in the Suzdal monastery, where he died in 1832 at the age of one hundred years. The doctrine of castration was not eradicated despite all the furious investigations of the Third Division of the Chancellery (the Tsar's secret police), and the rumours continued to flourish.

The sect was not restricted to the peasantry only. Its adherents included nobles, military and naval officers, civil servants, priests and merchants, and their numbers were continually increasing so that 515 males and 240 females belonging to the group were transported to Siberia as punishment between 1847 and 1866, and this did not affect in any way on the existence of the community. In 1874 the congregation numbered about 5,444, of whom 1,465 were female. Of these, there were 703 men and 100 women who engaged in female genital mutilation.

Many oppressive practices were practised against eunuchs besides ridicule, where males were forced to dress in female clothes and were paraded around the village wearing fools' hats. In 1876, 130 of them were deported. To escape these conditions, many of them decided to emigrate to Romania, where many of them mingled with the formerly exiled old believers known as Leibovans. The well-known Romanian writer Ion Luca Caragiale says that in the late nineteenth century, most of the people driving horse cabs in Bucharest were Russian eunuchs (Scopiți in Romanian). Although Russian law was strict towards them, as each eunuch was required to register himself, this did not affect the popularity of the sect.

Eunuchs began to be known as moneylenders, and there was a mastaba in Saint Petersburg known as the "Eunuchs Mastaba". Despite all kinds of oppression and trials to which the followers of the sect were subjected, this sect became close to 100,000 followers at the beginning of the twentieth century. Thanks to more pressures applied against them and thanks to the collective farming project in the framework of the Soviet Union, it was possible to reduce the number of followers of the group to reach a few thousand in 1929. The sect is believed to have nearly perished today.

At the level of all peoples and civilizations, part of the "eunuchs" serves, as it was in the era of the caliphate, in the offices of men, and others serve in (the haramik), that is, the palaces of the harem, and similar to those (Agahs) who are entrusted with guarding and monitoring the Two Holy Mosques and Jerusalem. They perform special work that no one else can perform, including separating the men from the women in the tawaf, the pilgrimage, and when performing the prayer.

Other Practices and Beliefs: The sect of eunuchs does not completely condemn the principle of marriage, as some of its members were allowed to have one child, and those in Bucharest were allowed two before they joined the congregation completely. The group was not pessimistic, nor did it have a desire to reach the end of the human race, but rather aimed at bringing the individual to the point of perfection. Their religious rituals include singing, the frantic dance that leads to ecstasy, as well as that of the Sufi Mevlevi. All members belonging to the group are required to take a strict secret oath, and these members then form what is known as a reciprocal cooperative.

369

Congregational meetings are held late at night in cellars and last until dawn. The men at these meetings wear long, wide, cropped white shirts with a belt and large white pants. Women also wear white clothes. All attendees wear white socks, and those who are unable to wear white socks come barefoot. They refer to themselves as "white pigeons."

The eunuchs believe in Christ, who in turn will establish an empire of saints, that is, the pure. The eunuchs also believe that the Messiah will not come until the followers of the doctrine become 144,000 [Revelation 14:1], where they combined all their efforts to reach this number. In 1911, there was a tendency among some members of the congregation that the tenets of their faith could be fulfilled through chastity and solitary living. [https://en.wikipedia.org]

Eunuch History: The history of the "eunuch" of man, with his white and black races, goes back to very ancient times, and at the level of all civilizations since the Byzantine and Greek times, even the Persian and Babylonian eras. It is believed that the Pharaohs were the first to use "eunuchs" to serve in their palaces, and it is said that (Yazid bin Muawiyah) was the first whoever used them in his palace, and the name of the first guard he used for his emirate office was "Fateh".

The "Secrets of the Two Holy Mosques" inherited the profession and have their own traditions and endowments. Some of them are married on the basis of the proverb "I possessed the kohl container without a dipping wand". The container here is the sex organ for the female, and the wand is the male sex organ!

In Europe, slave traders would buy captives from Germany on the banks of the Rhine and the Alps, and other places, all of whom, male and female, were beautiful and had white skin, and then transferred to Spain (Andalusia). Muslims were buying males to serve in palaces and females for concubinage, and when slave trading turned into a profitable trade, Jew traders castrated many of these slaves and sold them at high prices. These goods became abundant, and many worked with them, and they established what was known as "eunuchs' plants" in Europe, specifically in Verdun in the province of Lorraine in France.

Castrate Singers! In Italy, they would castrate singers and artists to refine, improve and elevate their voices when they switched between the female and male voice so that they would not tempt the women singers and be distracted from the singing. It is reported that one of the Umayyad caliphs in the seventh century - as mentioned by Al-Isfahani - ordered the governor of Medina in a letter in the Arabic language to "count the effeminate" singers; The governor saw a dot on the letter left by a fly so that the Arabic word census (count) turn into "castration" instead, so it was read as if the caliph ordered that all of them be castrated, and "Al-Dalal" one of the city's most famous singers, the most affable, beautiful, and good-natured was among the list of eunuchs.

Neutering Method: In the era of the Islamic State, a legal fatwa was forbidding castration but permitting the use of eunuchs if non-Muslims castrated them. They were therefore sent to Egypt to castrate them by the Copts. The process of castration was often conducted in the cities (Girga and Assiut) in Egypt. A group of Christians was conducting it, and they chose the victims from among the young boys, whose ages are between three and nine years, who are brought by the bringer convoys from different regions.

The bringing is usually done in the fall for health considerations, and those who perform it are not satisfied with amputating the penis alone, but all parts are amputated with a blade. Then they immediately pour boiling oil on the place of the amputation, followed by throwing henna powder, and fix a tube in the remaining part of the urethra, then bury the victim in the ground above his stomach, and after leaving him in this state for one to two days, they extract it from the dirt. They place a paste of clay and oil on the wound,

Caphoor Al Alhshidi: Since the "eunuchs" form the links between the women's palaces and the king's palace and transfer secrets to and from the women, they acquired tremendous information about the palace and what goes on behind the walls. It enables them to occupy the highest positions, whether in the palace or outside it, including leadership positions such as the Chinese Muslim traveller (Cheng), who led a Chinese fleet to the coasts of Africa. China still commemorates his voyage in 1405. Among these scholars are poets, geniuses, and people with extraordinary talents.

There are "eunuchs" who came to power, such as Kafoor Al-Akhshidi, who was enslaved from the Nuba. The governor of Egypt at that time (Al-Akhshid) taught Kafoor and trained him and earned him all political sciences and the arts of war before appointing him as an educator for his children, but after the death of their father, Kafoor distracted the children from the ruling with amusements and pleasures to win power for his self. He succeeded and led fierce wars that brought him to Aleppo in Syria to become one of the eunuchs who governed an empire. He had an immortal story with the poet Al-Mutanabbi after he was let down by Kafoor, who promised him gifts but did not fulfil his promise. Abu Al-Tayyib Al-Mutanabbi wrote one of the most famous satire poems in history that roamed the globe and are still preserved to this day.

Aghaat of the Two Holy Mosques: These eunuchs acquired a special position called (the Agahs) to work in the service of the Two Holy Mosques. They inherited this profession hundreds of years ago, and the word (Agha), an honorific title used in the Kurdish, Turkish and Persian languages, and is called the presidents, the sheikhs, and the eminence of the people, and is attributed to Muawiyah bin Abi Sufyan who was the first to use them to serve the Makkah, although there is another narration that Abu Jaafar al-Mansur is the first to do so.

The English orientalist "Burkhardt" mentioned them during his stay in Makkah and Madinah in 1814 when he found the Sheikh of the Haram was the leader of the "eunuchs", and he was the leader of the mosque and the main person in the city. He was sent to exile as a kind of punishment from the Ottoman Caliph (Saleem) after he was supervising the caliph's women - one of the first jobs in the Calipha's court. He mentioned that the "eunuchs" in the Holy Mosque wear special uniforms, including the brocade and the Constantinian Qawuq. They exercise the functions of the police and prevent disorder, in addition to washing the Holy Mosque, lighting lamps and extending the carpets. The public show them the utmost respect and appreciation, especially the Sheikh of the Agahs who they stop him whenever they see him kiss his hands, who also enjoys an important personality, and allows him to sit in the presence of the Pasha and the Sharif, noting that the number of "eunuchs" in the Holy Mosque was 40 Agahs, most of whom were sent from nobles and philanthropists as a gift to the sanctuary. Burkhardt expressed his surprise that all the Agahs were married to the Negro maidservants, and they keep a number of maidservants and maidservants in their homes!

Italian War Victims: Some of the Agahs of the two holy mosques, most of whom are Abyssinians, said they are the remaining victims of the Italian-Abyssinian war 1936-1948. During their conquest of Abyssinia and parts of Africa, the Italian invaders chased them, arrested them, and then castrated them in captivity by cutting off their genitals. They did it with children and boys as the castration of enemies was an expression of the desire to cut off their offspring and to suppress sexual feelings and aggression so that to work in the role of women without fear of them. Nevertheless, they marry one, two and three, as is the case with the Agahs of Makkah and Madinah, where many of them find someone who accepts him with full knowledge of his condition. And this is mentioned as one of the conditions of the marriage contract - according to their custom - when he says to her: "I possessed you as kohl container without a wand." This means that she has the kohl. As for the lukewarm, he has it, but it is disabled. The kohl is a package or bottle of kohl and the wand lubricant with which the eye is kohl.

They are Rich: "Eunuchs" are appreciated and respected by everyone, as they are considered wealthy and own endowments in the two holy cities of Mecca, Medina, Morocco, Yemen, and Basra, including real estate, towers, five-star hotels, and residential complexes worth millions if not billions of dollars, and provided them with a decent living, and placed them on the list of the country's wealthy. In their knowledge, the revocation inherits the revocation in these endowments, but it is a spatial inheritance, meaning that the revocation in Madinah does not inherit the revocation in Mecca, and its share is limited to the endowments allocated to them within the endowments of

374

Medina, and they are also ranked through the hierarchical ladder of the names of their jobs in the Two Holy Mosques. It begins with the Sheikh of the Aghas and ends with a son who works, and he is the one who sleeps in the sanctuary for seven consecutive years until he rises to the rank of (sheikh invalid) and deserves the title (agha), and within these ranks (my bread) and (half my bread).

Their Own Traditions: They are also protected by immunity that belongs to them alone, and to the exclusion of others from the human race - since the era of the caliphate - that does not allow any of the predecessors or the successors to interfere in their private and public affairs, and it has made them an independent group in their internal system, customs, traditions, property, endowments, and their freedom.

He Returned Without Testicles! The people of the Arabian Peninsula used to castrate their slaves who worked near women. There were three people who travelled from Najd to buy food from Iraq, but their money (dirhams) was stolen. They agreed that one of the claims that he was owned and brought to sell in Iraq. The volunteered guy was sold by the other two for a price sufficient to buy their food on the basis that he would manage any opportunity and escape. But what happened was that the buyer took him to the stage of a eunuch, and he castrated him and then managed to escape. When his friends came to bless him for his safety, he said, "I came back to you but without testicles." [www.alriyadh.com]

E. EUNUCHS AND IMPROVISED ONES IN THE THREE DIVINE RELIGIONS

I. Castration in the Bible for Jews and Christians:

The term eunuch, or eunuchs, or chief eunuch appeared in the Babylonian era, as there were texts talking about eunuchs in the Bible, and from these texts the following saying: "And all the princes of the king of Babylon entered and sat in the middle gate Sharezer, Samgerenbo, Sarsekhem, the chief of the eunuchs... and all the rest of the chiefs of the king of Babylon." And another text came by saying: Nebuchadnezzar, king of Babylon, said... "So Nebuzaradan sent the chief of the police, and Nebushuzban, the chief of the eunuchs...and all the men of the king of Babylon."

Other texts in the Bible dealt with the word: eunuchs or the chief eunuch, and it speaks of the Jews as the following text: "And the king (Josiah) summoned all the elders of Judah...and removed the priests of the idols...who used to burn sacrifices to Baal (an idol representing the gods of the Jews) and to the sun and the moon... He removed the horses that the kings of Judah had consecrated for the worship of the sun, and he burned the chariots... All these were at the entrance to the temple house, near the dwelling of Nthmelech, the chief of the eunuchs."

As for the Persians, the class of eunuchs is no less important than that of other kingdoms and other peoples, as it came in the Bible proving the importance of this class. The Book of Esther dealt with several texts that contained the word eunuchs or their chief, such as: "On the seventh day, when the heart of King (Ahasuerus) was blessed with wine." He commanded Mehman, Bizta, Harbona, Baghata, Abghata, Zitar, and Karkas, the seven eunuchs who served before him (King Ahasuer)."

376

It is mentioned in some literature that the Romans were the first to invent castration. This statement is certainly inaccurate because what was shown in the previous sections is that castration is a meaning and term that dates back to ages older than the history of the Romans.

Among those who said that the Romans were the first to do this is Al-Jahiz, when he said: "Every castration in this world originates from the Romans, and it is surprising that they are Christians, and they claim kindness and mercy, tenderness of the heart and liver, what no one of all kinds claims… Nor it was a crime that they sent eunuchs against themselves, asking for favours and remembering grudges… and we have never seen the enmity of (eunuchs against the Christians) justified by their enmity towards them. The eunuchs looked at the Romans with hatred and loathing, as they considered them to be the cause of their own eunuch because they invented castration, in their opinion. On the other side, the Roman practised and engaged in castration themselves.

Christians practised castration and earned from it. The Hadiah city in Abyssinia whose people embraced the Christian religion and they practised castration without other people from other Abyssinian regions until the twelfth century AD, and in Upper Egypt, there are two Coptic monasteries whose main income is from castration, which is widely practised, until it suffices to finance all of Egypt and other regions with eunuchs. A number of Coptic Christians worked to buy young black slaves, trade them, and castrate them. Many of these slaves died during the process of castration, as one out of every seven survives, but the rest is sold for twenty times its purchase price. It was by this process the number of eunuchs was reduced, and their prices raised. In Byzantium, the eunuchs were sold for four times the non-eunuch (ordinary) slaves, and some Romans castrated their children when they were young and put them to serve in places of worship to make them masters. They are careful not to damage the penis, as they are exposed for the testicles only so that their children cannot get their women and nuns pregnant though they can have sex with women and achieve pleasure, as they think that they reach in their sexual desire to a level that the stallion does not reach. Al-Jahiz described this by saying: "It is as if they claim that he is completely exhausting what she (the woman) sexually has and bringing her to the utmost of orgasm due to his excessive strength in elongating the intercourse time".

The eunuch who is suspended from working in places of worship, one of the works he performs is singing. The eunuch cannot be graded in religious positions in the Latin Church according to the instructions of the popes of that church, except for the Orthodox Church, so the eunuch can perform his work inside the church, such as singing, as it is possible to progress in religious positions until he becomes a priest and there are examples on this in the Orthodox Church as two eunuchs in the tenth century AD, took the position of Patriarch of the Church of Constantinople one after the other.

II. Islamic Religion Position on Castration:

Castration, in short, is the process of disabling the fertilization by dissolving the **male's** testicles when he is young or old without affecting his sexual desire, and he remains able to have sexual intercourse while the women he has sex with do not get pregnant.

The jurists and commentators differed about the legality of castration. Some of them prohibited castration at all, and others permitted the castration of animals for necessity, and the prohibition of castration of the uneaten animals at all, and the permissibility of castration of young uneaten animals rather than the old.

Many Qur'anic verses implicitly refer to the concept of castration. The matter was clarified by the commentators in their interpretation of the Qur'anic verses, and it came in the Almighty's saying: "The nature of God in which He has made people; there is no alteration of God's creation." Al-Tabari mentioned that what is meant by it is the meaning of castration and the Almighty's saying: "And I will command them, let them change the creation of God." In this verse, a group of them said that it is castration. Al-Hindi transmitted a narration that he attributed to one of the companions of Prophet Mohammed who said: "I was sitting with the Prophet [PBUH] in a group of his companions, so a group came and said: O Messenger of God: I have a relative of mine in ignorance and we were the share of sins and adultery, so we were permitted to castrate, and the Messenger of God disliked their question..." Al-Manaawi transmitted a hadith numbered (9697) saying: "There is no castration in Islam."

The Noble Messenger said that he forbids castration, saying: "Do not single out what grows God's creation." In addition, castration involves physical and psychological pain that may lead to the death of a person or make him a burden on society. Castration is a type of mutilation, and Islam forbids mutilation. He said: "...that mutilation is forbidden even with a stubborn dog." This is evidence that Islam's position on castration is that the castration is unsupported and forbidden, as well as it is disliked even if it is done by other than Muslims.

Jurisprudence rulings have been issued regarding eunuchs and those who are wanted from among human beings, and among these rulings: mutilate the penis of the stallion if he mutilated the penis of the eunuch stallion and if the testicles of the eunuch removed, the testicles of the doer are removed. The evidence for this is the Almighty's saying: "And the wounds are punishments." And if you punish, then punish with the same as you were punished with.

III. Eunuchs in Islamic Societies:

In the pages of the search for castration in language and terminology, we talked about the most important advantages that eunuchs enjoy and the methods used to perform the process of castration, in addition to the history of castration and the priorities of its appearance and the deep history of the emergence of castration, and with regard to castration during the eras of the Arab Islamic state, we must say That this phenomenon existed in the Arabian Peninsula before Islam, as the Arabs before Islam used slaves and black slaves to serve them in their homes and in housework, grazing and trade. Slaves were a layer of the constituent classes of Arab society before Islam, and among these slaves were eunuchs, who were frequently used In Mecca before Islam, as desirability to serve them and obey their masters, as they were owned by them, and in the days of the Noble Prophet when he was in Medina, Muqawqis of Egypt gave him two maidservants and with them a eunuch, and the two girls were Maria the Coptic and her sister Sirin and a eunuch named Mabour who he differed in that he was a servant to them, and it was said that he was their brother with many other gifts. That was in the year 629 AD, and Maria and her sister converted to Islam. As for Mabour, he embraced Islam in the era of the Prophet after a period of delay.

It should be said here about the Prophet when he accepts these gifts that include a castration. This does not mean that he allows or encourages castration, but it is a matter of accepting the gift because the position of Islam rejecting the

380

process of castration is quite clear towards this negative social phenomenon.

The noble Prophet's era inherited the phenomenon of slaves who were eunuchs within the pre-Islamic society, a society that relied on class in a social division, and a number of those eunuchs became Muslim and played an active role in it. He converted to Islam, and the Messenger of God (PBUH) realized and narrated a hadith from him, but in the Rashidi era (632-660 AD), there were narrations that indicate the presence of eunuchs and those who had a role in leading the armies, as the narration indicates that in the battle of Yarmouk between the Romans and the Muslims. The commander of the Roman army had been castrated and called: (Shalab the Eunuch), who led a hundred thousand soldiers, and another eunuch, who was owned by Heraclius of the Romans, was called: (Qiqlan the Eunuch). In the year 645 AD, Heraclius sent the Roman to Alexandria in Egypt, a eunuch named Ma'awil, and it was said Mandeel was leading Byzantine naval boats, and Omar ibn al-Aas confronted them.

But it seems that the main work of the eunuchs is to serve the harem and the women of the palace at the caliphs and the heads of the state and their masters, and they trusted them because they were not dependent on women (without the need for women). He played a role in isolating and appointing many officeholders who did not work in overly sensitive state institutions, so they were raised and lowered, according to the common saying.

The evidence for this is that the word eunuch in early Islamic times is a derogatory word that contains a lot of humiliation for those whom the word described. In the beginning, the word eunuch meant servant and such servants were called eunuchs out of defamation and belittling them, so that the common people always mocked them as confirmed by Al-Masoudi, who mentioned that the public was mocking them in the streets and shouting at them in disdain and saying: "O Agate, pour water and throw flour, O disobedient, O long-legged." It was practised by them inside the Caliph court. In the late Abbasid times, they were called: the teacher or the sheikh. Rather, the matter went beyond that until they became called influencers, and the elder and influential among them was called: the teacher.

Retribution was concerned with the subject of servants because of their funny situations and beautiful anecdotes until those servants became a subject for those writers or storytellers, such as imitating their movements and voices and striking situations with wit and joke.

IV. The Tomboy Woman

Linguistic dictionaries have dealt with the term masculine woman with many linguistic connotations, but in the end, the linguistic definition comes with one result, which is: the tomboy is the woman who tries to imitate men through dress, body, movements, and active, and from the linguistic definitions of improvised, Ibn Manzoor said: "A woman dismounted: she became like a man." It is said: "A masculine woman, if her features resemble the man, not in her creation." It is said as a woman's masculinity if she resembles in some of her conditions, and it was said: "… a woman who is male and masculine and man embodiment: resembling males." ".

The word masculine or male came in the idiomatic sense as the woman who imitates men and tries to enter their world and practice their actions, and Al-Aini said: "And the masculine ones, that is: those who are pretentious in manhood and imitate men in carrying a sword and spear."

The Position of Islamic Law: Islamic law is the monitor, adjuster, and regulator of the lives of Islamic individuals and societies, setting the rules of living through which life can be properly organized, and if the lines crossed, that transgression is considered in certain cases permissible and allowed and in other cases that are abhorrent and thirdly forbidden and not permissible. This is because doing forbidden action can negatively affect the entire community, not to mention the person who violates the established legal rule, and the phenomenon of resembling a man by a woman is one of the negative phenomena that affect societies. So Islamic law position as its debugger, the observer of its disadvantages, as communications were addressed Quranic verses and sayings of the Prophet this phenomenon came in the Holy Book: "And I would command them that they should change the creation of God, and whoever takes Satan as a guardian besides God has surely incurred a loss." Andalusian said: "It was said, the change of God's creation is that everything that God creates is for virtue, and any vice is considered as a change in God's creation, and the change in the character is a change in God's creation, and therefore it is vice, like the girl who imitates boys that she forbids what God permitted. The Almighty said: "The nature of God in which He has made people. There is no altering of God's creation. That is the right religion." By this, I mean the prohibition of the permissible and the exclusion of the forbidden, and the narration: God cursed the tomboy woman from among the women.

Historical Roots of Tomboy Woman: The phenomenon of tomboy is one of the social phenomena that have been present in different societies since ancient times, as this social phenomenon has been practised in different forms, sometimes through dressing the clothes of the opposite sex, and sometimes through the actions and behaviours of women, through which they try to enter the world of men, such as the roughness of the voice, the way of walking, and the process of flexing the muscles, an attempt through this to deceive others that she is a man. It must be said that there is a difference between saying that this woman is brave and saying that she is an improvised woman. The tomboy, and the courageous woman, society looks upon with veneration, respect, and greatness. As for the Tomboy woman, society does not accept her actions and does not respect her presence in such a form.

Permissible Resemblance of a Man in Muslim Community: The Islamic society was one of the many societies that recorded a prominent presence in the history of the world, and it was not far from the social diseases that afflict societies. Environmental and genetic factors help to form and shape the personality of each individual, and from this, it can be said that the Islamic society has negative social manifestations and among these manifestations is the phenomenon of masculinity among women.

But there are cases in which dismounting is permitted in Islamic society. For example, Khariji women would go out to war with their husbands, wearing men's clothes, wearing swords, trained to fight, fighting their enemy and fighting alongside their husbands and families without the opponent knowing them, imitating men in terms of dress and effectiveness. Women were sometimes used to deceive the enemy during wars and were commanded to imitate men's clothes to deceive the enemy by the large number, by wearing men's clothes and appearing on the fences with their weapons, so he deceives the enemy and believes that they are men, which increases the confusion of the enemy who

384

will expect that his opponent has prepared and prepared for confrontation.

Impermissible Resemblance of a Man in Muslim Community: Many novels dealt with the resemblance to man practised by a number of women, but it is difficult to separate at the time if the woman was actually a tomboy or accused of it. The received texts describe women as sassy who have the ability to confront and emulate men or when they act freely and lead a supposed lifestyle of men. It is considered a male if her femininity becomes impure and incompatible with the conception of the social system for her, such as having a beard or a rough and hoarse voice devoid of marble, and this is evidence that the concept of resemblance works in many cases, which would put women in unpleasant situations though they are praiseworthy in men.

It is worth noting that the phenomenon of tomboy women existed in the pre-Islamic era, as it was common in the Arabian Peninsula and remained well-known in Islam. It was also a well-known phenomenon in other cultures and moved from Persia and Constantinople through what was brought from the female slaves and concubines from those countries, especially during the Umayyad period. But it seems that the phenomenon of disembowelment was practised by young girls, and they tried to get out of the social system, but this phenomenon for them is temporary. Often the tomboy girls end up in the marital cage, where they are tamed by a very stubborn man, who returns them to the first place.

And considering that the Islamic society is a society that rejects women who try to imitate men, even if it preserves the characteristics of her femininity, beauty of her face, whiteness, and softness of her body, yet the society rejects every action that would lead a woman to the qualities of manhood. And if these actions appear from him, then they are good for him, and they are considered virtues, and if these actions appear from women, then they are defects because they are not suitable for women because they are specific to men according to social custom in the prevailing system.

As for the social justification for the existence of such a phenomenon in the male or tomboy woman, some have attributed it to rebellion and a departure from pressures towards liberation, as she sees that the man has the ability to enjoy life without restrictions such as the restrictions imposed on her from blocking, concealment and prevention, so she and her desire to get out of the reality that prevents her into a life of meekness and not being controlled by others. She works to imitate the actions, behaviours, movements and words of males and uses the trick to get a role in life that is better than the role she is, but this is temporary, of course, for the on-foot woman. Once she is discovered the associated agony in this role, she quickly returns to what she was before, and her act is nothing but a rebellion against femininity, and thus tomboy actions and masculinity is a charge directed at everyone who has left her natural feminine status in an attempt to rise to a better status. This situation has more impact on the woman herself than doubting her femininity.

The second type of woman resemblance by man is represented by a woman whose femininity was not complete for a physiological, structural reason. Signs and features of men are appeared on her, such as the growth of the chin and moustache, hair in the places where hair grew in men, or the coarse manly voice. When she realizes that she is of this type, she feels the embarrassment and causing crisis for her in social relations. Therefore, the resemblance of this type is an intentional attempt by the woman to keep her secret, and the choice to behave like a man is not more than a disguise to be in harmony with her manhood features or going into avoidance, isolation, and non-friction mode because friction causes the unintended mistake. The embarrassment which is accompanied by the looks of surprise, wonder and denunciation may occur, so the woman of this kind resorts to playing the role of a man to get rid of the unfamiliar features. Accordingly, she is forced to enter the world of men and considers herself one of them as not everything; her body is beautiful.

There are things that are anti-feminine, such as rough speech, excessive height, thick hair and muscles that are symbols of strength as they are masculine signs. If they are found in a woman, they must be corrected and removed in light of a society that strives to keep the distance established between the sex's constant. It excludes any causes that generate rapprochement between the sexes in a look or behaviour. Not all women are female, and they are not always in complete femininity. Poverty, destitution, sadness, and other factors remove the beauty features from women, not because the woman does not mind her beauty, it is only because she is far from caring for her body and beauty. A woman always needs to pay attention to her femininity and constantly subject her body to the conditions of customs and traditions prevailing in society. The more the features of masculinity appear in women, the more the society's disapproval and denunciation increases. Some masculine features are attributed to physiological factors such as hormonal disorders and the imbalance in the ratio of female and male hormones, which makes the masculine characteristics overcome the feminine ones.

And what is related to social conditions such as the severity of the veil, ostracism or need, especially if a widowed woman is in need, it sometimes forces her to adopt masculine values and assume the role of the male and carry out her tasks such as securing a livelihood for her children and entering the world of men. Such male characteristics and appearance is a protection mean for herself by being similar to them in their behaviour.

Sometimes the psychological disorders that are mainly resulted from upbringing play an important role in the masculine behaviour and appearance of the woman. Some parents who have no male child raise their daughter as masculine. The mother who only has daughters tries to raise one of her daughters in a masculine upbringing to replace her dead father. Or the mother, who lost her husband and have children to raise, adopts masculine appearance and behaviour to compensate for her dead husband. And as a result of getting used to want, hardship and the difficulty of life, the masculine woman integrates with the male society as a man, and after the passage of time, she disguises her female body, and she gets used to the new situation. The feelings of femininity change, and shame then leads to a feeling of comfort and a sense of victory and pride, so she feels pleasure and enjoyment in manifesting the role of a man, and her success in those increases her insistence on adhering to the desire.

With all the actions and impressions of males by the tomboy, the social system stands against her, and a woman cannot turn into a man, but she is an unclear image of masculinity and virality. The woman's departure from the veil and the numbness imposed on her by the legislative and social systems to become active and fast in her movement will bring her reprehensible and shameful fame, and it is a clear defect, and she will never be called a brave woman.

And here it must be said that woman impersonated man, whether voluntary or forced, she cannot in both cases confront the social system and obtain approval for her actions, but she does by disguising herself, and as soon as her matter is discovered, she is forced to dress like a woman and append her to women forcibly. Otherwise, she cannot coexist with society and becomes marginalized and is kicked out of it. Therefore, society understands her by departing from the function of femininity and rebellion against her, refusing to fulfil her duty as a woman. It provides the commendable qualities that men look for in a woman, and society has warned against the marriage of a tomboy or male woman.

It can be said that the female impersonating male losses many of the characteristics of femininity and gains a lot from the actions of men. She, therefore, remains with a vacillating personality between men and women, and it is reflected in her actions and behaviour. It is difficult to subjugate her and return her back to the quorum of femininity again. Therefore, looking at her is a look of slander and despicable because she looks to a value that does not belong to her, and thus she finds herself without a place among men, not even in the world of women. [www.uobabylon.edu]

COMMENTS

In order to avoid confusion in the use of modern scientific terminology about the third type of gender, it is important to know that this type is called intersex, which combines two sexes and is different from the transsexual (transgender) conducted through surgery of the genitals, and who is believed to belong to the opposite sex, and he or she is not considered a sexual deviant because he or she tends to

389

the opposite sex. Intersex is often males and has been transformed into females, wear women's clothes and behave in a manner consistent with their transsexual gender roles without hesitation, fear, apprehension, or disapproval. As for the individual's desire for the opposite sex or his or her sex in practising a sexual relationship, he or she is not subject to biological (masculine or feminine) influences, but rather to the cultural influences on which he or she is subject, such as social interaction and the requirements of the role he or she plays and his or her family and companionship upbringing. Then gender homogeneity occurs because the first represents cyclical cultural characteristics (changing from one culture to another) and the second represents fixed biological characteristics that do not change in all human societies. It is subject to the directives of society that change from time to time according to the speed of its development and progress and its influence on the course of public and private life, cosmic and regional. In light of this, the concepts of femininity and masculinity change so that they do not remain in their form and character but change successively. The physical strength and daring that distinguishes men from women and softness, tenderness and shyness do not remain. Adherent to the female, but masculinity has become associated with tenderness in dealing, elegance, and taste in the external appearance, carrying out household affairs and raising children inside the house, and the woman has become working outside the home and earning money to bring to her family and contribute to the family budget, and men argue about their rights and duties, so feminine and masculine concepts have changed, so they are no longer confined to biological characteristics. But this is not related to the third type of gender. Rather, there has become a third gender

390

identity that is subject to the material luxury and welfare of society, which affects the taste of individuals and changes it.

From case to case, we have seen this in the Greek Empire in the past, in the contemporary capitalist West, and in the civilizations that prevailed and then disappeared in the Ottoman and Roman eras, which did not adhere to one gender fixed concepts, but rather according to the directives of society to it, as it transforms gender and does not necessarily change sexually, like Al-Khanith in Oman whose gender is determined through his interactions with others. As long as he does not deal with women sexually, then he is not a man. Although he is a man, his clothing and external appearance are female, so he is a male who wears feminine clothes and behaves in a feminine manner and practices sodomy with him. This is the first form of the third type of gender.

So, we arrive at a summary that summarizes the issue of the third type of gender that we found in our study, these five forms: -

1. Al-Khanith in Omani society
2. The Mahus in Tahiti
3. Hijras in India
4. Bugis in Indonesia
5. The eunuch in antiquity and bygone eras

All of these forms are not stigmatized with bad or perverted stigma, or that is mocked or ridiculed, but rather they are recognized in their society, and they use them on important social occasions inside their homes, and their shortcomings in terms of social status and the positional roles that they practice in their society. It is important to clarify that society has produced these types, which is called the third type of gender, not the biological, genetic factor (male or female). It was not produced by the technological factor but rather the societal need to perform some recreational activities that social trends and orientations wanted. Then there is the wealthy and elitist royal and ruling class that they need in their palaces and families, giving them a distinguished position in their work and personal life, as is the case with eunuchs in all historical eras. Their role and development were prominent and distinguished, so they were neither marginalized nor excluded from social life.

It can be said that contemporary capitalist luxury and sophistication in Western society has transformed the traditional tasks of men and women into the contemporary, making women dress in men's clothes and act and work in the work of men. The man is adorned with the adornment of women, and the double clothing of both sexes has appeared without shame or shyness because the contemporary materialistic social culture has made this gender binary common, popular, and openly acceptable. So, it has become clear what this chapter says about the third type of gender, neither homosexual nor despised, because society and its culture produced it and announced it in its media, technologies, factories, administrations, and books, not to mention that it is a condition as old as the ages, through all phases and social horrors.

The importance of going through this topic makes me unveil a case that was absent in the works, research and theories of ancient and modern sociology, which it did not study or pay attention to it or judge negatively or positively, even though it represents a criminal behaviour that is not approved by the heavenly laws nor human morals, which is the castration of boys before they reach the age of majority by slave traders, rulers, sultans, Aghas and caliphs in order to use them in their service.

On the other hand, there are boys who have not been castrated but rather represent an exploited social segment that has no political or economic influence that society uses to perform festive practices that entertain the general public and make them different from their biological sex in their dress and behaviour. That is, they change their cultural gender. Note that the phenomenon of castration existed many centuries before the birth of sociology and prevailed in all ancient civilizations and empires.

But had it not been for the birth of the sociology of gender, attention would not have been paid to this phenomenon, which was produced by the society itself, and in particular by the ruling and wealthy elite. So, sociology did not defend it and did not condemn those who was and is exploiting them, nor did the social culture that dressed them in a new gender role and did not constitute a social problem for the general public, but it represented a criminal process. It is similar to the process of female circumcision, approved by traditional and backward social cultures in the African and Asian continent, in amputating the genitals of boys before they reach sexual maturity without taking their opinion or meeting their request in order to enjoy them sexually and recreationally and changing the features of their forms and clothing without their desire.

CHAPTER 8: THE STRUGGLE OF FEMININE AND HER SUPPORTERS AGAINST HER SLAVERY

INITIATION

A. FEMINIST MOVEMENTS THAT DEFENDED THE FEMININE AGAINST ITS SLAVERY

B. UNITED NATIONS ADVOCACY OF FEMININE WOMEN AGAINST SLAVERY

INITIATION

C. ADVOCACY OF WHO TO THE FEMININITY AGAINST HER ENSLAVEMENT

D. ADVOCACY OF UNESCO TO THE FEMININITY AGAINST HER ENSLAVEMENT

E. ADVOCACY OF WESTERN GOVERNMENTS TO THE FEMININITY AGAINST HER ENSLAVEMENT

F. ADVOCACY OF THE SCHOLARS TO THE FEMININITY AGAINST HER ENSLAVEMENT

G. ADVOCACY OF THE NATIONAL LEADERS' FIGURES TO THE FEMININITY AGAINST HER ENSLAVEMENT

H. ADVOCACY OF FEMININE REFORMIST MOVEMENTS TO FEMININITY AGAINST HER ENSLAVEMENT

CHAPTER 8
THE STRUGGLE OF FEMININE AND HER SUPPORTERS AGAINST HER SLAVERY

INITIATION

The forces of male slavery were faced the movements by the conscious feminine and her supporters among the national leadership symbols to defend her rightsHER which were usurped by the man who has concealed under a variety of covers (religion, culture, government, war, trade, industry, globalisation) because they realised and suffered from the man oppression to her and the prejudice to him via his fabricated trade-off over several centuries.

This topic leads to the clarification of the fact that changing the standards and values of a society does not happen suddenly or through a political decision, but rather through a bitter and multifaceted struggle due to the fact that it is a legacy that was developed by previous generations and passed on to the present generations. Therefore, when it is not in harmony with the spirit of the present age, it cannot be changed overnight and not through high hierarchical sites because there are conservative and advanced social segments that benefit from them and serve their personal and social interests. It is adopted by international and regional organisations, academic institutions, and research centres in order to change these inherited standards and values that are not in line with the requirements of the times. Therefore, it is important, difficult, and arduous for the generations affected by its legacy and constrained by its restrictions, which makes it take a long time to achieve the required change.

In order to analyse what was presented above about the reality of moral change, the historical events that took place in Western society are cited. The entry of women into the field of education and benefits from them in many professions that men used to do in journalism, literature, acting, art, medicine, engineering, and law are included. This has taken place in combination with the sympathy of some politicians (who were seeking their votes in parliamentary elections) plus the emergence of feminist movements demanding her freedom from male restrictions and the defence of her marital, family, and societal rights. Her demand for freedom continued so that she would not remain a victim of the oppression of the social system and the oppression of the male who practised on her through his occupation of leading hierarchical positions in constructive rhythms. Her success reflects the magnitude of the struggle of women in the Western world and the failure of the male to keep her as a victim controlled by the standards and values of constructive harmony in favour of men. It was expressed through:

1. The entry of women into the field of education.
2. The entry of women into the professional field.
3. Economic exploitation of women.
4. Some politicians sympathised with the submissive status of women, out of love to win their vote in the electoral process, not a sincere defence of them.
5. Formation of a feminist movement demanding the rights of women raped by males.
6. Some professions need soft hands more than rough ones, such as paediatrics and women, architecture, the arts of all kinds and types, media, fashion, decoration, elementary and primary education, and housekeeping.

On the other hand, the main reasons behind his response to women's demand were due to: -

1. The man's high level of education in foreign cultures.
2. His entry into the democratic political arena that calls for equality and his need for a woman's voice.
3. The need for education field for the female component after a man deserted him to go to work in factories.
4. Women's economic independence and their contribution to the family budget.
5. The disappearance of the pattern of parents choosing a wife for their son as it has become dependent on the two partners choosing each other without the interference of a third party, which made emotional feelings lessen the severity of abuse and violence.
6. The small size of the family (the nuclear family) which allows parents to take care of raising their children through their cooperation in raising them in order to cope with the spirit of the times.
7. Presence of a council for teachers and parents, P. T. A, in order to study the problems of children and not to use violence or ill-treatment in confidential and scholastic upbringing.
8. The advent of modern electronic devices and their use in the upbringing of the child, such as television, video, PlayStation, electronic games and computers, which made them avoid collision with their parents and gave them a new culture that differs from the culture of the parents and sometimes limits it.
9. An increase in violent behaviour on the part of the husband towards his wife and his children due to the weakness or lack of authority over his wife and their authority (husband and wife) over their children. The matter that made the partner spouses harden and

increased the violence so that each one of them did not lose his authority over the other. All this was apparent or worked to show loud voices calling for the reduction of wife abuse.

A. FEMINIST MOVEMENTS THAT DEFENDED THE FEMININE AGAINST ITSSLAVERY

The feminist movement's main tasks were to defend femininity and demand their rights. Their struggle in defending the female victim in the last quarter of the twentieth century has achieved a lot. Sociologists have been studying the goals of the feminist movement since its inception, which they defined in the year 1600 for a period of 360 years, after reviewing its actions and goals. They set and defined three stages which are:

The First Stage (Subservience and Submission): the woman's submission to the authority of the man orders and domination, whether in the family, in the market, in commercial, industrial, or medical work, in religious institutions (places of worship), or in military institutions, colleges, universities, publishing houses, and intellectual forums. In other words, if a woman is practising the profession of medicine, her professional status is subject to the direction and direction of her fellow doctor (the man), or if she works as a teacher in a school, her job and effort are subject to the management and instructions of the man regardless of the efficiency of her work, the seriousness of her style, perseverance of her effort and the success of her work. In other words, at the end of her work, she is subject to the domination and control of men over her work and way of life. This masculine hegemony over women is supported by the existing social system in all forms of the social structure and drawn on all layers of social hierarchy. This comprehensive domination in Western society continued until the year 1780 AD until matters and developments emerged that resulted in new cases.

The Second Stage (Grumbling and Criticism): in which the number of female writers, thinkers, literati, doctors, and nurses increased in Europe, which encouraged them to declare the disadvantages of comprehensive male domination and to express their dissatisfaction with the social oppression practised by society on them. In response to this, they put forward their criticism of their submissive and the total control and domination of men. However, these calls, propositions, and criticisms were not raised by all women of Western society, but rather by some literature and writers who have literary boldness and intellectual boldness, so their attempt has become a defence of the minority group within the society despite the fact that they represent half of the society. What is meant here by the minority group: the social activity and not the quantitative - numerical representation. The higher position of a man gives him power over the occupants of the lower positions, some of which are occupied by women. Therefore, as a supervisor and controller, the man confiscates the rights of the women occupying the lower positions within his management. This domination makes the woman weak and ineffective in her social action so that it does not make her equal and equal with the man. This, in turn, makes her withdraw from her struggle with him, making him a leader, and she is naturally becoming submissive and guided by him. Due to this social weakness of the woman, she becomes representative of a weak social minority dominated by men. Some men showed sympathy with her express their view that the progress of society is not possible without the participation of women in many professions such as medical, educational, industrial, and commercial. The woman, with this contribution, is considered as a valuable human element to help the man rather than under him as if he is her master. In contrast to this position, there are conservative men who believe that woman is an obstacle to the progress and development of society.

The Third Stage (Confrontation and Opposition): The first call to the work of women in the production process and their standing next to men in Europe was in 1780 and in 1790. As the call was organised in a controlled and delicate manner, its fruits ripened in the fifth decade of the eighteenth century 1850, after which it increased significantly and formed effective libertarian movements in the sixth and seventh decades of the twentieth century. Through this struggling chapter of women and the circumstances that accompanied them, three theoretical trends were formed, namely:

a. Focus on sexual differences.
b. Emphasising the sexual inequality.
c. Shedding light on sexual oppression.

It goes without saying that this formation led to the construction of a theory of femininity expressing multiple social issues, the most important of which are social injustice, social change, influence, interests, social beliefs, family educators (upbringing), law, politics, religion, and education.

This is what the two researchers (Patricia Madhu Lingerman, professor of sociology at George Washington University, and Gill Nybrug-Brantley, professor of sociology at Northern Virginia College) presented about the stages of the reality of women in Western society over 360 years in their tagged theory (contemporary feminine theory). [Omar 2009. p. s. 207 - 212]

1. Waves of Development of Feminist Movements

The movements went through phases in the form of waves according to specific periods of time in order to highlight the features that characterised each wave, as researchers in the affairs of these movements were able to identify three major waves (phases) for them that began at the end of the eighteenth century and continued until the nineteenth century and it reached the peak of its activity in the twentieth century.

The First Wave: It involved women's campaigns in the electoral vote between 1890 and 1920, which included new ideas and modern starting points. In 1890, many women in Europe and the United States were asked questions about their inferior status in a society characterised by their youth and advanced education, who describe themselves as "new women" who sought freedom from marriage and domestic responsibilities rather than staying in their homes who were supported by a father or husband. Unmarried and middle-class women who entered the labour market from the angle of official offices as employees and typewriters, so their new life was reflected and visible on their clothes and activities in how they occupied their spare time, which is completely different from the clothes of the housewife and her immersion in cleaning and household arrangement.

In 1895 the term feminism emerged coined and used to describe individuals who claim women's rights. There is no harm in referring to the social reformers who campaigned to improve women's lives for better education and job opportunities to reform marriage and divorce, property ownership laws, and social equality with men. Women have been active in supporting their moderate movements that oppose and struggle against the drinking of alcoholic spirits, considering them a major social evil against them and their children. In this struggle, they drew a vital picture so that men shall not spend their income and salaries on drinking alcoholic beverages in order to avoid their family's hunger, not to engage in violence with their wives, and so that their families do not disintegrate through divorce or desertion.

As for poor women, their situation was dry, as their visibility was low, with no guarantee for them, and living in poor homes with domestic violence and racial intolerance. However, in several countries, working women were involved in trade union movements opposing their oppression and contempt by the employees. This was noticeably evident in their strike in East London factories in 1888, but nevertheless, most of the women remained without union protection. There are some supporters of women who worked or joined new socialist parties that allow them to send their representatives to parliament. As for those who were more extreme, they became involved in revolutionary movements aimed at ending unjust and tyrannical governments in Russia and Eastern Europe. On the other hand, an activist movement of women's supporters emerged, and that was a year before the First World War, which called for voters to elect women and grant them the right to represent and elect members of the government, the same as for men. That was at the beginning of the twentieth century. As for young men, they had the right to vote in most European countries. The only countries in which women are able to vote are New Zealand, which granted women the right to vote in 1895, then Australia came and granted women this right in 1902 and in 1905, Finland became the first country in Europe which granted women this right. All of these countries were democratic in their rule and included strong trade unions, and accepted women's votes in the elections. As for countries with large population sizes and a wide gap between the rich and the poor, the authorities were openly opposed to the vote of women in the elections, and this situation continued for several decades.

We are now looking to the better world that women have entered, which is the issue of voting in the elections. It was more important and urgent to her than the election form that was placed in the secret ballot box. Yes, it is a public recognition of her rights and is a clear and explicit recognition of her existence. She was neglected, and no one appreciated her social input. Her voice has the power now and the influence in deciding the government and the party's election and hence the direction of the society. Respecting her voice became a must as they needed her, and she became the balancing element in the election scale. Relying on that, the government will be less selfish in its decision-making less fanatic for men. All this points to that the steps have begun to progress towards women's equality with men. The woman wouldn't remain the mother to give birth and be a housewife, but she became an active element in the life of society outside the home. And the men were forced to listen to her in peace issues, especially because she has does not like war and has sympathy for the weak than the strong due to her purity of thinking, clarity of mentality, and purity of body, which makes her rise above the selfish and corrupt man when he is in positions of power and influence.

As for the opponents of women's supporters, they used a language similar to this proposition in their drawing of the abstracts of the opposition. They defined what they think about women, where they said about them that they are smart and alert in insulting themselves in political matters that do not represent their competence but that of the man.

As for the extremists who oppose women, they see that the woman who is granted the electoral vote is the most dangerous woman because it will destroy the purity of the female by undermining the authority of men and crystallising conflicts and disagreements among the women themselves, which consequently lead to the breaking of the social system that coordinates social activities, and then life becomes chaotic and not regulated as there will be no organiser to life after the women are given the right to vote in elections.

One of the most famous election campaigns in Britain was precisely the one led by the National Union for Feminist Elections in 1903, where this union used direct actions. Between 1905 and 1914, more than a thousand women were arrested and detained, many of whom went on hunger strike and were forced to eat by prison guards because they were aiming to ignite the widespread revolution.

The American movement, however, was established much later than the founding of the British feminist movement due to the pioneering work of the National Feminist Elections Organization. This continued in reform until it reached the reform of American laws, but without benefit and success.

In 1915, fifteen of the forty American states in which women have voted prompted young American women to express their boredom and discomfort with this deficient state by practising more technical methods than their involvement in their arrest or imprisonment. This was in the form of an announcement about a meeting in which they used new and (at the time) media, namely radio and public ads in the streets, but they forgot to contact the labour movements, immigrants, and the coloured women in the big cities who are also fighting for racial equality. But when the First World War took place in Europe in 1914, it greatly affected women's activity, which was absent from the political and social arena.

The impact of the First World War was not expected on the advocates and defenders of women's rights. In the years prior to 1914, defenders of women's rights began activities outside the American continent in order to expand their activities and make it global, and the links between the United States of America and Britain became stronger than ever. Extraordinarily strong in the field of the feminist movement, and then translating the calls, demands, and goals of this movement into several foreign languages, it entered the political camps such as the socialist, the Pacific, and other countries of the world. However, World War I forced feminist defenders to choose either of the two issues, either patriotism with loyalty to the homeland or engaging in global communication. Societies with a large population have chosen loyalty to the homeland to the point that even the extremists abandoned the election campaigns and went to defend their countries opposing the war, so a thousand women participated in a peace campaign from twelve countries that they met in Holland, which was neutral in the war. In April 1915, everyone demanded that Governments stop defamation and grant women the right to vote in elections.

Although the urgent demand of women as outlined above was focusing on the right to elections and candidacy, the community movement was not unified. It was exposed to influences and obstacles that did their work on the interaction of society with it. The First World War, which lasted for four years, imprinted the standard of living of European women with various influences. For example, the rushing of young men to defend their country has created a void in the labour market that allowed women to enter it to fill this professional void. Similarly, it happened in public transportation lines and civil services, which required women to fill these needs and work in them for long hours in addition to her work in the nursing service as a nurse in homes and health centres. This was due to the harsh conditions imposed by the war that withdrew men from service and public work that was said to be dangerous to women and not suitable for females because they were of low degrading status. During the war, work became a matter of patriotism, duty and national honour, and this is what changed the balance of value and popular judgment on works that were restricted to women. In spite of these abnormal circumstances, the woman did not get equal wages to what the man receives for the same job. It was much less than the work related to cooking, cleaning, and caring for children. It goes without saying that the war has made the issue of women's right to elections a secondary issue, and there was little talk about it or demanding it because everyone is busy with war and its devastating effects economically, politically, and militarily. It is, therefore, right to state that the issue of women's right to elections flourishes in times of peace and prosperity. The government recognised this social fracture, and in the face of this limited change in the role of women, some neutral governments in the war, such as Norway and Denmark, guaranteed the right of women to vote relatively in the years 1913 and 1915.

Before departing from these developments that took place in this wave unless it is important to refer to the occurrence of revolutions within Europe, for example, Russian women, through the Russian Revolution, have obtained the right to vote in 1918, immediately after the emergence of the Austrian, German, and Polish nations. Some governments used a right to vote for women being rewarded for the services they provided in the First World War, such as Canada, which granted the right to vote to the military nurse in 1917 and then included all Canadian women in 1918. As for the British woman over the age of thirty years, she obtained the right to vote in 1918 as for men, while a young woman must wait until 1928 to vote equally as does a man when he reaches the age of twenty-one. That is, after 1928, all young men and women in Britain who had reached the age of twenty-one were entitled to vote. As for American women, they were granted the right to vote in 1920.

The travails that were happening in this wave have changed and transformed the role of women in electoral life and hence imposed many questions such as; Does a woman obtaining the right to vote lead to a change in society? And it makes women live a better life? Did wars and revolutions hinder or push women to participate in elections? Did the parliamentary, socialist, and leftist governments make women influence political life? In fact, despite the periodic transformations of women in political elections, they did not achieve much influence in political life, whether in parliamentary or socialist countries. Women were like men. They voted according to their political beliefs and based on their class decline. However, voting in the elections conveyed the message that when women enter the world of politics and public life, life becomes more regular, careful and less selfish. However, some politicians have become more sensitive to concern for women, so they forgot laws for the development of women's education equal to men in public life, like Denmark. On the whole, few women made it to political offices, and a few were then elected according to the vote and are still planning how to proceed to a better future.

The Second Wave: It held the title Feminism Turning to the Liberation of Women. In 1960 the feminist movement was living in the depths of the past and linked with its events and its historical heritage. In 1970 it became the goal of the feminist movement to take frank positions and enter into intense debates and discussions. This period was later called the second wave of the feminist movement, while the first wave was struggling to obtain the right to vote, but the term feminism was rarely used, and in 1970 it was replaced by the name of the liberation of women. In 1960, this movement included new reasons that came to it from the African and the Asian continents and from some countries that were struggling to obtain their independence from European rule. In the United States of America, there was the civil rights movement that did not use violent campaigns to attract or draw people's attention to the racial discrimination and poverty prevalent among African Americans. Some campaigns went even further, supporting violent methods in order to achieve the emancipation of slaves, in addition to the exit of many individuals in the form of demonstrations against the US government's involvement in its war with Vietnam (1964-1975).

Some individuals, such as Hippies (the existential beetles), rejected this prevailing trend in society (i.e. the movement to defend women's rights), so they removed it from favouritism and prejudice to simple, existential, immaterial living. On the other side, there are many who supported and helped this movement continuously for a long period of time. The beetles' attitude of existential appeared in their music, sex, drugs and clothing, which has become an organised part of their livelihood. While this movement emerged in North America, it spread widely and rapidly in

Western Europe and Australia alike and was supported by effective television programs.

It is striking that since the beginning, women joined this movement for change and translated their joining in their marches calling for civil rights and their demonstrations against the war with Vietnam, and then followed by the way the beetles live in their lives. All this led to their possibility that their struggle would achieve success in their demand for equality with men. But they discovered that women in extremist groups also face the preference of men over them, inequality, and a lack of respect for them in many parts of the world.

They realised that men think, speak, write, and women listen, cook, clean, serve, and respond to sexual intercourse as desired by men. When faced with this certainty, women were disappointed and freed from the illusion that prevailed over them when they faced discrimination in movements calling for equality and justice for all. The women realised that even the liberal and progressive movements that raise idealistic, exemplary, and utopian human slogans are a matter of false gain, lying and hypocrisy and that in reality, they discriminate against women as well, which shocked and freed her from the illusion that she had in her imagination. Therefore, she did not believe the movements' call for justice and equality between men and women. In other words, she encountered the true and practised reality in social, political, and professional activities.

We now turn to the topic of how and when the term "Woman liberation movement" appeared. Initially, it is more like the movement of people of colour and the demonstrations that came out hostile to the war aimed at achieving change in society to be fit with the developments of the age. This is what women did, similar to the colourists and those who object to the war with Vietnam, meaning there is no person or incident responsible for forming or establishing the women's liberation movement. After the middle of the sixth decade of the last century, women began to form small groups that discuss general problems and write an official statement regarding their goals, motives, and points of view, in addition to planning actions and positions that reflect their ambitions. Within several years, feminist groups have emerged in several countries from the world. These practices are carried out, then the term women's liberation has crystallised, which has become a global appeal similar to electoral voting. Several groups have tried to achieve change. It is worth noting here that the women's liberation movement includes an extremist minority and a moderate majority. The first (extremist) group believes that women will not be liberated except through revolution, and otherwise, they will not obtain their liberation at the same time. There is a lot of discussion about what kind of form will take its character in this regard.

For some groups, a representation of political violence was manifested. They seek to a coup, topple, or overthrow the capitalist system, especially since the extremist feminist movement tried to establish links and ties with trade unions and left-wing political parties. In 1968, protests, riots, and escalating political events appeared in Europe and North America, but they did not last for long, so the political system remained in place.

Then there are other women who rejected the communist and capitalist regimes together and saw the influence of the man and the patriarchal system as an existing problem for them. They tried to convince others on fabricated sayings that society is based on the needs of women even if there are many men and children in it. Not only that, but this group is

410

demanding separation from men when it focuses on rape, domestic violence, discrimination against lesbians and the exploitation of women in pornography.

There is no way to point out that most of the supporters and defenders of women's liberation do not belong to any group, but they are calling for change within the existing political and economic system. Organisations such as the National Organization for Women, called (Now) in the United States, and the electronic pressure group for women in Australia, pressured or exerted pressure on their governments to change the unjust laws that favour men over women and distinguish them. They also demanded the expansion of opportunities for women at work. The practitioners of these groups are descended from the middle class and whites. They supported thousands of women in their rights not to favour men, which led to the government responding to them by abolishing the preferential laws with new ones and policies in support of women's rights.

It is clear that that woman's liberation has never been representative of a unified movement, as many women of colour felt that the focus was mainly placed on the problems of the middle class and white women and the lack of defence of black women, especially those from the poor class who were plagued by poverty, racial suffering, and housing Lousy, miserable schools, a complex social system, and constant daily persecution. In this regard, one writer said that in 1967, a black woman in the United States earned only 40% of the average white man's salary, while a white woman earned 60 per cent. From then on, the black woman began to establish her own feminist movement called the Black Women Movement.

The women realised that if they wanted to express their interests and rights, they had to rely on themselves rather than depend on others. Hence the emergence of their awareness of their fate through their meetings and discussion of their suffering and the obstacles that stand in the way of their march. These meetings included small groups distinguished with brilliant awareness. They spoke freely about why they felt persecuted and upset and what they wanted to do. Their meetings took place in bookstores, public cafes, and places where they felt safe and comfortable, and this was the first time the feminist action was aware of their movement.

It is not surprising to say that the woman in the subject of her liberation focused on her own personal experiences such as her sexual relations, her pregnancy, and the breastfeeding of her children, but many women still felt that they had little control over their bodies and their lives. In many countries, it was difficult to obtain contraceptives or obtain a formal abortion and unwanted pregnancies. Women find it exceedingly difficult to get rid of them, and despondent and miserable women view abortion as illegal. That is, do not think of getting rid of it because it is a legal problem, and when it is illegal, it is not without health complications that the pregnant woman pays for, which sometimes leads to death due to the non-use of sterile and sanitary tools. Therefore, it is not surprising that safe, legal, or required abortion becomes one of the main reasons for a woman's right to raise her slogan, which demands control over her body without interference from the government, church, family, partner, or employees in official offices.

It goes without saying that the emancipation of women has not overlooked or forgotten the workers' wages that women receive, as they rarely get a job of equal status with that of men, or that the value of their wages is the same as the value of men's wages. Simply this difference is due to the fact that most works and services were classified according to gender. Any work that is specific to men, because it is characterised by or requires a special skill that is not found except for men, and women's work in which no men but women work because they have professional skill and women do not have advanced skills. Accordingly, the wages for their work are lower than that of men. On the other hand, people used to view the man as the breadwinner for his family, so more wages were paid to him than the woman, and her wages were lower because her work was seen as being surplus to need. The situation did not remain at this pace, as it changed somewhat due to women's marriage and exacerbated divorce rates with the support and strengthening of the women's liberation movement for women who carried out or called for a strike.

With what was said above, specific questions can be asked stating whether the demand for equality is desirable or applicable? Why does a woman insist on imitating a man? Why enter a losing battle at an end? Don't you know that the man is finally judging her work? Doesn't the woman know that society is biased in favour of men? Didn't the woman realise that she does not have the skills and abilities the way a man does? Didn't women see life activities imprinted on the nature of discrimination between men and women? These questions are answered in books and articles published by Feminist Publications and recognised by German Greer, Kat Melt, Cloria Stneem, Sheila Robertham, and others.

It can be said that the woman's liberation movement was very active and controversial as it had established great support from men and women. At the same time, it faced great opposition from both parties who see it as undermining the natural order and feminist values, as well as millions of women marching and demonstrations for change. In fact, the woman's liberation movement was a big movement for women without leadership, and there were few reasons uniting the wealthy, poor, white, black, married, single, lesbian, and normal women. In the eighties of the twentieth century, the movement split into several divisions and lost much of its vitality.

The women's liberation movement and associated groups played a vital role in the history of feminists. Although it was not always organised in a coordinated manner, it presented feminist ideas that served millions of women in their struggle and recorded important events in the history of humanity. Accordingly, women's rights emerged in Asia, Latin America, Africa, the Middle East, and other feminist movements, regardless of their colours and forms, and become part of women's lives in the world.

A summary is given here about the second phase (the second wave) of the feminist movement. It began in the sixth decade of the twentieth century, which was characterised by inspirations and innovators who recorded in their books the struggle of women against the injustice of men, such as Simone de Beauvoir in her book entitled "The Second Sex" 1953, Bette Friedan in her book entitled "The Feminist Mystery" 1963, Kat Melt in her titled publication " Sexual Politics 1970, and Jeremy Greer in her book entitled "The Castrated Female" 1970. The issuance of these books has fundamentally transformed the discussions and debates among people, which affected the writings of knowledge fields such as political, psychological, cultural and anthropology. This, in turn, expanded the movement's activity, pushing it further than it was in political rhetoric and making a defiant and blatant presentation of the most fundamental possibilities of culture and civilisation. These books came at a time when women needed the extremist social expression and the liberation of policies that they had wished for and demanded in order to be free from the oppression of men for thousands of years. For the extremist feminist movement, liberation and emancipation represent its urgent demand to improve its share in legal, political and social life in order to change people's attitudes towards gender and to equate the balance of influence between it and men.

In Britain, there has been a wide-ranging legal and legislative transformation that achieved a lot of equality between men and women when the abortion law reform 1967 was passed, the divorce law reform 1969, a statutory decision on equal work wages 1970, a statutory decision on sexual discrimination 1975, a statutory decision to protect employees in 1975, and a legal decision on violence domestic 1977. In spite of all these legal legislations, progress in dealing with the forces of the structure of gender differentiation in society is still weak. But the biological distinction between the two still exists. The woman is characterised by passion, cooperation, service and sacrifice that she gained from motherhood, while the man is characterised by strength, competition and limited emotion. These constants explain the biological paradoxes between them. Note that the history of mankind has recorded a lot of conflicting struggles between males and females. At the same time, we witnessed the involvement of the feminist movement in the peaceful movements and against the destruction of the environment and the nuclear war more than the positions of the male movements.

The Third Wave: Which began in the ninth decade of the twentieth century, supporters of women in this period discussed new topics, such as civil liberation, a reason for the legal advancement of women, medical and technical innovations that women use in their homes, such as contraceptives, menstrual hygiene pads, cosmetic and beautification, plus kitchen and household appliances that they use. The aim was to help her and lift the burdens of her responsibilities in cleaning and arranging her home and facilitating the cooking of food and ease her suffering with her children who were born without planning, so the troubles of the house and raising children did not remain as arduous and exhausting for women as used to be before. On the other hand, female writers have emerged and focused their attention on women's affairs and their requests for equality with men, such as:

1- Germaine Greer: Published a book entitled "Sex and Destiny" 1985, which dealt with compassion for women in their family life and raising children.

2- Jane Camellia Baghillian: who wrote about sex, art, and American culture in 1990, in which she inquired about the status of eunuch women.

In light of these evolutionary changes, the woman was called the "new female" after removing the prejudices that were hanging over her in several areas of social life. Also, during this period, the social and political atmosphere accepted the idea of equality between men and women, but the problem of gender discrimination did not completely and totally end. In British society, the wages of women remained lower than the wages of men, and they worked part-time, with low and insecure status, of low skill and temporary work more than men. But in spite of that, there were women who were at the top of the major professions in the legal and medical, academic universities, the media and the main civil services. In addition to that, in 2001 there were 40% of companies confirmed that they have no women in them, and the rate of employment of women decreased from 57% in 1999 to 69% in 2001. It is a wave or phase that differs from the previous phase in its qualitative and quantitative movement.

As for gender, it is marked by the cultural character that determines the different roles between men and women in general. It was imposed on behavioural patterns that are not related to biological or natural differences, which stipulate that woman assume their responsibilities in caring for children.

As for the political type, it represents a doctrine that reflects the oppression and injustice practised by one of the social types (men and women) on the other. It reflects the powers of men over women in a society in which the man has control over women in all activities of all social life. [Omar 2017. p. s. 162 - 179]

2. Schools of The Feminist Movement

When women have a mass movement, this means or must include a doctrine that reflects its goals, ambition, thought and logic. This is what has been made clear by those interested in studying social movements who said that they are an ideological movement as the mass movements that are included in society. Rather, the difference between them and the doctrines of the movements is the difference in degree, not by type. This is, in fact, what makes them extremely difficult to analyse and criticise. They include many ideological covers with distinctive experiences of women in society as well as their dealings with many fields of knowledge such as law, government, region, state, legitimacy, economic patterns, historical interpretations, language, ideas, and events extracted from other fields such as psychology, social biology, sociology, and anthropology. Nevertheless, there are criticisms directed at it in that it

417

represents a literary movement and others say it is an incomplete doctrine that other movements such as liberalism, socialism and conservatism have contributed to its formulation. Even so, it includes sharp and bitter goals, methodology, theories, and aspirations. Based on this introduction, the paths of the movement can be defined, and its objectives as a mass movement, namely the liberal, socialist, conservative, and extremist feminism movement, can be interpreted.

a) **The Liberal Feminist Movement:** This movement school emerged and arose in the arms of the first wave (first phase) throughout the nineteenth century from beginning to end. Leading names such as Mary Wollstonecraft, Harriet Teller, and J. s. Mills have all contributed and participated in its emergence and construction, focusing on the full ambition of civil and legal rights for women, reinforced in their focus on legal norms. As for the character of this movement, it is basically liberal, stressing equal gains and demands between men and women in terms of work and competition in the labour market and wages.

   In the second wave, Betty Friedan and others emerged who stated that women are directed by the myth of culture that made them a family member who has an appropriate role in life and that her education gives her a major role in public life. As for the feminist movement in Britain, it added the political factor to women's previous claims, so many legislations were enacted, such as the right to abortion legislation in 1967, the equal wages legislation in 1970 and the sexual discrimination legislation in 1975. In fact, such legislation gives women rights that help them - as human beings - to have freedom of choice about their livelihood in social life outside their home.

There are criticisms of the feminist movement, indicating that it cared about middle-class women and neglected working-class women. Nevertheless, many of their demands have been fulfilled in the Western world, particularly in the field of civil and political rights.

b) **The Socialist Feminist Movement:** Some (idealist) socialists of the nineteenth century, such as Forer, Saint Simon, and Robert Owen, believed that their ideas had important applications for women in terms of the widespread tolerance of the sexual environment in which they were free from the responsibility and burden of caring for children and domestic affairs by transferring most of the family functions to the local community. Abun said that religion is what subjugated the woman to the man, through her marriage to him and her humiliation by him, as he made her a slave to serve him and care for his stature, happiness, and well-being.

Marx was also interested in the emancipation of women, although he was living a conservative life within his family. Nevertheless, he believed that the socialist revolution would liberate women and that the communist system was not effective in granting women equality with men. Therefore, he took a conservative position on her, especially her political role. Therefore, women were more in their calls for emancipation were extreme when they saw the socialists and communist's conservative in their outlook and not serious about changing their role in politics and work. Whereas Engels defended women in writing entitled "The Origin of the Family" 1884, which identified the roots of women's oppression in the economic system based on private ownership and domination by men, so the woman became owned by the man, just as his feudal possessions were, and her position was lowered to a level lower than that of men. But it is possible to eliminate the injustice inflicted on women through her class struggle, which is part of her general struggle, and that the removal of the capitalist system means the end of women's oppression, as they are exploited by the capitalist system to a large extent with low wages and influence and allowing men to achieve the requirements of the capitalist system through her care for her children and her contribution in the family budget. It is therefore supportive of the capitalist system through its subservience and servitude to the man and the capitalist system, but it can obtain its demands for equality only if it is freed from the control of the man and the hegemony of the capitalist system.

Marxist activist Juliet Mitchell, in her book Feminists or Women's Affair in 1971 and her other book, "Psychoanalysis and the Feminist Movement," 1974, stated that the injustice and oppression of women in capitalist society is not only representative of economic exploitation but rather includes several psychological and cultural aspects that can be changed.

c) **The Conservative Feminist Movement:** This school emphasises the equal roles between men and women in a different way because it is subject to the division of human nature that men and women perform within the private (home) and public (outside the home) life, and thus it promotes male values and the interests of men. This represents the wide exploitation of women and humiliating dependencies that can be seen in her sexual relationship with men and her care for children. She is thus enslaved to men. The best example of this school is the Arab society, which restricts women to many responsibilities and at the same time by granting them respect and a visible status with a measure of personal freedom.

Therefore, the family is the best example of female activities and achievements, and there are conservative women who defend their conservative role in raising their children and taking care of their home affairs and prefer to be the core and centre of the family. They are happy with this responsibility more than their work outside the family and their wages for their work. An example of this type of conservative woman is Jane Bethke, M. 1981, in her book entitled "On the Public Man and the Special Woman", in which she published many points of view in which a woman's experience in life derives from motherhood, tenderness, passion, organisation, and cleanliness as a general quality in which all women share.

d) **The Radical Feminism Movement:** This school arose in the arms of the second wave (the second phase), and the substance of this movement focuses on the injustice and oppression that was practised on women. It was prevalent in the past and present that its origin was the injustice of the patriarchal system that covered the political, cultural, economic, religious, and social space through the role of women in the gender exploiting the woman by a man who permeates the entire culture and is challenged by politics, economics, culture, art, philosophy, science, and language.

Among the oddities of the demands that this movement demanded was to have a special language for men to speak to women. That is, the man should create vocabulary expressing his respect and appreciation for the woman when he speaks with her. It represents a new language that expresses gentle and non-violent tenderness. This is considered enslavement of the man, and this leads to healthy relations between the two.

Follow up and Comment:

It is indisputable that the stages of the feminist movement aimed at the end of its activities to change the role and position of women in society. Since the individual, whether a man or a woman, cannot change society, social movements through their continuous organisation and activities and obtaining support from some segments of society achieve part of the social change, provided that major changes in society, allowing these movements to progress and influence the overall movement of the society and change some of its expectations and obligations towards that individual whose social status is to be changed.

Since society consists of two main types of individuals from a biological point of view (male and female), any change sought by one of them is at the expense of the other party because they are socially and sometimes in blood interconnected (within the family). If the interests and needs of any party are damaged, he/she will not submit without resisting the change that has harmed his/her private and public interests and needs. And since the first and most important cell in society (the family) is mainly based on them, the interest of the family has the greatest priority in its position on this change that will affect it as well (constructively, functionally, and ontologically).

It can be said then that the feminist movement and the women's liberation movement are not going to be easy or welcome by the man and the family. This is mainly because they will be harmed in such a change, except the major changes that happen to the human society, such as the industrial revolution and what it has brought in terms of removing men from work in the field and the household and taking them to the laboratory and manufacturing plant led to the use of women in employment in the education and nursing line that the man left for her. The communication and information revolution were brought about by the speed of communication that made women interact with all women of the world in their liberation ideas, defending themselves and their social standing.

However, the war and patriarchy and capitalism did not free her from responsibilities but rather forced her to undertake patriotic work in military nursing, caring for the family and education. Changing the role and status of women through their feminist movement started by asking them to vote in the elections, which meant for them to enter areas that were not permitted because they were limited or restricted to men only, such as political organisations, official departments, political parties, and the labour market. Her first and last concern was her entry into the field of parliamentary and municipal elections, which began in 1890, and this was her first step to leave her traditional situation (at home and in the family) to turn into the new stage of women looking for freedom from marriage and household responsibility and relying on men to spend their livelihoods. The first thing that appeared this change was on her clothes, which became different from the clothes that she wears at home in terms of colours, fashion, elegance, and diversity. Not only that, but she took advantage of her free time for entertainment activities that she spends in cafes, resorts, public parks, and travels on family trips away from home and enjoying exercise and, physical agility and attention to her health after she spent her spare time sewing, knitting, embroidery and cooking food.

This challenge, which women started, attracted the attention of social reformers, so they supported some of her demands by allowing her to enter the education, nursing and labour market, demanding and defending her marital rights and stopping the use of domestic violence against her. What is striking is that they were opposed to men's addiction to alcoholic spirits because it threatened the family's existence in its budget and dismantling it, and the husband's disavowal of his family responsibility, wasting his money, neglecting his wife, as well as leading to the impoverishment of the family.

Her activity was not limited to this opposition, but she also opposed ethnic discrimination against her, which led to her involvement in trade union movements opposing her oppression and contempt by employees in companies and official departments. This led to the involvement of some of them in radical revolutionary movements to topple oppressive and tyrannical governments such as the Russian government and governments of Eastern Europe. However, her activity did not continue with the same enthusiasm and eagerness but was hindered by the occurrence of the First World War, and her calls for voting, elections, and equality with men were stopped due to everyone's preoccupation with war and defending the country and the soul.

For her, her demand to vote means recognition of her rights as a citizen, not just as a wife, as a member of society and not only in the family, as an industrial and economic producer, but not as a human producer - by birth - and as a political sponsor, not as a family educator, and as a social activist, not as a household cleaner, and as a writer and a thinker, not as a listener only, not a clown and a servant, and as a person with a voice heard by others, not as an individual who has no voice, and as a member in the decision-making process, not as a follower to the decision, and as a real contributor to building the social system that does not break her.

Such demands and pleading led to her being fought, arrested, and withdrawn by the governmental authorities because they considered such actions to break the social order and offend the woman's femininity. This is on the outward level, but on the real and deep level, it is to curtail the power and delegate his selfishness and greed to dominate her (his feeling) to stop her interferes in his manliness affairs, which he has become accustomed to and practised over the centuries.

There is no harm in saying that such a change in the balance of social forces within the first cell, the social structure, the position of the man, and the politics of the social and political system does not work in the interest of the man. Since a long time ago, he has been the dominator and therefore, he considers such demands by women are contrary to the human nature that God created. In reality, however, it does not enhance his influence, authority, and sovereignty, upon which he was raised and served his goals. But he forgot that the social, political, and economic conditions did not continue in this way all the time. Rather, major global events came that forced him to give up some of his powers and influence in the family, society, and politics in order for women to enter and take his place and help him in his social and political tasks not as a competition and conflict with him, but as a partner in the process Political, social and family.

This presentation reveals that social change was not caused by women or their social standing, but by major events such as wars, revolutions, and innovations, all of which created the society's need for the second half of the society to contribute to advancing change through her movement that led her to: -

- Achieving some equality in rights and duties.
- Entering the world of politics, elections, and voting.
- Entering educational institutions and acquiring education.
- Combating racial, national and class discrimination between her and men.
- Obtaining some financial gains to have wages from her work outside the home close to the wages of the man.
- She is economically independent and does not depend on men to provide for her.
- Reducing the number of childbearing in the family.
- Obtaining her rights in marriage and divorce.
- Stopping the violence practised against her by men.
- Her entry into the labour market, but she did not obtain professional leadership positions as the man got.
- Freed from the strict shackles of the past that restricted her outside the home.

It is worth pointing out that the change achieved by women was not alone, but with the support and assistance of the civil rights movements, movements against ethnic discrimination, slave emancipation, and movements against the war in Vietnam.

The context of the conversation requires me to say that the feminist movement and the women's liberation movement did not aim at separating women from work in public and private life but rather aimed at keeping pace with and following up on social developments in the social circle by transforming her limited function within the limits of the family (childbearing, upbringing, cooking and caring for the husband) to contribute to the productive and political process, the family budget, the improvement of its standard of living, and the livelihood of her children, in order for her not to be left behind and crushed by the wheels of change. Her demands, therefore, do not mean competition with the man or conflict with him, nor the acquisition of his authority, the withdrawal of his influence, nor his subordination to her, but rather equality in living and realising her or her feeling that she is a human being who has rights like her husband's rights and that her voice is heard and interacted with her thinking and she says her words not only on her children but in her professional work and to be rewarded as a man is at work, and for her voice to be heard in her pregnancy, raising her children and controlling her body, and that the professions are not classified on the basis of gender (this work is for women and that work is for men).

Finally, I do not want to leave this subject until I say my statement that the demand of women to equal their rights with men is an applicable requirement if she wants to assume the responsibilities of the man who was borne by them before the demand for equality, and if the man accepts to abandon those responsibilities. This is in terms of tolerance and abandonment by both parties on the logical and theoretical side, but on the real level, equality between them does not happen automatically and smoothly. Rather, the developments of the society and its articulated transformations within the structural system are what force men and women (alike) to change their positions, roles, and activities. Then obligate them to submit to these developments and break out of the patriarchal and capitalist system. This allows them to enter a new world that requires abandoning many traditional responsibilities and duties to assume modern ones that are required by the spirit of the times rather than what each requires because both of them are subject to this new and renewed spirit.

There is no fear of the rise of women to new levels that the man used to occupy, nor the man's fear of who would be taken from him. Before the spirit of renewal, it is a social responsibility that the man and woman pay for the benefit of society, whether they like it or not. [Omar. 2007. p. s. 180 - 190]

3. Treatment of Feminine Topic by Sociology

Sociology was always there and dealt with the issue of femininity continuously, but the densest was the period of 80 years starting from 1840 until 1960 when it analysed the movement and their associated changes. Historically, the feminist movements were not new in American society as their roots go back to the colonial stage, specifically on March 13th, 1776, before the independence of America. However, the first organised movements appeared in New York City in the town of Sync Avals on July 19th 1848. Its goal was to defend women's rights, demanding political and legal equality with men. With the advancement of time, the increase in political awareness and the decrease in the illiteracy among women, and the multiplication of their number in official institutional sites, the movement demanded that women shall be given the right to elect the President of the republic. That was in 1920 when this demand became her primary goal leaving her calls to lift grievances in the social and economic spheres.

This movement, therefore, did not reach the active and past state of pushing the wheel of social change in American society, and this situation was called the first wave of the feminist movement.

The second wave then came in the sixth decade of the last century, and its power greatly increased in the seventh decade of the same century, as it was manifested by the issuance of three books expressing her will, goals and

428

activity through her discussion of the rights of the disadvantaged women, which are the following: -

1. The second genus is called de Bouvard.
2. Betty Friedan's Feminine Mystic.
3. Kat Gillette's Sexual Politics.

This movement was not satisfied with defending women's rights against sexism but rather went to defend the rights of blacks (Negroes) who were disputed by whites and defined its hostile stance on America's war with Vietnam. This expansion was mainly due to the test of exercising their movement influence, and when it succeeded in that, an extremist feminist movement was born. Its name is the "feminist liberation movement", in which it called for the removal of submissive, obedient, and vulnerable roles in all institutions of American society. In addition to its other goals, which includes opposing the global hegemony exercised by the role of men in order to free her so that its role is lofty, not kneeling, strong, not weak, an active who is positioned in the foreground, not a careless person positioned in the shadows, primary, not secondary, and her role shall be the same as the man's role in the home, office, law, politics, economics and administration.

It is not surprising that the woman's social awareness has grown by her movement, which in turn pushed her to take a conflict position with the social system to obtain her lost rights, especially with regard to social and health solidarity, and representation in government councils to eliminate sexual discrimination in education and employment, They also, demanded permission for abortion condemning the abuse of a woman by the man in her family and opposing the imposition of contraceptive methods on minorities and the poor classes of American society. This means that feminism has become a past and effective mechanism in pushing the

429

process of social change by changing some of the formal and customary components of the social system.

The topic of femininity did not take its place in the sociology literature regularly and seriously in the period between 1840-1860 due to the opposition of society at the time. However, the matter changed in the period between 1890 - 1920 due to the events that encouraged and revitalised this issue. In light of these social transformations, three sociological treatments emerged due to the different periods of their treatments, which are the following:

1. The period between 1840-1960: Writings defending femininity appeared in the professional and political fields. And since sociology was at the beginning of its emergence and development, the writings of its researchers on the professional and political situation of women, not the sociology perspective, were included, so they were more mobilising and informative writings than a systematic methodology.

2. Containment of the issue of femininity marginally and not essential, mediated by theories that dealt with the role of men and women in society.

3. The work of some social workers interested in professions and career work, such as Herbert Spencer, Max Weber, Emile Durkheim, and Talcott Parsons, represented a conservative character. Their treatments of masculinity and femininity lacked the coherent ideas and common sense upon which sociology depends. That is, they did not deal with it in a critical manner but rather in a general and floating manner, according to what their circumstances dictated to them. In other words, they were not serious and serial writings but rather sporadic and in-depth.

430

Moreover, the first writings on femininity in sociology came from men and not women because the founders of this science were men, and their propositions were political rather than educational, economic, psychological, or social.

As for the second generation of sociologists, they wrote about femininity in a marginal and not essentially independent manner, such as George Zamel, William Isaac Thomas, Engels, and Karl Marx. However, the active act that revealed the issue of women in the field of sociology emerged with their opposition to society and their demand for equality in rights and duties with men. Talcott Parsons' writings on the family emerged as a social institution. That is, he deals with it as a fundamental and basic subject in sociology and not through other topics. He also stressed that it is the basic and the core for every social stability, but rather that it is a vital agency in the social educator (upbringing) process in which the human being acquires all the inhibitors of society (mechanisms of social control) on which social balance depends and give them emotional tenderness and social warmth.

Parsons then explained the system of division of labour in the family and the role of both men and women in it. Men link the family unit to the social system and nurture its members with ambition, motivations, and proper ethical directives and restrain themselves, while women accomplish internal family functions such as raising children, developing their tendencies of love and sympathy, and helping them to use expressive methods about their emotions and desires.

This sociological work done by Parsons explained to us the similarity of men and women in their family functions and caring for their children. Their competition and struggle mean the tearing of their family lives or the weakening of

431

their ties, which does not lead to social stability. [Omar. 2007. p. s. 207 - 211]

B. UNITED NATIONS ADVOCACY OF FEMIN-INE WOMEN AGAINST SLAVERY

Initiation

The United Nations, as an international organisation, protects human interests against extremism, discrimination, intolerance, slavery, trafficking and injustice between social groups, classes, and races (ethnicities, religions, sects and masculinity). It has stood as a sponsor and advocate for the rights of women in the world to defend her against intolerance, prejudice, and slavery, supporting her movement in several international conferences, calling on the governments of the world by not preferring the male over the feminine, and stopping violence against her and her enslavement.

In order to highlight the United Nations advocacy for femininity, statistical data on global gender inequality are provided in order to nurture gender awareness in all societies so that they can learn about it and stand against the abuse and prejudice practised on the feminine in the world.

The question that comes to mind in this context is, do biological differences constitute a global social problem that obliges the United Nations, as a global organisation, to take care of it and assign its specialised agencies to investigate and assess the size of this problem in the world and show its effects on human society?

The answer is yes because it caused biological intolerance by men against women in all societies, as well as crystallised racial discrimination between white, black, and yellow sex in American society. It has also achieved a professional comparison by men against women in all societies. Moreover, it has created two incompatible positions in the social hierarchy through the superior (male) and low (female) status in all societies. It has even created a social dilemma in American society even though the population of women is 51 %. And it is considered from the minority fanatic towards it. [Kendall. 2012. P.70)]

These differences highlighted the inferior and weak female (despite her active vitality in several families and social roles) who became oppressed, enslaved, and excluded by the man. All of this is due to the lack of wealth, influence, power and prestige that a man possesses.

These material and moral resources are the ones that wasted or weakened their entitlement to their legitimate rights, with no supporters and advocates for their rights by leaders, reformers, or international organisations.

Therefore, there is no success in addressing this problem, which represents a social phenomenon with a recent problem in the movement of changing society, which impedes its progress and paralyses the movement of the half of society in addition to the unfairness of the individual (women) who provide services and achieve basic periodic and coordinated functions for society and social culture. It represented unfairness, denial and obscurity of their rights legitimacy causes an imbalance in the dynamics and course of the actor's forces in the wheel of change.

1. **Statistical Data on Universal Gender Inequality**

The United Nations released statistical data indicating and expressing the masculine preference over the feminine in the world in 2013, issued by the Department of Foreign Affairs and Trade in Australia in the most important areas of life and the world in society, namely:

1) Health,
2) Education,

3) Electoral voting,
4) Contribution to economic food production,
5) Violence.

These five areas reflect the continuity of the contemporary qualitative differentiation in present civilisations (at the present time 2013). Despite the high awareness of the present woman and her assumption of leadership positions in advanced and developed societies, her percentage remained high in preserving her illiteracy while excluding her from vital work, and with her rich contribution to feeding half the world's population is with agricultural yields, but the masculine world continues in physical and sexual assault on them by 1/3 and 2/3. For men, male power outmoded traditions and nondemocratic political systems. It is a feminist social movement that is okay, but it still needs more and more in order to approach gender equality.

These are statistical data that reveals the situation:

a) In the Field of Health and Education:
1. Two-thirds of the 774 million adult women are illiterate and cannot read and write in all parts of the world. This percentage is the same as it was twenty years ago.
2. There are 61 million children who are not enrolled in primary school, of whom 32.1 million are girls.
3. There are gender gaps in education and employment that have impeded economic growth. There are countries that have not reached gender equality in primary and secondary education, leaving between 0.1 and 0.3 per cent per person in the growth rate.

b) Take the Leadership and Establish Peace:
1. By the end of April 2013, women occupied 21.2% of seats in parliament around the world occupying single and primary seats.

2. There are only 7 out of 150 women who have been elected women heads of government in the world, and only 11 out of 192 heads of government.
3. 40 women out of 271 are parliament presidents.

c) Economic Mandate and Livelihood Security (Livelihoods):

Peasant women produced more than half of the world's food, and between 60 and 80 per cent were from developing countries.

d) Violence Against Women:

1. On the global scale, one-third of women have been subjected to physical and sexual violence by a close and loving partner compared to two-thirds of women in some countries in the Pacific Ocean who have been subject to the same violence from permanent partners such as husbands.
2. At the International Labour Organization, statistics indicated that more than 43 per cent of individuals were smuggled across borders and then used forcibly to engage in sexual trade, where 98 per cent of them were women and girls. [Healey. 2014]
3. The United Nations was not satisfied with these official data, but rather presented other data that express disbelief and obscurity for the universal feminine rights to clarify the failure and that the woman has not been given the human importance, the failure to acknowledge their human fertility, and not recognising her economic merit and efforts.

2. Official Statements that Show Ingratitude and Ambiguity for the Universal Feminine Rights

The presented data here leads to clarification of facts issued by the United Nations expressing the denial and neglect of the rights of women in their work, remuneration and representation, which confirms that they are not accorded human importance and recognition of their human donation (in childbearing) and recognition of their economic merit, but rather a contempt them in boards representation, it all means:

a. A serious loss of human energy in the process of development and construction.

b. A financial loss exceeding billions.

c. Poor health, educational and family care for the future generation.

d. The taste, aesthetic and human deprivation in production and growth.

e. Promoting sexual intolerance that does not serve the balance of society.

f. Supporting the prejudiced tendencies that fuel the narcissistic self in the man.

g. Encouraging violent behaviour in feeding fanaticism and prejudiced tendencies.

h. Moving away from democratic representation in popular and parliamentary assemblies.

i. Expanding the circle of cultural and knowledge desertification.

j. The practice of authoritarianism, oppression and enslavement becomes familiar and desirable customary social controls in light of ingratitude and neglect.

In this respect, it is worth mentioning that Iceland is the most advanced country in the world on the issue of gender equality (particularly in increasing the political participation of women and her contribution to reducing the global gender gap and on the stage of the global economy.)

The following are examples clarifying the male, societal, political, and economic ingratitude, and disrespect of the woman in the world in 2013:

1. In 2011, 40 out of every 100 paid jobs in the non-agricultural sector were occupied by women globally.
2. There is research from (51) countries that revealed percentages of female business executives in the private sector ranging between 10% and 43% in most countries whose hierarchy in the United Nations ranges from 20% to 35%.
3. At the annual level, gender inequality has cost the Asia-Pacific region $ 47 billion each year.
4. Two-thirds of the 774 million adult population of the world are women, and the same percentage was 20 years ago.
5. At the end of April 2013, women occupied 21.2% of seats in parliamentary councils (all of them were of the lowest rank in the parliament).
6. Peasant women produce more than half of the world's food in developing countries, exactly between 60 - 80%.
7. The aim of the Australian aid program is to help to reduce gender levels and raise the morale of women in friendly countries.
8. The proportion of women in non-agricultural countries led to an increase in employment from 35% in the workforce in 1990 to 40% in 2011.
9. The conference on eliminating all forms of intolerance against women, which was adopted by the United Nations General Assembly in 1979, was considered a "universal declaration of women's rights."

10. Overall, females outperformed males in their school performance.
11. In 2013, the rate of women's financial gain was less than the rate of men's gains by 17.5%.
12. Australian women live longer than Australian men, with a life expectancy of 84.2 years when compared to 79.7 years.
13. Women who are pregnant and return from childbirth and from family responsibilities have rights under the heading of sexual intolerance (that is, they have the right to return to work after their interruption).
14. In the sixth month of 2013, the 2013 declaration of reforming and correcting sexual intolerance (gender identity, dual status, and sexual orientation) was approved.
15. At the level of leadership positions, there are more males than females in the private and public sectors and parliaments.
16. Although women make up 50% of Australia's population, there was only one-third of parliament representation of women (66 out of 226) in the Australian parliament in 2012.
17. In 1966 Australian women were forced to resign from public services upon marriage and were consequently prevented from advancing and progressing in their jobs.
18. Women were employed full-time in 2006 and spent 6 hours and 39 minutes every day to take care of their children, compared to a man's full-time work, who spent 3 hours and 43 minutes (in Australia).
19. On the global front, Australia has been rated extremely poor on the issue of women in parliament, on par with Canada.

20. In 2008, Australian women were recorded to spend 72% of their income on household expenses.
21. The income of Australian women whose annual income reaches 80 thousand dollars is 26%, while the percentage of Australian men who have an annual income of 80 thousand has reached 74%.
22. In the third month of 2013, the income of Australian women who work full time per week reached (1,252.20), while the income of Australian men per week reached (1,518.40). [Healey. 2014. P 57].

One of the oddities of matters is that capitalist, democratic, industrial, and civilised governments still practice the sexual differentiation at work, wages payment and political representation in the twenty-first century as if there is no influence of globalisation, free trade, global markets and the spread of democratic principles. I can state that the patriarchal power still has its domination over these kinds of governments in this century. So why criticise backward, conservative, and traditional societies (Eastern and Western) for their expression about the gender differences in all their behaviours and laws. Sure, they are not commensurate with the qualitative boom achieved by capitalist and democratic governmental systems. And with the increasing need for the human element and the increasing activity of feminist movements in the world, and the influence of the United Nations but the woman remains oppressed and disgraced her right to work, wages, and representation. Are we still in the patriarchal era? Or is it supposed to be in an era of democratic equality, respect for other opinions, and the valorisation of human competencies, not just male ones? Is the defect in the contemporary woman or in the modern man? Or in legal standards and rules? Or in human nature? Where is the cognitive change? And intellectual development? Where are they located in technological development? Criminals, fraudsters, and pirates have infiltrated modern electronic programs for their benefit. At the same time, the owners of administrative, financial, banking, and industrial businesses have benefited from these smart and accurate electronic programs to serve their businesses at their disposal. However, women are still unable to harness these electronic innovations to lift the injustice, bullying and oppression inflicted on them by various parties (human, cultural, political, and economic). They may not be able to do so alone, but rather they need help and assistance from those who are aware of intolerance and sexual prejudice against them.

We are not calling for sexual conflict, cultural rebellion, societal disobedience, or counter-violence, but rather for reducing the gap between the status of men and the status of women, recognising their efforts, respecting their role, and appreciating their participation with men in building the family, the first cell of society. Then, she reinforced her propositions by the existence of a gender gap in the world, introducing criteria and standards for measuring the global gap between males and females.

3. A Measure of The Gender Gap in Our World Today

This topic is often addressed in gender studies, and most of them are theoretical and conclusive. However, the United Nations, through its official agencies in the world, was able to obtain a report written by (136) countries representing more than 93% of the world's population in 2013. This report included: How political participation works to reduce this gap by dividing opportunities, resources, resources, and wealth in an orderly and fair manner between men and women. This report has classified the following four main

440

arguments to measure the size or breadth of the gap expressing the gender differentiation (the comparison of men over women):

1. The economic field: that is, participation in job opportunities, wages and salaries, contribution participation, and advanced and superior skill at work.
2. The educational field: that is, the educational achievement through which the attainment and maturity of women and men are known through the basic and higher educational stages.
3. The political field: meaning the actual representation in decision-making.
4. The health field: represented in preserving, caring and sustaining health.

The recent past years witnessed many developments that have occurred in the world, which have committed to bridging the gender gap by conscious and forward-looking reforms for the future of the human community in their countries. They have been persistent in achieving economic equality and political participation between the sexes.

The annual report that was published in its eighth year has included (136) countries that were able to bridge the gender gap in four areas, namely: women's economic participation in productive participation, their actual representation in political activities, health care, and their educational achievement. In the period 2012 - 2013, it was found 86 countries out of the 136 managed to bridge the gap. This report found that, as a whole, Iceland is the most outperforming country in the world in terms of gender equality over the course of five consecutive years, Finland came in with the second class, followed by Norway, where it ranked third, and Sweden ranked fourth. The gender gap has been closed by 80%. These countries participated in the first group of ten, i.e., the summit, while the Philippines entered the fifth place for the first time, Ireland ranked sixth, New Zealand ranked seventh, Denmark ranked eighth, Switzerland ranked ninth, and Nicaragua ranked tenth.

Other countries, such as Germany ranked fourteenth, as the individual enjoys the highest economic status, yet its sequence fell one place in 2012, then there is South Africa, which ranked seventeenth, the United Kingdom ranked eighteenth, and Canada ranked twentieth, while The United States ranked twenty-third, which fell in its rank in 2012, while Russia ranked sixty-first, followed by Brazil, which ranked sixty-second and China ranked sixty-ninth. As for India, it ranked one hundred. As for the bottom of the ranking, Chad ranked one hundred and thirty-four, Pakistan ranked one hundred and thirty-five, and Yemen ranked one hundred and thirty-six.

On the global level, the report revealed that in 2013, 96% of the gap was closed in the field of health and its care. It is only one out of four prospective and expanding lists since the beginning of the classification of countries in this report in 2006.

In the field of education, the global gender gap has stopped at 93% with a country as they completely bridge the educational gap. Then there is the economic gap, as it only reached 60%, 21% of which has been closed, as well as the progress that the world has made in this area, with political participation, which has decreased by 2% in recent years in developing and developed countries, as similar levels appeared between males and females in the post-secondary stage. In the workforce, however, few economic leaders emerged. (As in Table 1).

It is noticeable from the contents of this table that no country has achieved gender equality at a single pace but rather rises and falls according to its commitment to the terms of bridging the gender gap. For example, Switzerland reached the tenth rank in equality in 2012, but there was progress in its parity in 2013, and it rose to ninth. As for the Philippines, it was ranked eighth in equality in 2012, and it rose in 2013 to fifth place, while Belgium was twelfth in 2012 and fell in 2013 to eleventh. As for Iceland, Finland, Norway and Sweden, these countries maintained their hierarchy of equality in 2012 and 2013.

Although Europe is a scientifically and culturally advanced continent and some of its countries have managed to close the gender gap quicker than the rest, still bridging the gender gap did not take a single level and a similar path. As discrepancies appeared in this, for example, the report revealed that there is a polarisation in some European countries, such as Norway and Western European countries, which differed greatly from eastern and southern European countries. Spain ranked 30th, filling 72% of the gender gap, and France came in the forty-fifth sequence as it was filled 70%, while Italy came in the seventy-first place.

Country names	2012 Ranking	2013 Ranking
Iceland	1	1
Finland	2	2
Norway	3	3
Sweden	4	4
Philippines	5	8
Ireland	6	5
New Zealand	7	6
Denmark	8	7
Switzerland	9	10
Nicaragua	10	9
Belgium	11	12
Latvia	12	15

Holland	13	11
Germany	14	13
Cuba	15	19
Lesotho	16	14
South Africa	17	16
United Kingdom	18	18
Australia	19	20
Canada	20	21

Table 1: Ranking of countries according to their gender equality positioning.
(This table is taken from Healey's book. 2014. P. 1)

These European ratios show us that scientific and technical progress does not cancel, eliminate, or close the gender gap because it is linked to personal interests, mental knowledge, female vitality in the cells of the social fabric, the mentality of the community's elite, their elite, and their visibility towards anticipating the future of their society. Whenever it is characterised by liberal liberalism, human peace, and a civilised vision in the implementation of directed democracy, the gender gap in its four areas is closed, because the filling does not come from influential men alone, but from women who are aware, activists, and protesters in building their families and society away from its constructive and controlling disintegration.

When the sequence of Asian countries (in the continent of Asia) is considered, it was found that the Philippines alone has reached the highest level in bridging the gender gap in the field of health, education and economic participation, while the rest of the Asian countries remained in their low ranks, and this shows that the inherited social culture and religions in China, India, Korea and other countries It has the effective effect of not reducing the gender gap, which has made male power continue to dominate and limit the power and influence of women.

In Latin American countries, however, Nicaragua was the only country that managed to bridge the gender gap and ranked tenth and continued for two years, particularly in political participation. Then came Cuba, which ranked fifteenth, followed by Ecuador, which ranked twenty-fifth, and Mexico climbed sixteen ranks to reach the sixty-eighth place, due to the increase in the number of women in parliament and the number of professional roles, while Brazil ranked 62nd in bridging the gender gap In Latin American countries.

As for the countries of the Middle East and North Africa, it is the only region that does not have progress and development in the measure of the size of the gender gap that was applied in 2013. The highest rank obtained in this region is the United Arab Emirates in the field of educational equality, so the hierarchy ranked one hundred ninths, however, most of the countries in this region, including Bahrain, whose sequence came in the one hundred twelfth, and Qatar's sequence came in the one hundred fifteenth and the rest. They are still developing.

Finally, Africa came in the sixteenth rank Lesotho, South Africa ranked seventeenth, Burundi came twenty-second, and Mozambique came twenty-sixth, all of them in the group of thirty. Women in these countries were in the labour market in economic activity and had a position in making economic decisions and income, but they did not possess high professional skills and did not get high wages. [Healey. 2014. Pp. 1 - 2]

The United Nations was not satisfied with that but rather presented living and refreshing facts about gender equality.

4. Live Facts About Gender Equality

The United Nations has presented an international statistic on gender equality in the world that revives hope in the activity of the conscious woman's struggle to get out of her oppressive grievances and the ingratitude (denial) of her skill and competence to breathe the fragrance of liberation from the calcified heritage restrictions and the superficial and pretentious allegations of pious (formal) religious believers in the patriarchal power. These facts are as follows:

1. Gender equality is close to being achieved at the primary level only in two out of 130 countries.
2. At the global level, there are 40 of 100 jobs in the non-agricultural sectors that are occupied by women.
3. On 1/31/2013, the rate of women's participation in parliament in the world was more than (20) per cent. [Healey. 2014. P. 5]

Note here that the simulation or criteria that can revive the struggle of modern women are her work outside the agricultural sector, her participation in parliamentary membership, and her liberation from patriarchal power. These are alive harbingers that illustrate the success of the struggle of skilled and competent women in their quest to achieve equality and reduce the gender gap in modern life with fast rhythms and scientific excellence.

Thus, to achieve gender equality, the United Nations presented proposals to address the dangers of the disadvantages of gender differentiation on the human community.

5. Achieving Gender Equality

By strengthening the determination of the girl and valuing her will by eliminating the gender disparity in primary and secondary education. As per the advice of the United Nations, education must be compulsory for girls and

446

boys since 2005 in the primary and intermediate school levels. As for the rest of the educational stages, they were also subject to compulsion, provided that it does not exceed their obligation after the year 2015. In developing countries, gender equality has become the same in the elementary and secondary stages, and despite the fact that girls face obstacles in North Africa, Western Sahara and West Asia, the rate of girls' enrolment in school has increased dramatically, with a rate of 47% reaching 75% in the period between 1990. - 2011 The rate of males in this period also increased from 58% to 79%, and the girls of the African Sahara who were enrolled in school were 93 girls for 100 boys.

These basic steps that have been taken in developing countries make girls' education compulsory just like boys. In fact, it cannot be achieved without the United Nations intervention in obliging developing countries and adopting it in order to achieve gender equality since the beginning of educational formation, in order to improve their awareness, thinking and feeling that the male is not favoured by her at least outside her family in school.

West Asia is the only region in which more females attend primary school than males, but in other regions such as the Caucasus, Central Asia, Latin American countries, the Caribbean, Southeast Asia and South Asia, the equality between females and males at the primary level is equal. Convergent ranges between 0.97 and 1.03.

However, there is a gender disparity that is more paradoxical in secondary education, where the rate of female education has continued to decline. That is, less than the male average in Saharan Africa, West Asia, and South Asia. Nevertheless, West and South Asia have made progress in secondary education in the period between 1990-2011. In

West Asia, its level rose from 0.66 to 0.90, but the rate fell in the African Sahara, but there is an exception for Gambia, Ghana, Malawi, and Senegal, as they made progress in the previous period and between 1990 and 2011, their average increased from 0.5 to 0.9.

There is a greater disparity at the secondary level (post-middle school) when we compare it with the lower levels of education in terms of female education, whose enrolment is greater than that of males in a post-secondary school in Latin America, the Caribbean, the Caucasus, Central Asia and East Asia. North Africa and Southeast Asia.

In contrast to a young girl who is less than a young boy in pursuing post-middle school education in West and South Asia, the situation is more extreme in the African Sahara, which has a wide gender gap between 2000 and 2011. It is worth noting that there are only two out of 130 countries where information is available that has reached the parity goal at all educational levels. When analysing the gender distribution in school participation at the country level, the analyses show that girls are not always affected, but in general, inequality is a force that affects girls in an extreme way more than it affects boys. Girls in many countries are still denied their right to education (by public opinion), especially at the primary and secondary levels.

On the other hand, the gender disparity became wider and divergent as women advanced on the educational ladder, which changed the general picture of the level of post-secondary education, as the ratio reached 2/3 in countries with a low rate of enrolment in secondary education. This led to pushing women to work in the economic markets, obtaining regular financial income, economic independence, and a more self-reliant personality in housekeeping and family affairs, and the development of their personality in making influential decisions.

In 2011, 40 per cent of jobs in the non-agricultural sector were occupied by women on the global level. In fact, this is remarkable progress if it is compared with 1990 when it was 35%. Nevertheless, important differences observed in countries such as East Asia, the Caucasus, Central Asia, Latin America, and the Caribbean, in terms of equal numbers of women with men in occupying paid work has been achieved, but there is less participation of women in non-agricultural paid work in developing countries. The participation in West Asia, North Africa, and South Asia was below 20%, but in most countries, the participation of women in public sectors was much higher than their participation in the non-agricultural sectors, and there is a similarity to this participation as women are involved in the work of the local community where most of her work in government departments. When there is an increase in the opportunities available to work for women and gives them a good income, it does not mean that they have obtained reliable and appropriate work, nor does it mean that they are on equal terms with men. It goes without saying that the data available to the United Nations says that women in developing regions are more than men in their domestic work, such as agriculture, carpet weaving, sewing, handicrafts or blacksmithing, whose financial returns are negligible with a scarcity of social guarantees. This type of gender gap is endemic in West Asia, North Africa, and Sahara Africa, where paid wages are extraordinarily little.

There is no way in saying that the gap explains many facts, including the procedures and practices undertaken by the government and family life in which women are responsible for unpaid care, a lack of care equipment for children and other social rights, as well as their lack of participation in the workforce and the trade union.

In 2012 a slight feminist increase of 1% in the world in the number of women in parliamentary councils (higher and lower positions) from 19.6% to 20.4%, while the annual rate of increase in 2007 and the last two years was 0.5%. On the other hand, there are six countries in the world that do not have female memberships, which are: Haiti, Micronesia, Naro, Dlau, Qatar, Vanuatu. In 2013, 30 women were appointed in the Kingdom of Saudi Arabia in the Shura Council for the first time to form 20% of the council.

In 2012 there were 48 countries where women were elected to be a member of parliament, 22 of which the women elections were optional or legal. In the case of the voluntary quota, there was 22% women representation, while the legal quota was 24%, and when there was no share, the woman got 12% only. It is worth noting that the highest percentage obtained by women in 2012 was in Senegal, Algeria and Tumour, all of whom used the legal quota for the first time. In Senegal, women got 43%, and in Algeria, women got 32%, and in Tumour, women got 39%.

The question which imposes itself: Is the decision-making of woman linked to her role in parliament or popular, official, or family councils, or rather to her cultural and historical background imbued with oppression and deliberately suppressing her voice or by cultural norms that insist on not allowing her to express an opinion as these usually affect the legalisation of human development and the development of society. In the past four decades, women have made remarkable progress in their post-secondary education, which doubled their numbers in higher education. But unfortunately, this achievement has not been fully translated into the labour market and worker wages, i.e., were given marginal jobs and low wages that did not close the wage gap and did not allow her to have union representation.

The United Nations has a survey of (51) countries that the percentage of women as business managers ranges between 10% and 43%, and when women have influence in making their decisions, this is reflected in the improvement of the nutrition of their children, their fight against illiteracy and their high standard of living. But this survey included some African countries, revealing 37 countries in which women have the influence of their decisions in their homes exceptionally low in terms of expenses, family visits to friends and relatives, concern for health and participation in the family budget. This disparity in decision-making is a direct result of the differences between men and women regarding income and property affected by-laws and standards related to inheritance and property, all of which take a fanatical stance against women. [Healey. 2014. Pp. 5 - 10]

Very briefly, it can be said that women's decisions are not subject to their educational stage, nor to the official positions they occupy, nor to the popular councils that represent them, even in their families, because their decisions are linked not only to men but to cultural and social norms and material ownership of them. All of this influence her decisions on the family budget, her visits to family, relatives and friends, and the raising, care, and education of children. But despite all this, women in developing societies are oppressed because of their history and cultural background prevailing in them.

Elimination of disparities and differences between classes, spectrums, and gender is a difficult task. They have been planted by historical and cultural paths, class interests, and internal and external influences. And have been practised in all stages of the family, school, books, media, political and religious system over time for several centuries. Therefore, they cannot be removed by a political decision or a social reformer, but with thoughtful and patient planning, careful and gradual, starting from the easiest cycle, such as elementary school or kindergarten. The United Nations, as a global organisation, has managed to deal with intolerance and prejudice against women as a humanitarian mission and began to oblige backward and developing countries (rural, feudal, traditional, conservative, and racist) to make education obligatory for females and males. The result was very encouraging in many underdeveloped and developing countries and reflected on their health care and nutrition, raising the standard of their livelihood and social awareness, developing women's self-worth, increasing economic production, and reducing gender, occupational and wage gaps. This strategy adopted by the United Nations does not lead to the elimination of the differences between the female and the male, but rather as a first step to narrowing the gap between them. The United Nations initiative obligated developing governments to allow women to enter parliaments for the first time in their lives, and this was a fruitful achievement that the United Nations reached in reducing the gender gap, not only that, but also helped them to value women's decision-making on their own, even in principle, with regard to their families first, and this is a family movement. It helped the woman to become a pillar in family decision-making as a first step towards outside the family in underdeveloped and developing countries and the relative liberation of women from the domination of men, traditional culture, and patriarchal power.

C. <u>ADVOCACY OF WHO TO THE FEMININITY AGAINST HER ENSLAVEMENT</u>

Women differ from men with regard to health and disease due to their unique biological, social, and behavioural conditions. The biological differences vary from the cellular pattern to the apparent one, and it appears that women are more likely to be infected by some diseases and suffer health ailments. The World Health Organization (WHO) defines health as "a state of complete physical, mental and social safety, not merely the absence of disease or infirmity." Women's health is an example and reflection of public health, as it is "the health of a specific and defined group of the population".

Women's health has been described as a "patchwork quilt full of gaps". Although many issues centred around women's health relate to reproductive health, including fertility, maternal and child health, breast health, and endocrine (hormonal) health, including menstruation, birth control and menopause, the field of women's health has been expanded to include all aspects of health for women. All this led to the replacement of the term Women's Health in the English language with the term The Health of Women. The WHO believes that the unjustified emphasis on reproductive health is a major barrier to ensuring that all women have access to quality health care. Also, conditions that affect men and women, such as cardiovascular disease and osteoporosis, appear differently in women. Women's health issues also include medical cases in which women face problems indirectly related to their biology, such as gender discrimination in accessing treatment and other socio-economic factors. Women's health is a particular concern because of the widespread discrimination against women in the world, which leaves women deprived of some rights. A lot of health and medical research, such as the Society for Women's Health Research in the United States, supports this broader definition, rather than limiting it to issues related to the anatomy of human femininity, in order to include the anatomical regions in which a difference between the sexes appears. Women also need health care and access to health care systems more than men do. While part of this is due to her sexual and reproductive health needs, women also have more chronic non-reproductive health problems, such as cardiovascular disease, cancer, mental illness, diabetes, and osteoporosis. Another important perspective is the recognition that events throughout the entire life cycle (or life path) from life in the womb to old age affect growth, development, and health. One of the strategic keys to the WHO is a life course perspective.

Global Perspective: The gender differences in exposure, disease symptoms, and response to treatment in many areas of health are partially correct when viewed from a global perspective. Most of the information available comes from developed countries, but there are marked differences between developed and developing countries in terms of the role and health of women. A worldview is defined as "a field of study, research, and practice that prioritises the improvement of health and the achievement of health equity for all people around the world." In 2015 the WHO identified the top ten issues in women's health as cancer, reproductive health, HIV, sexually transmitted diseases, violence, mental health, non-contagious diseases, youth, and old age.

Life Expectancy: Women have a higher life expectancy than men, and they generally have lower death rates, regardless of race and geographic region. Nevertheless, historically, women have gone through stages during which their mortality rates have been higher, primarily maternal deaths. In the industrialised countries, especially the developed ones, the gender gap narrowed and was even reversed after the Industrial Revolution. Despite these differences, women still suffer from earlier and more severe illnesses in many areas of health. Despite such differences, the causes of death in the United States are remarkably similar between men and women, of which heart disease is the most prominent, with a quarter of deaths occurring due to cancer, lung disease, and stroke follow. While women have a lower incidence of death due to unintentional injury (accidents) and suicide, they have a higher incidence of dementia.

The main differences lie in the life expectancy of women between developed and developing countries are in their childbearing years. If women survive during this period, the differences will become significantly less, and considering that in later years of life, non-contagious diseases become the main cause of death for women all over the world. The mortality of cardiovascular diseases (one of the most important forms of non-contagious diseases) is about 45% of the deaths of elderly women, followed by cancer (15%) and then lung disease (10%). This creates additional burdens on the capabilities and resources of developing countries. Lifestyle changes such as diet, physical activity, and cultural factors that favour a larger body size for women contribute to increasing the problems of obesity and diabetes among women in these countries, as well as increasing the risk of cardiovascular diseases and other non-contagious diseases.

Socially marginalised women are more likely to die at younger ages than non-marginalised women. Women who suffer disorders from drugs intake and addiction, homeless women, prostitutes, or female prisoners, have significantly shorter lives than other women. And at any age, women in these overlapping groups are 10 to 13 times more likely to die than other women of the same age.

Cultural and Social Factors: The issue of women's health is placed within a broader set of knowledge mentioned by the WHO, which pays attention to gender as a social determinant of health. While a woman's health is affected by her biology, it is also affected by her social conditions such as poverty, employment, and family responsibilities. These aspects should not be obliterated.

Traditionally, women have been disenfranchised when talking about economic and social status and power, which in turn reduces women's chances of accessing the essentials of life, including health care. Despite improvements in women's lives in Western countries, women are still disadvantaged compared to men. The gender gap in health becomes wider in developing countries, where women are most disadvantaged. In addition to gender inequality, many diseases are linked to sex, that is, whether a person is male or female. The foregoing creates additional challenges in providing health care to women.

Even after successful access to health care, women face discrimination, a process that Eris Yang called "internal exclusion," a term that contrasts with the term "external exclusion" that describes barriers and obstacles that prevent access to health care resources. These issues remain invisible, preventing the grievances of groups previously disenfranchised by power inequality from emerging, which further entrenches injustice.

Behavioural differences also play a role, as women are exposed to fewer risks, including consuming less tobacco, alcohol, and drugs, which reduces the risk of dying from diseases associated with these behavioural patterns, including lung cancer, tuberculosis, and liver cirrhosis. Other risk factors (lower for women) include traffic accidents. Women are also exposed to fewer industrial injuries, although this is likely to change, as is the case in war injuries or deaths, and these injuries, in general, contributed to approximately 3.5% of women's deaths compared to 6.2% of men's deaths in the United States in 2009. In addition to the above, suicide rates are lower for women than for men.

A social view of the concept of health, coupled with the knowledge that gender is a social determinant of health, helps to provide better health services to women around the world. Women-oriented health services centres such as the Women's Community Health Centre in Leckhardt, which was established in 1974 and was the first women's health centre to be established in Australia, is an example of an approach to providing health services to women. Many feminist activists have addressed the issue of women's health, especially when focusing on reproductive health, and the international women's movement was responsible for many embracing agendas to improve women's health. [https://ar.wikipedia.org]

D. ADVOCACY OF UNESCO TO THE FEMININITY AGAINST HER ENSLAVEMENT

Gender equality is a fundamental issue in order to achieve human development, and therefore UNESCO seeks to achieve this goal and considers it one of its priorities. Thus, the equality goal was considered one of the millennium goals of the United Nations, which seeks to achieve gender equality and create parity for participation in development and community building.

The Convention to End All Forms of Discrimination Against Women indicates to Arab countries, despite some progress in the issue of equality, discrimination and inequality are still rooted in the legal framework, and girls and women still suffer from poor living conditions and a low social outlook, and discrimination is practised against them because they are women.

In response to the needs of the Arab region, the UNESCO Regional Office for Education in the Arab Countries increased focus on the issue of women's equality with men and granted them all rights and privileges. At the regional level, the office implements special projects to raise people's awareness and focus on the importance of achieving equality. Cooperation in this field is carried out with the rest of the United Nations organisations and civil society institutions.

Despite the available, encouraging indications, women are still underrepresented in the field of science, be it at the level of basic scientific research or at the level of higher decision-making. And facing the challenges of sustainable development at the present time and in the future depends on the mobilisation of scientific forces fully. Science cannot continue to deprive itself of the scientific potential of more than half of the world's population. Science is a key to knowledge. In order for women to access knowledge and achieve gender equality, they must be able to benefit from the sciences.

The UNESCO World Science Conference held in Budapest in 1999 devoted special attention to the issue of women in scientific research. One of the items that emerged from the conference indicated that inadequate preparation at the secondary level continues to be a barrier for young women seeking to pursue a career in science. The method

458

adopted for evaluating research underestimates women, who often assume significant personal and professional responsibilities, and that women's confidence in their academic capabilities is often undermined in unfriendly study contexts while women's views on environmental issues are not sufficiently encouraged.

The differences between the sexes are also the result of a lack of recognition of women's knowledge and know-how. In other words, a lack of recognition of the responsibility they assume in relation to half of the human knowledge and technical expertise as farmers, caregivers, animal keepers, forest users, and responsible for managing the resources and water needs of their communities and finally as innovators in technology and as catalysts for change.

The UNESCO has long been a pioneer in promoting gender equality, and the organisation's medium-term strategy 2008-2013 places us at the forefront of United Nations agencies that place gender equality at the top of their strategic priorities. A bilateral approach has been adopted, which is: gender mainstreaming and the empowerment of women in the Member States and within the Organization. "Mainstreaming a gender perspective" requires systematic efforts to consider the specific experiences and aspirations of both women and men and give them special attention in all stages of UNESCO's program, from planning to evaluation.

The partnership between UNESCO and L'Oréal for "Women in Science", the twinning program for UNESCO universities and university chairs, and the activities carried out in the field of basic and engineering sciences particularly focus on supporting female scientists, especially young women. Other specific examples include encouraging women to apply for grants from the MAB Program for young scientists, the increased assistance provided to the African Earth Women Scientists Association to encourage women to present their work at scientific conferences, and the efforts of the UNESCO Intergovernmental Oceanographic Commission to achieve Gender balance in capacity building activities in ocean science. [http://www.unesco.org]

F. ADVOCACY OF WESTERN GOVERNMENTS TO THE FEMININITY AGAINST HER ENSLAVEMENT

Its aim was not primarily to advocate for women but rather to reveal the extent of crime victims in their countries. Among these victims are women, especially housewives and employees who are harassed by their managers.

In 1966, the largest social survey of crime victims in the history of the United States of America, including girls and women, was conducted. It made a change in the direction of the course of criminal studies towards studying the victims in a detailed and accurate manner. It was the first comprehensive survey of crime victims in the United States of America, which was carried out by a body affiliated with the Presidency of the Republic in charge of law enforcement and criminal justice. Then the crime victims survey was conducted periodically as one of the important surveys in American society, and the aim of this survey was to measure the size of victims (at least against individuals) over time, to be aware of the increase or decrease in the crime and its impact on local and regional influences because the official statistics recorded by the police forces are insufficient due to the presence of gaps as not all victims inform the police and agencies of what happened to them. In 1972, a survey was conducted on 60,000 thousand houses distributed over three years during which they were interviewed, and questions were asked about the assaults and thefts of houses that took place with them, after which this experiment was applied in other countries to determine the size of crime victims such as Australia, Canada, Sweden, the Netherlands, Japan, and Britain. Then Britain conducted local surveys in some areas of London and Sheffield in 1981 and in Birmingham in 1982, as these surveys provided accurate details and general pictures of the societies included in the study. Other surveys were carried out in Scotland in 1982 and Wales in 1984, and Liverpool and Islington in 1988, showing where the victims were in urban areas. [Mawby. 1989. P. 6]

In the seventies of the twentieth century, extremist feminist groups became active in defending and treating rapists in an extreme manner, so they established special centres dealing with the rape crisis, opened hotlines to contact them immediately or after the occurrence of rape, and opened places to shelter rapists called shelters and places to accommodate refugee women to provide medical, psychological, and social treatment. This is in order to strengthen their positions, raise their morale, and reduce their psychological and personal pain by providing mentors and psychotherapists by volunteer donor specialists, which attracted the attention of the American public, who sympathised with them and supported them. Not only that, but it also refused to compromise with any party on the issue of rape of women and did not ask for the help of the police, and its mobile centres express the interests of the raped women. These acts carried out by rape crisis centres were not undertaken by or adopted by the National Union. Rather, the rape centres have adopted a method of their own to defend rape victims against the government by using a control and control agency (especially the police) that defends in an extreme manner the rights of women to the

461

extent that allows them the right to taking its decision at every stage of the case and not relying on the court or police decisions. This is a method not followed by the National Union, but by which the centres of rape crisis were unique, while the National Union resorted to a method of persuasion and the use of the police and their participation in settling the matter.

F. ADVOCACY OF THE SCHOLARS TO THE FEMININITY AGAINST HER ENSLAVEMENT
Initiation

This victory and relief did not come through their statements and media interviews but rather through the scientific field and analytical research by researchers and researchers' experiences in social investigations such as (Marigrid Mead, Anne Wakley, Claude Levi Strauss, Malinovsx and Benedict) emphasising the structural normalisation that imprints both genders in a different way and patterns them with different behavioural patterns that have nothing to do with biological differences, explaining the cultural influence on the normalisation of the genetic-biological base. So (Wakley) demonstrated that the biological factor has no effect or connection with the roles of women. These scholars have proven that biological differences do not separate or differentiate between men and women in the system of division of labour, but rather the culture of society works on that. In the sense of culture, it is that which determines the work of women and the work of men, not biological differences. More precisely, as (Wakley) sees, gender roles are culturally specific, not biological.

Charles Darwin emphasised that the differences in performance, thinking and action would be a factor in helping to acquire female and male genes and reinforce genes in their male and female differences. In the sense that the cultural acquisition of the individual's roles helps him to acquire male and female genes and the differences between them and link behaviour to genes. At the same time, there is a section of academic women who: -

1. Activists of Academic Community Against Enslavement

First Wave: Academic women conducted feminist research in which they announced the male differentiation over the feminine in the Western world, and that was in the sixth decade of the twentieth century, in which they tried to clarify the reality of women in society to educate people about them. The following topics represented their goals:

a. Confronting the male prejudice against women.

b. Determining the social position of women by reading legal texts and economic documents.

c. Defining the contributions of women to social and art history.

d. Exposing the oppressive and subordinate aspects of the legal restrictions and societal norms that prevented women from reaching the world of men.

e. Clarifying the patriarchal system that it is a global, eternal system of male domination in which a man controls the woman's sexuality, her reproductive activity, and his life in general.

f. The biological division (man and woman) is culturally supported by societal norms.

These major themes were represented in the first wave of feminist research in academia.

The Second Wave: This wave began in the late seventies of the twentieth century. It expressed the topics, trends, and academic theorising prevalent among academics in the West and how they approached the issue of gender. It was as follows:

a. The starting of studying the gender formula.
b. Addressing the problem of persecution that women used to live in societies.
c. Formulating methods for defining gender relations with society.
d. Considering gender, a central category in historical analysis.
e. Considering the concept of gendered roles as two complexes, socially constructed identities imposed on the biological sex, an essential identity located within the natural body.
f. Emphasising the authority of men and subordination of women.

There was a female hegemony prior to the emergence of the patriarchal system when the world was living a meek life in harmony with nature. Women were leading a life free of persecution as well as naturally controlling societies described as matrilineal or matrilineal societies. In prehistoric women, gender hierarchies were dominated by women.

The Third Wave: mid-eighties of the twentieth century.

a. This wave revealed the nature of the patriarchy and the oppression of women, and in establishing spaces specific to her only, saturated all of these concepts theorised as the common and unified experience of women.
b. Research on the third wave shows that the separation that arose between home and work, according to which family, marriage and what is there were analysed as the domain of women, is not only insufficient to understand the complexity of gendered relations, but it may also

464

contribute to the perpetuation of the binary structure of male / female arrangements.

c. Feminists resorted to creating a problem of the aforementioned structures and transforming them into power relations, and concepts of oppression, patriarchy, gender and identity began in a sense used by white middle-class feminists facing mounting challenges originating from the intersection of the new feminism with cultural theory and postmodern theories, especially post-structuralism and deconstruction theory.

d. The category of gender in itself as a separate entity is a social problem that has been superimposed over the natural gender prior to any discourse that suffers from some deficiencies.

e. There is no pre-existent gender or separate from its social structure upon which gendered criteria can be compiled since morphological differentiation is always a historical contingent.

f. This wave exposed the notions of sexuality and gender. [Bahrani. 2013. p. s. 48 - 66]

2. Med in Nature and Nurture

This title involves knowing how much of our everyday, habitual behaviour is determined by nature (heredity, genetics, biology) and how much is determined by nurture (the oceanic environment and culture in which we are born and live)? But the interpretations and analyses of sociologists interested in the study of sexuality (gender) go to the orbit of elaborative normalisation that imprints males and females differently and patterns them with different behavioural patterns, and that the differences between them are not only due to physiological influence, but also to demographic differences, attitudes, trends, and associated behaviour which all are sex-related. These differences are sufficient in the dominance of the patriarchal (male) authoritarianism, which is inevitable and absolute. However, the question that arises here is whether these differences outweigh the similarities between them? What is the biological role that determines these differences? The significance of these questions has emerged as a debate and discussion among scholars about which of the two has more influence on the behaviour of individuals? Inherited nature or acquired normalisation in determining these biological differences? We will separate and highlight the biological aspect in this chapter that will cover the biological explanation for this difference between males and females.

Before involving in the biological interpretation, let's work on an ancient study dating back a century by the well-known American anthropologist (Margaret Mead) to clarify the social background of gender and how the cultural variable affects the normalisation of the genetic-biological base whose impact varies from one group to another. The biological base has no effect on the cultural variable, so we made this study a prelude to what we will present later. Maed's scientific and research interest was focused on exploring and pioneering the issue of gender differences between males and females in the New Guinea community. That was in 1930 (a community living on an island located in the Pacific Ocean). She continued and said, "I travelled there for field study as a requirement to study for a doctorate at Columbia University - American, so I dealt with three tribes inhabiting it, the Arapesh tribe, and I found that their members are characterised by":

1. Warm and friendly relations, the gentleness of manners and tenderness.
2. Normalising men of this kind with a peaceful and obedient character, consistent with their cultural values, traditions, and social norms.
3. Tribe members spend most of their time farming, fishing, and caring for children.
4. The members of the tribe enjoy deep and broad satisfaction in the work they do, as they perform them with enthusiasm, longing and impulse.
5. The upbringing of the children of the tribe in light of these traits and temperaments, meaning they are imbued with cooperation and automatic response.
6. The desire and tendency of young men and women to meet the needs of vulnerable individuals, the elderly and young children.

In light of this exploration, Mead concluded that there are no periodic breaks separating the roles of males and females, as they are both imprinted in the nature of cooperation and spontaneous response in the agricultural fields, fishing and childcare, not like other societies that restrict the raising of children to women only, but at Arapesh, the man raises his children next to the woman and does not leave this matter to the woman only.

In other words, men of this kind share in their feminine behaviour and tend (men) and women accountability and cooperation, not aggression and competition. One of them responds to the needs of others, and the utmost happiness in this way is that a nice man marries a nice woman, and both sexes, that is, men and women, are powerless in the face of the temptation of sexual reality. Therefore, fathers warn their male children against immersing themselves in situations that include the love of others for them.

The second tribe on this island is the Mundugumor tribe. Unlike the Arapesh, both men and women are distinguished by masculine behaviour as well as aggressive behaviour. The highest happiness is when an aggressive man marries a violent, aggressive woman. There is no sexual temptation or sexual fondness. All that happens is violence and aggression. Therefore, the sons of this tribe are characterised by clear and frank aggressiveness.

Moreover, Mead found:

1. The sons of this kind are violent, cruel, and fierce.
2. They do not contribute with the woman to the upbringing of the children but leave them alone at an early age.
3. Teaching children aggressive behaviour, competition, and suspicion of others.
4. Parents act with simple and little flexibility with their children in order to give them social behaviour. They use harsh physical punishment for every behaviour that they do not approve of, and here the children quickly acquire cruel and aggressive tribal habits, and the tribe considers that behaviour acceptable. And not just that, it also considers it the safest and best solution in solving many of their family and social problems because both sexes, men and women, are characterised by this characteristic.

The third tribe is the Tchambuli tribes, as their sons act regressively, reflecting the gender role. Their men are characterised by a lack of sense of responsibility, but rather dependence and emotionality, while their women tend towards control and the predominance of the spirit to work on them and shun them in the personal and human aspects. Men dance and wear women's masks. In normal life, men adorn themselves with coloured necklaces, release their hair, and adorn themselves for their women, as they (men) are the masters of the family and the owners of the wives. The mother leaves her infant child taking her nipple in his mouth for a few minutes, and then throws him away from the breast, and from here, the aggressive tendency is generated in his old age while the mother breastfeeds her child in the tribe of Arapesh from her breast and this breast remains in the child's mouth for the length of time that suits him. If the child catches the breast From morning to evening, the mother does not show any distress from this behaviour and does not try to abuse her child. The women of (Tchambuli) do not adorn themselves with the adornment and finery of men, nor do they dress up for them, but they are subservient to the arrogant and conceited man who spends his time beautifying and adorning. At a time when women spend most of their time weaving mats, baskets and dishes from tree leaves, fishing and selling their products in the market in order to earn a living away from the man who does not participate in these activities but remains to reside in the village practising dancing, singing and decorating. While women enjoy each other's company (i.e. in women's councils), men attract women's attention and influence them, who respond to this foreplay with kindness and gentleness without pushing them back, and this is in contrast to the beliefs of the tribe that emphasise the natural differences of sex.

That is, the culture of the tribe does not allow gender equality but rather emphasises masculine masculinity, male virility, femininity, tenderness, subservience, and obedience in front of men. This is what Mead found in her exploratory study of sexual differentiation. [Lindsey. 2011. Pp. 23 - 24]

It is important to introduce the reader to this scholar (Margaret Mead 1901-1978) that she is an American scholar in cultural anthropology who studied the speciality of childcare in the Pacific and contributed effectively to the establishment of debate and dialogue about upbringing and nature and the study of culture and socialisation, considering and not denying the biological importance and the environment natural. Her study of culture in her book (The Coming Age in Samoa 1928), Upbringing in New Guinea 1930, Gender and Mood in Three Primitive Societies 1935 was especially important because it emphasised the importance of upbringing on nature. Her anthropological ideas gave important support to the feminist movement and her participation in the formulation of sexual policies that were later reinforced by both males and females in 1949. Her realistic study revealed the tolerance of primitive societies towards the sexual behaviour of adolescents and adolescent girls, and then she compared it accurately with the anxiety and tension associated with the stage of adolescence in Western society (Especially among Protestants) towards sexual development. Her interpretations and field explanations in the field of culture and commitment in 1970 contributed to a greater understanding and broader sympathy for the issue of generational conflict. [Omar. 2000. p. s. 293 – 294]

Before leaving this section, it is important to recap the three models presented by (Mead). It can be said that there is no single behavioural pattern for all women or all men in all societies, all times and places. Each society has its own characteristics for men and women, and this is due to the adoption of the masculine culture of society with its own setup, so there is a male culture and a feminine one, but no one defines social culture with its biological (genetic) characteristics, and hence there is no cultural femininity or cultural masculinity, but rather there is a masculine culture and a feminine culture.

We found the Arapesh tribe, its men, who were meek and peaceful, non-violent, responding to the needs of women and cooperating with them in raising children, but it was not like the man in the Mundugumor tribe, who is characterised by aggression, as well as the woman whose aggressiveness is a common characteristic of both men and women. We found the woman in the Tchambuli tribe submissive to the arrogant man, and she performs all economic activities outside the home, in addition to raising her children inside the house, and does not makeup, unlike the man who spends most of his time in the village, dancing, singing, and grooming.

These differences are not due to the genetic-biological factor but to the social culture that dressed up the biological factor. This is the state of gender among primitive tribes a century ago, but now the equation has changed. The culture is no longer cloaked in its dress of genetic inheritance. Rather, there has been a change in the feminine and masculine culture, where the female began to demand her political, economic, family, and professional rights much more than in previous times. At the same time, masculinity has turned into a reduction in its dominance over the family and society due to the economic independence of women, the small size of the family, and the reduced number of children in it, with the rise in the standard of living, technical progress, globalisation, and others. Therefore, normalisation prevails over nature in primitive, traditional, rural, feudal, and folkloric societies.

3. Wakley in Social Culture and Gender

Sex represents a biological difference that does not change, and gender represents a cultural specification, but it does change from one society to another, and it is not absolute, static and fixed in all societies and cultures. And that women's work is not confined to the home only but also to farms, factories, mines, the army, the police, sports, art, engineering, medicine and all the work that men do at the

471

present time. And what was said about her is that the woman is a minor, her energy is limited, and she cannot bear the burdens and hard work. But this is a myth launched by the man in order to limit the business to him and reap its profits and exclude the woman and marginalise her role outside the home to make her a prisoner of the house and imprisoned in it. It has been proven to dispense the biological mother of children with a nurse, a nanny or a nursery, and this is what is prevalent in urban and industrial societies.

What I want from this proposition is to say that biological differences do not determine or define specific tasks and actions, nor do gender actions determine and support biological differences because women have intelligence and energy like the intelligence and energy of men, and the needs of society do not differentiate between them, but rather that men release stories, gossip and myths against women for making her his seat in the house to serve him and comfort him throughout her life. Modern life has proven the myth of this masculine claim and the merit and efficiency of women in proving their presence in many spaces and areas that were forbidden to them by men, such as the air force, the navy, the military, security, sports, artistic, intellectual, and the ascent to the moon.

So, social culture is the explanatory container for everything that was said about it by the man about biological differences in order to remain in his ivory tower, domineering, controlling and pedantic in the role he described for himself to prevent women from proving their worth, wisdom, intelligence, and competition in his work outside the home. He did not manifest this exclusion himself but rather used fictitious and metaphysical beliefs, myths, and legends that were unrealistic in the social culture that he developed. I say the man used the cultural vessel to support and enhance his position, influence, and role in society. And that there is not a single cultural interpretation that emphasises the superiority of men over women and their inequality in rights and duties. Rather, it varies from one culture to another, and it is a fixed interpretation that does not change, such as establishing the biological difference between men and women.

However, the researcher (Ann Oakley) 1974, when she returned to the anthropological studies carried out by (Malinovsky, Benedict and Mead), found the absence of cultural determinism that separates the system of division of labour, roles and social sites on the basis of sexual difference. And she gave an example put forward by the modern French anthropologist (Cloud Levi Strauss) in 1956 when he said that every culture has its own organisation of work that goes along with societal needs and not for the biological difference. There are no boundaries and separations separating women's work from men's work or separating men's work from women's work. Then Oakley presented many examples from different societies that demonstrate and prove that the biological factor has no effect or condition on the roles of women, which are the following:

- In the Congo society, which is based on hunting and gathering in the rain forests, there are no laws that define the division of labour on the basis of sex. Men and women hunt together, and the role of mother and father is one in the care of their children.
- In the Aboriginal tribes in Tasmania, the woman is responsible for hunting seals and fish from the sea and collecting the vegetable crops found there.
- At the time being, Oakley noted the participation of women in the important military forces in China, the (former) Soviet Union, Cuba, and Israel.

- In India, 12% of the workforce are women working in the construction sector.
- In the countries of Latin America and Asia, a quarter of the labour force of women works in the mining sector.

For (Oakley), these examples clearly show that there is no obstacle or barrier that prevents women's roles and that what has been announced that the biological base of women renders them helpless and unable to bear the hardships and exhaustion of work is nothing but a fad and a false myth that has no basis in truth and that it is just empty chatter and has no support.

Finally, Oakley sees that gender roles are culturally determined and have nothing to do with biological determination and that advanced social events show us that there is no imposition or condition that emphasises the need to dispense with women's work and not depend on their energy and efficiency. Even the role of the mother is only a cultural determination because what is needed by children is love, tenderness, affection, warmth, and continuity of care, and this is what other people can do, not the biological mother, but from childcare homes and nurseries. [Van Krieken and (etal.). 2006. p. 310]

In order to clarify the impact of culture on the biological differences between men and women, it can be said that when society was primitive, women worked inside and outside the home in agriculture, hunting and gathering, and this was confirmed by anthropologists in their studies of primitive societies in Africa, Southeast Asia and Australia, even in the Bedouin and rural Arab society, where her work is not limited to childcare, but to herding (sheep and camels), agriculture and trade (selling animal and agricultural products in city markets). In the technical developmental stage, there is clear and active participation of women in the army, as is the case in China, America and the Soviet Union (ex) Cuba and Israel and in the mines and construction. Therefore, the biological aspect is not an obstacle to preventing women from developing economic, social and educational planning. Rather, it is the societal need that affects that and then is reflected in the culture of the community. It was found that the more women work outside the home, the smaller the family size, respectively, and that the extended family is found in feudal, religious, tribal and traditional conservative societies. Therefore, the role of women in society can be used as mercury in the barometer, which rises and falls according to the community's need for her outside the home. If there is an urgent need for her outside the home to work in the factory, the mine, or the army, her position becomes high in society, and the mercury rises in the barometer. And if the family's need for her in care and housekeeping is high, her position will fall, and mercury will fall with her, and then she will be enslaved by the man. Her leaving the house to work, therefore, leads to her economic independence, social liberation, and her cognitive enlightenment.

4. Darwin in Evolution, Genetics and Biology

The relationship of nature to normalization and their impact on human behaviour is often viewed from the perspective of Charles Darwin's theory, which sees sexual differences (such as gender, cognitive ability, and parenting) and gender differences (in play, performance, cognitive competence and choice of profession) as positive and beneficial in acquiring female genes and masculinity because it reveals and displays human tenderness and potential in activities and the enhancement of genes in their male and female differences.

Socio-biology is a scientific field that combines two disciplines, the first is scientific - biological and the second is societal, which involves explaining the social organization of animals and humans by referring to biological characteristics such as genetic formations and population influences in order to understand animal nature, asking questions about sexual differences, tracing the roots of social behaviour, benefiting from their studies of animals to reach conclusions about the nature and behaviour of humans, because they share one rule, which is the biological rule that involves internal motives that emphasize their genes associated with all their behaviour patterns. Humans and animals share the instinct of aggression and competition. As there is competition between man and woman in their life struggle, the woman wants to dominate the care of the family, and the man struggles in his work outside the family and even competes with his brother the man in order to gain a better position and money in life. This struggle represents an evolutionary legacy that pushes them towards the organization of their social lives.

Biological Perception: In fact, androgens are the main player in determining the masculinity and femininity of humans, including their brains. The sexual gender and the human brain are determined by the male stimulant, and the high-end type of this stimulant exercises the male type more than the female type. The difference in sexual perception is related to male ability more strongly than female ability. While the gonad is what determines the sexual gender, the female brain is more developed and growing than the male brain. However, there are genetic mutations that differ from what the male stimulant does. So, the biological perception is linked to the male stimulant.

The puzzle of hormones: Hormones are internal secretions released by the endocrine glands that circulate with the blood in the human body, affecting all parts of the body because both sexes (male and female) carry the same hormones, but they differ in their quantity. For example, the female hormone controls the female sex hormone oestrogen, which is secreted in a large amount by the ovaries, but in a small amount by the testicle. As for the hormone testosterone presents in the testicles, it is secreted in a large quantity by the testicle in males but in a small amount by the ovary of the female. Therefore, the difference in the endocrine glands in males and females is not inevitable but rather different for them, as it is more in males than in females.

As for the chromosome (which is a filamentous particle that appears in the cell nucleus at the time of X and Y division, both sexes have at least one X chromosome, but in females, they have two X chromosomes, while in males, they have one X chromosome and one Y chromosome as well. Therefore, the absence or the presence of The Y chromosome determines the gender of the fetus be male or female, because the X chromosome has a greater genetic background than the Y chromosome. It has a beneficial advantage in favour of the female who has the XX chromosome. The extra chromosome from the X is shared with a high immune system in immunity or her demise (i.e., the demise of female lower characteristics at all stages of life cycles due to domination of X chromosomes). As for the rest of the chromosomes, all of them are similar in shape but different in their genetic identity for the individual, and the chromosomes are a factor influencing sexual differences. In this respect, there is an important interaction between sex hormones and psychosocial influences on sexual behaviour (gender). It is known that sex hormones have two main functions that must be considered:

1. They shape the development of the brain and sexual organs.
2. They specify how these organs are active. Because hormones nourish the functions of the body's organs, their effect is different depending on gender.

Aggression: It is a behaviour that both humans and animals participate in when they are subjected to abuse, aggression, violence and defamation. Rather, both males and females share in its excitement, but it also happens when they want to express what they suffered from denial, aggression. It is clearly visible from both humans and animals that males are more aggressive than females, as it appears in males in the second year of their life, and both sexes of males and females are equal in their learning and acquisition of aggression, but female aggression does not appear publicly and clearly in front of people as males show it. The female is more inclined to suppress and hide her anger, upset and violence or to express it orally (i.e., verbally). In addition, she uses aggressive behaviour with the intent and intention of harming the other who abused her or assaulted her. She is more aggressive against an enemy of her gender, using her friends, colleagues, acquaintances, or individuals of her family in the performance of her revenge on her abusers. But this feminine aggression is not issued in vain, without reason, or provokes the occurrence of harmful reasons physically, legally, financially, professionally, or socially.

As for boys, they are more expressive of their aggression and implement it in physical ways by hitting, kicking, punching, and harsh speech. Often the opponent is males who are of a certain age, race or special nationality that occurs (aggression) in the workplace, home, school, pub or street or cafe, and there is aggression in the form of sexual harassment. Then there is the aggression of rodents from animals, which is caused by the influence of the male sex hormone in its aggression.

As for the cultural influence, it is clearer and more obvious than the biological factors explained above because it is acquired in the first stage of the upbringing of the child. The influence of the male hormone, which becomes active when the individual overcomes, succeeds, or wins over his opponent, and decreases his activity (the male hormone) when he loses. This condition appears clearly in males. In summary, it can be said that the male hormone plays a vital role in its influence on aggressive behaviour, emotional expression and sexual relations, and it is also clear to say that aggression and culture are important in the emergence of any biological tendencies or tendencies to aggression.

It is worth mentioning that disappointment and failure lead to aggression as well as expressing the inadequacy of the failure. Aggressive behaviour is also shown by individuals (males or females) who do not have the qualifications or skills that allow them to move up the social hierarchy, causing them to motivate in the direction of aggression against the other who owns what he does not own. In other words, aggression is not only motivated by the male hormone but also by frustration, disappointment, failure, or denial of possession of influence, money, social position, moral consideration, or physical background (hand or legs). It is not limited to males only but also includes females, who differ in their expression. The female does not show it publicly most of the time, in anticipation of social and material negatives, in contrast to the man who practices it publicly in front of others to highlight his muscular strength and masculinity associated with his gender.

Motherhood: It is an instinct that characterizes female humans and animal mammals. This instinct includes a maternal hormone, a hormone that prepares the uterus to accept the fertilized egg, and a hormone in the anterior lobe of the pituitary gland, which regulates the secretion of milk from the breast and pushes the woman toward motherhood. These hormones appear during pregnancy, which secretes secretions that bind the mother to her fetus, supporting abundant motherhood. The feelings of motherhood do not stop at this point, but rather the stage after pregnancy, which is labour and birth. All of this crystallizes a female's desire to have a child and responds to the man's desire to be a father. There is no harm in saying that paternity is acquired, except that motherhood is shaped by factors and developmental stages that the procreating mother undergoes (which are secretions of the maternal hormone and other hormones that do their work during the pregnancy stage to link the mother to the fetus, his care and breastfeeding, and hence the maternal instinct emerges as well as labour, birth, and depression after childbirth or abortion) all of this works to crystallize the feelings of motherhood in the mother who is not available to the father because he is not pregnant and is not affected by hormonal influences and he does not have labour, miscarriage or depression after childbirth and other things, but acquires the role of the father after the birth of his wife. Therefore, the barren woman believes that motherhood depends on maternal instinct and that her inability to conceive is linked to her failure to conceive.

It goes without saying that we refer to the maternal bond that protects and nurtures the fetus immediately after weeks of birth, and with repeated breastfeeding and care, the feelings of motherhood crystallize clearly. As for the feelings of paternity, they crystallize after the birth of the newborn, caring for him and his mother, bearing the burdens of health and medical care for the newborn, and the mother's participation in caring for her child.

In sum, the concept of motherhood includes physiologically developed feelings with the mother's body that pays for her health and physical, expressing a pureblood bond that arose in her womb and grew up in her arms, drinking from her breast milk and interacting with her psychological, health and physical care. It is a sophisticated emotional and physiological concept that the concept of paternity does not possess, which is different in its composition from the concept of motherhood. This is what makes the female desire to be the mother of a child growing up in her womb, and in the face of that, she responds to the desire of her husband to become pregnant by him and for him to be the father of her child. It is a feminine instinct that men do not possess. This is a unique distinction in its kind that women boast more than men and feel a lack of their femininity when they are sterile, as well as the case with men when he is sterile. Motherhood, then, refers to the human existence and immortality of the mother and the father. Had it not been for motherhood and paternity, there would be no female presence in the family, nor the presence of a man in it. Rather, there would be no immortality for her or her husband. Motherhood is the natural source of human immortality.

G. ADVOCACY OF THE NATIONAL LEADERS' FIGURES TO THE FEMININITY AGAINST HER ENSLAVEMENT

When governments established feminist organizations or unions that included women, their establishment was not an expression of preference for them or granting them their rights or exploiting their energy or equality with men. It is rather a government front to support its rule and ruler from a segment of some opportunistic, factional intrusive, and professionally unskilled women. They use them as propaganda mouthpieces for the ruler's rule, not to defend women's rights or their equality with men. It is a dishonest organization in its advocacy of women's interests. Such feminist organizations are usually found in totalitarian and dictatorial regimes. They have no presence in regimes controlled by the ruling family, the ruling tribe, or the ruling sect. It can be said that these regimes exploit women to whitewash the face of the ruler and his government in return for paying the expense of women's unfairness in rights and duties, granting them their right to the family and eliminating domestic and legal violence practised against them.

Lenin in the former Soviet Union granted many rights to women, except for her entry into party leadership and sovereign positions. Also, (Suharto) in Indonesia legislated many positives for Indonesian women in order to prevent the practice of extremist and conscious feminist movements from exercising their activities against the government. The situation is similar in Arab countries such as Iraq, which established the Association for the Defence of Women's Rights during (the rule of Abdul Karim Qasim) and the Women's Union during the rule of The Baath and (Saddam Hussein) and the situation applies to Syria, Egypt, Tunisia and other Arab countries whose clients appointed their

482

agents to establish a women's organization to support their rule and rulers only and freeze women's awareness and human rights aspirations, not to defend their rights and not to exercise violence against them or grant them their rights in marriage, family, appointment, wages, work, etc. till then. Because rights are extracted from the inherited social culture that the ruler uses to support his dynastic rule. Are women's voices and positions equal to men in popular, municipal, union, parliamentary and party councils? Was her opinion taken in making corrective decisions? All of this did not happen because her position and role were not exercised in all patterns and structures of the social structure, because the man does not want that, and it is not in his interest as his masculine, family and cultural authority will be reduced. If it happened, and if a woman entered his fields, such as what happened in education, nursing, and social service, it was only because he left these fields of his own free will and went to fields that pay higher wages rather than confessing or fairness to woman rights. Therefore, there are many and varied gaps between them, such as the wage, the professional, the educational, the legal, and the expressive linguistic gap (which favours men over women in written and oral expression), all of which still exist in all human societies despite being taken by force and with constant urgency and with great merit. High positions in advanced societies have been recognized by men and women, the media, international organizations, the United Nations, and international politics. Her dissolution of what she won was not easy, facilitation, or sympathy on the part of the man, but rather through fierce, serious and persevering competition. It is the public interest that has brought her to what she has reached in leadership, prudence and pragmatism, without arrogance or condescension to the man who underestimated her rights for centuries, such as (Angela Merkel) in Germany, (Theresa May) in Britain, and (Melinda Gates) in technology Information, and (Christine Lagarde) in Paris and (Yuxiu Hua) in China, (Serena Williams) in America, and (Jacinda Ardern) in New Zealand and others.

1. **Chinese Leader Mao Zedong:** He considered the patriarchal family a microcosm of the oppressive capitalist society. And considered the feminine the right hand in family, economic and agricultural development, and construction, and made her position and work equal to and equal to her work within her family. He made her an economically productive element in the socialist system in the sense that he freed her from the bondage of society and raised her economic status, stressing that social reform must start with equality between men and women, and when this is achieved, reform takes its place in society.

In 1950, he issued reform laws for the Chinese family in which he removed the customary and situational controls that oppressed women and enslaved their freedom as human beings in order to make them like Chinese men in terms of gender rights, for example:

1) He abolished the family's interference in choosing a life partner for a woman and a man
2) Granting the woman, the right to divorce herself.
3) Not allowing a man to marry more than one wife at a time.
4) Not allowing a man to dominate a woman.
5) Preventing sexual intercourse without a legal marriage contract.
6) Not to marry a minor.
7) Cancellation of the bride price.
8) Abolishing the restrictions imposed on the remarriage of a widow.

Then a law was issued in 1980 abolishing many restrictions imposed on women's right to work, study, and participate in social activities, as well as preventing violence against women.

In 2001, Mao issued a law that considered illegal sex (without marriage) outside the law, granted division of property upon divorce, and allocated a monthly stipend to the divorced woman.

2. Gandhi And Nehru in India: During the rolling of Gandhi, Andera Gandhi and Nehru, Indian women achieved many milestones on their road towards her liberation, equality with men, and social participation.

1) Gandhi granted a radiant national consideration for women in opposition to political movements and groups to play a vital role outside the home.
2) Nehru granted women the right to inherit, divorce and vote in elections.
3) Andrea Gandhi made women the mother of India, a national symbol in Indian traditions.
4) Andrea Gandhi worked to equalize the rights of women with the rights of men.
5) Gandhi granted women equality with men in all Indian castes, regions and regions.
6) Gandhi Granted women's participation in and leadership of political opposition movements.

3. **Suharto In Indonesia:** From 1966 - until 1989, Suharto launched a development program in the economic, social, and demographic fields to serve the interests of women. His main achievements were:

1) Offer many job opportunities for her.
2) Providing medical, health and educational services

3) He considered her the symbol of the mother in her work on the cohesion of family members and the preservation of their traditional ties and customs.

4. **Lenin in the Soviet Union (Former):** Since 1917, Lenin worked on:

1) Upgrading the status of women through the abolition of all forms of discrimination and intolerance against her that the Russian Tsarism used to practice.
2) Ensuring their full equality in employment opportunities, education, property rights and family affairs, and their competition with men in the management of government
3) Elimination of intolerance and prejudice against her at working institutions such as labour unions and political positions.
4) Her employment in the labour market has reached the highest percentage of the workforce of any industrial country in the world.
5) The income of a woman is 2/3 of the average income of a man.
6) Closing the wage gap between her and the man.

H. ADVOCACY OF FEMININE REFORMIST MOVEMENTS TO FEMININITY AGAINST HER ENSLAVEMENT

In the face of the unfairness and injustice that the feminine has suffered in enslavement by men of religion, politics, social culture and patriarchal authority, feminist reformist organizations have been formed to educate society about the reality of injustice, ingratitude, and humiliation of them at work, their wages, family, inheritance, and marriage from violence. Feminist groups have emerged opposing these ungrateful and unjust practices against them in both India and Indonesia are the following:

1. **Indian Glaring Movement:** It emerged in the nineteenth century:

a) It attacked and criticized the marriage of minors and the neglect of women's rights to property.

b) It attacked the blocking and isolation of the widow from public social life.

c) Raising awareness of women in their role as a mother.

d) Urging women to educate and remove their illiteracy.

e) She reduced the pressures of family life on her.

2. **Contemporary Indian Organizations:** They helped the women throughout India to tackle their problems and called them to live their lives in civilized style with trouble-free. Their activities were known by:

a) Addressing the high rate of women's death in India.

b) Elimination of women's illiteracy.

c) Applying health awareness and combining modern treatment with traditional treatment.

d) Medical education dissemination to combat AIDS.

3. **Contemporary (Wife Power) Community:** This is a reformist feminist movement in Indonesia. It is the most influential feminist group in the world that includes the wives of civil servants working behind the scenes. It enjoys an influential power due to its mandatory membership and has a wide network of contacts, which makes it exert pressure on government decisions as a pressure group, particularly on family matters such as polygamy for government employees. That is, a man married to more than one wife should not be appointed to a government institution. This group includes six million wives who have an influence on government policy in local communities, with the aim of:

1) Raising the level of Indonesian women, especially the wife, and freeing her from the burdens of the family by legalizing childbearing and health care for her.
2) Preventing violence against her.
3) Grant her union membership.
4) Receiving leadership positions in government institutions.
5) Putting pressure on the management of factories in favour of women.
6) Participation in popular strikes and sit-ins in order to obtain their rights.

CHAPTER 9: FEMININE PHASES IN ANCIENT CIVILIZATIONS (THE DEITY WHO BECAME A SLAVE)

INITIATION

A. THE GOLDEN AGE OF THE FEMININE (THE AGE OF ITS SANCTIFICATION AT THE PHARAOHS AND MESOPOTAMIA IN BABYLON AND SUMER)

B. THE ERA OF HER ENSLAVEMENT (AT THE TIME OF THE GREEK, ROMAN, PERSIAN, AND CHINESE CIVILIZATIONS)

C. ARAB WISE WOMEN THROUGHOUT HISTORY

CHAPTER 9
FEMININE PHASES IN ANCIENT CIVILIZATIONS
(THE DEITY WHO BECAME A SLAVE)

INITIATION

The ancient Babylonian, Sumerian, Phoenician, Roman and Pharaonic civilizations showed that their phase (their state, type, class, or entity) represents the goddess worshipped and the first mother giving birth to a life, exceedingly beautiful and more perfect than the man. This is how her existence was within these ancient and authentic civilizations and therefore called (the divine phase).

In the Greek, Roman, Indian, and Arab civilizations in the pre-Islamic era, Persian, Judaism, and ancient China, it was found that she was considered a commodity subject to dealing in buying and selling, a degenerate being, and a demon Satan whispers to humans' beings, subject to men in a despised, humiliating and deprived of rights. Her condition, type, or entity is therefore called (the slavery phase).

Accordingly, the title of this section is (the feminine deity who became a slave) because she was worshipped by men of six ancient and ancient civilizations in the history of humanity at the same time, then she became a slave owned by men in seven ancient cultures in human history.

As a matter of enrichment, elaboration, and specification, and in order to be clearer about the above, astonishment is raised about these two phases of a single creature whose sex and it's biological genes have not changed. Even her social roles in all ancient and modern civilizations (eleven civilizations) and among millions of different people culturally, religiously, ethnically, and evolutionarily in terms of being a daughter, a wife, and a mother who raised her children have remained constant.

Four main roles, sometimes considered by civilizations as a worshipped goddess and as the first mother who gives birth to a child (such as Ishtar, Anna, Asharut, Aphrodite, Venus) who has the right to inherit own property, children were affiliated to her rather than to their fathers, she has guardianship over her husband, and she assumed the rule and to be a queen. Yet, she was treated in a very contradictory way as in the civilization of the Pharaohs, Babylonian, Sumerian, Phoenician, Greek and Roman. On the one hand, she was considered a queen, and on the other hand, she was considered a second-class citizen though she had not changed in her biological type, as can be seen in the following treatment by the same civilizations:

1. Of the animal family (in the Greek civilization).
2. The source of evil (in the Roman civilization) she is buried with her husband upon his death while she is alive.
3. Drowning in water to death (in the Babylonian civilization) if she disobeys her husband's orders.
4. She is owned by the legal heir after the death of her husband (according to the Arabs in the pre-Islamic era).
5. She is completely isolated from her natural roles, such as menstruation and postpartum bleeding (in the Persian civilization).
6. She serves her husband and is sold and donated (in Judaism).
7. To be cremated (according to Hindus) after the death of her husband.
8. Sold at birth in ancient China.
9. She is infanticide and buried alive in the pre-Islamic era.

It is important to point out that if these attitudes and dealings were issued by one individual, it could be attributed to personal attitudes or self-interest, but, they come from an inherited social culture and different peoples and nations in their stages of development and have civilities and cultures attested to deal with a creature that represents half of the society and nourishes it with new human elements. Even religions such as Judaism, Hinduism and Zoroastrianism need a human element that feeds their population size. They dealt with the feminine like an animal!!! Why such extreme variability towards the same creature? Sometimes she is worshipped, and sometimes she is excluded!!! And she serves the man (brother, father, husband, and son). Why this inhuman collective contempt? Is there a reason for it? So why does a man accept to be served by an afflicted creature and incomplete? What is the reason that makes six ancient civilizations worship her and grant her rule, inheritance, and a family title? Is there an alternative to her in society? Why did ancient civilizations not do justice to her, deny her, and oppress her? Is it correct that civilizations fall into a cultural or human error? And why were there civilizations that worshipped the same creature and considered her the mother who gives birth? Is there a civilized misunderstanding and misunderstanding of the feminine? Why this confusion for them? And why did the feminine continue to play the same roles over centuries (wife, mother, nanny)? So, she is the constant in her cyclical, biological, and family functions. Without her, the family would not have been established, and there was no social cell, and the transmission of social culture from the previous generation to the next through her upbringing of her children by teaching them the language, religion, customs, and values of her ancestors, would not take place? Why does human civilization oppress the

492

permanent partner of man in building the family and society? If there are external influences that do their work in this regard, is it conceivable that these influences have been going on for several centuries, working to despise women, marginalize their status, and place burdens on their role in housekeeping procreation, and upbringing? When are the rights and duties of the feminine equal and equal to the masculine? Because this extremism between its phases (the slave and the worshipped) does not represent the civilizational, cultural, and human maturity and the imbalance of human relations that God Almighty created between men and women, why does society deny feminine services to it and its social cells? And why does he exaggerate her services and consider her to be the gods and worship her as he worshipped Ishtar?

So, there is an impairment in the judicial system for her and an imbalance in their vision of her. For this reason, the current era is seen as if it makes attempts to be fair to the feminine. In this respect, it does not underestimate her position in the family and the society, not denying her service and productive role or denying her position in the family or her systematic functions in the social structure.

The discussion concerns the feminine culturally and not individually, civilized and not personally because this reality constitutes a socio-civilizational dilemma that sociology has to tackle as a deep and far-reaching macro dilemma that concerns not only women but society, reformers, leaders and political leaders interested in human and social affairs and the liberation of women's slavery by the inherited calcified legacy that does not serve society in the era of instant rapid communications and the information revolution.

After this definition of the concepts of the subject, the ancient civilizations that represented the golden age of the feminine in those ancient civilizations are detailed in the following sections:

A. THE GOLDEN AGE OF THE FEMININE (THE AGE OF ITS SANCTIFICATION AT THE PHARAOHS AND MESOPOTAMIA IN BABYLON AND SUMER)

The feminine went through a golden age, in which she was an example of sanctification and worship, prehistoric in the totemic stage and then agricultural societies where they sanctified her and made her a god, a goddess symbolizing fertility, growth and love. [Al-Khaqani. 2013. p. 126]

In the Pharaonic civilization: The Pharaonic civilization ranked first among human civilizations in terms of its treatment and appreciation of women. The Pharaonic woman had the right to inherit, and she owned and took care of her family in the absence of her husband. They believed that the woman was better than the man, and the husband wrote everything he owned to his wife. Children were related to their mothers, not to their fathers, just as the woman's guardianship was over her husband, not the man over his wife, and the husband had to pledge in the marriage contract that he would be obedient to his wife in all matters. In the era of the Pharaohs, the woman also had the right to take over the rule if there were no male rulers. Despite this, only five queens took over the rule of Egypt, compared to four hundred and seventy kings, due to the woman's feeling of her femininity. [Wikipedia. Societies' view of women in different civilizations]

Not only that, but there is also the goddess Ishtar in Mesopotamia (currently Iraq), who represents love,

494

motherhood, fertility, sympathy and tenderness. So (Sumerian Inanna), the first of them being (Babylonian Ishtar, Egyptian Isis, Phoenician Astarte, Greek Artemis, Roman Diana, and even the pre-Islamic Arabs who had their Ishtar, which was the Pharisees that did not stay with them for a few centuries before leaving them and turning into Venus) and there is an exciting story in the book of idols by Ibn al-Kalbi about destroying Khalid bin Walid for the statue of Ishtar Arabia in Wadi Harad. [Latakani. 2012. p. 24]

It is (Ishtar) the goddess of sex, love, beauty and sacrifice in wars for the Babylonians, and it corresponds to the Sumerians (Inanna) and (Astarte) to the Phoenicians and (Aphrodite) to the Greeks, and (Venus) to the Romans. It is the morning and evening star (Venus) whose symbol is an octagonal star erected on the back of a lion, on its forehead a flower and a bouquet of flowers in its hand. Its depictions and symbols were numerous and appeared in most ancient legends, poets sang about her love, and artists excelled in painting and sculpting her depiction.

And (Ishtar) of the feminine deities in all primitive religions was symbolized and referred to by symbols such as the eternal flame, the pentagonal star, the rose and the moon.

She is the mother goddess: generally symbolizing the first mother goddess who gave birth to a life. And one of her symbols was the lion, and her main temple was in Nineveh, near the city of Mosul. The Sumerians called it Anah, the West called it Athtar, and the Greeks called it Aphrodite.

Ishtar, according to the Sumerians, is the daughter of the god Sin, the sun god, and her sister, the goddess (Arshikigal), the goddess of the underworld, the world of death, and she is the greatest of the gods, the most stature of them, and her original centre of worship was the city of Uruk (Al-Warka), the capital of Sumer.

It is said that (Ishtar) is of a dazzling beauty, the like of which has not been witnessed, even (Usis) her love, and the people of the earth were not far from that love. (Ishtar) was going around the human world in search of victims until she reached the kings of humans. She used to take everything they owned and promise them marriage. Even if she took what was dearest to them, she left them crying day and night. [Wikipedia, the free encyclopaedia]

For more information about the matriarchal society, it needs to be explained as a society where Ishtar was the Great Mother.

Until the mid-nineteenth century, it was believed that society was a patriarchal society. And it prevailed even in ancient societies, which were as old as human society. This hypothesis collapsed in the face of scientific criticism by a number of pioneers in anthropology and human sciences. They provided sufficient evidence for the existence of an older form of masculine society, which is the matriarchal society. It was not based on masculine values and the authority of the father but on the feminine values and the position of the mother. This is based on the first human assembly that was not established under the leadership of the warrior-hunter but crystallized around the mother who was tightened through her emotions, taking care of her children in the first united human unit, which is the matriarchal family as the largest cell of the matriarchal society. The most important characteristics of this society are:

1. That the man handed leadership to the woman not for her physical superiority but in appreciation of her human characteristics, spiritual powers, supernatural abilities, and the rhythm of her body in harmony with the rhythm of nature. She was the first priestess, fortune-teller and first witch. She was responsible for the lives of children

and securing livelihoods for them, and she was responsible for preparing animal skins and turning them into clothes, mattresses, and covers. Also, she was the first weaver and the first to make pottery, and because she spent a long time searching for roots and edible herbs, she learned the properties of magical herbs in healing diseases, so she was the first doctor and she was the one who built the house and made its furniture. Moreover, she was a merchant who exchanged her products for the products of others. And from the presence of the sacred fire flame in the temples of late civilizations and the temple's maidens guarding it and keeping it burning, it can be concluded that the first flame of fire was kindled by the woman and was the first guardian of it and the preserver of its secrets, until the woman crowned her economic role in this society with the discovery of agriculture and the transfer of man from the hunting community to the community Food production, while the man maintained throughout this stage his traditional role of hunting and moving in search of large game.

2. The men of the matriarchal society were more honourable, noble, and chivalrous than the men of the patriarchal society, as they gave women their status in respect and appreciation, not out of submission or fear.

3. By tracing the forms of the maternal family and the pattern of the sexual relationship between a woman and a man, we conclude that sexual relations were completely free without any regulation or law, where every woman is for every man, and every man is for every woman.

4. In this society, it is not possible to know the father of the child because the children are attributed to their mothers,

and each child is known by his mother, not by his father. This is what he called (mother's right), and children have the right to inheritance from their mother and not from their father because the father is considered a stranger, and his inheritance and states go to his brothers.

5. The woman had the right to separate from her husband whenever she wanted, and the children would return to her, not to the husband who left the house empty-handed.

In Babylon, for example, the man, until extremely late periods in the history of the patriarchal society here, could not place under his guardianship the sexual life of the woman before marriage, so the woman's virginity was the property of the goddess Ishtar, not to her future husband, and she was blowing her virginity in the temple where she practised sacred sex under the patronage of the gods before committing to married life.

Likewise, the matriarchal society was clear to the ancient Egyptians, as well as to the rest of the eastern civilizations, so we notice the remains of the matriarchal society clear today. [Gateway of Babylon of the Gods]

Women between the matriarchal and patriarchal eras, in the matriarchal society, as the writer (Firas al-Sawah) says, children belong to their mother and their clan, not to their father, who was always viewed as a stranger. Based on the (mother's right), the children inherited nothing but the wealth of their mothers. The matriarchal principle in this society includes the life of commons, justice, and equality, and it unites people with nature and makes them submit to its laws. As for the patriarchal society, which is led by a man, it relies on ownership, domination, and discrimination, as it is a departure from the path of nature and subject to artificial laws: (The maternal principle unites and unites, and the patriarchal principle divides and sets barriers and borders).

498

In the matriarchal society, the groups surrendered their leadership to the mothers due to their important human characteristics and creative abilities. The position of women has been enhanced because of her important economic role, as she is the first producer in the community because she is primarily responsible for the lives of her children to secure their livelihoods. She was the first to plant and produce food, weave, and make pottery, mattresses and covers, and the first to know the properties of medicinal herbs in cure diseases; As for the man, he maintained his traditional role of hunting and catching game.

The woman in the matriarchal society was established for the spirit of justice and equality among the community, as she instilled love and equal affection among all her children and all her group, who are brothers in a large family. She also instilled the spirit of peace and pacifism because she hated physical violence and shunned it, which spread peace among the matriarchal groups, but when the father patriarchal society, in which we still live today, peace was lost, and we lost our beautiful paradise. Today, the mother is blunt, meaning that she always gathers her children around her and unites the family.

Women are currently suffering from many forms of discrimination against them, starting with the way they dress and ending with the smallest details of their personal life and freedom of expression.

Here, some cases are mentioned as an example, starting with the family and how to deal with childbearing:

Every family wants to have a boy, he is the one who will carry the family name, and he will immortalize the name of his father or grandfather when he grows up and gets married and has children. Even today, there are men who marry after their wives if their wives did not give birth to them or if they only gave birth to daughters. Whoever does not divorce his wife or does not marry another woman in order to have a boy tries with her to repeat the children until the boy finally comes, and he may not come, and the number of family members increases dramatically, which is not desirable in the current time that most people suffer from of great economic and social difficulties, in addition to its great impact on the increase in the population and the population explosion taking place in the third world, which is accompanied by a massive shortage of natural and food resources to meet the needs of the huge increasing numbers of the population in the third world.

If a girl could carry the name of her first family and pass it on to her children, thus immortalizing the name of the father or grandfather in her family, was there an urgent need for a boy in this family?! Do not be surprised, there is a clear example in European countries, for example, Spain: a girl in this European country, just like a young man, her nickname consists of both the nickname of her father and her mother, and when she gets married, the nickname of the husband is added to these two nicknames, and she must choose one nickname in addition to Her husband's nickname: either her father's or her mother's, and she can carry it to her children when she gives birth...

Thus, it is true that when she marries, she is forced to choose between the surname of her father and her mother, which will be added to the nickname of the husband, but if this practice applied in the East, the girl can, for example, choose the nickname of the father, as long as the system is patriarchal, to be carried by her children in addition to the surname of her husband if her first family was devoid of male siblings... Thus, the father can be assured that his family's nickname will continue, and he will be satisfied with having girls if that happens, and his wife has not given birth to him males. Therefore, the parents are not forced to have many daughters and not stop childbearing only when the male child comes, which is one means of birth control to avoid an increase in the population rate.

Another example that illustrates discrimination against women is that many rural areas in Syria, which are still controlled by the tribal spirit, in the northeast, middle and south of Syria as well, are, in many cases violating Islamic law by not giving the girl her legitimate inheritance from her father. Or from her mother, because if she gets married, she will marry the (stranger) from whom she will have children (strangers) from the clan and the family, and thus her father's inheritance will pass to these (strangers) children. But if she does not marry, then it is sufficient for her to remain in her father's house and under his care, then with her male brothers and their families to eat, drink, sleep and also "serve" her brothers' children, and there is no need for her to be economically independent or to have her inheritance from her father to dispose of!!

This is not only a violation of the explicit Islamic law applied in the Arabic countries, but it is a humiliation for the woman and a disregard for her human being. The importance of women's economic independence is very well known now a day, and Islam, in particular, has honoured the woman by giving her the financial responsibility that is separate from their husband.

The strange thing is that there are a lot of talk shows on satellite channels and religious programs about matters such as purity, Islamic dress and how to perform acts of worship so that women and men do not fall the risk of violating Islamic law and rarely does one of the specialists mention such violating practices absolutely and explicitly. It is clear

501

to Islamic law!!! Note that several contemporary commentators have interpreted the noble verse "God enjoins you in your children to have the male equal to the share of two females" (an-Nisa 11) within its context, that the female can be inherited to the minimum amount.

And if the application of Islamic Sharia is implemented in these clear and explicit matters that preserve the entity and dignity of women, it would be possible to abolish such discriminatory practices against her, which are exemplified by the following line of poetry, which many recite as martyrdom and boasting: "Our sons are the sons of our sons, and our daughters' sones are the sons of distant men". Another example is the problem of nationality. A woman in Syria, at least, cannot pass her nationality to her children, and this is considered flagrant discrimination against women.

French women, for example, and European and American women, in general, give their nationality to their husbands and children, and this is normal in the countries of the wide world. If The mother unites the family, and without her, there would be no family, how could it be that she cannot pass her nationality to her children or her husband? Why is this discrimination, which amounts to persecution?!! Also, in some Arab countries, a sharp debate still exists about allowing women to vote and run for office. Unfortunately, it has been raised again, under foreign pressure in the implementation of the so-called "empowerment of women."

Women's work these days is no longer a luxury. It is an economical, cultural and social necessity. A woman bears the burden of work inside and outside the home, often without help inside the house, on the pretext that this is the field in which they have been experienced, knowing that most of today's youth will not be able to bear the burdens of the family alone, and that woman's work is necessary to carry out and share some of these burdens. She has the right, then, for a man to help her with the burdens of domestic work, just as she helps him to bear the burdens of working outside the home for the family.

However, it seems that people still consider woman's work unnecessary, and some claim that if the woman returns to her home, the problem of unemployment in the country will be solved. Of course, this is wrong thinking, and it is clear discrimination against women and has no reasonable justification as the causes of unemployment are numerous.

Here I mention an example that happened to us when we were working in one of the governmental, cultural institutions in Damascus, and it is supposed to be a pioneering institution in the field of culture and thought. At the end of the eighties and the beginning of the nineties of the last century, a senior near retirement man took over the management of the largest directorates in this institution, which is dominated by women in the number of employees. And he, in particular, would persecute any girl who worked, especially if he saw her for some reason, health or physical, and stopped working for a moment to rest a little. He would take the initiative to deduct 5% of her salary for several months... This is, of course, inhumane treatment, especially since the first generation of this cultural institution has made great efforts in establishing it.

On one occasion, one of the active female employees protested against the deduction from the salary that accrued to her, just because he saw her sitting due to a sudden illness that she suffered, so he said to him: "Professor, we are like your daughters, so why are you so hard on us? Do you treat your daughters like this?"

He replied immediately and without thinking: "I never allow my daughters to work outside the house!!!" Here we concluded that he oppresses women only because they dared to go out to work. So, how many directors and department heads are still at the head of their work in the cultural and official departments and institutions and carry such a sick attitude?

In the matter of marriage and choosing a life partner, women in Eastern societies are still, in general, under pressure from the father or brother in marriage, without leaving them the right to choose their life partner. And if she happens to choose a husband from outside her sect or social environment, her fate may be ostracism or death in many cases.

Islamic law gave the woman the right to have infallibility in her hand until the third divorce. However, it is rare for a woman to use this right no matter how high her social and economic status is, so it is not appropriate for a "man" that his wife holds infallibility in her hand.

With regards to Islam, the marriage contract conformed to the principle that (the contract is the binding law of the two contracting parties). In his book (Circles of Fear), Dr Nasr Hamid Abu Zaid published an example of a marriage document from the fourth century AH, i.e. from the eleventh century AD in Andalusia, and in it, the husband made a promise not to marry a second wife and to be responsible for his wife maintenance and clothing. There are conditions to her domicile and place, and if all these conditions are violated one day, or if the husband does not respect them, then the marriage contract becomes void, and the wife can divorce herself directly. In some cases, in married life, the husband may disguise his wife's struggle hand in hand in bearing the family's burdens, neglecting her and neglecting

504

her opinions, or marrying another woman on the pretext that she is no longer keeping pace with the requirements of his new material life.

Returning to Professor Firas al-Sawah's book "The Ishtar Mystery", which stated that all religions began as Ishtar, and thus women played the role of the first teacher in the history of human civilization. For the advancement of any society, a woman must regain her right and her lofty role with the elimination of discrimination against her.

The patriarchal society, in fact, has been inherited from the Jewish religion, which considered the woman a disgrace to the man and, in some cases, underestimated her human status. However, the demands of the subordination of the woman to man as he was featured as the head of the woman were inherited from the Christian religion. The Islamic religion, in this respect, was considered a social revolution. The Qur'an has addressed the men and women equal in human speech: "And one of His signs is that He created for you spouses from among yourselves so that you may find comfort in them. And He has placed between your compassion and mercy. Surely in this are signs for people who reflect." (Ar-Rum / 21). "He is the one Who created you from a single soul, then from it made its spouse so he may find comfort in her. After he had been united with her, she carried a light burden that developed gradually. When it grew heavy, they prayed to Allah, their Lord, "If you grant us good offspring, we will certainly be grateful." (Al-A'raf/ 189)

When stewardship is mentioned in the Holy Qur'an, it is mentioned within the context of what is often neglected and is not mentioned: "Men are the caretakers of women, as men have been provisioned by Allah over women and tasked with supporting them financially. And righteous women are devoutly obedient and, when alone, protective of what Allah has entrusted them with. And if you sense ill-conduct from your women, advise them ˹first˺, ˹if they persist,˺ do not share their beds, ˹but if they still persist,˺ then discipline them ˹gently˺.2 But if they change their ways, do not be unjust to them. Surely Allah is Most High, All-Great." (An-Nisa /34).

Unfortunately, Islam was not able to prevent pre-Islamic customs that infiltrated Islamic society and are still deeply rooted in Arab societies. It is true that female infanticide is an untouchable custom. However, female infanticide continues to oppress her socially, economically, intellectually, and spiritually... It is a "female infanticide" of another kind.

So, what is the solution to get out of this situation?!

The only solution is the just man-made law that considers woman and man to be human beings, and both are subject to equal rights and duties in a free atmosphere of justice, democracy, and secularism, which considers women to be men's partners in the family. It is a law that recognizes and does not deny the other, regardless of the other's religion, gender, or colour. It is a law that preserves human dignity in a healthy, cohesive, and free society. It is not permissible for a woman to be treated with this discriminatory insult to human dignity... The ideas presented here may be contrary or inappropriate to some people. It does not matter as far as the intellectual discussion continues in order to have a liveable society for all its members. Multiplicity and diversity in thoughts are healthy!! [http://www.rimalattrache.com]

The Extreme Patriarchal System (Stagnated Arabic Society): The father-patriarchal system is a distinct social and psychological structure rooted in the collective memory that characterizes the family, tribe, authority, and society in the Arab world. It is a hierarchical relationship based on irrational authoritarianism and submission that contradicts the values of modernity, civil society and respect for human rights that resulted from historical, social, and economic conditions and circumstances and through a series of historical stages and interconnected social and economic formations. Each stage is linked to a previous stage until it reaches the stage of the modern patriarchal system, which is a specific pattern of a social and economic organization prior to capitalism. It differs in its social, economic, and cultural structures from the structure of the Arab patriarchal system that adopted a distinct type as a traditional society and was in stark contrast with the modern society. This is characterized by scientific and technical progress. The Arab society's characteristics include its ability to resist the change of its original structure from the Middle Ages until now and its ability to continue to preserve its traditional values , such as belonging to the tribe, sect, and region, and its connection to the desert environment, which resulted in a patriarchal system that dominated the Arabic region many centuries and still.

If most of the societies prevalent in the world today, whether democratic, socialist, capitalist or otherwise, are patriarchal societies, then the Arab society is more patriarchal than other societies because it is a stagnant, past traditional society that lacks the internal strength that motivates it.

On the social level, the patriarchal system dominates the social, cultural, economic, and political relations that are dominated by tribal, sectarian, and local affiliations because the patriarchal society is a type of traditional society in which patterns of values, behaviour and distinct forms of organization prevail. Therefore, it constitutes a distinct qualitative structure that takes different forms, including the structure of the Arab patriarchal society, which is more masculine than other societies, more traditional and more besieged by the individual's personality and culture, consolidating his traditional social values and norms, marginalizing women and alienating her personality, because it has a qualitative and specific character. And a historical extension linked to the pastoral desert environment and the prevailing tribal values and fanaticism. It is well known that the Arab world is the greatest homeland for Bedouins, just as it is the region most affected and suffering in the conflict between Bedouin values and the values of civilization, as indicated by (Ali Al-Wardi) in his book (The Nature of Iraqi Society), a conflict that still affects the structure of culture and personality. Arabic.

Maternal System: The matriarchal system represents an ancient stage in time when the power of the woman-mother prevailed in society and monopolized economic and political leadership as well as religious authority. This corresponds to the patriarchal system, which later replaced the mother's authority.

Although the woman is physiologically weaker than the man, she had occupied a high social position in the family, society, and authority and assumed a high spiritual position in an ancient historical stage in which liberal sexual relations prevailed in which affiliation to the mother line, that is, the affiliation of children to their mothers, because it is not possible to know the real father of the children. Anthropologists have termed this system the matriarchal system, meaning the power of women in society.

Children at that stage were related to their mothers and not to their fathers because it was not possible at that time to

508

determine the father as there was no kinship system that determined sexual relations, and for this also, women, as the only known mothers with confidence and affirmation of children. She enjoyed a great deal of respect and thus gained social status and was highly religious.

Woman acquired their high status in the beginnings of human settlement and derived their high status from nature because she was the first to settle in the land and discovered agriculture and domesticated animals, and because the principle of fertility in the land is the same as the principle of her fertility. Thus, the power of a woman in society developed, which is, in fact, a natural right for her because of her acquisition of spiritual significance, came the religion, the duty to give at birth. Therefore, man sanctifies the earth as he sanctifies the female, for the female is an image and successor to the original mother - the earth. The land did not imitate the female, but the female imitated the land, and it became sacred like her. Religious respect and sanctification became the basis for her authority, the rise of her religious and social status, her state policy, and her management of religious rituals.

And the female is the origin because she is ahead of the man with her giving and because the man is the result of that giving. The son is the future husband, who in turn fertilizes the woman and becomes a father. The kinship organization finds its place in the arms of women, and from it, all other social organizations have developed. Thus, the mother's right becomes a natural right for her.

Transformation into the Power of Man: The power of woman did not last long after the right of the state took control of her natural right, after the development of the city-state, which created the first new social organization for sexual life, that took the form of the marriage system and

509

later developed into the form of monogamy and was linked to a religious system that had defined sexual relations between the man and the woman. The development of another stage adopted the male authority and affiliation in the paternal line instead of affiliation in the mother's line and the transformation of sexual relations that regulate agriculture, marriage, and kinship. At this stage, the religious system was transferred from the worship of the moon to the worship of the sun.

The beginnings of regulating sexual relations between men and women were the beginnings of the establishment of the state, which gave power to the man and forced the woman to gradually lose her natural right through the discovery of minerals, the development of the property system, the spread of organized agriculture and the emergence of cities. On the ruins of that system, the beginnings of a new civilized stage in the history of the development of societies mankind which is the stage of "father's authority", began. As a result, the mother-woman lost her golden age in which her social and religious status was elevated through the magic of motherhood and her biological function.

The stage of the father's right is the stage of (metaphysical right) as it is called (Bachofen), which was represented by the decline of the mother's right, which is her natural right, that appeared with the rule of the patriarchal system in its highest forms in the Roman state and before it in the Babylonian state, and still exists until today in most societies in the world.

The Roots of Arab Patriarchy: The roots of the Arab patriarchal system extend back to the pre-Islamic stage, where the (Sheikhdom) system dominated the Arab society. Such a system was the product of socio-economic relations specific to the pastoral production pattern in the Arab desert based on tribal fanaticism and on the system of kinship and blood ties. In this system, the individual conforms with the tribe by exchanging loyalty and protection as it is responsible on a social and political level for each member of the tribe. This led to the strengthening of the tribal system based on tribal fanaticism, which makes the family the cornerstone of the social structure that expands its circle to include the clan. Its entity is double control: the father's control over the family, the man's control over the woman, and the sheikh over the tribe, and the dominant discourse becomes the father's discourse, command, and decisions.

Although Islam tried to change the tribal structure and came up with the concept of (nation) as an alternative to the concept of tribalism, the tribal system remained dominant over society and the state, where values and traditions persisted.

The roots of the Arab patriarchal system therefore formed from historical, geographical, and cultural conditions through the control of the Bedouin culture over social, economic, and political life through the tribal system (the sheikhdom), which was an alternative to the state and its management as a social organization based on Values, fanaticism, and tribal relations.

The Arab desert also continued to supply the villages and countryside with continuous Bedouin waves to which the inhabitants of the countryside and cities were subjected and affected by their values, customs, and fanaticism due to the weakness of the central state, after the fall of the Islamic Arab state and its capital, Baghdad, at the hands of Hulagu in 1258, which caused the dominance of the tribal and local system over society, especially the family structure. It extended in its social and economic relations and continued until the modern era in one way or another, despite the entry of many elements of modernization into it. This is because the modern state has not completed and matured yet, as well as the concept of homeland, citizenship, and identity, which are still gelatinous concepts. And because the structure of the Arab family in Its initial form does not differ much from the structure of the Arab tribe of the pre-Islamic era except in some of its external manifestations that were affected by modernization, and not in its behaviour, contents, values, and mentality.

As was mentioned earlier, the patriarchal system is a psychological structure resulting from specific historical and civilizational conditions, and it consists of a set of values, norms, and patterns of behaviour that are linked to a traditional economic system. Thus, it has a specificity and a living social reality and is not just a characteristic of a specific production pattern in the Arab world.

Tribal Fanaticism: One of the most important characteristics of the traditional Arab patriarchal system is that it is based on tribal fanaticism and the identification of the individual within the tribe.

Fatherhood has taken its character from kinship and blood and the need for the son to respect his father and serve him. The tradition of the son offering the duties of obedience and respect to his father continues to this day. A son's respect for his father is the same respect for his clan concentrated in one person represented by its sheikh. In fact, the authority of the father is only an individual manifestation of the authority of the tribe. Despite the passage of hundreds of years, Arab society remained a tribal society consisting of social units based on kinship, which is represented by the family, which is part of the clan, the thigh, the clan, the tribe, and the union of tribes that constitutes the society in its broadest form.

The Arab family consists of several families in general. It is a large extended family, which constitutes the basic feature of the structure of the Arab family until the middle of the last century. It includes all the descendants of one male grandfather and fuses into one unit, and all its members bear the name of the first grandfather of the family.

In fact, the authority of the father is only an individual manifestation of the authority of the tribe. Despite the passage of hundreds of years, Arab society remained a tribal society consisting of social units based on kinship, which is represented by the family.

In the Arab countryside, the structure of the family is intricately linked to the prevailing economic production method and social relations that constitute the land and agriculture as its first and basic pillar and clearly reflect the structure of the kinship system, which is based on solidarity, cohesion, and family fanaticism in the face of problems, burdens and conflicts with other families and with governments and others. Therefore, the family needs to multiply offspring to supply the land with many male labours, early marriage and from within the family (cousin and cousin), as well as polygamy imposed by the unity of work on the land. Thus, the extended Arab family remained until a short time as a productive social unit due to the continuation of the structural conditions and conditions for its development until the end of the nineteenth century.

One notices the persistence of behavioural manifestations that are still doing their work in reproducing kinship relations, which appear in the tendency to residential rapprochement in one area or one city and the strengthening of kinship relations by attending various family occasions, especially on the occasions of marriage, holidays, deaths, and others. Internal marriage is still the preferred model for many extended Arab families. The Arab father-patriarchal system also extends to power formations that still depend on familial influence, and family and clan blocs still play an important and prominent role in many villages and rural areas and even in many Arab cities.

Patriarchy and Woman: The cornerstone of the patriarchal system is based on the male domination over the female and the enslavement and oppression of women, and the denial of their social existence. This is the norm as it is a patriarchal society in which the man controls the woman considering her of a lower degree than him. It forms a patriarchal mentality with an authoritarian tendency that rejects criticism and dialogue and punishes anyone who disobeys this patriarchal system.

Since the dawn of the first high civilizations in history, women have been victims of the patriarchal/patriarchal-masculine society that codified values, customs and traditions that made women inferior to men to a degree, which made them oppressed, and the one who oppresses them is the man, although life is not complete without them.

Persecution Takes Three Forms:

First- Specific oppression is based on a man's superiority and dominance over a woman in order to achieve his private and public interests. This led to the obliteration of the personality of the woman and the downgrading of her importance and social role, and the alienation of her personality in the latter, which caused the lack of integration and social solidarity between the sexes.

Second - patriarchal oppression - masculine, which manifests itself in the domination of the male over the female in the family, society, and power. This domination and oppression are expressed by the father over the mother and children, irrational domination that necessitates their submission and obedience to him blindly, just as the boy controls the girl even if she is older than him and more rational than him.

Third - Legal oppression that emanates from patriarchal oppression and is reflected in man-made and customary laws. It oppresses the woman in her social, economic, and political rights, which hinders her progress and equality with men in humanity.

In fact, the oppression and dispossession of women were not due to biological, religious, or psychological factors. It is rather due to social and class factors and masculine values that resulted from the interests of man in dominating, possessing, and subordinating her to his will, which is the basis of gender inequality and the eternal conflict between them.

Patriarchy and Political Domination: It is not rare to find members of one tribe, one sect, one city, or one region who control power, the state, influence and controls the fates of people, as in most Arab countries. This is evidence that patriarchal authority is based on the extended family, which is the dominant kinship pattern that extends to the modern political system and derives its legitimacy from being a patriarchal kinship system in which the ruler presents himself as (the shepherd) and (the leading father) and that all members of the people are his children. And he addresses his subjects with "my children," and they all have the duty to offer loyalty, obedience, and submission to him always, and at the same time, the "leading father" awaits from his children absolute loyalty to him. In this way, he embodies the patriarchal-male system that dominates Arab society. In fact, the ruling father is the first beneficiary of this (fatherhood), which helps him to control his flock and subject it to his will and tyranny.

On the other hand, paternalism supports the idea of a similar and obedient group that helps to submit to the social and political system, just as it helps to lose sight of the concept of the individual citizen and his individual independence from the group, as well as the absence of his privacy and the assimilation of his personality in the group. The more a person loses his individuality and independence, the more he feels insignificant and weak in responsibility because the collective responsibility rests with the family and the clan, which dominates all individual responsibility.

The personality, which is more concerned with means than ends, establishes the dominance of (the shepherd) and prevents individuals from establishing any social contract between them and accepting what exists so that they become helpless and paralyzed and cannot refuse and say (No). All traditional institutions stand behind, support, and entrench this deficit.

In fact, modern civilization is based on a social contract and the concept of specialization and the division of social work among individuals, where the right person is placed in the right place, which contradicts the values of family, clan, kinship, sect, neighbourliness, and the like, which do not place importance on the individual except that he is one of the groups. Contrary to modern civilization, which gives a person his appropriate place according to his capabilities, competence, and capabilities. It is these incentives that have enabled advanced societies to develop and advance in civilization.

The relationship that controls the chief and the subordinate in the family, the tribe, the sect, the society and the state is a form of hierarchical, patriarchal control that establishes a duality of domination and submission, not only between the individual and the family but between the ruler and the ruled, as the Arab ruler is still tyrannical in his opinion. He is the Caliph, the Wali, the Emir, the Sheikh, the President, and the Leader, who issues orders and prohibitions, and the subjects, residents and people must submit to his commands and prohibitions and always say: Hear and obey!

This unequal relationship between the boss and the subordinate is bound to generate a social conflict that exaggerates masculinity and underestimates femininity, and makes the eldest son (the firstborn male) a domineering man even over his older sister, who is older and more educated. It is a hierarchical, authoritarian relationship that grows under a strict moral education that teaches individuals blind obedience, where the father represents strength and authority, and the mother is obedience and submission. When the boy grows up, he imitates his father and takes his authoritarian role, and the girl imitates her mother and takes her role of submission.

Domination and subjugation are transferred from the family to the school, the street, the job, the factory, the security, and military institutions, and even to the top of the hierarchy of power. It is an authoritarian relationship that may lead to conflicting responses. It either leads to excessive submission to the authoritarian or the complete rejection of his authority and rebellion against him. Also, this authoritarian relationship abolishes freedom just as it cancels dialogue and understanding in the family and in society as well as in power; that is, it cancels politics, as it is an act of dialogue between independent individuals that transcends the family to the ruling authorities, which are essentially family authorities as well, concerned with the interests of the family, not the interests of the people and the country. Thus, despotism and authoritarianism are transferred from the patriarchal family to the ruling authority.

The authoritarian relationship also strengthens the bureaucratic organization, which is based on oppression, obedience, and submission, and turns individuals into mere machines, distorting their personalities, usurping their rights and tainting their humanity. In this sense, this type of tyranny does not mean reaching maturity, but rather lack of maturity, which does not liberate a person, but rather chains him with chains of ignorance, fear and submission so that a person loses confidence in himself and mutual respect with others as well as with society. Thus, patriarchy reveals its authoritarian and oppressive face and consolidates the power of traditional heritage.

Linked to authoritarian paternalism are obstacles and challenges that have faced the political issue that is still up until now, where freedom and the crisis of the state and authority remained unresolved to determine the relationship between the ruler and the ruled. It remained just a wish far from achieving since the independence of the Arab countries and the pursuit of a nation-state with a socio-political content and the establishment of rules a stable legal basis based mainly on the separation of powers, justice and equality before the law and the achievement of free citizenship. The Arab world is still witnessing an almost complete absence of such legal and constitutional rules and even a significant decline in the legitimacy of authority, its exclusivity and decision-making, which allows for the reproduction, and even consolidation of the prerational state with its ethnic, tribal and sectarian components and shifted loyalty to it at the expense of the nation, the state, and identity.

One of the results of the authoritarian (patriarchal state), backwardness and suppression of freedoms in this civilized reaction that the Arab world is experiencing today, which has produced states that dominate by force and oppression over all state institutions and society with their totalitarian ideology and monopolize power to dominate social, economic, political, and cultural systems, as well as social forces in the name of the nation, the people, and the law. It is also the identification of the chiefs as symbols of deification that transcend control and accountability, using all tools of force and oppression to subjugate individuals and force them to obey and submit.

In father-patriarchal societies, as in Arab societies in general, the family constitutes a patriarchal-male structure that works to build a subordinate personality that tends to submit to adults and submissive to the family as well as to authority through a strict patriarchal education that teaches individuals indoctrination, submission, and blind obedience. When the children grow up, the boy imitates the father and imitates him and takes his role in controlling his sister first and then his family after marriage secondly. The daughter imitates the mother and takes her subordinate role, and obeys the male's commands and prohibitions. Domination passes from the family to the clan and from there to the school, the street, the circles, the factories, and all formal and informal institutions.

Submission and non-violation of orders make the individual carry out those orders without any thought, refusal, or protest. Thus, the obedient child (a good boy who always hears words). But when the obedient boy grows up and adapts to the necessities of situations, he has contradictory reactions and begins to develop intense aggression against the father and the teacher, as well as against the employee, the policeman, and others. This is because he is forced, due to fear and excessive respect for values and customs, to suppress this aggression, which is dangerous for him to show. But this aggression gradually turns into a dynamic factor in building his personality and creates anxiety and turmoil for him, and pushes him to submit to more than one side. At the same time, it creates challenges and aggressive reactions sometimes directed at others and life itself in general.

These reactions also negatively affect his personality, and over time he develops new traits that become part of his personality.

It is known that tyrannical authority often searches for weak and submissive human beings. It tries to adapt his mind to ensure his body and uses various mechanisms, including the killing and distortion of the rational and critical dimensions. And the development of justifying postulates, such as conspiracy theories and new enemies, to justify imposing restrictions, taboos, and obstacles to restrict thought and pour new habits into ready-made templates in the mental structure so that they stand as an impenetrable dam against any resistance shown by the oppressed social groups. Over time it leads to the subjugation of the body and mind and the weakening of the sense of responsibility, which facilitates the process of submission.

If a weak and helpless person cannot evade the domination of the authoritarian patriarchal force imposed by the ruler, the policeman, the Sheikh, the teacher, or the employee who owns the decision-making power, he has no choice but to acquiesce. Thus, losing control of his fate and future. Instead of resistance and rejection, he performs compensatory behaviours such as adulation, surrender, and exaggeration in respecting and revering the authoritarian in order to avoid his evil on the one hand, and greed for his approval on the other hand, and the hope of living in peace because he cannot refuse, rebel, and confront on the third. In this case, the relationship of equivalence ceases to be replaced by the relationship of reification because there is no recognition of the ego as a human value. Thus, a new relationship of another kind develops, where "the other is hell". The more the authoritarian self becomes inflated, the helpless loses its importance, consideration, and effectiveness until it almost loses its humanity, as it loses the sense of suffering and sympathy for others. Also, fears of the other and the need for security and tranquillity increase, and man becomes prey to anxiety and indifference. [https://aljadeedmagazine.com]

It remains to mention at the end of the matriarchal society the reasons that led to the demise of this society and the emergence of the patriarchal society and the patriarchal authority, which are the following: -

1. The development of the city-state, which created the first new social organization for sexual life, took the form of the marriage system and later developed into the form of monogamy.
2. The establishment of the state gave power to the man and forced the woman to gradually lose her natural right through the discovery of minerals.
3. The evolution of the ownership system.
4. The spread of organized agriculture.
5. The emergence of cities.

Those are the fundamental reasons that led to a woman losing her golden age.

B. THE ERA OF HER ENSLAVEMENT (AT THE TIME OF THE GREEK, ROMAN, PERSIAN, AND CHINESE CIVILIZATIONS)

It seems that the manmade it as if it is the fate of the woman to suffer in pain and agony. Throughout history, the feminine had not been spared from oppression and aggression. So, despite the scientific progress of the Greek civilization, the feminine was considered one of the animals of the family that humans needed as the horse and the donkey. And despite its democratic progress, the Roman civilization believed that woman was the source of evil, and it would shut her mouth so that she would not speak, and evil would occur. And if the husband died, they buried his wife alive with him. Babylonian civilization, however, was known for its progress and its first legislation by (Hammurabi). Even so, they did not save the woman; instead, in his law, he sentenced her to drown in water to death if she violated some of her husband's orders.

Among the Arab tribes, there are three of them infanticide girls, for fear of dishonour or poverty. Generally, in the pre-Islamic era, the woman was a commodity, goods that were subject to dealing. And if a man dies, his wives are owned by his eldest son, if he wants, he can sell, and if he wants, he can keep them or marry any of them. [Al-Khaqani. 2013. p. 128]

Before Islam, and throughout the ages, the man considered a woman a degenerate being, as well as a diet demon who whispers evil. She was greatly humiliated, as she was bought and sold in the markets as goods or as livestock and belonging. She was forced to marry, to prostitution, to inherit, but actually not to inherit, own, or actually not own. She was always submissive to the man, father, and husband. Her husband owned her and owned her money and set up a

522

trustee over her before his death, while the man had power and dominion in everything and considered the woman for them to be nothing, dealing with her like other belongings in the house and had no rights but she has many duties.

Men differed in some countries over the nickname of a woman: is she a person with an immortal soul and will enter heaven like a man or not? In the end, one of the groups decided in Rome that she is an unclean animal, or that she has no soul or immortality, but she must worship and serve, and her mouth should be muzzled like a camel or a sterile dog to prevent her from laughing and talking because she was in their eyes a demon.

As for the position of the feminine in the civilization of the Greeks: they had her like a poisoned tree, and she was despised and humiliated until they called her an abomination from the act of the devil. She was sold and bought in the markets, usurped her rights, deprived her of the right to inheritance and the right to dispose of the money. She was so degraded that she was not spared from the Greek philosophers.

The opinion of the philosopher Aristotle about the feminine: He said about her that nature did not provide the woman with any mental preparation to be considered, and therefore her upbringing should be limited to the affairs of housekeeping, motherhood, nursery, etc. Then he says three things are not for a woman to dispose of by herself: the slave has no will, the child has an incomplete will, and a woman has a will, but she is helpless. And he said that a woman is an imperfect man, and nature has left her at the bottom of the ladder of creation. He said that the woman to the man is as the slave of the master, the worker of the world, the barbarian to the Greek and that the man is of higher status than the woman.

The philosopher Socrates said about her: The existence of a woman is the greatest originator and source of crisis and collapse in the world. A woman is like a poisoned tree where her appearance is beautiful, but when the sparrows eat from her, they die immediately.

And the Romans forbade the woman to speak, and they ordered her to put a padlock on her mouth, which they called (the Mossler). So, all the women were from the highest and lowest families walked in the streets with a padlock in their mouths, and she went and went back home with an iron padlock in her mouth apart from the physical punishment she exposes to because she is a seduction instrument used by Satan to corrupt hearts. They would pour hot oil on a woman's body and tie her to the tails of horses, then drag her at full speed as they tied the naughty women to posts and pour hot oil and fire on their bodies. [Wikipedia. Society's view of women in different civilizations. https://en.wikipedia.org]

As for the position of the feminine among the Persians, they preferred the male over the female because males were the mainstay of the army in the war, and girls were brought up for others, and others benefited from them. The ancient Persian women were subjected to the three religious currents, from Zoroastrianism to Manichaeism to Mazdakism, and each of these religions left its clear mark on the family entity. The woman lived in humiliation, oppression and enslavement, and she was under the absolute authority of the man, who had the right to sentence her to death or to enjoy her life according to what he saw and pleased him. She was like a commodity in his hands, as she was cheap in natural roles such as menstruation and childbirth. Women are kept away from the house in their time, and they live in small tents that are set for them on the outskirts of the city or town, and it is not permissible to mix with them at all.

As for the feminine among the Indians, she was in the worst conditions. In the laws of the Hindus, she is worse than the prescribed patience, wind, death, hell, poison, and snakes.

As for the Jews: some sects of the Jews considered the girl to be in the rank of a servant, and her father had the right to sell her as a minor. She would inherit unless her father had sons. Otherwise, she takes what was donated to her by her father during his lifetime. In the Jewish Sharia, a woman is part of the inheritance estate of the deceased.

If her husband dies, his heir (son or brother) inherits her with the rest of the estate, and he may sell or withhold her. Then the woman is not pure to them on the day when she begins to feel that her period is approaching, even if there is no visible trace. The husband must not touch her, not even with his little finger, and he is not allowed to handle her anything, and he does not take anything from her hand or the opposite. She is not allowed to eat with her husband at the same table, he is not allowed to drink what she prefers from the cup, and they are not allowed to sleep in the same bed or ride with him in the same car. [The position of women in some ancient civilizations and other religions - Alukah Network. https://www.alukah.net]

China swallows cups of humiliation morning and night, and an ancient Chinese song depicted the true status of women in China, which included (Except for the miserable fortune of a woman, there is nothing in the whole world of less value than her. The boys stand leaning on the doors as if they were gods fallen from heaven. As for the girl, she is not pleased with her birth, and if she grows up, she hides in her drawer, afraid to see a human face, and no one would cry for her if she disappeared from her home. The Chinese father, for example, if he was preached about a female, he would go to the market offering her for sale at low prices, and if he did not find someone to buy her, he gave her to the first passer-by without return or deliberately killed her by suffocation in a deserted place, or drown her, or bury her in the dirt, and if he has not been disposed of her by any means, her feet are mutilated to prevent her from leaving her father or husband's house or even a man from the relatives of her husband in lineage [https://said.net Women through the ages]

It remains to refer, in this context, to the phenomenon of (Haramlek), which means separating women from men, which was used in ancient times, as this isolation was used by the Greeks in the third century BC. Roman women usually occupied the first rooms of the house and the most visible, where they received many of their acquaintances. As for the Greeks, on the contrary, their women do not participate in a banquet unless it is with their relatives, and they always occupy the most secluded part of the house, the entry of which is forbidden for all men. That is, they despised women, and Aristotle believed that the reason for the decline and collapse of Sparta was due to the men of that city being lenient with their women and allowing them to go out to the markets to buy their needs, unlike the women of Athens who did not go out of the house except to the grave. As for Socrates, he said that the existence of women is the greatest source of crisis and one of the reasons for the collapse of the world is that it resembles a poisoned tree, its appearance is beautiful, but when the birds eat from it... it dies.

In the Akkadian civilization (in Mesopotamia - Iraq now), the Akkadian king Sargon used the name (Harmtu) for the priestesses of the temple who were serving the moon god in the city (Ur). Akkadian and Babylonian men were allowed to marry only three women, but he was not entitled to marry begotten by a priestess wife. That is, it is not permissible for her to give birth to the man that she married and loved. [Latakani. 2012. p. s. 121 - 122]

Finally, (Zainab Al-Bahrani), a professor of ancient arts and archaeology at Columbia University, says: in Mesopotamia and the ancient Near East in general, it was not rare or surprising for a woman or girl to be the main heir and to actually inherit. Women in the Middle East and Egypt in ancient times enjoyed legal rights and social freedoms incomparably better than what their peers enjoyed in the countries of Greece and Rome, and when the Hellenistic dynasties that inherited Alexander the Great ruled in Egypt and the countries of the Middle East, the women who moved to live in the mentioned region preferred to marry according to local laws and not according to Greek laws Because the latter was strict in protecting the rights and independence of women and gave them the right to decide their own life affairs and activities. They were also able to own property and social centres and move about in cities without any restrictions on travel or movement. This situation provided them with a much wider space of freedom than was available to women in ancient Greek and Roman times, and consequently, the restrictions imposed on women's lives appeared in late antiquity. They came from outside the region and from intrusive cultures. These restrictions were not representative of the original local attitudes of women shown by the records of ancient texts. The original conditions experienced by the women of the ancient Near East afforded them independence and legal rights much better than what was available to women in other ancient

527

societies and even in many contemporary societies. [Bahraini. 2013. p. 18]

Finally, I refer to the main reason for the difference in the position of the feminine in human society, which is not due to her feminine roles in the family and working in it, to the scientific developmental stage of society, and to the human need for her outside the home. When society is in a state of constant wars, it needs the man more than the woman, and since she represents the weakest creature in war, the warriors fear for her from captivity and imprisonment, so they do not attach great importance to her but rather assigned her for procreation and housekeeping, as the Romans, Greeks, Persians and Chinese were among the fighting peoples who were in need of men, therefore, they despised and enslaved her because she is not a warrior, but rather easy prey for the enemy, so her social position is not high in society. But in the case of peace and stability, her position is high and respected, symbolizing love, sex and beauty, and this is what happened to the Babylonians, Sumerians, Phoenicians and Pharaohs who needed it in building family, civilization, luxury, and prosperity. A transformation of the feminine was taken place from the stage of worship to the slave to the forfeiting of the mother's right to lineage and inheritance. That was the major defeat for Ishtar. [Latakani. 2012. p. 27]

In conclusion, it can be said that society's need for technical professional jobs used in industry and agriculture with the formation of new official organizations such as parties and huge military armies led to society's need for muscular strength. Therefore, the man emerged in his continuous investment and independence at the expense of women, so he turned from a subordinate to a master and from obsidian to be obeyed, and the idol turned into a slave.

C. **MIDDLE EASTERN WISE WOMEN THROUGHOUT HISTORY**

The change that happened to the traditional gender identity is a call to address the subject of Middle East wise women in the old gender, but they were a minority whose work is unknown. However, for scientific integrity and objective honesty, they have addressed her in order not to overlook their rights. The women of the ancient (Arab) gender were not pragmatic, they were creative and wise women, and at the same time, they represented the historical background of Arab qualifications and competencies in ancient times of Arab history. As for the situation of Arab women now in their gender identity, it is miserable and oppressed due to political instability, civil and international wars, revolutions, and the ossified mentality of the rulers who control Arab society, making them represent the congruence between gender and sexual identity. This is a shameful thing though it fits with the spirit of the current era, which is characterized by liberation, civilized friction, and the dominance of technological sciences in public and private life.

Wisdom is the ability to think and act using knowledge, experience, understanding, common sense and insight. It is therefore associated with important traits such as emotion, experience-based self-knowledge, moral virtues, and benevolence. The righteous wise: is the one who has the ability to deal with issues related to life and behaviour and is distinguished by sound judgment and the choice of means and goals that lead to the most appropriate solutions. The ancient Greeks considered wisdom one of the most important and noble virtues. A wise person has the ability to overcome feelings of helplessness, anger, and hatred and enhance his insight. Therefore, he had a great reputation among his people due to his good opinion and his impartiality. History has also preserved many names of the (wise) women, some of whom are mentioned in the following:

1. **Shajarat Elddor:** She was nicknamed Issmat al-Din Umm Khalil. She assumed the throne of Egypt for 80 days after the death of the Sultan (Saleh Ayoub) in 1250 AD. She was characterized by intelligence, strength, and wisdom, so the righteous king assigned her the reins of power to act on his behalf when he was outside Egypt. One of her most prominent positions that prove this is her important historical role during the Seventh Crusade against Egypt. During the battle of Mansoura, she hid the news of her husband in that critical situation so as not to weaken the morale of the military. She told everyone that the Sultan was ill and could not meet anyone, so she used to bring food into the room where the Sultan slept so that no one would suspect anything. With her wisdom, she was able to lead the army and besiege the Crusader forces. The battle ended with the defeat of the Crusaders and the capture of Louis IX, King of France.

2. **Hatshepsut:** She lived in the period 1479-1458 BC. She is one of the most famous and influential queens who ruled the Pharaonic Palace. Her dynasty dates back to the 18th dynasty that ruled Egypt and ruled the country after the death of her husband, King Tuthmosis II, and her rule was a prominent point in the history of Egypt. Hatshepsut learned ethics, correct behaviour, reading, writing, arithmetic, philosophy, religious rituals, grammar, and novels. Her reign was characterized by peace and prosperity, and her reign was marked by the strength of the army, construction activity, and the great sea voyages that she sent for trade.

3. **Zenobia:** The Queen of Palmyra, who lived between 240-274 AD. She led with her husband a rebellion against the Roman Empire and enabled it to control most of Syria. Zenobia, with her wisdom, was able to lead her people to a comprehensive renaissance and an ambitious military force. She played a major role in the East and in Rome itself. She was highly educated and spoke the Palmyrene language, an Aramaic language, as well as Greek and Egyptian. Queen Zenobia issued the currency of Palmyra and minted money. What most people do not know is that she took power when she was only 14 years old, but she was able to build a great empire that shook the Roman throne.

4. **Bilqis:** The Queen of the Kingdom of Sheba was mentioned in the Holy Qur'an, where (Bilqis) received a message from the Prophet of God (Solomon) in which he asked her to worship God and desist from sanctifying the sun. Among the manifestations of her wisdom is that she rejected tyranny in her opinion and sought advice from the public, who assured her of their confidence in their military capabilities and left the final decision to her. "She reasoned, "Indeed, when kings invade a land, they ruin it and debase its nobles. They really do so!" (An-Naml/No 34), and then she sent a gift from the good and precious stones and gold to (Solomon). He rejected the gift and decided to go with his army and fight Sheba. Balqis realized the fact that she is in front (A prophet) who calls to worship God Almighty alone and is not tempted by gifts and money. She, therefore, turned to her intelligence, acumen, and her ability to distinguish between right and wrong—a great role in turning her people from prostrating to the sun to worshipping God Almighty alone.

5. **Cleopatra VII:** The Queen of Egypt lived between 69-30 BC. She ruled between 51-30 BC. She was beautiful,

charming, intelligent, cunning, and wise enough to make her assume the throne of Egypt. She defeated her brother, who monopolized the rule, and to strengthen her thorn, she married Caesar of Rome in order to invade the country. After his death, she strengthened her position by marrying (Marcus Antonius), and her misfortune ended in their defeat and suicide.

6. **The Blue of Yamama:** An ancient Arab figure, a Najdi woman from Jadis, the people of Al-Yamama. She had an extraordinarily strong sight that it is said she can see a person from a distance of 3 days. She was distinguished by wisdom, knowledge, and fortune-telling. She warned her people against small moving trees, and the enemies had learned by the power of her sight, and they cut down the trees and covered themselves to camouflage and to be disguised so that she would not reveal them. When she told her people about that, they did not believe her and mocked her, and when their enemies caught up with them and surprised them, they realized her truthfulness, but it was too late.

7. **Hind bint Khuss bin Habis:** She was one of the Arab women with eloquence and sweet logic that no one could compete with her eloquence and the authority of her tongue. She was one of the Arab women famous for reasoned proverbs, perfection, and eloquence.

8. **Sohar bint Luqman bin Aad:** She is the daughter of Luqman al-Hakim, who took wisdom from her father, and it was said that she was famous for her intellect, perfection, eloquence, and wisdom and that the Arabs were adjudicating with her regarding quarrels and disagreements in lineages and others. [Saydity magazine. Issue 1915. dated 18/1/2017]

These eight models of Arab women have proven their wisdom and their prudence in making difficult decisions in managing the affairs of society. It is clear that despite the existence of patriarchal authority dominating women, there were distinguished Arab women in ancient times far from globalization, the internet, technical progress, and freedom of expression and thought. Their decision in guiding society in times of crises saved their people and society, so what if the doors of patriarchal authority, labour markets and leadership were opened for her, and the man gave up his selfish narcissism? For sure the man can rely on her outside the house more than inside it and devote himself to helping her in her new tasks!!!

This is a picture of individual blogging of women and not blogging of all women, as half of the population pyramid is written by men and not women historians, which allows us to say that this is both a historical and a feminist flaw.

CHAPTER 10: THE POSITION OF THE FEMININE IN THE HISTORY

INITIATION

A. HISTORICAL THEMES OF THE FEMININE
B. DEFUNCT SOCIETIES
C. THE POSITION OF THE FEMININE IN THE MIDDLE AGES

CHAPTER 10
HISTORICAL POSITIONING OF THE FEMININE

INITIATION

History, in general, has not done justice to women. A lot of events had been missed and absent in the writing of the women's history as a group rather than as individuals. This issue is highlighted here because the interest in this context is in women since the start of human being history rather than since 1960 when the organization of a feminist movement was established in the West. Yes, this movement for sure has acted as a motive, and in fact, it motivated many women who are interested and specialized in sociology and history to start with the movement and begin to generate a new field of knowledge for the study of women because there is a vast difference between studying woman as an individual and as a group of all women. When the recorded history is reviewed, side and marginal references to women can be found. They are looked at them as an accessory to men. And if they are referred to, they are described as (brilliant beauty, intelligence, shrewdness, cunning, deceiver, or they have an influence on leaders and kings). They have never been recorded as an entity, as it happened with men who were recorded in their races, classes, and movements. Sometimes there were referring to women's deviations and their tampering and trafficking, their shortcomings in public life, but no mention of their contributions to the private social movements, and if some of the events and activities of women were written, they were mostly written by the man and to serve his own goals.

The purpose of this initiation is to highlight the fact that no historian woman has written about the women of her gender, and there was no history specific to women before 1960. All that was written was about the elites that emerged through male historians and considered them to be attached to the man by class, ethnicity or religion. This would be her position in society and her identity in history, even if she was not written but rather inferred.

It is not unreal to say that the influence of women as a social force represents the history of women. It was intentional that the African and Latin Americans were averted and avoided in codifying the chronicle of the American. Similarly, there was a duality in dealing with the writing on man and on woman as it is full of forging and distorting manner. Since the American society is multicultural and multi-ethnic, the writing about the women specifically through their race, class and culture does not exist, and if so, they refer to them as they attached to the men. Moreover, they are rarely writing about the fact that, for example, they are of African origins to compare them with white women. If women did not have political or economic influence, they would never be referred to or written on them in history, and hence they do not have a written history. But when they organized themselves and began to demand their rights, history began to be written about them because their influence represents the key to writing their history in human existence.

A. **HISTORICAL THEMES OF THE FEMININE**

The aim of writing this topic is not to take revenge and settle scores with historians who have fallen short in their attention when recording feminist events, their activism and raising their awareness. The objective is to review the historical stages of the woman's action phases and their influential initiations plus their subservient behaviour to

536

men, as it is the reason for such dependence that can be attributed to men's hatred, contempt, and contempt for women. Therefore, her overall reaction as the motive for the woman against her oppression, subjugation, and submission to the man's adherence to the patriarchal authority to strengthen his domination over her and make her a victim of society. This topic is the focus of women's attention today, regardless of their scientific specialization.

The context of the conversation requires addressing the rest of the special historical topics in Western society, which is the topic of the dualities which is crystallized through woman's resistance to the patriarchal authority, with her focus on the stories of courage, valour, bravery, boldness, struggle, and the women achievements to restore their usurped rights.

In fact, this alternative view indicates that women's history is still undiscovered and uncovered because it involves issues that challenge the bold and travelled traditional thinking about gender roles; on the one hand. On the other hand, there is a stark challenge faced by the symbols of the feminist movement in crystallizing a gender binary that has nothing to do with class or race but rather a dualism that reflects two contradictory sides, such as nature versus naturalization, work versus family, public affairs versus private affairs, and the environment of men versus the environment of women similar to the symbols of the feminist movement in sociology. There is a topic that reflects the overlapping elements of several fields in one field, such as (the field of social history), which uses theories and methods of sociology to understand the link between patterns.

Historical and social, this, in turn, crystallized an additional duality called (cultural pluralism versus single culture) that sheds light on the relationship of gender to class, race, religion, and region. Gender culture is linked to multiple cultures such as class, ethnic, religious, and regional culture. This is the multiculturalism associated with gender culture.

Social change, however, often reveals the grievances, prejudices, discrimination and fanaticisms that women face when they contribute to daily life. Although they have been ignored and overlooked by history, the movement of society reveals this no matter how obscured by the man or his patriarchal authority.

B. **DEFUNCT SOCIETIES**

They represent the societies that lived thousands of years before the birth of Christ. Most of the information that is known and has been obtained about those societies was taken from what men wrote about that era in arts, philosophy, politics and religion. The life of these societies began from the Bronze Age (copper) in the period (3000 - 1200 BC), and this period became a witness to what societies presented about democracy, literacy, beauty and health. It contradicts the roles of women who lived in that period, as well as the presence of a dark side that dominated this period, such as wars, slavery, deadly competition and brutal living alongside democracy and beliefs philosophical. It is a contradictory state that continued until the Renaissance.

1. The Ancient Greek Society

There are many contradictory images of women in Greek society due to the place and time in which these images are interpreted. Where there is the Amazon and the matriarchal society, others refer to the superstitious women of the warriors that Greek mythology claimed to have resided near the Black Sea, tall, tomboyish, warlike, and strong. Similarly, the maternal family is a feminine group of mothers whose authority is handed over to the mother. Even lineage and heredity are attributed to her as a stage of the development of human society.

The history of Greece promises riddles and legends displaying Amazonia as a warrior capable of wielding a bow and arrow in war. As for the Greek warriors, they were sent to remote places far from their country in the barbarian realms to test their courage and strength against the Amazons women, but the Amazons women lost their strength after marriage, and the Greek warriors were trained in weapons and struggle to conquer and defeat the Amazons women.

Greece was one of the most civilized and most developed ancient nations. Scholars, thinkers, and philosophers emerged from them, such as Aristotle, Plato and others who established schools of thought and philosophical curricula until they reached a position where they were the destination of scholars and thinkers, and generations of scholars and intellectuals learned their curricula. But if we look closely at their first era, we find that the condition of women in it was extremely degraded in all areas of their life, and they did not have a noble status or position in that society. Rather, it was believed that women are the cause of all human pain and calamities and that they are creatures in the lowest depths of the world. The position, therefore, was extremely insulting, humiliating and a waste of dignity, to the extent that they did not sit with her at the dining table, especially if they had strangers' guests, as it is the same as slaves and servants.

It continued like this, then things changed, and the position of women in society rose, and she became better off and higher in rank than before, as she became a housewife, in which she had complete influence, and her chastity and honour were among the most precious and valuable things he owned, and what was looked upon with appreciation, respect and glorification. He considered a woman's marriage and her attachment to her husband without any other man's sign of honour and chastity. And they looked at the life of immorality, prostitution, and debauchery: a look of hatred and contempt. This was in an era when the Greek nation was at the height of its glory and the splendour of its strength and youth, and what they had of moral corruption was restricted to a limited scope.

Then, the psychological lusts overcame Greeks, and they were swept away by the current of bestial instincts and unbridled passions, so whores and prostitutes assumed a high position in the society unparalleled in the entire history of mankind, and the homes of prostitutes became a centre visited by all classes of society and a reference to which writers, poets, and philosophers' resort.

Then their love for beauty and their fascination with it increased them further in adoration, smashed into the sludge of vice, and kindled in their hearts afire of lust that would not be extinguished. The nude statues, which they mastered in perfect craftsmanship, were the ones that always stirred their desires and extended their bestial instincts, and it did not occur to them that surrendering to desires is something reprehensible in the law of morals, just as the rush to follow the current of passions is a disgrace and hypocrisy.

Their standards of morality have changed to such an extent that their great philosophers and ethicists do not see adultery and immorality as sins for which a person can be blamed or reproached.

This shift in thought was accompanied by the formulation of myths about women, as they adopted a deity of love, which they called: the god Cupid, the god of love (KUPID), and the general people of the Greeks looked at the

540

marriage contract with indifference and disrespect because women became available to anyone and in every hand, and any man could satisfy himself sexually by her in public without fear or apprehension, and without contract or marriage. The matter continued with them in this way, and many people refrained from marriage in order to escape the family bond and to bear its responsibilities and consequences. The repercussions of this moral decay, social corruption, and the severing of family ties were awfully bad, and every day that passed, a part of this ancient civilization collapsed until it disappeared after it had prevailed, and it did not exist after that.

In the ancient Greeks, women were robbed of freedom and status in everything related to legal rights, and they were replaced in large houses at a place separate from the road, with few windows, guarded doors. The singers' clubs became famous in the Greek metropolises due to the neglect of wives, mothers of houses, and rarely allowed to accompany men in polite clubs and forums, and the philosophers' councils were devoid of women's gender, and no brilliant woman known besides the famous singer women, or free sex enjoyers maidservants' women.

The Athenians of Greece looked at women as merchandise, and they may offer them in the market for sale and sell them, and this was within the rights of the husband familiar to them. In addition to that, they considered women, in general, an abomination of the work of the devil, and on that principle, they were deprived of their legal and human rights. As for the ancient Greeks, they believed that calamities lie in hopes, and failure to achieve demands comes from the wrath of the idols they worship. Therefore, when a catastrophe, calamity, or failure in society came, they would offer girls as an offering to those false gods in order to repel harm from them.

History narrated: that when a dispute occurred between Greece and the people of Troyes (Anatolia) and they were forced to enter the war, and they prepared their forces and warships, but the weather did not help the movement of the ships, and they stayed on the coast waiting for about three months, and no relief came to them until they became fed up and terrified, they complained about their condition to the head of the church and asked him to address the crisis, so he decided to present the daughter -Aja Memnon- the Emperor of Greece during his reign as an offering to the gods.

The Latins from Greece also permitted the man to marry whomever of the wives he wanted, without limiting the number, and in the days of the Greek conquest of Egypt - the time of King Philopatry - the woman was prevented from disposing of the money except with the permission of her husband, and everything became for the man, and the woman had no right to own property, because the man is the source of wealth and the first owner of it, and whatever right she has, she still below the man.

The Greek woman was not entitled to direct legal actions, and she was subject to the guardianship system or the permanent resurrection of her father before the husband, then to her husband after marriage, and then to her eldest son after the death of her husband, and the husband had the right to choose through his will a guardian or curator of his wife, as The Greek woman was deprived of the inheritance, and the dowry came to obtain it from her father before her marriage in exchange for that inheritance, unlike the isolation in which the woman lived far from society as if she were a household item.

Among the most prominent descriptions of women by the Greek philosophers is what was said by (Justine), the famous orator of Greece - where he said: We take wives only to give birth to legitimate children to us.

Aristotle: The woman is an imperfect man, and nature has left her at the lowest level of creation, and that the woman is to the man as the slave of the master, the worker of the world, and the barbarian to the Greek, and that the man is of higher status than the woman. Nature has not provided women with any reasonable mental preparation.

Plato saw in his virtuous city: that women with healthy bodies devoid of physical defects should be common goods for healthy and strong men to bear healthy children. He also saw that the woman was an abomination from the work of Satan, far from God's mercy, because she carried the sin of her supreme mother, Eve.

Chloritlus: who was one of the great historians of Roman civilization, was amazed at why men in Greek civilization would feel shame if a husband took his wife to a feast.

As for the Spartan sect from Greece: they forbade men from polygamy, but they allowed the woman to marry many husbands as she wanted, so the Greek women of this sect practised this despicable custom, and they came to it freely, and this was the treatment of women in Sparta more humane than in Athena. They were giving her the right to inherit, the right to appear and the freedom, and this was what Aristotle blamed them for, and he attributed the fall of Sparta and its decay to this waste of freedom granted to women in Sparta.

And the granting of this freedom to the women in Sparta was not the result of an acquired right for them but rather came as a forced result because men were working in combat and were preoccupied with it. So, in their absence, they would leave everything to the woman's disposal, which made way for women to go out to civil society and liberation from their isolation.

The deterioration of the status of women in Greece, their contempt, and their neglect by men led to the spread of homosexuality between the two parties of the sexes so that the love of boys was recognized by Greek law.

And because Eve in Sparta got many benefits by going out into public life, women shone through frequenting clubs and mixing with men, which led to the spread of immorality, and abnormal relations between men and women abounded.

The Greeks' view of women was full of contempt, as the woman was used as a tool for procreation, while the man devoted himself to his mistresses, maidservants, and servants and buried her under the veil to reduce her movement.

The Greek woman was robbed of her will in everything, especially her social position. She was deprived of reading, writing, and general culture, and the Greek law oppressed her, preventing her from inheriting, and she could not obtain a divorce from her husband, and she had to remain an obedient servant to her master and the head of her house.

The Greeks looked at the woman as they looked at the slave and saw that her mind did not count. The Greek girl did not leave her home until her wedding, and the wife did not see her husband's face except on the wedding night. The wife would disappear from the house if the husband hosted a friend of his.

Although the Greek civilization advanced and the name of women shone at the end of the Greek era, women did not gain their freedom or obtain their rights in the correct sense due to the preoccupation of leaders and thinkers with a life of luxury and the spread of moral decay.

Even her progress was at the expense of her physical constitution and her moral appearance, so they excelled in sculpting scandalous statues and engraving exposed images and made women a symbol of beauty, love and adoration, and a source of sex lusts and brutal passions. Thus, they restricted looking at women as if they were fallen human beings that were nothing more than porn images or a statue. Made of bronze, they kneel between his hands in reverence for the aspects of beauty that they highlight in it. It was as a result of their pursuit of sensual lusts that matter overcame them, and they were swept away by the stream of bestial instincts and dominated by unbridled passions, and what remained of their women's history was only a scandalous picture engraved by a creative painter whose brush admired everyone who preferred debauchery, which spread very widely in the ancient Greek civilization. This has not changed the view of the Greek woman in the present era. It is still seen as the owner of the tongue, which resembles a sword, and does not rust.

[mrx540.blogspot.com]

Partner: Specialized archaeologists wrote in the Neolithic era until the Bronze Age about the birth of the Greek city and the rule of the Matrilineal inheritance based on the lineage of the mother and the reference to it. And they considered her a goddess of high importance and worshipped by everyone with a powerful force representing the priesthood and the queen. There was no unique authority in the matriarchal authority, nor was there a unique authority in the patriarchal authority, and since the woman enjoyed a high position, the man was in a lower position, but it was not subordinate to the position of the woman, and the peak of equality between men and women was when they were in the worship of the gods on the island of Crete, where the

Minoan civilization was in the period between 3000 - 1100 BC is one of the oldest Greek civilizations. In Europe in general, it goes back to the Bronze Age, the birthplace of civilization, and it became at the height of its fame in the third millennium BC, during which arts, literature, social complexities, scientific and technical prosperity, and the rule of peace flourished there. The Mennonite civilization in Crete was characterized by:

1. A social construction based on the behavioural participation between men and women.
2. Both are allowed - in part - to engage in sexual relations.
3. When she flourished, women became more involved in exercising their sexual freedom
4. because of the few restrictions imposed on their modesty and chastity.
5. This civilization focused more on interaction and communication than separation and isolation between the sexes.
6. Absence of wars, private property, class construction, violence, and rape.
7. There is no social hierarchy based on gender that was not defined in it.
8. The time of this civilization was described as the Golden Age, and this was confirmed by Greek myths.
9. The man works with the woman as a participant and not as a boss and subordinate, and each supports and helps the other in work.
10. The continuation of the influence of women does not mean or represent the maternal authority - the domineering feminine, but rather the moderate one.

2. The Latin Society (Athenian Society)

An Athenian woman can be described by the following qualities:

1. She is seen as a movable commodity or piece of furniture.
2. Concubines occupy a better position than the wife and the husband's child-nurturer.
3. Divorce of the wife rarely happens, but it is possible.
4. Athenian women are classified under the category of minors, as are children and slaves.
5. The husband has the power of life and death over the wife.
6. There is a class of women, wives of warriors, who enjoy the wealth and property of their husbands when he is away from her on a military or government mission for a long period of time.
7. The Athenians oppress women so severely that neither wealth nor possessions compensate them for their excessive cruelty to them.
8. A man has the right to seize the property of his relatives' women, and she is forced to relinquish them to him.
9. Women represent a low, degraded, and exploited class, economically and socially. [Loraux. 1998. Pp. 25 - 29]

In order to be exclusive with what has previously been mentioned about Athenian society, it is pointed out here that the man used to exercise strict and direct supervision of women outside and inside the home. He does not tolerate her in front of people and in public places, except on mourning-funeral occasions for women only. As for inside the house, they are secluded and wearing mourning clothes, and they have their own corner or section inside the house in which their movement is restricted, and they are subject to direct and continuous monitoring, particularly their sexual

547

behaviour, to the extent that the Athens government has special police to monitor women and focus on their chastity.

But despite these severe restrictions, there were two types of women's groups in Athenian society:

The first group - was a group that plotted and planned the political intrigues and conspiracies of men in order to deliver their sons or husbands to positions of authoritarian influence.

The second group - was made up of the concubines who possessed a higher degree of beauty, intelligence, elegance, grace, wit, and stage-humour than the concubines.

This is on the level of women, but on the level of men, homosexuality has spread as a fashion for them, so they went to accompany young boys to practice sodomy with them. At the same time, he can transfer his sexual pleasure from boys to women.

Not only that, but another phenomenon also appeared among men in the fourth century BC, which was the preference of concubines over wives, so that the man would not bear family responsibility with his wife and children.

3. The Spartan Society

A military society in its public life raises its male children on military and war training to the extent that it uses (infanticide) if they cannot bear or possess physical fitness and physical health, then he is killed. It is similarly for the girl. If she is not characterized by physical and aesthetic qualities, she will also be killed when she is a child.

Males are trained in martial arts and war, and this training continues until he reaches thirty years of age. He is isolated from his wife but is interspersed with some visits by the wife to her husband. In the event that the husband is absent from his wife while he is in the field of military training or on governmental missions outside his town, the women (wife and daughters) enjoy personal freedom, but this does not prevent him from continuing their responsibility for raising children and housekeeping in order to continue their upbringing to prepare for the military training stage, and the same is the case with girls to be healthy and beautiful. However, the women of Sparta enjoy more freedom than the women of Athena, and this is what made the women of Athens criticize the women of Sparta, as they said that they are taken by young men to the wrestling arenas while they are semi-naked, and their hips are completely naked, and this is shameful and disgraceful. The Spartans have superior privileges over the ethnicity, and they have the right to inherit, that is, the inheritance of property and dowry (the dowry), but they remain under the supervision of their husband, brother, and father.

Finally, the most prominent of the Spartan women is that they are subservient to the man and oppressed by him.

4. The Greek Society

The history of Rome begins in 753 BC, when it was an empire that transcended the development of Germanic tribes, especially in the fifth century BC, when it reached Rome in its development, acquiring cultural, social, and political components and continuing to influence gender roles. In the late days of the empire, it was in contrast to the powers that were issued in its beginning, but with all these developments, the woman remained subordinate to the man. Her image cannot be separated from his image because he is domineering over her, and she is dependent on him. Despite this, when compared with the Greek woman, the Roman woman has an amazingly high rate of freedom that exceeds the rate of Greek freedom.

On the other hand, there is the authority of the man, which at the beginning of the empire's life was strongly supportive of the position and role of elderly men in the family, as he has absolute authority and influence over all members of the family, male and female, to the extent that his authority reaches the death or execution of one of his family members if he is rebellious against his authority. If the family is exposed to financial hardship, no one will deter him from selling his children as slaves to meet the family's financial needs. As for the daughters, they are under the authority of the father of the family throughout his life, but when he dies, the sons and daughters are freed from his authority and domination, but if he is alive, the sons and daughters remain under his authority even after they marry and leave the house to live in a separate house. The father, husband, uncle, or brother has the status of the father of the family over the women. This means that husbands exercise a limited rate of control over their wives because the old man is still alive, and he has absolute power. However, this absolute power has advantages that belong to women in the long run, and it is at their will, and financial assistance is provided to them if the situation requires it or if their husband suffers a financial crisis that impedes their life with luxury and ease.

In light of these conditions, the father of the family exercised his care responsibilities with great caution, especially with his guardianship and care for the woman. This absolute responsibility caused him many burdens and a variety of responsibilities, and in the first century BC, legislation was approved that allowed a woman to be freed and freed from the care of a man if she was responsible for the care of three children. This was a measure of her independence later on. But Rome, like Sparta, had many wars, which led to a decline in the birth rate and the abandonment of paternity in the family in exchange for a new job for women, which was to have three children to take care of.

Women's Power and Influence in Rome: The Roman woman, like every woman in ancient history, has a strong influence but is free from the exercise of power over men, but when we compare her with the Greek, we find that she has a wide role in the city life only does not exceed the religious field, as it remained fossilized by religious worship through the Vestal virgin (She is a venerable virgin for the service of Vestal, the Roman goddess of fire) and through this venerable virgin a few women are chosen for public duties. She knows that she will eventually be a wife, mother, and housewife when her husband is busy with military and war missions and inherits the inheritance. Upper-class women have great opportunities to learn, perform music, dance, and art because they defy the system provided. They have a husband or father. Finally, the Roman was granted the right to divorce and given responsibilities that the Greeks lacked. She has freedom in most areas, except for the religious field, while her existence remains linked to the existence of the man. [Lindsey. 2011. Pp. 104 – 108]

It is deduced from the aforementioned presentation that the man and woman are linked to each other, although this link expands and narrows according to temporal influences and social, military, and religious developments. This link turns from biological between man and woman to social through roles, positions, influence, classes, gradation, professions, and religion, all of which are subject to the system of division of labour in the family and society.

The most prominent issue in the literature on women in human history is that she is missing, unwritten, and documented because human history is written by men first and that their interest is focused on their interests, power, strength, wealth, and activity. As for the second half of history, it is not concerned with it and is not mentioned (about the role and position of the wife, her upbringing of her children and her assistance to him in the field, the workshop, the factory and the wars), meaning they did not write down her position in the history of society not because she was hated, but because she is far from hot events in politics, wars and discoveries because of her preoccupation with management home and childbearing. Shortcomings fall primarily on women before men, as there were no female historians compared to men historians before the emergence of feminist movements after the middle of the twentieth century. Moreover, history is written about the great leaders, the powerful, the influential and the wealthy, and not about the weak or the squandered of their rights. Thus, history is not objective in its recording or neutral in its monitoring of events, and this is a second reason for the absence of women's history through time.

There is no sin in saying that it is not a disadvantage for a woman to do housekeeping and to be a wife and mother who helps her husband in his work (field or workshop), but rather it is a superior and distinguished ability that a woman enjoys, where it is not for these four main roles, the family would not continue to live. Therefore, it is a positive score for the women rather than a negative against them.

However, there are writings that demand women to have a role in politics, the economy, and parliamentary representation in order to write their history. This demand comes at the expense of her four constructive roles in the family (she is confined to her housekeeping and is a circumstantial or temporary wife and a biological mother more than if she is a nanny social and separated from her husband in his work) and here there is a benign family disintegration, heading towards separation, leading to divorce, delinquency of children or addiction to drugs and alcohol by the sons or parents.

C. **THE POSITION OF THE FEMININE IN THE MIDDLE AGES**

This stage begins from 306 to 337 BC when the Roman Empire, during the reign of Constantine, was in a dire state, suffering from the throes of death, disintegration, and dissolution. In the face of this deteriorating situation, Constantine proposed a marriage between the empire and Christianity to save the former through the support of Christianity, which represents the strengthening force for the non-disintegration of the Roman Empire, because the latter was in a state of accelerated collapse and Constantine's insight was in influencing Christianity of an effective and distinguished role. He did not invade Europe, and his grip on it was tight, and here came the common role between the Renaissance and feudalism, as they were not extremists in reducing the influence of Christianity and saving it, but it was influential on the role of women compared to the old role, which was deteriorating, and was depressing the situation that prevailed in Europe when Christianity dominated Europe During the Middle Ages.

1. Christianity

When the dissolution and disintegration of the Roman and Greek empires occurred, the following happened:

a. Churches and monasteries became a repository for looted, plundered, and stolen items during the chaos that followed the collapse of the Roman and Greek empires.

b. Churches and monasteries became trusted and safe places.

c. The forces of the intellectuals disintegrated, and they left the cultural arena, causing the readers, writers and teaching to fall into the hands of those in charge of the church, which had confidence in knowledge, interpretation and translation of events and issues.

d. At that time, the church became a witness to the course of events that could not be challenged or suspected of witnessing. It became the absolute trusted guardian among the people at that time.

e. The priesthood of Christ recognised the spiritual equality of gender.

f. They did not accept the misogyny that was prevalent in Jewish teachings.

g. The women provided charitable services of evangelical value and taught social services to the newly established institutions.

h. In view of this openness to women, the door was opened for her to enter the ecclesiastical hierarchy and to occupy positions in it for those who chose religious life as a curriculum in their lives.

Monasticism and monasteries played an active role in serving women, especially those of the upper class who did not want to marry. This service consisted in educating them and directing them to worship without conditions and restrictions. The talented ones became poets, composers, and artists. The education of nuns eroded and diminished when restrictions were placed on women's ownership of land, but the women of Catholic Europe served the nuns sector in their independence, and the women of Protestant Europe were left without acceptable alternatives to marriage.

As for misogyny, it has recently emerged as a church game approved by those who acquired the old traditions with strict restrictions on women. Women were dispensed within the new charter, and they were not taught to read, write and interpret the Bible, which now includes cultural beliefs that display the degeneration of women and place the blame on Eve when Satan was whispered to her to eat the apple, so mankind was brought down to earth.

It remains to be noted, in this context, that Christianity has changed its position on marriage and divorce in a manner different from what was prevalent in ancient societies. Because marriage cannot be annulled or its bond severed, as divorce cannot be obtained, and the church does not allow the violation of the sanctity of marriage, whatever the reason (real or not). This is because marriage is considered a sacred bond in the church's view, and a man cannot leave her even if they have no children, so divorce does not happen, and this is a protection for the women and their immunity by the church.

2. Witch Hunt

There is a period of time characterised by the most brutal in women's history, the medieval period when misogyny prevailed and emerged in the form of witch hunts. Women have deviated from the prevailing social norms, and new social norms have been placed and have crystallised, expressing superstitious beliefs that do not exist in real life, such as if a woman remains celibate and unmarried after her divorce (for the divorced) and has no children, she is seen as sexually provocative, cannot be trusted, and not reassuring in her as well. She is seen as very liberal, independent, and influential, in her opinion, so she is a witch but in disguise. In the old society, women who came from a social class and loved their sisters were domineering over the other positions of the sisters. So, witch hunts can be identified in that time period for everyone who owns:

a. Money, prestige, and power.
b. Therapists, midwives, and counsellors.
c. Divorced women who have no children.
d. Descendants of a high social class.

These are the goals of witches in their pursuit of others, so their position is respected in their local communities, and they are avoided because they symbolise Satan and the wrath of God. In turn, it means that money, prestige, and profession do not protect a woman or a man from witches, but rather they are a direct target for their pursuit. Hence, people's hatred of these women emerged because of their association with witchcraft and sorcery that contradicted Christian religious teachings. Female influence is based on scientific practices that are subject to the desire and mood enhanced by Christian theology and its view of sexual passion and lust in women who cannot be rational. This is, in fact, what caused women's hatred (because they are irrational and subject to their moods and emotions) and their use of magic in chasing others. Most of the victims of Europeans were women, as thousands of witches were burned because they were hostile to God and his will and provoked his anger, and the witch's confession of her magic required burning, torturing, or killing her.

3. Feudalism

The reality of feudalism and its continuity is linked to the perpetual occurrence of wars and their hostile effects that capture many prisoners to serve the victor. The feudal society consists of feudal lords (lords - landowners) who own the land and the workers, agents and slaves on it. The feudal lord protects and supports both sexes. Here, women become submissive to enter them by the feudal on their wedding night before their husbands enter them, and the feudal is the one who chooses the wives of his agents, not them because their marriage means the union of two families and lineage. When a woman gets married, she kneels before her husband as an expression of her obedience and submission to him. After that, this woman joins in her cohabitation with the feudal lord and the husband because he (i.e., the feudal lord) is the owner of the land and whoever works on it and lives on it. There is a case where the father or brother exchanges his daughter or sister and presents her as an alternative to the dowry in exchange to marry the father or brother of the girl he wants to marry. This is because marriage for them is an economic and relative union or unity and not an association of two lovers as the wife is owned by the husband. There is a category that comes after the feudal lords, who are the agents or nobles who represent the feudal lords and represent them before the slaves. And that the woman (wife) is the property of both the husband and the feudal lord together, in the sense that she is an acquired commodity that does not exist as a human being with an opinion, a ruler or a position, but rather a service role for the husband and the feudal lord for childbirth, raising children and housekeeping. All this is not done by her will or by choice but rather imposed on her by the male authority enslaved to her and in control of her virginity, dignity, and energy.

In conclusion of the foregoing, it can be said that the subservience of women and their low status are subject to material poverty of their lack of property and money, the continuation of wars that need men as a striking force, the captivity of women, bringing them to the victorious society, and using them as a commodity for the rich in the slave market, which in turn degrades the position of the warrior's wife. All this is coupled with customs and controls.

Customary serves the benefit of the man through which he transcends the woman and degrades her position.

Therefore, poverty, customary patriarchal controls, and war represent compelling and pressing factors on the position of women in using them as a commodity offered for sale, purchase, use, enjoyment, and enrichment (human, material and moral). Here she is a victim of the cube of influences practised by the perpetrator of the cube of superiority, in the sense that this society degrades the status of women at the same time and raises the status of men to make them sublime and lofty.

4. The Renaissance and Religion Reforming

The European Renaissance was a transitional movement in Europe between the Middle Ages and the modern era that originated in the fourteenth century in Italy and continued until the seventeenth century and was characterised by the influence of classical concepts, the flourishing of literature and art, and the dawning of modern science. It is a movement or an era of intense artistic and mental activity, which had general benefits and privileges that benefited women at all levels in their aristocratic education, and they became exemplary models in literature and the arts, and many of them were references in their lives regarding their rights, especially women who emerged as scientists, writers, artists, and intellectuals - of noble blood. All of this earned them consideration and prestige for their accomplishments. At the same time, there were women who resisted the challenge of old traditions.

Martin Luther and the Reformation: With the Reformation (Protestant movement) in the sixteenth century, an astonishing idea emerged that struck the hierarchy of the church, which was to exclude people from worship and preach theology and liberation from the church because it was too restrictive and strict. Then Martin Luther put forth his explicit claim that Christianity receives all people on the basis of faith and then criticised (Thomas Aquinas) because he saw the woman as immature and incomplete and accused her of being a monster. Luther defended the woman and said that she is God's creation, so she is beautiful and not a monster. As for the texts of theology, it was emphasised that she bears the greatest burden of sins because of Satan's temptation to her like Eve. And the divine natural order determined her function, which is confined to procreation, carrying out domestic and marital duties, and accompanying and cohabiting with a man. But she overturned the natural order, brought it down, and distorted her image when she committed adultery, and this is not justified except by stoning her to death. This does not extend and apply to the man when he is not faithful to his wife. However, the reconfiguration set back and guided it throughout the Western world, so there was no complete change that revealed the Christian image of women and their events.

Going back to the Renaissance, it can be said that it did and actively re-born art, literature, and music in the world quickly, then moved to trade and communications, the growth of cities and the standard of living of people, so women emerged in most scientific and cultural fields and closed the doors to the clergy, nobles, and feudal lords. Therefore, women achieved economic progress through their work in shops and offices and produced products in their homes for sale and trade, and when the policy of barter instead of money was introduced, a new class appeared that did not depend on agriculture and the feudal lords for production.

When you pay attention to the issue of gender in ancient history, the active influences on the deterioration of the status of women can be identified. It includes the elevation of the status of men over her in the social barometer, which did not deviate by a single degree over time, nor through the social variables that occur in a society that was not aimed at women. Specifically, she is affected sideways by the effects of these variables. Sometimes it was found the deterioration of the status of women and the expansion and multiplicity of their roles in contrast to the high status of men and the shrinking of his roles. These macro variables (global and dimensional) are the following: a) wars, b) feudalism, c) individual property, d) clergymen in misogyny, f) priestly texts, g) the dissolution of the empire and its disintegration.

This historical background took a vast time-space between 306 and 337 BC until the seventeenth century AD. At the same time, there were influences that raised the status of women to a good level, but they did not reach the level of equality, including:

a. Monasteries in her education and learning.
b. The European Renaissance.
c. The Protestant Reformation movement.
d. Martin Luther.

It was concluded that the clergymen and not the religion, the feudalism and not the material property, and the warriors and not the war. They interpreted the priestly texts to serve their interests and ambitions and their authority to enslave women sexually, reproductively, educationally, and administratively. Because she does not possess power or money but rather possesses aesthetic appeal and sexual pleasure, without authority and with no domination over men and over children. In view of that, the men adhered to religious texts directed toward women, and they called the "natural system of the gods" in intercourse and intimacy with a man, procreation from him and raising his children, so they invented a metaphysical reason to humiliate and despise her after the passage of centuries, which is what Eve did in eating the apple and descending to the earth under the devil temptation of her. This is an interpretation that neither reason nor humanity accepts, but the ultimate narcissistic interest and they did not punish the man when he betrayed his wife. Which religion approves of this? This is a distortion in the teachings and prejudice against the rights of women, as well as the clerics' use of the phenomenon of witches in society to attach them to the position of women, claiming that it is a premeditated act of Satan that only women can do. This is what increased men's hatred of women and their treatment of degenerate and contempt. The question here is, was there no magic of men? Were there not deviants from the married life of the man? Why did the clergy not take the same position with them as they stood against women? Wasn't this passive and feigned prejudice against women and the promotion of men? Is it because she does not have money, land, or influence? This is another factor in the enslavement of women during the feudal period. It means that when she gets rid of the enslavement of the clergy and stigmatises her with the worst and most humiliating stigmata in the name of the religion whose interpretation of its texts has been distorted, then comes the enslavement of the feudal lords to her, and we do not forget the warriors who capture women in every war and enslave them in the slave market and use them as concubines. These three influences engendered the patriarchal and masculine-enhancing power over her. But when the European Renaissance and the Protestant Reform Movement came, women were emancipated from the grip of the clergy and the domination of the feudal lords. Women then benefited from these two eras, so they excelled in science, literature, and art.

Finally, it can be stated that the intolerance and prejudice against women are impulsive and fabricated by men who have power and money to enslave women for sexual enjoyment, have children for them, raise them and manage their homes. However, this is not removed automatically, nor by the man, but by regular, coherent, and admirable feminist forces in performing their work outside the home and in workshops and laboratories. Then the man is excluded from his fanaticism and prejudice, and the restoration of women's rights to citizenship is achieved. It requires an intense and intelligent effort and a long time.

CHAPTER 11: GENDER PHASES IN PRESENT SOCIETIES

INITIATION

A. THE CRUSHED VICTIM IN THE RUSSIAN GENDER

B. THE CHINESE GENDER... AND THE REVERSAL OF ITS REFORM

C. THE JAPANESE GENDER… A TEMPORARY, NON-PERMANENT, AND NON-IMMUTABLE GOOD

D. PATRIOTIC SACRIFICED WOMEN, THE INDIAN GENDER, TO MAKE HER A NATIONAL SYMBOL

E. WISE IN INDONESIAN GENDER

F. THE LATIN GENDER....THE MOST SUBMISSIVE AND OBEDIENT

G. GENDER IN THE ISLAMIC WORLD... BETWEEN TWO VEILS

H. THE ARAB GENDER... SURRENDERING TO ITS CULTURAL PATTERN

I. THE ISRAELI GENDER....EQUALITY ON PAPER ONLY

J. THE SCANDINAVIAN GENDER... THE IDEAL MODEL FOR ITS EQUALITY

CHAPTER 11

GENDER PHASES IN PRESENT SOCIETIES

INITIATION

The area of this phase starts at the beginning of the twentieth century until the first quarter of the twenty-first century. It covers the factors that reinforce and nourish sexual differences (between feminine and masculine) and their fight against gender equality in the present societies, including the following:

1. The second globalization, which led to the dispensation of women's work in factories and advanced technological sites and the sale of their farms, and the abandonment of the man from his family and the search for another place of work outside his country, with the push of women into the home and volunteer work without pay.

2. The collapse of the socialist camp and the demise of the Soviet Union, which lost the feminine economic and political influence in work and the government and stopped her wages, which increased her working hours inside the home with the erosion and fragmentation of her feminine rights to the extent that it no longer has any influence or consideration as it was before the collapse and demise.

3. The rule of the Russian Tsardom before 1917.

4. Confucian principles in China, which viewed the feminine as inferior and considered it stupid, naive and narrow-minded.

5. The patriarchal authority in Japan, Indonesia, Israel and the Arab and Islamic countries.

6. The laws of "Manu" in India and the sect of the Brahmins, which favoured men over women and made women dependent on men.

7. The dominance of the Roman Catholic religion and the Spanish and Portuguese colonial heritage in Latin American countries that allow men to dominate the feminine and invoke social restrictions to humiliate her, glorify the role of motherhood, and bear the misery and cruelty of men over her without complaining.

8. The politicization of religion in Afghanistan, Iran, Iraq, Yemen and Libya.

9. The multiplicity and diversity of political conflicts, wars and revolutions in the Arab countries and their support for the patriarchal authority.

10. Ignorance of the Indian woman in sexual and health education, which made her subject to male domination and control over her.

All of these factors hindered the implementation of the equality of feminine rights with men's rights and supported his authority in the family, work, elections, and all aspects of life. It remains to be mentioned that not all of these obstacles impede gender equality in every country. Rather, each country has its own obstacles stemming from its history, culture, and educational levels, but they are not as effective today as they were a century ago.

It is also noted that religious principles (Confucianism, Manichaeism, Catholicism, and sectarianism) support the authority of men, as well as the Spanish and Portuguese foreign colonization in Latin American countries and American in Iraq, and all kinds of political and military turmoil, all of which led to the male's help and the enslavement of the female to make her his father, housewife and nanny for children.

But after 1917, big and notable changes occurred, such as the revolutions, World War II, and the American occupation of Japan that crystallized the emergence of leaders of national leaders with modern visions and human needs to call women to the process of new construction in all institutions of structural systems, starting from the family and passing through the school to the political leaders such as Lenin in Russia in 1917, which set a policy that abolished all forms of discrimination and intolerance against women that the Russian Tsar was fighting in education, work, administration and trade unions. Then the policy of (Mao Zedong) in China, who implemented reform between the feminine and masculine in marriage, education and work, as well as (Gandhi and Nehru) in India, who worked on the independence of women and gave them a shining national consideration in the opposition political movements as well as (Suharto) in Indonesia 1966-1998 where an integrated development program was establishing to serve women in work, education and services. Then there is an Indonesian feminist organization called "Wife Power", which includes wives who work behind the scene and have a wide network of contacts and have an influence on government decisions that practice intolerance and prejudice against women by applying equal rights to men's rights.

It can be inferred from all of this that the societies present today did not establish gender equality automatically or voluntarily, but rather by the presence of popular leaders in the leadership of the nation to stop the inherited power from many previous generations and reduce its influence and domination over the feminine. In return, it supports the role of women by eliminating the usurpation of their rights to choose their life partner, divorce, inheritance, election, attendance in municipal and parliamentary councils, work outside the home, and raise the wages of their work in conjunction with the support of the largest international organizations (the United Nations) and a strong government such as the US government when it occupied Japan. Had it not been for these effective leadership forces, the authority of the man would not have diminished, and the power of the feminine would not have been strengthened in family, professional and political life. It is humanity's need for a woman, and it is not the end of her struggle with a man, but rather the entitlement of her usurped right, the payment of her fees at work, and dealing with her as a human being like a man who provides services and achievements like him, but without her, man would not have been born.

A. THE CRUSHED VICTIM IN THE RUSSIAN GENDER

Gender usually includes men and women, but the situation in Russian society has different sides from the situation of gender in other societies because of the overwhelming chaos that afflicted Russian society after the fall of the communist political system and replaced by a non-communist political system. Between the fall and solutions, social chaos has occurred, in which the society lost its control and security. Consequently, multiple and varied disintegrations have resulted in the organization of the society, including turning the Russian woman into a victim in front of several perpetrators (the husband, the family, the society, the social system, the employers and the government).

This is an introduction to what will be present in detail about this gender equation in Russian society in the last decade of the last century until now.

When the collapse of the Soviet Union happened, there was a tiding in the spread of democracy in the world, and the former President of the Soviet Union (Mikhail Gorbachev) worked to implement the policy of openness (Glasnost) associated with reconstruction (Perestroika), which was a key to the transformation of the Soviet Union into the democratic capitalist nations accompanying the economy free market. However, Gorbachev's vision of capitalism was not available to him. This meant that the Soviet Union had turned into an independent nation's government without democracy. As Russia had the most influence on the economic and political life of the former Soviet Republics, it remained firmly on its path of transformation towards a prosperous economy. Since 1998, the financial crisis occurred with the tyranny of global globalization. There has been a change for many Russians who were enjoying prosperity and a good financial level. However, this situation did not continue during the phase of transition and transformation because the aid, health aid and social welfare were excluded and cancelled for them, which affected their standard of living, including gender (this is the motive of the Russian gender). [Clements. 2004. Pp. 122 - 128]

In the face of this transformation and abolition, Russian women became rapidly moving towards poverty, affected by the effects of globalization and the shift towards a free-market economy, as all the republics that were under the umbrella of the Soviet Union, such as Azerbaijan, which cut educational aid and health care, and government jobs were also reduced, and jobs occupied by women were abolished. With cutting government aid to care for its children and the elderly, which increased the poverty of women, children and the elderly, Azerbaijan fell in the United Nations ranking of developing countries from 71st to 90th.

It is appropriate to point out that Soviet laws and legislations had done justice to women since 1917 when Lenin's policy announced the elevation of the status of women by eliminating all forms of prejudice and intolerance against her that were practised by the Russian tsarism against her, as he ensured their complete equality in employment opportunities, education, property rights, and family affairs and their competition With the man in the management of government institutions. That is, half of the positions and jobs were guaranteed in government legislation, such as the trade union.

However, the influential political positions were devoid of females; that is, they were not filled, so the equality policy was a mask for the continuation of the injustice and oppression practised upon it in the former Soviet Union (this is the Soviet Gender barometer).

The attention in this regard is focused on female employment in the Soviet Union, which has a high percentage of women in the labour force than any other industrial society. It emerged through its rapid vital activity, as no country in the world has passed laws in favour of the female, as it happened to the Soviet workforce, which was legislated very quickly. There is no harm in saying that Russia today includes the vast majority of female civil servants. There are widespread gender patterns around the work of the female competing with the man and her preference over him. However, factory owners and business managers see women as less productive and useful. The working mother receives specific assistance for her children in the field of health care and attention to childhood, as they consider her a burden on their work because the working mother and wife are not fully and completely accomplished like a single woman. In light of this, the time allotted to her

569

in training is less, then her skill is not unique and high quality. Therefore, she is considered a second-class worker. However, in the official legal legislation for respected female workers, such as engineers, doctors, and intellectual workers, they were fair with her as they did not underestimate her. However, her wages are lower than theirs, and their professional consideration is not distinguished and high-level to the extent that they are not taken into consideration for recognition of their professionalism and merit.

Therefore, on the ground of practicality, there is hidden prejudice and intolerance toward women. But during the communist rule, working women earned two-thirds of the average income of a man, and now her earnings are less than half of the man's earnings. Hence, there is a serious wage gap in the salaries between men and women. This gap became wider and deeper during the financial crisis of 1998 and doubled during the economic recession of 2008. It especially became much worse in modern Russia. In fact, this wage gap appeared in a clear, prominent, and fanatical way in the women's work related to education, nursing and social workers, where it is low despite their skill in these applied professions more than men's and fanaticism has emerged more widespread and entrenched against her in unskilled and unprofessional jobs.

Russian gender inequality still exists and persists even in the unemployment crisis. Globalization, however, created a labour movement in industrial activities that went to new fields and used new innovations that were not known before. As for companies with quick benefits that have spread in all industries, they are far from being monitored by government agencies, and government bureaucracy and their subsidies have ceased to exist. This, in turn, had made the heaviest fees imposed on women, which led to a high rate of unemployment in the Russian labour market, especially in the transitional period experienced by Russia (i.e., When she moved from the communist system to the new capitalist) where the government was unable to monitor commercial and industrial activities accurately and continuously. The women were harmed more than the men because they were working in companies with quick benefits more than men. But the Russian peasantry benefited from this new circumstance, particularly when the gardens were exploited and turned into places for small commercial work. This new exploitation was able to absorb the unemployment of Russian peasant women working in them.

The incompatibility of social culture and social policy resulted in serious disagreement and conflict between the family and work and its outcome (in the Gender barometer), in addition to the glaring disparity between masculine and feminine in the field of the workforce explains the double burden on the women. The Russian social fabric poses solid and authoritative obstacles that hinder the work, progress and development of the female when compared with men in developing societies. A Russian man enjoys family duties that represent a minimum of responsibilities when his wife, sister, or mother receives wages from the labour force as he works 30 hours a week with free hours in which he works no more than his wife. The rural and urban wife has few hours outside the house, but her work inside the house takes long hours every day, and hence they are crushed between the jaws of a mill (their household-family responsibilities and what was left by the state of transformation that created complete chaos in the lives of Russians, which burdened them with a lack of working hours outside the home).

On the other hand, the Russian government is concerned about the decline in the birth rate, the increase in the number of families of small size, and the economy's dependence on women's cheap work that they obtain from part-time and temporary work. In the face of these shocking problems, women have become respected in their specialization outside the labour market, unlike the female manual labourer who is still in high demand due to the advantages of her hand at work, with her low wages. Then, the failure of employers to provide financial aid to the mother when she gives birth or breastfeeds her children doubled the mother's burden and the Russian wife. It made the couple neither want to have children nor to form a large family because of its high cost. The availability of affordable contraceptives helped them in controlling births. However, abortions have increased at a high rate, and according to official figures, there are two abortions for every birth. This number is not a secret because illegal abortions are estimated to be more than that, as for every eight abortions, there is one child. The government is not serious about birth control or paying social security to the parents of newcomers to society.

Crushed Victim

It is clear that the Russian woman has become an official and societal victim that pays the price for the chaos caused by the political and economic transformation phase. The government did not rescue her from her drowning in a rough and turbulent sea of troubles, including the prevailing collisions and conflicts between the new costs of living, the male preference over her, family burdens, and the government's negligence of her. They placed her in a difficult position in every fronter, while there were no women's organizations to defend her against the injustice and her new, diverse and multiplied misery. The biological

572

differences are clear and sharp between the masculine and the feminine, but what has increased the gap between them is their diversity and proliferation. It has become repetitive, leading to the congruence of gender differences with biological differences, so that they have become in their social position, multiple and diverse in their manifold roles due to the disruption of social life resulting from the collapse of the old political system and the emergence of a new political system. Many of them became poorer and a few richer, making the rights and duties of the female in a wide and deep dissonance more than the biological differences. The latter increased the injustice and oppression on her and her professional and material poverty, and her double toil suffers from the existing struggle between family necessities and political and economic chaos.

When it comes to the family, the Russian woman is quite aware of her role, which she handles very well, and it is the same everywhere in the world. Therefore, she is not seeking equality in this very role. This is right as in the sense of the enormity of her tasks, she is not concerned with this equality, but the villagers (peasant women) are more inclined to the romantic relationship, preferring it to the equality between them and the male peer. But in general, the Russian feminine places a high and precious value on raising her children and building a family because Russian society places an especially important value on this and on the social system more than anything else. All these heavy responsibilities are not matched by high labour wages, but rather low significantly because Russian society painted a vivid picture of the Russian feminine as a housewife and mother at the same time, drawing a distorted picture of her in the workplace, drawing her as if she was a rough man who endures toil and fatigue. It is unfortunate and sad that she is blamed when she gets family and behavioural problems such as divorce, pregnancy during celibacy and adolescence, drug addiction, or deviant behaviour.

On the other hand, the woman's work requires comprehensive national productivity in order to obtain a high financial income to spend on her children and family, unlike the Russian masculine, whose society did not paint a picture of his responsibilities towards his family and, unfortunately, the social disapproval of women continues. But the truth is that when a woman works outside the home in a factory or workshop, she loses her femininity, which prompts the modern man to blame her for such a loss, knowing that the unfairness on the part of men, society, and Russian culture.

This is the contemporary Russian feminine because the feminine as a human being has equal rights and duties to man in citizenship and imbues her with cultural norms. She exercises her individual and personal freedom and is frowned upon if she loses her femininity. From what I have seen about its social and cultural reality, the description (victim) or the concept of victim applies to her because:

1. She was robbed by society.
2. She was stripped of her society's culture.
3. She was used and abused by the family.
4. She was mocked by her husband.
5. She was created by the family and society.
6. Blamed by society.
7. She was disapproved by the man.

Therefore, she was subjugated seven times to torturing at the hand of society, her culture, the husband, the family, and the man, so she became the seventh victim. In the sense that she was crushed severely and heavily, this is an anomaly, as what happened to Russian society was the fall and collapse of the ruling regime that lasted eight decades. It turned into another regime that contradicted its previous regime, which led to its turmoil and the prosperity of chaos and the absence of positive and moral controls in controlling behaviour. The daily and moral calls were made to the gentle, kind, and sociable human element, namely (the female) who was not merciful to her, who treated her away from her legitimate rights and blamed her when she was not subject to him and the underestimating, so she loses her femininity and put her in the service of the man, the husband, the family, and the society. Therefore, she is robbed of her will and enslaved to men, society, and its culture, and she lives in the twenty-first century, the era of personal freedom, democracy, and freedom of expression of free opinion.

After what was mentioned about the Russian feminine, the negative and positive reactions to the trend of gender equality can be explained. In the traditional stage, the Russian feminine faced many economic restrictions and suffered a lot from the preference of men over her inside and outside the home. The period of openness policy (glasnost), however, represented a window that was opened to claiming her rights, particularly for the rural women, who began in practice on university campuses and in the daily newspapers by talking openly about women's rights and the feminist movement criticizing the former political regime (the Soviet Union) in withholding talk about gender equality which was deliberately neglected.

Meanwhile, the position of popular culture has opposed equality and considered it a hostile movement against Russian values. It was a declared war against the Russian man, and when the man's financial and professional situation worsened, the woman rose up to respond to the man who was exploiting and oppressing her. She was violent and harmful to him, which made her control him. But the Russian feminist movement was clearly suffering from the lack of young and dynamic elements in taking leadership positions, organizing its activities according to solid rules, and getting a foothold in universities and regions. It practised its activities outside and inside Russia, and its activity abroad was more vital than inside.

In general, both men and women were sceptical about the sincerity of their egalitarian intentions because the woman who performs the chores of the house is not able to work full time (forty hours a week) simultaneously. However, the central government issued a decree mandating gender equality. Finally, the openness policy (glasnost) paved the way for women, but it revealed many problems that they were not aware of before that time, and this policy revealed the rights of women that were absent from them.

[Clements. 2004. Pp. 161 – 178]

Through this study of the Russian gender, it was concluded that poverty does not make a woman demand her feminine rights because she did not find provisions to fill her and her family's stomachs. Therefore, what is the value of the call for equality with men when she is hungry and her children suffer from diseases and do not have health care or a healthy residential shelter? So, it can be said that poverty becomes a thick and towering wall to isolate the woman from thinking about her legitimate rights, such as intolerance, prejudice, violence and occupying powerful government positions while they are hungry. Poverty has no voice other than hunger and thirst and does not think without stopping the agony of poverty.

Poverty, which is an internal and external cause, is usually linked to unemployment that is stronger in its spread. For example, modern technological innovations have laid off a lot of traditional labour, and globalization and free international trade are global influences that have increased the poverty and unemployment of women before others, especially because there is no political or economic support for them. Then there is the "double burden" on women resulting from traditional family responsibilities and their work outside the home. This variable is cuffing, gagging, and pulling her from both the family and professional sides, and this does not make her free to express her rights and equality with men.

The local and global influences of the Russian gender can be featured by:

1. The Soviet Revolution of 1917.
2. The collapse of the political system and the tyranny of the second globalization in 1998.
3. Influences of businessmen and owners of factories on female workers.
4. The incompatibility of social culture with social policy in Russian society.

These variables highlighted the fluctuations in realizing woman's rights and their deprivation of them, each according to his interest and need.

The Soviet Revolution of 1917 took place in:

a. The abolition of all forms of discrimination and intolerance against women that were practised by the Russian Tsardom before 1971 AD.
b. Equality with men in employment opportunities, education, property rights, and family matters.
c. Opening the way for her to compete with men in the management of official institutions.
d. She held distinguished positions in the trade unions.
e. Covering it with social security, health and educational care.

f. Providing health care for her sponsors.

g. Enact legal legislation that guarantees her right to work and civil service.

h. Her professional wages are less than the wages of a man with the same experience and skill. (This is the Soviet motive until 1989)

This situation continued until 1989, when the Russian female enjoyed rights close to the rights of men, except for not being employed in high political positions, and this shows the persistence of prejudice and intolerance against her. That is, she enjoyed the rights granted to her by the Soviet government for 72 years, and this is a good thing to be reckoned with.

But with the advent of (Gorbachev) and his policy of openness and new construction, woman's rights flourished, but this prosperity continued for nine years when this prosperity stopped due to the occurrence of the global financial crisis and the tyranny of globalization in 1998 and the collapse of the political system in which the following was done:

1. Cancellation of aid for women and others.
2. Cancellation of health aid for her children.
3. Cancellation of her social security.
4. Cut off educational aid for her children.
5. Reducing the government jobs that were occupied by them.

Then came the influence of businessmen and owners of factories and industrial, professional workshops, which had a great impact on the working mother and the working wife so that they were not seen as first-class products but rather as second or third-class products, so they were dispensed with, and women professionals were not looked at with a professional eye with distinct professional merit. The following gaps appeared:

a. The wages gap.
b. The working hours' gap.
c. Occupational gap.

Finally, there is the incompatibility of social culture with social policy in Russian society. The first places obstacles that hinder the work of the woman and does not place them on the man. These global and local variables gave rise to new problems that were not known to Russian society, such as:

i. A drop in the birth rate.
ii. An increase in the number of families of small size.
iii. Women's dependence on low-paid work and part-time and temporary work.
iv. Employers do not provide assistance to the working mother or the working wife during pregnancy, childbearing and breastfeeding.
v. The high rate of legal and illegal abortion.

This is what resulted from the inequality of the rights of the female with the rights of the Russian man. The gender difference in his rights is not related to the biological difference but to the local economic and political conditions associated with the universal, globalization and technical development that the local standard of living must submit to and respond to its influences. This, in turn, nourishes and revives some of the popular beliefs and practices inherited in society, such as the roles of the wife and mother in the family, which doubles the burden placed on her by society and the social culture that considers the family her kingdom. It also makes her not pay attention to the call for equality between her and the man while emphasizing the contractual relationship between her and the husband. On the maternal relationship, she considers it a mechanical and interconnected relationship between her and her children, focusing on the family unit to the main degree more than her focus on the low wages of her work (if she works). In addition to that, the Russian society does not encourage her to work in the factory and bureaucratic circles, so society blames her:

1. When she loses her femininity by working outside the house.
2. When she is divorced from her husband.
3. When she becomes pregnant while she is celibate.
4. When she deviates behaviourally.
5. When she opposes her husband's orders.

In conclusion, it seems that the rights of Russian women have been greatly affected, and they have lost many of their rights due to the fall of the ruling regime, which has achieved many social, professional and political gains for her with global external influences, which deprived her of many of her legitimate rights.

B. THE CHINESE GENDER ... AND THE SET-BACK OF HER REFORM

Chinese women have a prestigious and high value in building the socialist system. This was confirmed by the President of the People's Republic of China (Mao Zedong), as well as by the Communist Party, who considered her the right hand in development and construction, even for the peasant revolution, giving her priority in the family and economical building process and occupying the large space in the government's thinking when building its society, the new.

The Chinese goal is to get women to work in economic projects for the beneficial benefit as well as the benefit and benefit of their families. The patriarchal family (with male domination) represents a microcosm of the oppressive and oppressive capitalist society. Therefore, the woman's exit from her home to work outside it means that she has become economically productive under the new socialist system, and this, in turn, liberates her socially and improves her economic position and equals her with men. Reform must start with equality between men and women, and this, in turn, will reform society. This is the Chinese communist doctrine like that of the former Soviet Union.

The Reform and the Family (The Motivator and the Incubator in Chinese Society)

The tradition of the Chinese family is based on Confucian principles that grant full authority to the male-dominated man (Patriarch), taking patrilineal lineage, and dwelling with the father. One of the ancient Confucian writings is that it looks at women with an inferior look and considers them stupid, with a naive, limited, and narrow mentality, without any wisdom and jealousy, so men despise them, as they have no occupation other than the temptation of innocent men. It is neither strange nor surprising for the life and living of women in Chinese society, which is subject to strict and rigid restrictions on their family life that do not allow them to express their opinion on family matters and has no right to inherit from the family inheritance of property and material and when she marries, she goes to her husband's house to serve him under his authority without discussion or controversy. And such behaviour is not discussing her husband is an extension of preventing her from discussing and arguing with her father, brother, uncle, maternal uncle, or any man from her relatives. For her son-in-law, and in special cases, the mother-in-law can sell her daughter-in-law if she disobeys her orders or runs away from her home. Therefore, the daughter-in-law has a lower family position in the ancient Chinese family hierarchy.

There is a case of tying a woman's foot, which is one of the practices of the upper class, which is obligatory for her to limit the movement of her foot in walking, provided that her walking steps do not exceed three inches, and this means that walking at her is impossible. This situation was valid and prevalent until the last decade of the last century, when it was one of the requirements of the upper class for women, except for women who work in manual labour or in agricultural fields.

It is necessary to point out the emergence and decline of Chinese marriage in 1950, which was issued a reform law that year specialized in reforming Chinese family laws through the passing of a law that removed customary and status controls that oppressed women and excluded their freedom as human beings in order to make her like the Chinese man in his gender rights. This emergence led to the disappearance of many unfair and equitable practices of women's rights in the family. So, this decline did not come smoothly or automatically, but rather with reformist legal texts that led to the abolition of the following:

a. The family's interference in choosing the life partner for the woman and the man in the sense of making the marriage free and independent of the parents of the newlyweds, i.e., giving the woman the freedom to choose her husband without the influence of the family or relatives in her marriage, which was called feudal marriage. This emergence led to the demise of many traditional family practices with old beliefs, including:

b. Not allowing a man to dominate a woman.

c. Granting the woman, the right to divorce herself.

d. Not allowing a man to marry more than one wife at a time, meaning that the new law does not allow polygamy or husbands.

e. Sexual intercourse without a legal marriage contract is prohibited.
f. Not to marry a minor who has not reached the age of majority.
g. Abolition of the bride dowry.
h. Abolishing the restrictions imposed on the remarriage of a widow.

Moreover, in 1980, the law of 1950 was purified in order to develop and promote it, especially for the institution of marriage. The 1980 law equates the husband and wife to have one status within the family. At the same time, they were granted the right to work in any job in which there is a wage or permission to enable registration in schools and universities and participate in social activities. Moreover, this law prevented the husband and wife from imposing restrictions and restraints or interfering in the affairs of each other. It can be seen from the foregoing that the 1980 law strengthened the status of women, especially urban ones, in their families, while rural women's share was slightly less than urban ones. But after two decades, that is, after the year 2000, the Chinese family witnessed many unexpected practices, behaviours, and problems, such as:

(a) The practice of domestic violence against women.
(b) Leaving children under the care of one of the parents.
(c) The divorce rate is four times higher than it was previously.
(d) The high level of poverty.

In 2001, the 1980 law was discussed in order to promote it, even though it was protecting the woman in their family. The modification stipulates that illegal sexual intercourse is considered an outlaw and counts sexual pornography as illegal. It granted the women broader division than before of property upon divorce, as it included all the property received after marriage, including the monthly salary, financial allowances, and inheritance, all of which the wife deserves after divorce, while forbidding husbands to marry more than one wife at a time, and considered forced marriage illegal. In spite of all this, the use of concubines and girlfriends continued in practice as it was in the old law. Nevertheless, these reforms faced opposition resistance in their implementation.

The abolition of an inherited traditional law based on the choice of parents as a partner for their children and its replacement by an opposite law based on the free choice of partners is not a very simple and smooth matter for Chinese feudal, rural and kinship families, because such social bond requires a temperamental, personal and intellectual preparation of young people who did not experience it. Hence the legislation modification faced serious resistance to the conditions of equality between the sexes. This is because equality requires equal standing and the presence of loyalty and sincerity between and among the two partners. It goes without saying that the rich were subjected to a reduction in their freedom to marry more than one wife or one husband at a time, and kinship relations were also subjected to cracking. Therefore, the practice of parent's involvement in choosing a life partner for their children continued for a period because it contradicts their kinship relations, and those marriages of free choice depend on knowing the privacy of the two partners, which was not available in Chinese society due to the strict cultural restrictions on young people. And the Chinese reality was not prepared to accept such conditions because of its dependence on the parents' choice for their children in marriage and on kinship and traditional relations. The new law cancelled all major obstacles was to the success of early free-choice marriages.

The One-Child Policy

The ancient Chinese traditions have left great importance on the birth of a son and low values on the birth of a girl accompanied by an ominous impression on her birth. However, since the birth of the People's Republic of China, it has focused on raising the status of women and eliminating injustice imposed on them. At the same time, it has put forward a strict program to reduce the growth of the large population size in China. In fact, these two goals were contradictory and difficult to implement. In 1979, the central government began implementing the policy of one newborn (child) in the family under the name of owning one child or allowing the family to give birth to one newborn, with severe and severe punitive restrictions on violators of this policy. Then there was another law that the Chinese government placed on violators of the restrictions on population growth, and it was more stringent and severe. In fact, the one-child policy in the family is unique, with severe punitive restrictions placed on non-compliance. Therefore, the government has launched a comprehensive popular campaign to implement it and make parents aware of it and the consequences of violating it.

The couple receives a document stating the birth of the first newborn that authorizes them to receive annual financial child aid and cash. But if a second birth occurs, a deduction will be made for the financial aid provided to them, which imposes compensatory burdens on them in school, feeding and treating him because the government does not take care of the aid of the second child, in addition to deducting the aid given to the first newborn. During the first newborn and the second pregnancy, she is obliged to abort. If she refuses to have an abortion, she faces criticism, ridicule, and mockery from her co-workers. This is, on the one hand, and on the other hand, there is a great preference for the male sex and the perseverance of the man so that he is exempted from sexual sterility. At the same time, since Chinese society includes multiple customs, ethnic and religious minorities, they are exempted from the birth of one child, i e, exempted from the application of the one-child policy. Among these minorities are Muslims, Tibetans, and Euphoria.

This policy has many shortcomings and negatives, including that the one-child policy will increase the number of centenarians in the period between 2006-2050, increasing their percentage from 8 to 24%, with no increase in the number of children of one child within this same time period. Moreover, this policy is not successful in rural areas because the farming family does not take it seriously and continuously because of its need for government financial aid. It is not urgent because it grows food yields for itself and needs labour from members of its family to help them in farming and agriculture. There is also a failure to implement this policy among the rich who live in urban areas and cities such as Beijing and Shanghai, as they do not need government aid or pay school fees for their children. Moreover, the peasant families who have two female children want to have a third male child.

Preference of the Male Over the Female (As a Gender Motivator)

Regardless of the economic and social status of the two partners, they prefer the male over the female, and even under the one-child policy, this trade-off remained. It is associated with the mentality of the Chinese because it is a remnant of the ancient and sacred Chinese heritage in the ancient cults that prevailed in China in the past. As the grandparents have a blessed influence and authority in the belief of the children and the view of the grandchildren, they are blessed in it in order to bless their livelihood. It goes without saying that a woman acquires the status of her ancestors from her husband and her male children (not in the family into which she was born), and when there are no males in the family, the grandchildren have no place in the other after their death. It is worth mentioning in this context that the lonely and gloomy state of doom appears on the psyche and personality of the wife who does not give birth to a male or remains without marriage or the widow without a child. Therefore, we find that Chinese women are very interested in the family tree, whose roots extend back to three thousand years, in which no female names are mentioned in the family. Even under the one-child policy, there is a preference for males over females. Historically, there has been a practice of female infanticide in Chinese society. It has been practised for several centuries, but it diminished after the outbreak of the Chinese Revolution in 1949 because it was linked to the one-child policy and considered (the revolution) that an infanticide is an illegal act, and the abortion of a pregnant mother with a fetus whose gender is known was also considered illegal. Not only that, but even polytheists who adopt a child from outside China prefer to adopt a male over a female. [Potts. 2006. Pp. 333 – 361]

Despite the aid and benefits received from sticking to the one-child policy, the modern generation in Chinese society does not support this policy. The new families consider it as a temporary measure to accustom the partners voluntarily to reduce their family size. Although the population size is huge, the cultural and financial influences on gender lead to disruption of the unified commitment of the Chinese to it. If the rich and famous people in China fail to abide by it and pay fines for this violation as a punishment for them, which includes even the Chinese who had more than one child and were not condoned when they return to China. But there are many changes that have occurred since 1979, such as:

a. There are 75% of those who supported the one-child policy and justified their support as being necessary for their country and its economic and population development.

b. Those who support the one-child policy do not favour the male over the female at birth, and this serves the future of the female, mother, and daughter together.

c. It was also issued with support from graduates of Chinese universities that it is not only for the one-child policy but rather that the male is not given preference over the female. Instead, the girl is preferred over the boy.

d. But the hidden function of the one-child policy involved:

   i.   Reducing interest in inherited paternal lineage.

   ii.   Encouraging women to work in non-traditional businesses.

   iii. The one-child policy has strengthened the position of women in society and raised their grip high.

   iv.   The one-child policy demonstrated a blatant demographic and economic challenge to modern China.

   v.   This policy resulted in an economic benefit to the family, society and the country.

Finally, a large percentage of the rural population and the outskirts of the poor cities remained committed to the old traditional beliefs regarding the preference of males over females, but in general, this differentiation is subject to the level of individuals' culture and the breadth of their thinking.

New Chinese Slogan: "When You Become Rich, You Become Revered."

In light of the application of capitalism in modern China, the Chinese were eager to implement it, live under it, and consider it their inspiring slogan for them. It spread very quickly, influenced by the material motive and luxury living. This slogan was the product of the effects of globalization that opened the doors wide for women with wages paid in cash with a material motive and a luxurious living. In other words, this globalization slogan was a motivator for the Chinese (both spouses and women). It prevailed in the last decade of the last century, and both the urban and rural people were affected by it. Despite women's domestic work and their low wages, there was great flexibility in the conditions and restrictions on migration from the countryside to the cities, where women's wages rose in agricultural fields and industrial factories, so they quickly turned their work toward industries produced in factories as the capitalism opened the doors of Chinese investment, that poured huge benefits and liberated them from the many restrictions of internal migration. Women were looking for more paid jobs, and internal migration constituted for them the largest in the history of peoples and nations.

Illusioned Paradoxes by Contradiction (Globalization and Development)

The government's policy and economic reform expressed their support for promoting equality between men and women and the integrity of the women's economy. As in both urban and rural areas, her work increased due to the migration of her children to areas other than their areas of residence, so she became the master of the house and the family together. She entered the labour market as it became flexible in its restrictions and conditions towards her, which freed her from male domination over her. Therefore, she became free from patriarchal control (man-father authority or husband or brother), and the freedom of her work is now wider than before, subject to her level of education and the skill of her professionalism. All this helped to equate her with men in his rights and duties.

On the other hand, it has appeared in China that there is no difference between the old patterns and the negative aspects of globalization and development for women, as globalization has widened the gender differences (between men and women) in government departments that employ women more than they were affected by the negative aspects of globalization and development, where many of them were dispensed. In this aspect, the agricultural fields have turned into places of work for the elderly and the less educated women because professionally skilled and well-educated women migrated to the city and became an auxiliary element in urban work that separates women from men and pays them lower wages than men. In fact, on the official and legal level, the government emphasizes gender equality, but in practice, it is weak or absent in the workplace.

However, the illusory paradoxes of the effects of globalization on Chinese women have manifested in many keys of different dimensions, including:

a. The high rate of women's work and at the same time, there was a high rise in unemployment for both sexes.

b. There are major gains in the incomes of housewives, especially in rural areas, yet their earnings are less than that of men.

c. The most suitable place for women has become the home and the kitchen as a means to solve the problem of unemployed men.

d. China's need for manpower is exceptionally large because of its large population and its many abundant natural resources. Hence, it needs women in development more than any other country. [Lindsey. 2011. Pp. 145 - 149]

Follow Up and Comment

The Chinese gender does not differ from the Russian gender in terms of the collapse and fall of the political system and its replacement by another political system that differs in its belief and the nature of its rule, but they differed in their time. In China, the popular revolution took place in 1949 and in Russia in 1917, which changed the status of women from her enslavement in the rigid cultural heritage to liberation. She has been pushed into economic projects outside the home in order for her to contribute to the process of social and economic reform and to get rid of the Confucian teachings that digest and oppress the rights of women in favour of men, worse than the patriarchal system. All this came through the 1950 law, which freed her from many restrictions in choosing a life partner and her right to divorce and not to marry more than one man at a time. Then the amended reformation came in 1980 for what was not reformed in 1950. However, such gender reforms did not appeal to many Chinese men, especially among the rich and feudal lords, because they were against their traditional customs. The major obstacle that faced gender reform is the one-child policy in order to reduce the huge China population and modify the family economy. This policy did not succeed at many social levels, especially among the rich and conservative rural people. It shows that the application of equality between men and women in a society that has been against women for centuries does not recognise the multi-coloured opposition by its practitioners because it is contrary to human nature and the spiritual beliefs of a society that has a legacy in its culture that adopts the patriarchal system and Confucian principles.

The preference for males over females remained in place for all Chinese because it is linked to the mentality of China that descends from the ancient and sacred cultural heritage to be blessed by the ancestors who prefer males over females. Demanding equality between males and females under this mentality is almost impossible because it is linked to the people's view of the male and their history, which has been leading the girl for several centuries. One of the strange things about the issue of gender equality of women with men is that all the reformist decisions of the Chinese government regarding women's rights, about freeing them from the shackles of the ancient and sacred cultural heritage, liberating them from the patriarchal authority and Confucian principles are for involving them in industrial production. However, globalisation and development programs pushed the wheel of gender reform back in terms of her dispensation for its services. It widened 1) the professional gap between men and women, 2) the wage gap between them, and 3) the official-governmental gap. So, after more than half a century of narrowing the gap between them, reforming their family and economic status, and their approach to men's rights, external and internal influences came to crystallise the three types of gaps between them.

It was found from what was mentioned above that the equality of women with men is not subject to internal influences and governmental reforms only, but to international and external influences that do their work in favouring men over women in work, wages and official laws, while they have been, before 1949, subject to sacred historical influences and teachings contemptuous, inferior and condescending to them. It can be attributed to a differentiation of the man over the woman in terms of belief, legal, professional, wage and official. Equality does not come primarily from leaving the house to work and obtaining a material income that is equal to a man, but rather from the popular and visible family mentality in upbringing. The people's revolution in 1949 and the legal reforms in 1950 and 1980 did not underestimate the gender reforms, but this is at the level of internal reform, which lasted fifty years, striving to bring women's rights closer to men, and they succeeded to a large extent, but the international and external pressures attributed this gender equality to biological differences (between male and female) because women have duties that are more important than material benefits, which are forming a family, raising and caring for children, and contributing to building society from the smallest cell of society, which is the family. This is not against the equality of women with men, but rather that it supports the construction of the family and society by both sexes, not in one place of work, but eliminating two different places, because when a woman leaves her family to work outside it, who will manage it and take care of her children? There must be a division of labour for both in building the family and society.

The Chinese People's Revolution, led by Mao Zedong in 1949, tried hard to bring women's rights closer to men's rights through its giant reforms, but in the end, it did not achieve what it wanted to equalise between them due to the influence of factors beyond its control and planning, namely globalisation and comprehensive development, so gender differences remained parallel to the biological differences between men and women in China are much better than they were before the 1949 revolution.

Before leaving this section, let's dig further into what happened to Chinese women before the outbreak of the popular revolution in 1949 and after it. Reforming laws were enacted to remove injustice brought by the ancient spiritual and cultural beliefs. It resulted in the two reforms proposed by the popular revolution in 1950 and 1980 to cancel the many inhumane practices imposed on her. However, the third stage in which the effects of global globalisation appeared and the freedom of free international trade plus the merging of giant commercial companies in the world led to a setback in reforms and a return to the biological difference between males and females, leaving the Chinese gender suffering from inequality and the crystallisation of professional, wage and government gaps after the revolution succeeded in easing the equality of her rights in work and public life.

If the society does not need manpower, it dispenses with her because she has other work to benefit from within the family and at home, unlike a man who does not find a place for him to work at home and the family if he is laid off. This is a natural procedure that serves the gender-based division of labour (male, female) and has nothing to do with gender and biological rights and duties. It is the needs of a society in its development that determine the equality of rights and duties between the sexes. The popular revolution desperately needed labour-intensive hands to build a growing and developed society, so it sought help from her. Since the Chinese society was subject to sacred religious and spiritual rituals, so it dispensed with her when it did not need her work, and it would kill her in enslavement and contempt.

The Chinese society is the same, it did not change in gender but was changed by a popular revolution that wanted new social construction, so it continued when external factors came into conflict with the labour density with the use of modern technological devices in production and communications. Then workers in factories and laboratories were dispensed with, and the first was the dispensation of unskilled and uneducated women. So, she returned to the house and the family to work in and did not dispense with the man. This is not a bias in favour of the man so that the problems experienced by the community do not multiply because if the man is dissected from work, his place is not at home like women who become pregnant, breastfeed, and take care of children. It is a pure biological task since the social inheritance shows that the man is the shepherd of the family, responsible for its livelihood. It is a matter of the fact that he continues to work outside the house to bring bread to his family members, and the woman serves them inside the house. It is a natural condition commensurate with society's needs for manpower and the distribution of jobs according to the biological differences between men and women.

However, with regards to the triple motivator, its gender data concerning the women for the period before 1949 are as follows:

1. Adopting the paternal lineage and residing with it.
2. The inferior view of her, and his superiority over her, considering her stupid, naive, unwise, and jealous, who is good at sexual temptation.
3. Not allowing her to express her opinion on family matters.
4. She has no right to the family inheritance; that is, she has no share in that.

5. When she gets married, her main task is to serve and obey the husband without question.
6. She does what she is commanded by her husband.
7. Her mother-in-law has the right to use her as a servant, beat her, and sell her if she disobeys her woman.

This is, in fact, human enslavement to a creature that represents half or more of the population and raises children according to its low status, so how can the education of children be at the hands of an enslaved and despised? Her upbringing is expected to be the same as her husband and his family treat her, and she does not know other than them. She was brought up in the same educational style, so the male child will follow his mother's style, being imbued with a servile and submissive character that does not know the freedom of expression or normal interaction with others. She breeds deprivation, subservience, and humiliation in the emerging personality. Although she represents the status of the wife and mother in the Chinese family, which was crystallised by ancient religions and they have the traditions of the Patriarchal system, this reinforces and supports biological differences and makes gender differences identical to the biological difference between males and females.

On the other hand, the following points illustrate the reality of Chinese women after the popular revolution that took place in 1949 with the issuance of the Reform Law in 1950 including:

a. Not allowing the family to choose the girl's life partner, but rather the right to do so.
b. Liberating the marriage from the family chains of the two partners.
c. Not to allow the man to dominate and abuse the woman.
d. Granting her the right to divorce her husband.

596

e. Not allowing a man to marry more than one woman at the same time.
f. Prohibition of sexual intercourse without a marriage contract.
g. Not to marry a minor girl.
h. Abolition of the bride dowry.
i. Abolishing the restrictions imposed on the remarriage of a widow.

These reforms came to restrict the man and his domination over the woman because they prevented him from restricting women and violating her rights in marriage, expressing opinions and divorce, and preventing from marrying more than one wife. This reform of women by restricting the man who represents the strongest party in the gender differences granted to him by the inherited heritage and the patriarchal authority while amending and abolishing some unfair traditional controls on the marital relationship. We conclude from this that reform is not carried out by the victim only (the woman) but starts from the perpetrator (i.e., the man) and the values of society. This is not easy work, so it requires its implementation by a popular revolution and an explicit and bold law in establishing gender equality, not just a word or a media announcement. Moreover, it also requires a practical application on the ground.

In 1980 two laws were implemented to grant women freedom in education, work, and social activities and respect for their privacy. This reform came for her, not for the man, in order to feel the right of his position as a human being who has a place in her society.

It goes without saying that these cases before and after the 1950s, 1980s, and 2000s were subject to global developments such as political, technological, social and economic movements that directly affect gender. Therefore, when the events of globalisation, free global trade, the free market, and the movement of international labour all affected what the Chinese reforms carried out in terms of equality between Gender regression in it, as she was dispensed within factories, companies and government works, so she returned to the house and her family worked in it, and she continued to work outside the home, her wages were very low, less than the wages of men.

Therefore, it has become clear that gender differences are affected by global influences, global trade, technological innovations, and international politics because they create new professional and economic interests that attract skilled specialists and innovators and exclude those who do not know them. Thus, winning men into new businesses and pushing women to go to their old places of work (the home and the agricultural field). When they are dispensed with, there will be a contraction and a decrease in the women's need for them in the labour market, and so on. In addition, neither the patriarchal authority nor the inherited traditions have an impact on determining the characteristics of gender in modern society but are rather effective in rural-agrarian, conservative, traditional and sectarian societies.

As for the preference of the male over the female in Chinese culture, it reflects the human possessive nature. When she bears and gives birth to a male, she feels he is part of her womb, and he fed on her breast and embraced in her bosom and raised him according to her upbringing of obedience more than her husband obeys and loves him more than her husband, as well as her realisation that he will be a support for her when she is old. By her nature and her desires, she finds her first love in him and that he belongs to her and not to anyone else. Even if he marries a wife, the mother will still feel that he is the son of her womb, and she is not indispensable or favoured by anyone over her.

Finally, the one-child policy that it is a patchwork policy to treat population inflation as if the Chinese government is treating cancer using headache tablets. It is unaware of the class, ethnic and religious hierarchy in a huge society and neglects the desire of the Chinese family to have a male and prefer him over the girl according to the ancient Chinese religious rituals. Rather, when the mother gives birth to a girl, she has a desire to transcend one child in order to survive a male and bear the government sanctions imposed on her. After the birth of the second child, and thus this policy does not reduce the huge population size in this miserable way, the Chinese Government forgets that the man and woman want his marriage to immortalise him after his death through the birth of a male more than a girl!!!

C. THE JAPANESE GENDER... A TEMPORARY, NON-PERMANENT, AND NON-IMMUTABLE GOOD

When comparing gender role patterns in Japan with other societies, it was found a series of contradictions between them. But during the Second World War, Japanese and American women had much in common with them, as both refused to depend on government and industrial leaders but tolerated dependence on them to take care of family and household affairs.

However, under the American occupation of Japan in 1945, the workforce decided to implement a policy that supported democratic practice in harmony with the values of Japanese culture. The successes of this individual experience have emerged in the economic, health and higher education fields. There was comprehensive prosperity that expresses the amazing success of this experiment in leading the social change that prevailed during the American occupation of Japan. However, the major shift in attitudes about comprehensive social equality, particularly in the equality of men with women, has benefited Japanese women more privileged than Japanese men.

The policy of the American occupation was characterised by a superimposed imposition by the American government in an agreement concluded in July 1945, emphasising the democratic application of freedom of expression, religiosity and respect for human rights. These paragraphs were required and supported by the Japanese themselves, which was announced in March 1947. It includes clear support for women's rights and equality under the law away from prejudice and intolerance of any race, nationality, religion, political party, regional social status or family lineage, in addition to the general guarantee of youth in their educational equality based on competencies while ensuring the rights of women to work in government departments and granting them freedom In a marriage dependent on the consent of both partners. Finally, the 1947 agreement guaranteed the rights of Japanese women more than Japanese men in an unprecedented manner, thus enhancing their position in society. This is the gender motivator in Japan after 1947. [Brooke. 2005. p. 212]

It goes without saying that gender equality is subject to the general trend that expresses the government's policy on long working hours, pregnancy, childbirth, and monthly menstrual leave. The public policy made it clear that the new Japan needed to raise the status of women, support their legitimacy, and embrace their feminine peculiarity from a biological point of view because they are the birth and originator of the Japanese individual. In brotherly terms, the health, maturity, and wisdom of the next generation depend on the care of its mother and the support of its patron (which is the mother). These feminine gains took 30 years to be approved, so it was issued in 1986, which called "equal pay in wages and employment."

The delay in ratifying these feminist gains is attributed to the outdated standards of Japanese culture, the calcified social system, and the interest in Japanese stratification. In a sense, these obstacles were to the emergence of such changes in favour of Japanese women. This case reveals the fact that changing the interests of the old generation, which carries the standards of its time, the criteria of its social upbringing, and the controls of its inherited culture are not achieved by officials, leadership, or military police decisions, but rather it takes a long time and patience in order to witness its different temporal stage from the generation of its fathers and grandfathers. It is associated with the weakness and weakening of control and directing the old generation to the new so that the events will then make them withdraw from the path of the rising generation. Thus, it takes years which is not free of emotions, revolutions, and conflicts until the forces of the old generation are exhausted, and its status declines, to be replaced by the stardom of the new generation, full of vitality and activity. Then the non-gradual and unacceptable changes are achieved by the ageing generation.

Gender Equality Plan

The Japanese government focused on the issue of gender and equality between men and women in the last decade of the last century, specifically in 1994, when it created a department specialising in gender issues and the equality of its two poles (men and women). Then, in 1997, a decision was issued to upgrade its authority to support the status of women and their future role in the twenty-first century. This strategic plan was drawn up after defining its base in 1999, which included a series of visions to change the traditional values that restricted the position of women in society, allocated a budget to spend on their activities and involved men of high stature who had broad horizons in contemporary female affairs. This department is supported by voluntary civil organisations that have, in addition to the support of the United Nations for it. All these attempts helped women improve their decision making regarding their affairs and problems in Japanese society.

The government's support for the priorities of the plan constituted a positive event at the official and civil levels. It was directed at everything related to human rights, civil violence against women and their equality with men. It also involved training teachers in teaching the principles of these issues. This serious and official support met with the approval of world public opinion, as it found universal support for its financing, in addition to helping global women. All of this drew the attention of popular and official segments and spectra to welcome the world for their gender equality in the family, home, workplace, neighbourhood, and the local community. At the same time, these practices revealed gaps that were prevalent in the past, which were wide and persistent gaps that occurred between housewives and female workers. This is a new problem that appears on the surface of gender that was not known to gender in other societies, but rather there is sympathy, cooperation, and coordination between them.

Meanwhile, the men of Japan clarified the economic burdens of living on working women and housewives. This burden was supported by women workers in social welfare programs for the elderly and lineages (i.e., mother, father, husband, and wife), and what women do is offer tea and secretarial work to the arrogant man and with them a level primary education and initial professional experience. Therefore, in this sense, the Japanese worker was more like a maid or a maid to the man who cursed illiterate and unskilled at work. However, the major problem that Japanese society was suffering from was the great shortage of manpower, so its treatment of this problem was to open the door for foreigners to immigrate to Japan and fill this large gap in the workforce, and here the Japanese did not break the Japanese cultural taboo. That is, they did not exceed the standards of Japanese values.

Despite the fact that the decades passed since the issuance of legal legislation expressing gender equality in rights and duties in employment and payment of wages to them and their equality with men, it has not been implemented on the ground, in addition to the emergence of negative attitudes against the aspirations of women and their liberation as a negative reaction to them because these attitudes represent opposition to social norms and are not expressed. In the face of these negative attitudes and the neglect of legal legislation on equality, they remained ink on paper. One of the goals of issuing these legislations was to ignite and raise awareness of gender issues, but awareness was not achieved and was not seen in daily life, though it has not been disputed or removed. In other words, the legal legislation was not in conformity with the traditional standards of society but rather contradicted them, which reflects that the social norms have an effective force and are stronger than legal legislation because the first is imbued with the thinking, judgments, and behaviour of the Japanese for several decades, while the legal legislation is new and has not been practised by any generation. Therefore, such legislation is not taken out in the daily practices of the

Japanese, proving that customary standards are stronger than legal legislation in Japan and in every human society because the former is more deeply rooted in the conscience than legislation, and this is one of the reasons for the non-application of gender equality in Japanese society.

The Feminine, Temporary, Unstable Good (The Japanese Gender Barometer)

There is a well-established and prevalent view in the Japanese cultural belief related to the work of the female in the labour market that she represents an emergency and temporary commodity until her marriage as a fixed fact that does not represent a difficult problem, whether it is for a woman or for society because it represents a realistic behaviour in the life of Japanese society in particular in the labour market and the family, where she enters the labour market while she is single (unmarried girl) looking for a source of livelihood to earn from, but she leaves it when she gets married, so why discuss this recurring topic every day and everywhere in Japan. It is a work biography that represents a pervasive and permanent behavioural pattern as if it is a temporary non-permanent guest, so why is it considered a permanent resident on the work ground?! But the Japanese couple began to express their regret about this issue, which is caused by women leaving work after their marriage, and a married woman knows what her role as a wife and mother is who determines and legalises her work opportunities outside the home, but this issue is resolved or addressed in the interest of the home and family and outperforms the workplace. In this, the woman declares that the guillotine comes down on her neck and separates her head from her body when she gets married, meaning separating her from the labour market (this case is not only in Japanese but prevalent in all developing societies). As the

Japanese worker is restricted by the restrictions of gender-stereotyped roles, so it is found them focusing on lower types.

On the other hand, the situation of sexual segregation in the workplace is prevalent and strong, and gender equality at work does not have consideration and respect. They are not paid high wages, but rather low, which men do not desire and accept. However, in a few cases, the women are not subject to this segregation.

It is not surprising to say that there is a large wage gap between the wages of women and men, not only this but that the positions of the director of the administration are excluded from being occupied by women because employers see that they represent a disability in production, easy to obtain, ease of dismissal and dismissal, in addition to the fact that their work is expensive and not continuous. However, their work provides benefits to employers through low wages, lack of professional benefits, and marginal benefits such as permanent, full-time work. Japanese women have entered the labour market on a large scale after returning to work after the end of the period of raising their children while they are in their middle age and who focus on part-time work and low-level work commensurate with their educational attainment. Therefore, they face intolerance and prejudice against them. All of this is due to a set of reasons, namely gender intolerance, age, and status. The social situation of the family and their desire for a permanent and full-time job, but they face permanent cultural barriers that prevent them from entering the permanent labour market. The returns to work are nothing but permanent professional positions because they leave work when they marry, become pregnant or breastfeed their children, and this is a strong reason why the Japanese labour market has taken sexual segregation without challenge or relentless. [Hori. 2009. Pp. 25-30]

The cultural beliefs influence gender equality which is mirrored in the convergence of scientific and technical development with the development of society because the movement of the former is always faster than the movement of the second in its progress, which causes cultural and social backwardness, but it is possible to reduce the gap of backwardness through social awareness. In this respect, the role of the wife and the role of the mother. The first is that if her role is performed in proportion to the role of the husband, then the family will not be threatened with disintegration and dissolution, and if the role of the mother is performed in a responsible educational and social manner, then this serves the levelling of the next generation away from deviations and behavioural misdemeanours for them. However, if inherited cultural beliefs, the interests of employers and the interests of narcissistic men punished these two roles, in light of scientific and technical development, and considered them as a "temporary commodity in the labour market." This crystallises the following (in the gender barometer):

1. Dysfunction of the role of the wife.
2. Dysfunction of the role of the mother.
3. Delinquency and deviation of children.
4. Family disintegration and dissolution (abandonment, separation, divorce)
5. The high rate of spinsterhood.
6. The exploitation of the masculine by the feminine in his sexual relations.
7. The crystallisation of a gender gap that does not serve scientific and technical development.
8. The crystallisation of a professional gap that does not serve scientific and technical development.

9. The crystallisation of a wage gap that does not serve scientific and technical development.
10. Forming feminist movements rebelling against gender barriers that are exploited by opportunistic political figures, not to serve them and achieve their rights, but to use them as votes in elections for these symbols.
11. Conscious females' rebel against these calcified standards and deviate from them in an extreme way, which poses new and emerging problems that the hypocrites, flatterers and political reformers cannot control.
12. The ossification and calcification of cultural norms that are opposed to the criteria of social development and awareness of the value of women in modern life.
13. Women become social and cultural victims of politically reformist, personal narcissistic and culturally backward men, as well as from inherited cultural norms, patriarchal domination, and employers.

As for how to address this dilemma between (family and work), it is done through the government's intervention in terms of social and health security by aiding the wife and mother who left her job because of these two legitimate roles through which she provides many humanitarian and social services that enrich the present and future generation. That is, for her generation and the generation of her children, she serves the interests of the family and society and does not make the material influence imposed by employers on the future of the next generation, on family upbringing, and on not disintegrating the family. Therefore, for a healthy society free of social diseases such as (divorce, desertion, delinquency, crime, addiction to drugs and alcohol, school dropout, early child labour, prostitution, beggary, family disintegration) both sexes shall be equal in their rights and duties, and not intolerance to any of them. It must be done away from inherited cultural influences and patriarchal authority (Patriarch) in order to ensure that the behaviour of the next generation is levelled. These accumulated principles were formulated by the interests of reformers and cultural standards set by generations that prevailed and then died in guiding the behaviour of neighbourhoods in subsequent generations. Therefore, the planning for the prosperity of the coming future generations has to start in the present life and not be subject to the constraints of the past because it is not appropriate and is not dependent on the changing and developing reality far from the past.

Marriage and the Family (Gender Incubator)

It was said in the past, and what was known about the Japanese feminine, that her feet are programmed to walk towards and enter the house and not leave it, and that there is a strong attraction that pulls her towards it, and this attraction works together with family life to attract women. This is the reality of the Japanese feminine in most parts of the country. Since the girl is brought up from a young age to acquire family and home values as if she will work at home throughout her life, she is carefully taught as if she will be subject to a severe and careful selection. She also learns these standards in school and the family together because society wants her to be a successful housewife throughout her life. When this situation is compared with women in other societies, an anomaly in the labour market can be found. However, with the progress that happened in Japanese society, the method of her upbringing made her better than what she was before, and her sexual fertility in procreation also decreased.

The Japanese feminine was able to control her sexual fertility to the lowest level if her condition was compared with the fertility of women in the countries of the world. This Japanese feminist ability confirms that the educated feminine can control the number of children she has and takes care of her home affairs and taking care of her children at the same time. However, Japanese cultural beliefs focus on or centre around an initiatory goal above all, which is that the mother's concerns are primarily about raising her children. In a sense, the goal of Japanese social culture is to take responsibility for the role of motherhood that constitutes and represents the public image of the social and personal identity of a Japanese mother. In other words, Japanese social culture is concerned with the role of the mother first, then the role of the wife, and then the role of the job in the profession. This is the periodic gradation of the Japanese mother in her personal identity. If the mother works outside the home and has children, her mother helps her and takes care of her daughter's children while she works. That is, she does not give up her maternal and marital role, but she can give up her work if her role as a mother or wife requires her family before her work.

As the population shifts affect one way or another marriage and the family in Japan, in addition to the effect of the minimum sexual fertility rate (i.e., having children), where Japan has a high rate of elderly people (i.e., life expectancy with the longevity of the individual) and in 2030, Japan will have the highest rate of the elderly in the world aged 85 years and over. And those Japanese women now do not want to marry early for their age, but to marry early from their work, but to marry later than their age at the same time. If they marry, they do not give birth immediately after marriage but rather postpone it for a while and prefer to go to university studies than marry and have children because a university degree gives them more job opportunities in clerical, engineering, medical or bureaucratic professional work.

Therefore, it can be concluded from the foregoing that the contemporary Japanese feminine is subject to two strong influences in her life, namely: an inherited cultural influence that cannot be overridden: the interest in raising her children before her interest in her husband because her culture looks at the future of the next generation at the hands of a full-time mother.

As for the second influence, she is subject to the requirements of the new era in working outside the home, which requires university studies in order to be able to work in modern and technical professional jobs.

The pressures of these two influences on the Japanese feminine resulted in the following:
a. The delay in the age of her marriage.
b. Delaying the birth of children.
c. An increase in the life expectancy of her
d. Her preference for university studies over her desire to marry and have children.

All of this led to a reduction in the size of the family, her fertility and increased life expectancy. It is a positive response that serves the position and role of the feminine in the family and society, and it is not subject to traditional influences that hinder her development and make her responsive to such traditional inherited norms and values. In total, it is a healthy condition for her.

Therefore, the delay in the age of marriage for Japanese females leads to and produces large numbers of male bachelors. In Tokyo, for example, 40% of men in their thirties who are unmarried, live with their parents, have a college degree, work full time, prefer being single and parasitic on their parents' life and livelihood. There is a fact about these men that although men are not expected to have the necessary civic skills (such as manual labour) to live on their labours, they would rather remain that way than women, knowing that the Japanese view these men with contempt because they represent dependency, laziness, and like parasitises. In the old decades, the Japanese husband worked all his life in one job full time at a rate of 10-14 hours per day, but this kind of work has disappeared and was replaced by the modern man who is keen to live outside the limits of the traditional job and traditional marriage (parents choose a wife for him). He became involved in household chores to help his wife, in contrast to the old husband, who was nicknamed the "salaryman" [Tsuya etal. 2005.P.174]

It is important to point out that there are contradictions in the role of women within the Japanese family. However, the Second World War removed many laws that challenged the efficiency of women, as their position was low in the family and lacked influence, and their role was limited to family hardship and toil, carrying the service of the husband and children and the mother of the husband, and being obedient and submissive to them. This is what the Japanese social culture was like before World War II, but then it became effective and unlimited independence, and her status and role were liberated, such as:

a. Her consent to her husband.
b. The consent of both parties upon divorce.
c. She receives equal rights upon divorce.

This is what is new in the gender barometer after the II World War.

No doubt that Japanese woman is adept and skilled in housekeeping and maternity care. But nonetheless:

a. Dominated by a man.
b. And her social consideration is low.

c. Her influence, power and privileges are few when compared with men.

d. But women as a group do not have influential power in society because they are isolated and feel an inferiority complex.

e. As an individual, she has an influential position within her family and is considered a decision-maker by her family members.

f. She is active in building her marital and maternal identity.

[Liddle and Nakajima. 2000. p. 22]

Japanese Motherhood

Nothing is superior to the sanctity of a Japanese mother by her children and her mother because she originated from childhood caring for and caring for children (with her sisters or relatives), so she (the mother) sacrifices for her venerable and venerated family and her children. In Japanese culture, the child is seen as a sacred creature because everyone who takes care of him is revered and respected. When comparing Japanese childhood with American, the former is more dependent and less independent than the American child, and the more the child is dependent on his mother, the more the mother becomes a necessary and inherent creature for him. This is for the children and their mothers. As for the husband, he is also cared for by the wife as if he were one of her children. As for the patriarchal authority (patriarchy), it is present outside the house and the family, where there is a system of regulating domestic work that the husband and wife share in doing because if the husband manages the house, he will deprive his wife of maternal authority. Therefore, both of them share the affairs of managing the house and the husband work outside the house and earns money for the family while the wife is responsible for

612

managing the family budget, domestic affairs, and the husband's authority lies in paying the family bills. [Notter. 2002. p. 224]

Before moving on from the Japanese gender, a picture of the Japanese feminine from its perspective is presented. Its image can be classified into two types. The first includes periodic family-maternal behaviours that reflect:

a. Those that respect and value family life and give it high family and social consideration.

b. Do not think about divorce, even if her marital life becomes bad, miserable, and incompatible with her husband.

c. She is proud of her family role when she makes her decisions regarding financial spending and planning the family budget.

d. He realised that she is better than the Japanese mother who lived in the sixth decade of the last century in her independence and personality, but she does not reach equality between her and her husband in terms of rights and duties.

e. She works outside the home until the birth of her first child and then returns to work again after her child enters secondary school.

f. She sees herself as a respectable housewife, enjoying a position characterised by a good wife and a wise mother.

The second image of the Japanese woman involves the young woman yearning for personal and financial independence and choosing her own husband through mutual romantic love rather than the choice of parents. However, this love is not easy to choose and find because after graduating from university, they enter the labour market that separates the sexes, and in the face of this obstacle, the girl postpones her marriage until she chooses a person whom she is proud of financially, professionally, and personally. In front of this picture, the Japanese man sees that this girl does not possess feminine vitality and is not worthy of a Japanese man because he wants to marry a housewife. At the same time, the woman wants to marry a man who recognises gender equality and is qualified for marriage.

In summary, it can be stated that the Japanese gender is still in its embryonic stage, expressed verbally and vocally. It is called out and chanted not because it is faced with a fanatical challenge from customary, ceremonial, and cultural distinctions where cultural norms still control the behaviour of men and women in the workplace and wages. Therefore, the international feminist movements worked to support and strengthen the Japanese feminist movement in order to liberate Japanese women from the grip of the inherited culture and the tyranny and domination of men over them. She has now become a temporary and non-permanent commodity in the labour market that is needed when the market lacks male labour, and they are dispensed with when the market is hit by economic crises and men's unemployment.

D. PATRIOTIC SACRIFICED WOMEN, THE INDIAN GENDER, TO MAKE HER A NATIONAL SYMBOL

When the Indian society is studied, the challenges and threats to its economic and political stability cannot be overpassed. The challenge lies in its population size of more than one billion and three hundred million people (the second population size in the world comes after China), which represents an incompatible lightning strike linked to food, housing, unemployment, and economic classes (between the poor and the rich). Indians often look at their demographic, social, economic and health problems and attribute them to the heterogeneity of the religious, ethnic, and cultural groups of their society, but they have forgotten or ignored that the woman can have a large share in solving their problems and she can be relied upon in their planning.

Religious and Political Heritage (The Gender Incubator)

There is a similarity between Western societies and Indian societies historically and religiously. It includes an inconsistent contradiction in the role of the goddess in the female religion and her precarious economic role in the pre-ransom stage (a Hindu philosophical system based on redemption for the indigenous Ceylon 2500-300 BC) that displays a high level of social consideration for women coupled with technological change, which excludes women. This was what was prevalent among the Hindus, but it gradually became extinct and fragmented, so the woman was turned into semi-movable baggage capable of settlement when the religion had a foothold other than the religious institution.

But by the beginning of the first century AD, the power in India was decentralised, and every state or territory started to govern itself. The supreme and influential Hindu sect in the lives of the Indians was the Brahmin sect, which had a very strong sectarian, political and economic influence to the point that only they translated the ancient laws of India, which are the Manu laws that prevailed in India. These laws made women completely dependent on the man (husband, father, son). Not only that, but the Manu law prohibited the remarriage of a widow after her husband's death and degraded her status, calling for her to be expelled from society or burned. Moreover, they legislated the preference of men over women and made them below the status of men. They also promoted and safeguarded the interests of the ruling Brahmin sect. [Mitter. 1991. p. 87]

Social Reform Movement (The Gender Barometer)

It was only in the nineteenth century that a new reform movement emerged in its ideas about women, such as the Glaring movement, which attacked and criticised the marriage of minors, the pattern of their rights to property, their withholding and segregation, and the sad and depressing conditions experienced by the widow. But the reformists were more successful when they took into consideration the religious prohibitions and customs responsible for the conditions of women in terms of education and removal of illiteracy, which pushed her towards reading and writing and made her a wife who understood her role and an ideal mother and reduced the pressures of family life affecting women. But not all the women of India were included in the reform movement. Rather, the village women and the women of the lower sect were not included in the movement and did not take care of them. Divorced, widowed, and single women remained in an unenviable position due to the lack of a source of livelihood provided by a man who takes care of them and spends on them, and at the same time, she cannot afford it. She works outside the home and gets paid because of the cultural traditions of women, their marriage and the patriarchal system in India, combined with the extended family imposing huge economic burdens and family troubles on them.

Gandhi and Nehru (The Gender Motivator)

Mahatma Gandhi had focused on the role of women in independence and social justice, based on their importance in liberating society and giving them a shining national

616

consideration in opposition political movements and groups in order to play a vital role outside the home and in national and political affairs in particular when Jawaharlal Nehru came who supported Gandhi. In this vision, he was the first Indian Prime Minister after independence, granting women their rights to inherit, divorce and vote in elections. On the other hand, the women's liberation movement existed 30 years before independence, but it had a weak impact on gender equality. This is due to pressures and opposition from British colonialism and the Indian national presence, who were supporting women verbally and not in action and deed, only when they needed to support their interests and not the interests of women. Then there was the Patriarchal system that supported her inequality with men. All of which made the Indian woman the victim of factional conflicts with which she had nothing to do, so she did not feel any change in her daily life. However, Nehru worked to equalise it after independence, and when (Andrea Gandhi) came and occupied the position of Prime Minister in 1966, she was one of the supporters and pillars of the (Nehru) movement, and she worked in a smart way to make the Mother of India a national symbol and one of the traditions of India. In other words, (Andrea Gandhi) granted Indian women a privileged position inspired by the Indian traditions of the mother of India in the new era. This grant lasted for fifteen years, that is, until she was assassinated by one of her guards in 1984.

Andrea Gandhi was characterised by her intelligence on the issue of equal rights for women and men (gender equality), stemming from the ancient Indian heritage, which considered women as the mother of India, the giver and sacrifice for the sake of her family, society and country. She imbued the role of contemporary Indian women with this national idea to raise her status, which was obliterated by

British colonial control, the Patriarchal system, and the interests of the Indian private groupings. The main arteries that liberated her according to the vision and decision of (Nehru) were granting her the inheritance right from the family, the freedom from the unjust husband's restrictions if she wanted to get rid of him, and the right to vote in elections for those who represent her in government councils.

This was the liberation rule from which Nehru started, and then his daughter (Andrea Gandhi) crowned the achievements of her father in imbuing the role of the Indian woman by attaching her to a traditional symbol in the Indian heritage which is the Mother of India. Mahatma Gandhi, however, was an outstanding charismatic leader as he granted women equality with the man in all religious sects, areas, and regions throughout India and let her participate in political opposition movements and leadership roles in them with active involvement.

Note here that the liberation of Indian women came from national leaders who wanted to advance their society through national elements equal in their rights and duties, namely (women and men) and not only men. Because of their noble belief, they were able to change women's positions and activate their roles outside the home in politics, the economy, and their legal rights in the family. As for women's movements, they alone are unable to achieve women's rights in society because the interests of men conflict with their interests, so they need charismatic leadership positions to help them achieve equality in rights and duties, and this is what happened with the gender of Russia and China during the rule of (Mao) and Russia during the rule of (Lenin) and India by (Gandhi) effect.

The Gender Gap in the Human Development (The Gender Barometer)

In order to clarify the gender gap, we rely on the data on human development in Indian society. As there are 50% of educated Indian females when compared with 75% of educated males, among which 20% of boys are continuing their secondary education. These educated ratios translate the use of women in paid work, especially when comparing them with the huge numbers of unskilled women in Indian work since most of them work in agricultural fields and the skilled of them - the minority - work in small factories. However, there is an expansion in the employment of women in general, but this does not affect the reduction in the number of unskilled employees, as there are informal jobs in which women work. The Department of Human Development in the United Nations has three areas to measure women's achievements: the health department, the education department, and the employment department. Through these areas, India was included in the list of poor countries because it is ranked 128 out of 177 countries.

There is no point in referring to some demographic facts related to the gender gap and human development, such as the high mortality rate and the low life expectancy in some regions of India, despite the efforts made in community development. This case is similar to the Chinese case in this regard. As the birth rate of males is more than females, especially since Indians prefer males to females, and this often helps to raise the death rate for females more than males due to poverty, which affects the nutrition of children, causing neglect of female care, which in turn affects their lack of continued survival. Life is caused by the mother's interest in her favourite male at birth. This case explains the high dowry of the girl upon marriage, which constitutes a sharp class hierarchy and a socio-financial mechanism of social mobility that men use to influence women and drain their rights in order to reach a higher social status. The dependence of the dowry on the girl and the preference of the male over her greatly affects the female mortality rate.

The existence of influences that are reflected in cultural beliefs has exerted force on the wife in increasing childbearing and the husband's right to have sexual intercourse with his wife. Then the wife's ignorance in not using contraceptives, as a quarter of the wives are ignorant, not only that, but most of them do not know the duration or time period between births. All this leads to high mortality at birth, which is followed by the death of the newborn, all of which negatively affect the failure of family planning and the desire to reduce the number of children.

Also, one of the reasons for the high death rate in women in India is AIDS (acquired immune deficiency syndrome), as it is infected faster than men, and it is prevalent in rural areas and among religious sects, where many of them have not heard of AIDS, and others are more ignorant of it and are not aware of it. They had not seen their husbands use condoms. The infected woman, in fact, has been infected by her husband, but she cannot escape from the request for sex by him, as she is forced to submit to intercourse because he is the head of the family and the supreme authority. Rather, even her knowledge of AIDS does not diminish the inevitability of the Indian wife. As in this case, she either submits to her husband and earns a living, or she dies of AIDS or starvation if her husband divorces her if she opposes sex with him. This is her destiny. [Roy. 1994. p. 22]

Gender (Equality of the Sexes) In the Eyes of the Indians

Non-governmental organisations are interested in the movement for gender equality (men and women). They are highly active in drawing the attention of government institutions officials to the need of raising the status of an Indian woman to help her in eliminating the negative side effects which are produced by the economic restrictions applied on poor women and those who drowned in the sea of poverty.

This Indian feminist movement became known among the segments and classes of Indian society and civil society, and the public awareness of the domestic violence practised on her by men. It attracted their attention to the disparity in power that exists between men and women rather than its call for the liberation of women in their families. These movements closely monitored the unjust laws issued to women in public life. In the face of this call issued by non-governmental feminist movements, the government proposed a five-year plan (implementation within five years) in which the following feminist aspirations would be achieved:

1. Addressing the high rate of women's death.
2. Eliminating the illiteracy of women through their education.
3. Applying health awareness and combining modern treatment with traditional treatment in a way that is acceptable to the rural family.
4. Disseminate medical education to combat AIDS and introduce its dangers in order to control it by raising women's awareness, attention, and attraction.

The importance of accessing the Indian gender issue makes it possible to address its diverse activities in the social, pastoral, and political fields to raise awareness of poor, marginalised and excluded women from their productive work in order to improve their energies by self-reliance, support the Indian family that owns workshops and activate its role in the local community. This is on the internal level, but on the external level (outside India), its activity is extremely limited. It is worth noting in this context that the impact of the gender equality movement had an impact on poor women, but it could not pull women away from sectarian influences and cultural restrictions as activists were doing at the beginning of the twentieth century against British colonial control. [Lindsey. 2011. Pp. 149 - 153]

Comment and Follow Up

In order to understand this abundance of knowledge about this virgin subject in the field of sociology in several different societies in sizes, development, culture, sects, and systems, it is required to reveal the first human half (the woman) in every society because she bears double the burdens than the other half in human society (the man).

It is preferred to go back to the roots of the Indian restrictions on women in making them subordinate and dependent on men, not because of their weakness, but to look at them as secondary creatures in existence. It started with the old Manu laws, which stipulated that the woman should be dependent on the man and prohibited widows from marrying for the second time after the death of her husband. These laws remained in control of women for centuries until the nineteenth century. The first reform movement on women emerged that did not go beyond the boundaries of religious sects and cultural restrictions in restricting women's freedom and legitimate rights but was limited to reading and writing and raising awareness of their family role. The activity of this movement was limited only to urban and not rural areas for a number of reasons, including the beginning of its activity in light of antiquated customary and sectarian restrictions and controls rooted in the life of society. The sectarian and cultural restrictions of Indian women prior to political independence are attributed to British colonialism as per the following points:

1. A woman is not entitled to work for a wage outside her home.
2. The laws of Mano that restrict her freedom and legitimate rights.
3. Marriage to underage girls.
4. Not to marry a divorced woman and a widow for the second time.
5. Subject to the authority of the Patriarch.
6. Her dependence on the man in every action she takes.
7. She was a victim of factional struggles between Indian groups.
8. The high death rate for females.
9. Decreased life expectancy for females.
10. The Indian society's preference for a male over a female.
11. Ignorance of the wife about sexual education and sexual health.
12. The number of people infected with AIDS is higher in women than in men.
13. The illiteracy rate is higher for women than for men.

But 30 years before India's independence from British colonialism, the need to use the woman as a human element in confronting colonialism and liberating her country from it arose. This was the beginning of the need for her as a national element. But the fact and confirmed in making the biological differences between men and women conform to the gender differences are the following:

1. The ancient laws of Manu.
2. The power of the patriarchal.
3. Religious sectarian restrictions.
4. Cultural controls - ethnic inherited and traditional.
5. British colonial domination.
6. Poverty, unemployment, and illiteracy.

But with the advent of the reform movement (Glaring) at the beginning of the nineteenth century, the following reforms were proposed:

a. Opposition to forcing underage girls to marry.
b. Opposition to isolating women from society.
c. Demanding her education and removal of illiteracy.

   Then came independence at the hands of its leaders (Gandhi) and (Nehru), who worked to transform women into a national symbol that helped to resurrect society from its backwardness, poverty, ignorance, sectarian, and sexual bias, so they made the following reforms:

d. Freeing her from the unjust restrictions of inheritance, strict divorce, and fanatic and extremist electoral voting.
e. Linking women to the Indian cultural symbol (Mother India), which holds the highest national, political, and cultural status.
f. Addressing the high rate of women's death.
g. Fighting illiteracy among women.
h. Health awareness against AIDS.

So, why women were restricted? And who took her hand and broke her chains? What is the benefit of liberating her? Without a doubt, the woman has a strength no less than the physical strength of a man and intelligence less than a man, but her biological nature, which she carries out during pregnancy, breastfeeding and upbringing, is what occupied her in competing with men in earning a livelihood. This seems to be what made her focus more on what she produces and what surrounds her in her place of residence before anything else. This is a biological effect, but it is not a biological constraint. It is rather a biological advantage that men do not have, which gives and allows women the structural and functional privacy to build the smallest human-social cell in the emergence of society. The man is an auxiliary element and a component in this building and not functional because his job is outside the home.

On the other hand, her restrictions came from religious sects that focused on sectarian interests. They needed the woman to increase the number of their human elements by procreation and hence placed strict restrictions on her to deliver this objective and also to teach her children the teachings of the sect. At the same time, this is an acknowledgement that her upbringing work cannot be carried out by the man. Despite all this, she was lucky that she got who took her hand and partially liberated her from the restrictions that prevented her from her legitimate rights after the oppression she suffered. She was the oppressed and the submissive element, which was entrapped by more than one restriction and barrier by the mass and not by an individual, such as (sectarian, religious, cultural, social, and patriarchal restrictions). She is embedded in the slavery of man, the culture of his society, his religious sect, and his political system.

However, with her learning to read and write, the effects of technological progress and her civilisational friction, the man leaving some of his handiwork and his need for it in some of his handicrafts, and his unemployment with the financial and economic influences and international political changes, it has fuelled women's awareness of her condition and her periodic, positional, productive, and humanitarian situation. Here came the need for national leaders (not partisan, sectarian, or regional) in need of half of society in order to awaken her from her slumber and calcify her vitality, so they sought help from this neglected and forgotten half. Inheritance, Divorce and Electoral Voting, this liberation trinity makes her more aware of her financial, family, and political freedom. This is what both Gandhi and Nehru demanded. Then Andrea came and placed the fourth pillar on upgrading her national position, which she called (Mother of India), which marked her position with the purest and most sacred and authentic national and heritage characteristic.

The objective of this commentary is to attest that there are tough, solid, and deeply rooted barriers in human existence that support the biological difference of women and make the gender difference conform to it, which are the following:

1. Religious sectarian teachings.
2. Sociocultural restrictions and controls.
3. Patriarchal authority.
4. Political interests.
5. Intolerance and categorical prejudice.
6. Ignorance of health and education.
7. British colonialism.

Finally, the detractors of the intractable barriers are the following:

a) National leaders, not sectarian or partisan leaders.
b) The professional and economic need for manpower.
c) Perseverance and feminist competition for men in the political and scientific fields.
d) Secularism and objectivity.
e) National liberation.

E. **WISE IN INDONESIAN GENDER**

The title reflects the position of women in Indonesian society, which made her come out of her subjugation, servitude and domination by the patriarchal system and the culture of society, religion, and government. This was achieved by the formation of a pressure group on the government after Suharto's rule representing her strength throughout the country to remove many of the policing and arbitrary governmental and professional family practices. She worked with calmness, sobriety and decency without going beyond the religious limits or the domination of the government on the whole. So, she got support in the exercise of her liberation from their shackles, and thus she deserved to be called "wise" after she was oppressed and subservient to the custom and law.

Indonesian society is characterised by more distinctive features than others because it includes an ethnonational diversity of varying foundations that reflects a complex social structure. It includes inherited and rooted ethnic divisions in the history of its existence, which makes the Indonesian feminine does not descend from a single origin or root. In addition to the existence of an economic and occupational class division that identifies with him. These affiliations are:

1. The elite and the middle class, which consist of property owners, wealth, and social and economic influence.

2. The working class, which includes workers in agricultural fields, street vendors and markets, and workers in home workshops, including handicrafts and commodity sales.

As for the size of the females in the Indonesian population pyramid, it is estimated at 85 million women, 20 million of whom belong to the elite and the middle class, and

65 million women are from the poor, and they represent the second group in Indonesian society that includes the wife, mother, and daughter, and they are in control of the market trade. They differ from Muslim women in Islamic countries such as Iran, Saudi Arabia and others due to their influence on ethnic-national diversity, which makes them different from the Muslim gender class in Arab and non-Arab countries. The following table shows the gender differences in Indonesian society to illustrate this fact.

The table on indicators of gender differences in Indonesian society.

Women in public life: The percentage of women in government institutions is 11.1%

Education in 2005	
For women	Reached school years with an average of 6.5.
	The illiteracy rate in the 15-24 age group is 4.9%
For man	Reached school years with an average 7.6.
	Participation in middle school reached 59%

Illiteracy in 2000	
For women	The adult illiteracy rate is 17.9%.
	The illiteracy rate in the 15-24 age group is 4.9%
	The illiterate rate over the age of 25 is 33.5%
For man	The adult illiteracy rate is 8.1%.
	The illiteracy rate among them in the 15-24 age group is 2.6%
	The illiteracy rate of those over 25 years old is 15.8%

Work 2002	
For women	The adult female workers are 51%.
	Her participation in the workforce is 37.5%
	Distribution according to types of work:
	Wages and salaries 28.3%
	Workers in their own business 29%
	Agricultural and domestic 37%
	The female managers is 18%.
	The unemployment rate is 12%.
For man	The percentage of working men is 84%
	Distribution of men by types of work:
	Wages and salaries 33%
	Self-employed workers 53%
	Agricultural workers in their homes 8%
	The unemployment rate is 8%.

This table was taken from the Society and Culture resource for authors Howitt, Julian. 2009. P. 313

Through the four criteria in the table, it became clear that the rights of Indonesian women are much less than the rights of men. It seems that women did not fulfil their role as an individual as it was allowed men to achieve their roles. In education, there is a wide gap between them. As for illiteracy, the rate of illiteracy among women is double that of men, and the situation at work is similar. This is mainly due to the opportunities for work available for women being much less than those available for men. Also, her participation in government institutions is minimal, meaning that Indonesian gender is similar, if not identical, to the biological sex differences between them. The preference of men over women in education and work is clear and gives an indication that the Indonesian social culture plays a major role in the sexual differentiation between them, as well as religion, both of which emphasise the patriarchal (male) authority.

629

Factors Affecting Gender Differences (Gender Barometer)

The intention of this title is to show how gender differences are crystallised and nurtured in Indonesian society, which is subject to many powerful influences such as ethnic diversity, education, economy, religion, and government.

In the field of ethnocultural diversity, the Indonesian acquires the ethnicity that presents to him what is expected of him by the Indonesian society. Not only this, but it also tells him what his specific limits (for both males and females) are. As for the educational factor, all Indonesian children up to the age of 15 are obliged and committed to going to formal government education. It teaches them the concept that the best and most appropriate place for a girl is home. At the same time, it teaches the girl the mechanisms that can be used to challenge traditional patterns and the needs that can be fulfilled by not yielding to traditional inherited behavioural patterns and habits. The economic factor, however, such as globalisation, have affected the Indonesian woman greatly, as she became involved in factories for the garment industry and trans-oceanic projects, but this involvement and prevention were at the mercy of the global economic crises as it happened in 1997, which affected her and destroyed the Indonesian economy. On the other hand, the field of religious fundamentalists has affected women's society, their status in the family, marriage, education, and ways for them to work outside the home. However, the government's political and legal programs' effect is manifested in women's participation in education, work and society, which pushed them toward these areas.

The sexual gender is, therefore, imprinted with ethnocultural, educational, economic, and religious stamps that make it in their personal patterns, inclinations, tastes, beliefs, feelings, behaviour and thinking. The biological difference has nothing to do with this gender normalisation because, as was indicated at the beginning, the diversity of the Indonesian society in cultural races makes normalisation subject to each cultural race different from one other, all of which focus on masculine authority (patriarchate) over the female in interaction and dealing. As for the economy, it is the position of women in businesses that are not independent by themselves. All these variables made the Indonesian woman subservient to the man and not to the biological difference.

United Nations Council is aware of the mistreatment of Indonesian women and their lack of protection in government legislation. The Indonesian government was informed in 1998 by the UN about the following information and data:

1. Abusive and oppressive cultural attitudes and tendencies to stereotypical roles of mother and housewife.
2. All government legislation, policies and programs reinforce the gender stereotype that prefers men to women.
3. The prevalence of violence against women and the lack of documentation in government records (security, police, and justice).
4. Severe harassment of some religions.
5. The high rate of low wages and unskilled work among women.
6. Lack of women's participation in public life. (These are gender motives)

In 2007, the Amnesty International Committee revealed a report on the exploitation and abuse of Indonesian women. It covered their involvement in domestic service work, the sexual, physical and verbal violence practised in the home on them, and not reporting to the police. These practices are rarely appearing before the eyes of the people, but even within the walls of the house where violence and abuse take place in the shadows, it is seldom investigated even if they are reported, particularly if the worker is dismissed from her job. Even in 2003, a new law was issued, but it did not protect the civil rights of the working woman, and neither it obtain her rights from the abuser and the aggressor, nor did it specify her working hours and even did not do justice to her appropriate wage for a reasonable and comfortable living.

Cultural Attitude (Gender Barometer)

Being civilised in Indonesian society brings a lot of options and opportunities for elite women and middle-class women. In the past, the life of the elite was devoted to the family and the home, i.e., motherhood, the requirements of married life, but now, after the financial and educational gains that have occurred in Indonesian society, she has many opportunities for the participation of men and works in influential positions that have social consideration, and the situation is similar with middle-class women, if not less. It's a simple thing. As for the workers in the rural agricultural fields who represent the lower class, their chances of obtaining influential and highly regarded positions are exceedingly small because their daily requirements are predetermined in specific traditional occupations, and they are not allowed to ask for other responsibilities because their main responsibilities are confined to the home and family. Many Muslim women interpret their lives as being determined by the nasibe, i.e., the destiny determined for them by God the Creator, so none of them can discuss their lot.

The Government's Position on its Development Policies and Programs (Gender Barometer)

In the period between 1966 - 1998, during the rule of (Suharto), who established an integrated development program in the social, economic, and demographic fields that served the interests of women by offering many job opportunities and providing medical, health, educational and other services to them. It was considered the "symbol of the mother", whose mission was to work on the cohesion of family members and preserve its ties and traditional customs, meaning that women were the highest goal in the plan (Suharto). However, this plan worked to freeze many of the feminist movements that were demanding equality with men and mobilising the Indonesian street. For example, there was an extremist feminist organisation called (Jerwani), which was banned, and then there was an organisation that included the wives of state employees. Then the marriage law was issued in 1974, which granted women an alternative right to Islamic law, which granted the Muslim man dominance over them. Two decades ago, middle-class women got support from the International Conference on Women's Rights, which became a pressure paper on the government to create a special ministry for women's affairs. After that, women got the chair of the government presidency, and a feminist movement interested in family affairs emerged to help the government to establish development plans such as population regulation by determining the number of children in each family in order to serve the economy of the family and the nation. It provided free contraceptives for rural women. However, these decisions were criticised and accused the government exploited the mother in carrying out her projects and not for the love of the mother!!! In this regard, women's associations demanded to educate the mother about the side effects when using this technique and the drug while guiding her on how to treat its effects.

So, there are government attempts to develop the mother before the daughter and the family above all, whether the goal is to reduce the population size or health education. It is not government exploitation of women as much as it is an official and collective awareness necessary for society, especially among villagers and illiterate women. This is positive and better than leaving the mother without important guidance and assistance, granting her the title (symbol of the mother) and reminding her to preserve the cohesion of the family and its traditional customs.

Wife's Power (Gender Incubator)

One of the most influential feminist groups in the world is the Indonesian group, which includes the wives of civil servants who work behind the scenes. It has an influential power because of its mandatory membership and a wide network of contacts. This group is called (the Power of the Group), which in Indonesian culture means the duty of a woman because she exerts pressure on the decisions of the government as a lobby group with regard to government employees (i.e., marrying more than one wife at the same time, which is permissible in Islam), that is, not appointing a man married to more than one wife in a government institution. The vitality and position of the members of this group are linked to the status and the positions of their husbands who work in the private and public sectors. As for the number of members of this group, it exceeds 6 million wives. Its activity has an effective influence on the government's policy for its promotion in local communities throughout Indonesia and has influence outside it when there are Indonesian communities working in other countries. It is worth mentioning that the members of this group do not describe themselves as feminine but rather as active and energetic who are able to exercise their influence indirectly by describing the influence of wives as representing the old model that prevailed in Indonesian society, which was participating in the labour market. In fact, this group has a great resonance throughout the country. On November 27, 2007, the wife of the Indonesian Prime Minister, Madame Ani Bambang Yudhoyono, gave a speech at the International Conference on the Destruction of Earth's Heat (Conference on Climate Change). On the Indonesian woman, through her praise and praise for giving a group the influence of the wife and the rest of the women's groups, she said, "We know that women have natural characteristics in their own person, such as nurturing, care and bringing up, and that we do not like to cut trees, but rather we prefer planting them in the gardens of our homes next to flowers and trees, and if there is no garden in our house, we must try to replace it, such as pinecones, pots or cans. These natural characteristics are represented by the Indonesian woman, whose population is about 115 million women. I believe most in saving the earth from global climate change and global warming.

It is inferred from the foregoing that this group really aims to raise the level of Indonesian women, in particular the wife. They want to get her rid of family burdens by rationalising childbearing and health care for her. They also want to prove her strength through her husband, who works outside the government institution. Her voice should be heard and not subject to the authority of men. She demanded that polygamy should not be adopted and applied to those who want to work in state institutions, and she did not demand its abolition entirely out of respect for Islamic religious teachings. The beautiful thing about this group is that it includes the wives of workers in service work, not the government, out of respect for government institutions as a first step to prevent polygamy and to know the society's reactions towards this partial ban. It is indeed a group that expresses and represents the power of wives, but not all wives of Indonesian husbands.

Violence Against Women (As a Gender Motivator)

The violence against Indonesian women was practised publicly and terrifyingly. In the pre-independence period, the army and military militia were carrying out horrific acts of rape, displacement, and treachery of women in East Timor and West Papua. A non-governmental organisation called Fokupors has over 2,000 cases of violence against women in Balut, East Timor.

Moreover, a woman who declares or publishes about violence practised by a member of her family (her husband, brother, or father) is considered a disgrace for her because it is part of the family's secrets that cannot be disclosed publicly according to Indonesian Cultural Taboos.

The Influence of Religion on The Indonesian Wife: she is required, according to the teachings of the Islamic religion, to obey her husband and abide by his instructions. But what is the degree of her obedience to him? It depends on the degree of his commitment to the teachings of religion and belief. The wife who represents IBU has a strong influence on the family environment and its affairs and controls the family budget, influencing the husband's decision-making. However, the authority of the conservative husband over the wife is represented by his consent when the wife wants to obtain official documents such as a passport or

636

needs his permission to work outside the house at night, to perform an abortion or birth control and use its means. Nevertheless, the Islamic religion recommends that the husband who marries more than one wife establish justice and equality emotionally, financially, and socially, and not trade-offs between them, and if he cannot, then one should suffice. However, in 1983, the government issued a law prohibiting the marriage of government officials to more than one wife in order to prevent the squandering of family income on more than one family. This is a justification for the prohibition and prevention of polygamy.

Woman's Position on The Professional Level - Work: it reflects the Indonesian women who have secondary education in the agricultural fields. Their traditional role has begun to change due to the agricultural use of modern machines. However, half of them aspire to work in the cities, which made these women gradually reduce their work in the agricultural fields. But there is another large category of families represented in local trade, such as selling food, fruits, vegetables, and handicrafts produced in their areas, which they sell in small kiosks inside their residential areas, but this type of work is also considered a low social position.

Job opportunities are available for women who are looking for work within cities. Mainly, they work in workshops and factories of mass production, such as sewing clothes, making shoes, preparing some food, or manufacturing electrical machines, which need low educational attainment and initial experience. However, most of the female workers in these businesses are young and leave their job if they get married or have children. Therefore, their work is temporary according to a contract rather than permanent, and it is not guaranteed as they can be dispensed with at any time. Moreover, there are downsides to their work, such as:

1. Poor working conditions.
2. Her upgrading and promotions are scanty compared to the promotions of men.
3. She is granted few vocational training programs.
4. She does not receive strong support from the trade union.

On the role of the female in the labour union, it was noticed that she did not have any cyclical practice during the rule of (Suharto), as the union was managed and controlled by men only. After the end of the rule of (Suharto) in 1998, the Indonesian woman was able to challenge the old reality and enter the labour unions to exercise her effective role in conveying her voice to officials and to the world. She obtained leadership positions and brought many women to these unions to become new members. She was also able to exert pressure on the management of the factories and workshops for the benefit of women and their interests. On top of that, she participated in many regional and international conferences and contributed to labour negotiations and occupational strikes. All textile and shoe factories became completely occupied by women in all parts of the country, but the power and influence of working women had reached to level that they could employ their husbands and the rest of their family when they lost their jobs. As for their wages, they are paid every month and are sufficient to cover their personal and domestic needs, while they get to work overtime after their regular work to the point that they do not have enough time to attend their union meetings twice a month. The Indonesian woman achieved financial gains related to maternity and childbirth expenses and was granted leave when she had her menstruation period, along with the costs of their education outside work regarding her rights.

This is the feminine challenge to the old traditional pattern, which she worked hard to remove from her way and her professional and social mobility. As for the women of the lower class, some of them work as prostitutes in cities such as Jakarta and Surabaya, where there are 650,000 prostitutes, except for those who practice prostitution outside the country. As for middle- and upper-class women, they bring maids to the house to help them with the house cleaning, and this affects the family budget. [Howitt and Julinn. 2009. Pp. 312 – 322]

Indonesia's gender was strict in its biological, cultural, and ethnic differences in favouring men over women. But after she paid the price for the strictness of male and female differences supported by cultural, ethnic, religious, patriarchal, and political differences, she began to demand the removal of this biological strictness, especially after the demise of the (Suharto) system in 1998, which was reinforcing biological differences. The "Wife Power" group appeared, which became a pressure group on government decisions to prohibit polygamy for government employees and participating in the labour union membership. She entered factories and workshops and earned gains that were not obtained before 1998, such as additional wages at work, payment of maternity expenses, and granting her leave during menstruation. These gains were the result of her struggle against the representation of the unjust cultural, ethnic, and political customs and traditions which were instated by men and government institutions. Therefore, her struggle, insistence on change, her jostling with the man, and her competition for job opportunities in factories after being away from the agricultural fields were very fruitful. It can be said that the changing of the gender balance did not happen from the man or the conservative traditions or culture, but rather from the woman who is aware of her oppression and deprivation of her legitimate rights over which men dominate. Accordingly, she developed her society and pushed its wheel forward and brought it out of darkness into the light in addition to realising her interests and rights and reducing her duties and leaving some of them to the man who had the same interest in home affairs and raising children, because urban and industrial life is not limited to men alone, but also to women.

F.   THE LATIN GENDER - THE MOST SUBMISS-IVE AND OBEDIENT

Latin gender has a special character that shows the huge diversity that combines the environment, politics, and culture, despite the presence of common features in the characteristics of gender, which makes them not united in their rigid class structure and the spread of the Catholic religion and the Spanish and Portuguese colonial heritage. At the same time, the Latin feminine pretends to have diverse and common features that unite and separate them for now. However, this does not eliminate the clear and prominent gender gap between the feminine and the masculine Latin.

The Gender Split

The upbringing of the feminine and the masculine in Latin culture is characterised by the presence of a major joint in the concept of masculinity and femininity that is clearly seen because it is spread between the two extremes of gender, where masculinity focuses on virility, sexual boldness and domineering physical and ideological control over the feminine as well as the legitimate violence practised on it.

It is appropriate for us to point out that the spiritual Catholic religious belief reinforces the preference of the male over the female in all social institutions, as it allows the man to dominate the housewife and invoke social, economic, and sexual restrictions and other ways of living in the humiliation of the feminine. At the same time, feminine femininity requires her to glorify motherhood and bear the misery of her marriage and the cruelty of her husband towards her, and not to complain but to remain silent about what the man does towards her. These feminine traits are prevalent in all Latina feminine in their behaviour and thinking, but these religious requirements are out of the question for males in Latin America because he is transcendent and domineering over their position and social role.

But when the Spanish conquistadors came and occupied some Latin American countries such as Brazil, Costa Rica and Chile, they brought with them very ancient beliefs and visions dating back to the new world religions. Over time, women became economically dependent on men, and even efficient and skilled women with an advanced level of education received wages less than the wages the man. This condition was prevalent in Brazil, Costa Rica and Chile. In Nicaragua, women were equal to men, especially among uneducated men. There is no point in pointing out that the Spanish conquistadors degraded the status of women in the countries they invaded and occupied, making them inferior after they were equal to men, unlike the Americans. When the Americans invaded Japan in World War II, they raised the status of Japanese women, but when they invaded and occupied Iraq, they degraded the status of Iraqi women. So, it can be stated that there is serious influence by an external invader in raising or degrading the status of women in the occupied society.

The United Nations, in its conference held in Beijing - China, tried to persuade governments to review their policy regarding family planning and the issue of birth control, politically and culturally. However, Latin American governments insisted strongly on remaining bound by the decisions of the Catholic Church, which did not support the policy of birth control. In Chile, for example, the close relationship between the government and the Catholic Church, which has a significant impact on women's lives, the Chilean government has strongly disrupted the use of family planning, in contrast to Peru, which persisted in adopting a family planning policy, but it collided with the Vatican's policy of spreading birth control that the Vatican demanded. It is necessary to take a woman's opinion on this and consult her in achieving her desires regarding birth control, knowing that the Peruvian woman and society benefit from the birth control policy because its population is large, and half of them live below the poverty line and are illiterate and that the fertility of Peruvian women has reached 6.2, but the family planning policy In Peru succeeded in 1990, and the birth rate reached 4.1, but in 2008 it reached 2.4, due to the practices of women who reached hierarchical positions - powerful government, who helped and supported the birth control policy and the adoption of the family planning strategy.

However, the government of Nicaragua has considered the demands of the United Nations on birth control, health care, education, sex education, provision of services in family planning, and an emphasis on women's rights to determine their offspring when they want to have children, how many and how to get them? But at the same time (the Nicaraguan government) denounced abortions to prevent pregnancy or to reduce the size of the population. These measures did not challenge the church's policy on birth control and did not conflict with cultural norms that do not seriously challenge gender roles. Even the more conservative Chile advocated gender equality, human rights, and unfettered birth control.

It is appropriate to point out the erosion and decreasing importance of the role of Latin women in light of the effects of globalisation, as it negatively affected their work in the labour market, which prompted the Latin governments to put forward a reform program that restores women's activity in work, thus opening the doors for foreign investments, and raising the level of women by addressing her unemployment in the labour market, her poor nutrition and poor health, this treatment was prominent in Mexico and Costa Rica. [Anastaskos. 2002. p. 11]

On the other hand, the impact of globalisation on these countries has been effective on women's income and productive activity in the agricultural sector, forcing their husbands to migrate to cities in order to work there and leave their women and children in villages and countryside. This undoubtedly made the status of women more religious in addition to the influence of religion and the feudal system on them, especially in Brazil and Argentina, after five hundred years passed by European colonialism on them. Even after its independence in the nineteenth century, the rule of dictatorial regimes came over it in the twentieth century. It remained backwards in its economy and society, including the relationship between women and men, which was not equal. The influence of the global market and its fluctuations shall not be forgotten as it has negatively affected Latin societies and, in particular, women. Such fluctuation n the market was a real disaster because these societies and their regimes are not immune, culturally, and scientifically, and easy to penetrate. Therefore, the economy of these countries has eroded badly, and their foreign debts have worsened, forcing their governments to cut their aid to women and stop the agrarian reform, which undermined the status of Latin agriculture. So, the internal and external influences were catastrophic thunderbolts for the Latin woman, namely:

1. The Catholic religion.
2. The Vatican.
3. The feudal system.
4. European colonisation, which lasted 500 years.
5. National dictatorships.
6. Globalisation and its economy.
7. Fluctuations in global markets.
8. Stopping financial, health and educational aid for women by the government.

All of this weakened the position of the woman and made her be inferior to the position of the man, and her role was more active and broader than the role of the man in the family, the field, and the factory. Even though she still kneels to him following religious rituals, patriarchal, feudal, and colonial domination, and the effects of globalisation, culture and religion, which denied and did not consider all her family and economic services to the family and society.

The Latin woman was distinguished by her struggle to advance her position and role in society through the formation of feminist organisations that defend their wasted and exploited rights. After the establishment, they obtained popular support from all levels and feminist social and economic backgrounds, especially among the symbols of rural women in the Latin countryside. Not only that but they

644

were supported by international feminist organisations because they were calling for the application of democratic principles in central and southern Latin America. These demands constituted great strength and political acumen in a loud sound calling for economic and political reform and the elimination of gender intolerance. This made her more intelligent and astute in class and gender awareness. This case is not similar to the case of the Indian feminist organisation, which faced obstruction by the reform movement of the Indian peasant women, which made it perpetuate its activity and struggle in society because it found positive responses welcomed by the spectra of the Latin community.

Whenever one gets into the orbit of gender, he will find himself in harmony with current events, which are opposite to the biological difference between men and women. There is a prevalent and widespread belief among many writers and intellectuals about the lack of economic and professional independence of women and their continuing dependence on men for their livelihood, making them submissive and docile to the man in all societies and their developmental stages. However, this alone is not sufficient because there are social and cultural facts that precede the economic dependence of women on men. Namely, religious teachings such as the Catholic, Hindu, and Jewish religious faith that allow men to dominate women, freeze maternity roles, tolerate men's cruelty and harsh treatment, and not complain about them but rather keep silent. Then there is the freezing of cultural norms for the man's role as the family's breadwinner and representative of the family's name and position in society backed by the hereditary patriarchal authority.

These two pillars (religious and cultural) are used by the man to support and reinforce his superiority, tyranny and enslavement over the woman who is in harmony with her upbringing in her childhood by her family with the entitlement of these pillars (religious and cultural). In the social mirror, the more she detaches from these pillars, the lower her position in the social woman becomes. Then comes the role of her work outside the home and its kind, which is not only her desire, but the effect of her husband's need for financial assistance for the family budget, and this doubles her social, marital, domestic, and relational burdens, which exhaust her physically and mentally. This is a third economic pillar that men use to pressure women to be more submissive and compliant with him and his desires in the name of religion and culture. and family.

So why was it that men, society, social culture, and the political and economic system have not recognised these enormous sacrifices made by women? Was not this unfair to her? Ingratitude for her sacrifice? Under the pressures of these three nightmares, can the woman alone get rid of them easily? The answer is no. It needs a great power such as the United Nations and bodies defending human rights, women, democracy, combating racial intolerance, birth control and non-abortion in order to reduce the size of the population through international conferences that oblige governments to adopt these contemporary humanitarian principles and get out of the dark corridors that are not suitable for living in the era of enlightenment and the scientific renaissance. This is what happened with all Latin American countries, India and Arab countries. The challenging religious institutions such as the church and cultural heritage are not an easy matter to change or convince, but if it comes from a strong national leader who is determined to achieve a radical change in society, such as what was done by (Mao) in China, (Lenin) in the former Soviet Union and (Nehru and Gandhi) in India, all restrictions and restrains can be paralysed. Having said that, no one denies that gender equality cannot be achieved overnight. It takes decades and generations of people because it is rooted in people's lives and minds. Its change requires intelligence, acumen, and accuracy in applying modern requirements. Expecting opposition to it is a reality or fighting it is an expected thing, especially from the old generations and their owners, religious, economic, and political interests.

It is also important to emphasise the necessity of women's participation in forming free and voluntary organisations in raising women's honest awareness away from courtesies, flattery and political bidding for rulers to regain their rights in inheritance, marriage, divorce, childbearing, electoral voting, higher education, intellectual expression, professional committees, and freedom to make their decisions. It is the task of generations, minds, and owners of influential positions in society to respect the inverted upbringing of the new generation for the old and accept the other opinion. Otherwise, society is subjected to rupture in its relational fabric, disintegration in the joints of its construction patterns, generational and ethnic conflicts, whose restoration is difficult to restore, requiring its reconstruction after a renewed social and cultural revolution in its leadership and principles, expressing the spirit of the age.

G. GENDER IN THE ISLAMIC WORLD... BET-WEEN TWO VEILS

The first veil expresses national solidarity and the second one represents the suppression of Islamists. The Islamic world possesses abundant wealth, the source of which is oil, and it has pioneering development programs in reconstruct-tion, agrarian reform, huge job opportunities for foreign workers and professionals. It has an ancient and strong social culture, though the position of women is low. The women in this society suffer from patriarchal authority and Islamic interpretations issued by men and fundamentalists to separate them from the man educationally, professionally and in representation. These discrepancies reflect gender congruence with the biological differences between men and women. It can be said that there are rich material resources working on the civilised development of the country, but there is an ancient inherited culture with old standards and values that do not fit the standards of the current era and the presence of clergymen who translate or interpret the Islamic religion according to their patriarchal interests against women and without justice, contrary to the teachings of the Islamic religion and Qur'an. The Muslim woman is at the mercy of the man who exercises his authority and keeps her oppressed, deceived, marginalised, excluded and enslaved in the name of religion and cultural traditions!!!

Among the social phenomena that attract attention is the entry of the variable of social movements between men and women. This is what happened in some Islamic and Arab countries, where the social movement took the Islamic religion as an excuse to shed its rule and mislead the society, which adheres to the religion, by submitting its symbols in ruling them. They interpreted and translated Islamic teachings in a false way as a pretext to serve their authoritarian, domineering ambitions. It was exercised by the Taliban regime in Afghanistan in 1996, Khomeini in Iran in 1979, the Shiite Da'wa Party in Iraq in 2005, and the Houthis in Yemen in 2015. Their Islamization movement was expressive of their hostility to urbanisation and confronting Western culture because their movement invoked extremist Islamic fundamentalism instead of moderation and the application of idealistic ideas devoid of realism and used as a shield and weapon against Western ideas. This pragmatic and false practice had a resounding resonance in south Asia (Pakistan and Bangladesh) and in the Middle East and North Africa. These extremist movements, in their pretext and false in their calls, affected all aspects of social life in these societies, in particular women (daughter, wife and mother in her home, work and school), who became the biggest victims in the enslavement, the humiliation and the contempt by the extremist movements.

It is clear that social movements are not always working towards developing and advancing society to a broader and more affluent level. Sometimes and in particular in severe, critical, and bad conditions, a group appears and presents itself as the saviour to lift the people out of their misery and the injustice. It exploits such conditions by using the excuse of religion and claiming that it is capable of leading and reforming the way of life that the majority yearns for. In the face of this urgent social need, the group adopts the horizons of what this majority aspires to ride the wave, seizes the authority of government, and declares that it will achieve the masses' objectives. With their blatant stupidity, they rush in applying ignorant religious teachings, expressing their cognitive ignorance, narrow-mindedness, social naivety, and behavioural stupidity. Its positional extremism, citing its false claims, confronts urbanisation and antagonises

649

urbanisation, and targets, desecrates and destroys every cultural forum, a civilised legacy, free opinion, and respect for others. This is what happened to the Islamist movements in Iran, Afghanistan, Iraq, Yemen, Libya, Syria, Sudan, and the rest of the Arab countries. In the end, women were the major victims and the first target of this fundamentalist movement. Using the phrase "the true Qur'an," they were misleading Muslims because they used it as a pretext to serve their political, individual, and masculine ambitions.

Under the false pretext, the Taliban movement launched the application of Islamic law, so they used the woman as a wheel to ride in order to restore the Islamic identity by confining her to the home and exercising her role without leaving her except with the accompaniment of a Mahram. People are doomed, and if the woman does not dress modestly or she walks with a stranger (not from her family or close relatives), she will be executed in front of the people. Not only that, but she was prevented from teaching in schools and working outside the home, and if she worked, she was not paid to the extent that she was prevented from working in the hospital or as a domestic servant. Several schools for female students were burned, with beatings, executions, and harassment of female teachers who teach there. All of these inhuman and anti-Islamic practices claim that the Taliban group is applying the Islamic identity to the girl, and this is a deliberate distortion of the Islamic religion, if not ignorance of it. These practices were the biggest stain on the forehead of the Islamists because Islam does not oppose civilisation and civilisation. Was there not an Islamic civilisation in Spain (Andalusia)? Wasn't there an Abbasid civilisation? And another Umayyad? This is a deliberate distortion supported by the anti-Islamic trend and opponents of the progress and development of Islamic society.

The Islamists in Iran were not extremists at the beginning of their rule in Iran. Women were given medical and educational care in their own schools, but they remained under complete and restricted control over the tyranny of their father, husband, and brother and were obligated to wear the Islamic dress for women, which is the veil, and that her role is exercised in the family, motherhood, and marriage. However, one of the paradoxes of events is that during the days of the Shah's rule, she used to go out to public demonstrations against the Shah's rule while she was wearing a headscarf for fear of her identity being discovered by security men so that he would not arrest her. In the sense that the veil was a symbol of national solidarity against the rule of the Shah and an expression of national unity, in addition to being a respected Islamic consideration, at the very least, for her to obtain her rights to work opportunities and to make decisions regarding her private and public life. This means that the veil was not in Iran during the Shah's rule as a conservative demand and an expression of Islamic traditions, but rather for fear of the secret security man discovering her identity and arresting her. Therefore, it was a unifying symbol for all opposition to the policy of the Shah's rule, unlike in the days of Khomeini's rule.

It is worth noting that Iranian women during the rule of the Shah supported Khomeini because he was calling for and claiming equality between men and women and that the Shah's rule robbed them of their freedom and authorised them the right to choose their life partner, work and education. But after the advent of Khomeini and the expulsion of the Shah from power, in less than a month, the illusions of gender equality that Khomeini was calling for emerged, so he issued unjust legislation against women in all aspects of public and private social life, and the saddest was the permission to marry a minor girl, as the minimum age for her marriage during the rule of the Shah was (18) years, then it was amended in Khomeini time to be 13 years of age and then to 9 years of her age. Then he stripped the woman's freedom of expression and dress, as he punished her with flogging and imprisonment if she violated the wearing of the veil and ordered the execution of the adulteress and the transgressor, and obligated women to wear the veil so it became a symbol of injustice and enslavement after it was in the time of the Shah a symbol of national solidarity against injustice and slavery!!! [Mir-Hosseni. 2001. p. 125]

Therefore, it seems that the scheme of Khomeini's revolution was implemented after the revolution and after deceiving the Iranian. In the sense of suppressing all her ambitions, which she dreamed of when she was demonstrating in the masses against the rule of the Shah. He worked with all his might to withdraw her from public life to languish at home and treat her harshly and impose restrictions on her movements outside the home. It is not known whether Khomeini feared the woman because she was aware of her oppression and succeeded in her demonstrations against the strongest rule Dictatorship of the Shah? Or because she is able to mobilise the Iranian feelings against him? Or is the conscious man more attracted to her consciousness as he was in the days of the Shah? Or is it the ploy of political brokers when they are outside the government, demanding its change and raising ideal slogans of national equality, freedom and democracy, and when they take control of the government, they apply the opposite of what they were asking for, and they apply discrimination, factionalism, authoritarianism, patriarchal authority and democracy?

However, the impact of globalisation on the Iranian regime has frustrated its practice of encircling and besieging urbanisation and against Western and American urbanisation excessively. When President Ahmad Najati was re-elected for the second time to the presidency of the Republic, tens of thousands of Iranian women came out without veils, protesting in a demonstration condemning the government for rigging Ahmad's election. So, despite the government's practice of oppressing women, confining them to their homes and removing them from work, they remained energised in their awareness against unjust practices and their refusal to continue restricting them and the regime's domination over them in the name of the Shiite community. It is clear that Iranian women are aware that the symbols of power are nothing but policy brokers, using the Shiite sect's robe to achieve its greedy ambition to rule and continue their takeover of society. But the woman was more courageous and determined to go out to the streets publicly to reveal the supply of symbols of power and bring them back to power in falsified reality.

They do not have more than a slanderous and dishonest method of using the religious Shiite sect in their rule because they are not qualified to manage the political system except by intimidating and terrorising the society with a spiritual-religious factor, as is the case with all criminal rulers who invoke religion as a quilt to wrap them before the people. The Islamists are ignorant, and Islam disavowals of them because they are hypocrites, awake and hostile to Islam principles.

But the question that arises in this context is whether or not Iranian women are excluded from working in government departments? The answer is no, for fear of her, because she has Islamic and legal arguments to support her blocking against fanatics, and it has a historical background that goes back 30 years during the rule of the Shah that attests to her activity and effectiveness in mobilising the Iranian street and revolution against the unjust ruler. However, the problem facing the Iranian feminist movement is that it is divided and not united. This is what made some of the symbols of the authority bargaining with them and widening the gap between them. The situation is similar for women in Afghanistan and Pakistan.

In sum, the acquisition of the chair of the ruling by an adventurous group ascending to it by means of the electric elevator (religion) occurs in modern Islamic countries but going down and leaving the chair does not take place in the same electric elevator, instead of by throwing them from their chairs to the bottom in ruins. That is exactly what has happened in many countries as the Islamization of politics or the politicisation of religion is one of the worst mistakes because every one of them coordinated its fields, goals, motives, and doctrine. Religion is a divine belief that does not change, while the political belief has a human ground that changes according to the change of fractional interests, and because religion does not accept bargaining and prevarication, but rather direct and direct, while politics lives on bargaining, evasion, twisting and turning. They do not represent two sides of the same coin because they are mutually exclusive in goal and motive. I mean, the life of religion is longer and more ancient, while the life of politics is shorter (so to speak and analogy), and the thought of religion is humane and merciful, while the thought of politics is narcissistic (selfish) and aggressive.

Whenever one enters the orbit of gender, he encounters new and effective events that differ from one country to another and from one society to another. One of the common mistakes made by the rulers of third world countries is that they do not realise and understand the waves of change that drive the wheel of social change. These waves come in the form of globalisation, regional war, modern technological inventions that serve man in the course of his daily life and push the history of the society from one phase to another. History shows the winds of change are blowing with storms that change the speed of social movement and do not exclude the regime, economic policy, ideological camp, or military force, but rather overwhelm it to replace it or place its opposite as societies requirement.

The rulers of the Islamic and Arab world rejected the urbanisation and modernisation achieved by the Western world under the excuse that such modernisation is against religion. This, in fact, represents one of the shortcomings of these rulers and their limited and shallow mentality and their short vision of the future, as well as their loss of awareness of the outside world and recognition of human lifestyles.

In the face of the dilemma of seizing power while not qualified to rule their people, the rulers dealt with it by clinging to the strongest authoritarian authorities over their people, which are the religious (spiritual) and patriarchal (male) authority on which the rulers were brought up. Their pretext was authoritarianism, prejudice, and arbitrariness, and this is one of the greatest tragedies of their people that their rulers are intellectually superficial, narcissistic in behaviour and forced to confront their compelling reality.

It seems that the "weakest and largest" component in these complexes is the woman (the weakest because she does not have military, financial, political, and organisational influence, and the largest because she represents half or more of the population of the community). They work to enslave her by excluding her from the labour market and controlling the first cell in society (the family) with the support of the husband or the father to transform her into a childbearing resource, educator and servant to the husband or the father, and an ignorant, submissive illiterate who has no backing. The males interpret the history of their culture according to their self-interest and translate religion according to their domineering patriarchal service to terrorise and subjugate her in his name and in the name of the inherited patriarchal culture. The men in Islamic countries succeeded in establishing their authority via these mechanisms:

1. Translating religion as masculine, not spiritual and human.
2. An exaggerated reading of the inherited social history in support of the patriarchal authority.
3. Isolate society from the movement of urbanisation and urbanisation prevailing in the world.
4. Fighting technological progress and not bringing it to the country so that it will not be used by the woman and open new doors that the man cannot close.
5. Their fear of her history of struggle against injustice and abuse.
6. Transforming the veil from a religious symbol into a symbol of injustice, oppression and abuse.
7. Using public punishment in front of the masses to terrorise them, claiming that this is God's punishment on them.

The problem of the Islamic gender is different from that of the Western gender. Woman in the Islamic world does not suffer from low wages, fanaticism in their work in the labour market, or the withholding of some academic and scientific disciplines from them and restricting them to service work. No, they made the Islamic gender's problems to wear the hijab, restriction of modern clothes does not drive a car, lack of electoral representation, preventing her from education and marrying her while she is a minor (i.e., nine years old). This is the reality of gender in countries ruled by Islamists who do not know the truth of the Islamic religion. They do not allow the woman to interpret the Qur'an spiritually and humanly. And when they do, it is rather the interpretation in a masculine context!!!

H. THE ARAB GENDER... SURRENDERING TO ITS CULTURAL PATTERN

Westerners hear and read events involving Arab women being forced into marriage, domestic violence, and isolating or withholding from men, and they interpret this as representing contempt and humiliation for women in their society. This is an unfair interpretation because there is a cultural interpretation of these cultural practices of women that have nothing to do with religion, and Arab women and men do not see that these practices mean one of the aspects of injustice, but rather they are aspects appropriate to the nature of woman, and they do not find them to be strict and sharp, not belittling, or contemptuous of woman, but rather a protection for them. It represents danger and pressure on her, and there is no need to discuss, tempt or insult her outside the home, as most Arab women see that this is protection for them, a guarantee for them, and respect for them.

There is no reason to point out that the traditional Arab gender is condemned by patriarchal authority and the kinship system from several centuries ago. At the same time, there is a difference in the status of the woman due to local traditions such as the veil, which the man must spend on her and his family members until they marry. The children must respect their parents and not leave their parents' home before marriage. Also, an Arabic woman sees that the family is the main source in which she lives, and she does not want to fall into the same problems as Western women. They do not want to be liberated as Western women and fall into the same mistakes, "this is the statement of the President of the Iraqi Women's Union." [Nydell. 2010.P. 45]

This title includes the Arab community in the Middle East and North Africa. Women in these countries have a prominent role outside the home to work in health, education, engineering, political reform, media, art, journalism, the peacekeeping force in the world, the army, commerce, and administration, which means that she is not at home and that the veil is considered one of the unjust symbols of some activists. But the unfair thing about Arab women, especially in North African countries, is the amputation of the female genital tract as female circumcision, which is done in order to reduce or eliminate the girl's sexual desire and enjoyment when intercourse with the man, but it expresses her virginity and chastity. If she is a virgin, the chance of her marriage will be high, and if she is not, she will be condemned and live as an outcast. And sometimes, she is killed by one of her family's men or relatives out of shame. This is what is prevalent in North Africa, some countries in the Middle East and some regions of the African Sahara. According to United Nations statistics, the total number of females who have undergone genital amputation (circumcision) ranges between 80 to 100 million girls, including children aged four years. [Lindsey. 2011. P. 170]. It is a cultural-social custom that is practised in rich and poor rural and urban families because it is considered a tribal custom, healthy purity, and a religious custom that preserves the honour of the girl and the family.

At the procedural level, a section or all of the organ is amputated by removing it, leaving a small opening for urination and the exit of menstrual blood from it. When married and on the night of the wedding, the vagina is returned as a sexual organ, and this is usually accompanied by pain, infections, and health complications that the girl loses her sexual pleasure. It is an inhumane procedure that is practised in Egypt, Sudan and Somalia and some parts of Ethiopia. For this amputation of cultural concepts necessary and important in these societies, which are the following:

1. A social, religious, and cultural testimony to the honour of the girl and her family in her virginity.
2. A social, religious, and cultural testimony of a girl's chastity.
3. Increased chances of a girl's marriage.

The amputation of her clitoris is considered a high honorary and nominal testimony in the eyes of the people of these societies. She brings shame to her and her family if the girl refuses or objects to amputating her clitoris. Most of the people who encourage this operation are the authorised midwives who defend it vigorously and forcefully and force the girls to undergo the painful operation.

The United Nations tried to study and treat this harmful and disfiguring process of the female sexual organ through an international conference that obligated the governments of these societies not to practice this process in health centres and hospitals. However, it continues to be practised in homes without the knowledge of the official authorities. On the other hand, shelters have been opened for girls who refuse to perform the operation. However, such superior and official measures do not stop the practice of an inherited social and even religious custom. It is real stupidity to place the status, reputation and consideration of the family honour on a circumcised clitoris of a girl.

However, the hijab (veil) for girls and Arab women has another problem because it is seen by some girls as a restriction on the girl's freedom, adornment and taste and interference in her privacy. Others consider the hijab as a religious and legal action that gives the girl the character of conservatism and femininity and support for Islamic culture and the teachings of Islam.

Interfering with the issue of gender equality as a matter of social and cultural customs (circumcision and veiling) does not work because it is linked to masculine authority and inherited culture. Therefore, it is not surprising that equality has been subjected to a lot of objections by men and even by females (the old generation) because the Arab society is still traditional and conservative despite its development in modern technological uses. It goes without saying that the Arab society has lived through a long period of political turmoil, wars, revolutions, and military coups from the middle of the last century until now, which has made it difficult and impeded the Arab woman's exit from her traditional cultural and social cocoon. This is what they say about her and made her a seat in her home with her family and, at the same time, strengthened the male authority of men. She was forced to live inside and outside the home, and in the face of these harsh and prolonged conditions, she became satisfied with her culturally, religiously, and socially framed lifestyle.

Therefore, the gender gaps in wages paid to workers outside the home, the occupational gap, the electoral gap, or domestic violence have not been addressed because they are all obtained in light of her satisfaction with her three-pillar lifestyle (cultural, religious and social).

But does the satisfaction of the Arab feminine derive from her conviction to dominate her in satisfying her desires, needs and ambitions? Or is she resigned to the many aspects and ways she faces (from illiteracy, poverty, unemployment, tyrannical rule, patriarchal authority, and social stigma imposed on her by society if she does not respond to it in circumcision or veiling)? Then there was no sincere help for her from the government in equating her rights with the rights of a man. Rather she was there are fictitious organisations, not to equal them, but to use them to polish the image of the ruler. In addition to the preoccupation of the ruling regimes with military coups, internal revolutions and external wars that enhance men's power and push women towards the home to manage it, take care of children and serve the husband. And what makes matters worse is the effects of the first and second globalisation and the information revolution that worked to completely dispense with her in the factories, so they used her in the white slave trade and the slave market, forcing her to migrate, asylum, and displacement to the countries to work. In addition to the class disparity generated by globalisation and technological progress and what happened after the Arab Spring, revolutions of structurally disjointed secretions systematically opened the doors wide to political, administrative, financial, judicial, educational, military, medical and engineering corruption. The major victim was the feminine who was in the face of these giant influences that afflicted the Arab society, making the feminine submissive due to her weakness in front of these non-individual forces represented by the (male) patriarchal authority. Moreover, it also led to her ignorance, unemployment, low wages for her work outside the home, the instability of the labour market and eastern values regarding honour and ostracism associated with her marriage. This is the case of the Arab feminine, defeated and resigned to the pressures of her social culture, and there is no one to support her.

I. THE ISRAELI GENDER - EQUALITY ON PAPER ONLY

Israel has worked to recruit women because they need the human element in building their institutions, in particular, the military establishment and collective farms (Kapotz), with the appointment of a woman as Prime Minister (Golda Meir). This is just an apparent constructive need before the world, with women enlisted in the army being given maternity leave and opportunities for education and work. However, the Israeli activists struggled hard to achieve real and realistic gender equality because military conscription has been imposed on all Jewish women since the establishment of the state in order to protect its internal and external security. However, the reality of the situation does not allow Israeli women to rise to the military ranks of advanced, high-ranking, and highly paid positions. Remunerative but initial and limited military ranks with exemption from military service if she gets married, gives birth, or has a religious permit to exempt her from military service.

On the other hand, there is gender segregation between men and women in military work and duties, but they are employed in clerical, secretarial and nursing work. The military institutions and the political system identify with the patriarchal system (male domination). As for employment opportunities for them outside the military institution, they are limited and regulated and not open, as some think, as the Jewish religion, the government and the family are arrogant in the exercise of patriarchal authority over women. This is on the real level. On the external and media level, however, the government claims that gender equality exists and there is no difference between the feminine and the masculine. But this is a misleading and deceptive claim, and what is true is only a flimsy claim.

The Jewish family occupies a high-ranking position in the Jewish society because it represents the core and essence of the Jewish culture as its roots in the traditions of the ancient Jewish religion, which is undoubtedly a question of nature in a way and based on that, the Jewish family is embodied in the role of women. In that sense, the woman represents the centre of the family but is subject to the authority of the male. The government of Israel, which is supposed to mind the gender issues, is neither religious nor secular but rather a legitimate rabbinic-Talmudic vessel that transcends marriage and divorce. This vessel serves the interests of the Jewish traditions stemming and rooted in Orthodoxy Judaism, where all women in all branches of Judaism are obligated to carry out all forms of housekeeping and to practice religious rites that free men from study and education to engage fully in religious life. However, women contribute to local economic and social life, but they see that these tasks entrusted to them are unfair. But religious teachings have priority and the upper hand over gender claims in women's equality with men. It was found that this vision is prevalent among most Jewish families in Israel. [Sasson. 2003. P. 440]

Kibbutzim: It is a Jewish collective farm whose mission is to raise Jewish children according to gender equality between males and females and to make their parents available for the development of their local community. At the same time, it is an experiment carried out by the Israeli

663

government to get the Jewish children out of the domination of the patriarchal authority and the system of division of labour based on the sexual difference (male and female) in order to eliminate the discrimination and segregation between the work of men and the work of women.

This collective experience expresses collaborative activity to reduce gender differences and focus on popular group upbringing. The Israeli government takes the children one or two months after their birth to live in their own house for twelve (12) years, cared for by nurses and nannies, to raise them on the same soil without class, racial, or gender differences, after which they are transferred to other houses called (Sabbath) in which the children live with their parents to get love, affection and family warmth that exempted them from the responsibility of raising their children for 12 years to devote themselves to the activities of the local community and make the work of men and women one in the local community.

These basic rules did not continue because the upbringing of children in collective farms made women grumble and slander this community because children live far from men (fathers) and negative feelings crystallise in them, and the parents' satisfaction increases a lot if their children live with them in one house much better than they live with their peers. An alternative idea has emerged saying that a family centre will be established, bringing together parents and children in one house. Regardless of this alternative idea, women will leave the kibbutz because the second and third generation of kibbutz children will leave them to go to modern life and the small nuclear family. The loss of agricultural interest will lead to the outward migration of young people and increase occupational segregation. Women's work is concentrated in childcare, nursing, education, and working in kitchens as cooks because they only know the work they do on the kibbutz, although the kibbutz focuses on cooperative relationships, love and equality. It is an experiment that does not address gender differentiation as much as it works to raise an Israeli generation linked to what the Israeli government wants to build a society that has nothing to do with sexual differentiation. The disadvantages could be more than the benefits because it undermines the family relationship between children and parents and strips women of their non-domestic activities, such as acquiring non-domestic professional skills. And non-structuralists such as engineering, medicine, and technology.

With regards to the field of education, the gender gap has disappeared between the sexes at all educational levels. But there is an exciting debate between religion and education, and the latter greatly affects the beliefs and perceptions of marriage and family among Israeli youth because religious schools instil religious concepts and teachings about the femininity defined by the divine law in the male world. At the same time, education has a great and strong impact on the aspiration toward modern life and conscious female currents. At the same time, the number of females is increasing in religious institutes in all their branches except for the Orthodox.

The Israeli woman suffers, with regard to work, several gender gaps in a blatant and recurring manner that expresses her unemployment and the separation between her and men at work regardless of her skill levels. She also experienced a loss of her work in the public and private sectors (as one of the effects of globalisation on her) and her lack of equal wages for a man, but much less than him, and when a conflict occurs between the family and work, the latter is abandoned because the conditions of work do not meet the conditions of the mother or the wife who faces pregnancy, childbirth, and motherhood. There are laws approved by the Knesset (Parliament) in 1988 that stipulate the prevention of intolerance and prejudice against women in advertisements, training, promotion, salary cuts, harassment, and sexual harassment of women in the workplace and not giving them additional benefits. This is on the theoretical level - the paper does exist, but on the practical level it does not exist and is not considered because the Israeli woman is still seen as a wife and mother above all, and then as a livelihood earner. In fact, there is a gender gap in Israeli society and an occupational, wage and family gap though there is a law prohibiting it.

It is important to point out that the government's general policy does not interfere in helping women with the burdens they bear or in confronting their contradictory roles that hinder the performance of their role, particularly those obstacles that stem from ancient Jewish traditions and prefer the man over the woman. However, this policy does not include culturally and officially legitimate decisions to help women. The following are among the biggest problems of the feminist movement in Israel:

1. The movement did not originate from an Israeli feminist organisation but rather was imported into Israel from the Western world (i.e., imitator of it and did not arise because of the Israeli woman's need for it).

2. It does not express the cultural, ethnic, and class components of women in Israel.

3. Rather, for the middle class of European immigrants to Israel.

4. It did not express the Jewish feminist unity if it excluded the women of the poor, marginalised, non-Jewish, Arab

and immigrant classes from the Middle East and North Africa and from Asia.

5. It was dominated by Ashkenazi women (women from Eastern, Central and Western Europe, i.e., Western Jews).
6. It does not include women of colour but only white.
7. It is an immature movement like the maturity of feminist movements in the world, in particular in its dealings with marginalised races, nationalities, and classes. [Lindsey. 2011. Pp. 160 – 164]

It seems that the patriarchal authority is the master of gender life in Israeli society and that racial intolerance and national prejudice against women and from other races and nationalities is the master of gender life there. These are irrefutable facts, no matter how much the media claim to deny them. It can be seen in family relations, official offices, and job opportunities because the Jewish religion, government and family take the patriarchal authority as their backbone, and the sexual segregation between men and women in the workplace expresses the occupational gap followed by the wage gap in paying women's salaries less than men, and without any consideration from the management of the work about the conditions of a mother when she is pregnant, giving birth, nursing and caring for her children, and even obliges her to quit her job without financial compensation for that.

On the other hand, the feminist movement in Israel does not deal with women's problems in work, family, and public life, nor does it address their ethnic, national and class suffering as it is an imported movement from the Western world, in form without substance. It did not defend against racial discrimination or factional intolerance because it is dominated by the generation of the middle class, with the

667

European race superior to the rest of the races. This alone does not reflect the goals of the feminist movement but rather reinforces racial discrimination and isolates the women of the poor from the middle and the rich. Therefore, it can be said that the Israeli gender is identical in form and content to the biological differences between men and women and is inhuman, but rather class and racial and is full of anomalies from the rest of the feminist movements of the world that demand the rights of women in their equality with the man. It also indicates that the Israeli society is a patriarchal society that is biassed toward the male and intolerant against the female, and this crystallises the imbalance of the components of the modern society because it lives in the scent of outdated inherited traditions that are inconsistent with the spirit of the age in gender equality as if it lives in its past more than its present and future.

J. THE SCANDINAVIAN GENDER...THE IDEAL MODEL FOR ITS EQUALITY

This region includes Norway, Finland, Sweden, Iceland, Denmark. The societies of these countries are known as Scandinavian peoples, and Their societies differ from the rest of the world's societies in their policy of equality between the feminine and the masculine. They scored 5/7 position in the index of the countries of the world, which was used by the United Nations to measure the gender gap worldwide, especially in the participation in economic activities, job opportunities, educational presence in schools, health care, and active participation in political activities. Scandinavian women occupied between 35 and 45% of the legal government seats, in addition to occupying half of the seats in municipal councils. They benefit from the privileges of gender equality in terms of generous support in childcare

668

and support for women in the workplace and their own organisations. In fact, there are strong links between civil society in these countries and their governments. Thus their setup has been considered the ideal model for gender equality in the world.

Gender Norway and Sweden

Through the Prime Minister of Norway, Mrs Harlem Brundtland, who has been in her position for sixteen years, one can learn about the nature of gender in Norway. At the end of her term, no men compete with her as she is supported by women in government positions with the presence of an open understanding between government institutions and gender equality, where the doors are open to different ways of living spontaneously without cultural, ethnic or political disabilities, and having a permanent presence in politics and benefiting from education, health and work. All of this was not at the expense of men's roles but rather equal to their rights. The same is the case in Sweden, with the Swedish mother focusing on managing her home and taking care of her children in front of her work outside the home in the areas of care for children, the elderly and the disabled while raising her children on gender equality and benefiting from government aid for her and her children with no gender, wage or professional gaps. [Bergqvist and Nyberg. 2002. p. 221]

CHAPTER 12: WAYS TO LIBERATE THE FEMININE FROM SOCIAL SLAVERY

INITIATION

A. SELF-AWARENESS AND THE COMPLEXITY OF THE PREFERENCING EXPOSING
B. THE PARADOXES IN SOCIETY AGAINST THE FEMININE IN THE FOUR WORLDS
C. THE TRANSFORMATION OF GENDER
D. LIBERATING THE FEMININE FROM THE CONSTRAINTS OF MASCULINE POWER

CHAPTER 12

WAYS TO LIBERATE THE FEMININE FROM SOCIAL SLAVERY

<u>INITIATION</u>

Injustice or differentiation is not based on differences and paradoxes only but on intolerance, prejudice, discrimination, marginalisation, exclusion, superiority, belittling, contempt, and disrespect (these are collective practices rather than individual ones) that occur between individuals, groups, parties, tribes, classes, races, nationalities, minorities, sects, religions, and cultures.

These collective practices express imbalance, lack of moderation, unevenness, and unfairness. One of the parties represents the possession of influence, money, power, knowledge, or status, and the second represents a person who lacks influence, money, authority, knowledge, or status. It is not called the term inequality, but the dissonant and conflicting difference based on normative nihilisms that form the basis of the gradual construction called (Social Stratification).

It is a fact that there is no human society free of social classes, religious sects, scientific specialisations, party affiliations, regional residences, sports teams, companion paralysis, criminal gangs, and economic incomes. Rather, there is a gradation specific to each of these categories. When it comes to justice, equality and balance is a form of idealism and a fictional utopian logic that only occurs in theorising and not in the realm of application. It is the norm of life that is constantly in motion, changing, and progressing. What is dominant becomes defeated, and what was high is sacrificed low, and what has become strong becomes weak. On the contrary, this is how the vocabulary of life is not subject to the balance of balanced and equal justice.

Since the subject involves the inequality of the masculine with the feminine, which is the product of natural roots and nutrients such as religion, social culture, political system, work, money and profession (internal factors), war, economic crises, and natural disasters (external factors), the forms of equality and balance are missing - realisation - It is followed by injustice, exploitation, enslavement and marginalisation, expressing ingratitude and prejudice on the weak and poor side by the powerful and the rich, reinforced by internal pillars such as religion, social culture, and patriarchal power. In other words, justice does not exist and does not exist as long as there is a difference and disparity in abilities, power, influence, and authority between groups of society, then the sexual difference is supported by natural, professional, religious, regional, and tribal differences, which closes the door to qualitative equality between male and female and keeping the latter at the mercy of the former. However, with recent technological developments and major human changes such as war or globalisation or fluctuations in global trade in international markets coupled with the presence of instant contact between peoples, gender responds to that and demands a change in the equation that was against women in order to obtain their stolen and usurped rights by the religiously supported man culturally and politically. He demands the lost (justice) just as it is demanded by the races subject to fanaticism and racial discrimination, and as the poor (lower) class demands against the rich and ruled class against the ruling class. Thus, the woman's sympathy with the man who she does not want to remain under his control, independence, and marginalisation of her.

672

The demand for justice and equality means that there is exploitation, extortion, injustice, reaping and usurpation of rights, desires, interests, and benefits. Is there a state of force equilibrium between them? The answer is no, or is there equality in rights and duties for them? The answer is also no. It is a conflict between the possessor and the loser, the ruler and the ruled, the victorious and the defeated, the hungry and the full, the female and the male. This is a problem that is added to the responsibility of sociologists to study, as long as there is a rape of rights and physical and sexual violence against some members of society, It needs diagnosis of its causes, analysis of its reality, and an anticipation of its effects, future, and harms on social life.

The inequality between the rights and duties of women and men, however, differs from racial discrimination between one custom and another because it is neither related to religious teachings, patriarchal authority, values, and cultural norms, nor the social policy of the political system. In other words, gender inequality is more complex and disruptive than racial discrimination, tribalism, regionalism, and partisanship because it exists everywhere, in family, tribe, clan, religious sect, economic class, village and city. It is broader and more widespread in the social fabric. Although the inequality is between economic classes, religious sects, and ethnic dynasties, it is confined to the boundaries of class, sect, or dynasty only. However, the inequality and equality between men and women is not confined to or is not limited to only the material - economic and political factor, but in all aspects of life.

The basis of the differences is not biological difference but the response of men and women to cultural and religious judgments on their social roles. In other words, the injustice did not come from the ruler, the leader, or the man himself, but rather from the historical, cultural, and religious background of the society. On top of that, the absence of justice does not lie in class, race, or in nationality, gender, or age.

Therefore, inequality between men and women does not represent a personal - individual problem but a cultural - societal problem, and this is what makes equality between them a requirement that includes several diverse internal and external efforts such as liberal external international pressures and internal oppositions by active elements in the daily cultural and media life. The balance leads to the stability of society and progresses it forward, while the difference leads to conflict and strife, which in turn hinders and impedes progress and development. It is simply because the balance makes both sides cooperate in building each of them rather than destroying and undermining each other. The authoritarian man exerts violence on the woman and prevents her from being creative in work and making smart decisions. Rather, he degrades her value under the guise of distinction and social contempt for her, and when she is enslaved to him, she does not have the right to see what she is not allowed to see or to think about what she is not allowed to think. She acts like an owned slave. Therefore, it can be stated that the inequality between men and women reflects the imbalance of rights, duties, influence, property, power, money, prestige, status and role. The man owns all of that, and the woman loses all of that, and this alone is enough to generate a structural and unilateral deficiency that is (for the man's side) as opposed to what is required of him to be two-sided.

Finally, justice cannot exist in reality but is a theoretical and epistemological requirement. Rather, there is competition and conflict between the affected and

674

beneficiary stakeholders. So, what to do in the face of justice lost in society? Work is:

A. SELF-AWARENESS AND THE COMPLEXITY OF THE PREFERENCING EXPOSING

Equality between men and women represents the complex complexes of the decade since ancient times and ages and still is... So, for how long will it last? When will the dawn of the desired gender equality rise?! Will it ever shine?! Then what are the principles of gender equality? And what are its terms? And who is responsible for achieving it? The woman or the man? Or both?

It seems that equality is not in the hands of men and women but in the hands of forces greater and stronger than them: the patriarchal authority that dominates the masculine over the feminine, then the religious brokers who interpret religious teachings to serve their interests, influence, positions or money, as well as the intruders in politics who use the preference of men over women in support of their rule, then the socialisation emanating from male authority and supported by male and female toy factories. Not only that, but for those responsible for official and public work opportunities such as state departments, factories, laboratories and workshops, their interest is to favour men over women because of their female biological composition, which causes them not to work outside the home (such as menstruation, pregnancy, childbirth, and breastfeeding) and then comes the issue of her wages that are not equal men's wages at work.

On the other hand, this aspect of her femininity and beauty makes a man assault her in sexual harassment and rape because she has no authority, influence or physical strength to defend herself. As for her conditions, they are represented in the self-awareness that falls on each of them in order to fight the law of nature and move according to it, which shows that the man does not lead her or her leadership of the man, but rather they walk equal and equal towards equality in duties and rights so that it comes from the inner feeling, conviction and general appreciation to do towards the opposite sex and not exploitation of each other in particular the exploitation of women by men in work, wages, education, sexual harassment and climbing the social hierarchy. As for who is responsible for achieving it? In the first degree, the feminist organisation itself is the one who can impose on the government and the community leadership to respect their rights, grant them what is usurped from them, respect their opinion as human beings, trust them as a citizen, and gain a place through their efforts and competence, not by inheriting them and not transgressing their duties and rights. Also responsible for achieving equality are the national leaders and leaders who take the hand of their citizens without fanaticism, prejudice and discrimination between one race and another, or religion and the second, or nationalism and nationality, if they want to build solidarity and interdependent society in the functions of their society. Otherwise, inequality will continue to infinity, and the dawn will not rise—the desired equality between them.

It goes without saying that only men or women are able to achieve gender equality, and this is a figment of the imagination because the modern man is burdened with manifold responsibilities in work and family and facing the pressures of the second globalisation with rapid, contradictory, and aggravating transformations. The woman's situation is also overloaded as she is facing the transformation cube fatigue in the family, work, and home.

In other words, both of them are not able to achieve equality on their own, but with their joint efforts and with leadership planning, as Lenin did in the former Soviet Union, Mao in China, Suharto in Indonesia and Nehru and Gandhi in India, provided that he starts from the stage of igniting self-awareness. The man must be aware that his existence is linked to the existence of the feminine at the same level and not inferior to it. They must cooperate in building the first cell in society (the family) and revitalising the market, the farm, and the factory because gender equality represents a diversified complexity in various aspects of life, which are rapidly changed, with their roots are deep in the subconscious of both sexes.

B. THE PARADOXES IN SOCIETY AGAINST THE FEMININE IN THE FOUR WORLDS

These growing paradoxes reveal that the structural patterns of human society favour the masculine and the feminine, regardless of whether the society is rural, urban, industrial, simplistic, capitalist, or informational. And since the building does not want to change the policy of its layout, nor does the system desire that its status becomes stable, and centuries of time have passed since its dormant and stagnant state, but society does not know stagnation and hibernation, but rather permanent and perpetual movement because it is affected by the external factors and influences that provoke the internal components, so their balances change and change its interests. The first to crack with this change is the smallest cell in the social system, which is the family consisting of the husband and wife.

However, this cell represents a transmission agency that transmits the social culture inherited from previous generations (such as language, religion, morals, standards, traditions, customs, and others). What the family does in its upbringing is reflected in the economic activity in the economic, industrial, and political system, and this is unmistakable, except that what is dusty is the following:

The woman who is the wife gives birth to children to provide the society with new members. This is a social act worthy of appreciation and sanctification. Then she transfers the cultural and social components of teaching her children standards and disciplinary values, and this is a more worthy and solid work that perpetuates the heritage and morals of the society. So, without her, society would not have become developing and bearing the culture of its generations. Then comes the task of domestic affairs in managing, organising, and feeding family members, and this is an indispensable household responsibility that is associated with her and accompanied by the responsibility of working outside the home to help the husband in the family's livelihood. All these responsibilities are carried out by the woman - the wife. There are biological processes that accompany her female roles, which are the period of pregnancy, childbirth, breastfeeding and menstruation. These are natural biological burdens that every female faces, which are carried out by the wife, which the husband does not carry out, and their responsibility affect the aforementioned male. The burdens and responsibilities that occur to the woman - the wife (the five) is:

1) Biological burdens - female.
2) The process of childbearing.
3) Housekeeping.
4) Work outside the home.
5) The process of family upbringing.

All of these burdens and responsibilities do not do justice to her, nor do her social culture, her family, her life partner, her children, the rulers of society or the employers. Rather, they consider them:

1) A temporary basket in the labour market.
2) Unworthy of professional skills.
3) Weak in a professional production.
4) Frequent absenteeism from work.

It resulted in low wages, preference for man over her, the dispensation of her if unemployment occurs with the man, and he grants her half of the family inheritance or deprives her of it. So, here is a reward for a creature who gave everything for her partner, her children, her family, and her community? It is a human tragedy in which the most powerful elements and the most difficult collective barriers (cultural, male authority and social order) participated, and society does not pay attention to it and is in dire need of her giving because she is "the giving land", she is the nourisher for the human... No one did justice to her!!!

In studying the topic of gender, it is necessary to differentiate between what culture, authority, order, and system impose on the preference of the male over the female and what the male himself prefers over the female in terms of material interest and moral exploitation related to what is imposed by the first influences (culture, authority, order and coordination), but rather physical strength, social influence, political and family authority, financial income and management position.

This type of personal-individual differential is studied in the field of criminology, juvenile delinquency, and victimology. As for the first type, it is within the competence of (gender) because social, cultural, political, economic, and industrial differentiation does not exclude anyone from it and is practised openly and without hesitation, but rather boasts about it before the people because it is supported by the overwhelming majority and by its standards, values, and social system.

Two questions may come to mind why does the individual agree with society, its culture and its coordination in favouring men over women? Who are the most generous in her sacrifices for men, family, society, systems and culture? The answer is that the family realises and is more aware of the woman's marital, maternal, upbringing and disciplinary responsibilities than the man and knows the gravity of its human responsibilities in her feelings than the man as she is more emotional than him. These sensory perceptions, which she naturally has, make the man jealous of her. He, therefore, uses his physical strength to exercise it over her and exploits his work outside the home, using his financial source to be superior to her and subject her to his authority. He deliberately and intentionally marginalises her role in the family and society or obscures her, but he cannot exclude her from the family because she is its pillar and the security of society as she is half of it. He can only enslave her to achieve his dominance. Therefore, the woman who is aware of this marginalisation and enslavement urgently demands equality in her rights and duties with men. In other words, she demands some of the duties that she had assumed to put on the shoulders of the man, such as taking care of housekeeping, children, taking care of her feelings and not using physical and verbal violence with her. At the same time, she takes some of the rights that the man had held alone so that they become parts of her rights, such as allocating part of the family budget to her personal expenses, giving her the right to express her opinion and giving her freedom to make family decisions, and her right to the family inheritance and not seizing it or depriving her of it. She must have the right to divorce her husband and the right of taking care of her children even after divorce, to marry after being widowed or divorced, and the right to choose the man she wants to marry (if she is unmarried). Also, to have the freedom in travelling outside the country on her own, to have her own bank account, to attend parties and theatres alone and with others.

It is right to say that the preference of men over women is a mirror of the prevailing norms of society and the values of its culture. This is permissible, but it is not permissible for a man to claim his right to rape a woman, make her a victim, deprive her of an inheritance, or not grant her the right to divorce her husband if their relationship became difficult or he physically and verbally abused her, or he committed incest. It is not reasonable for a society to be lamer or to look with a single eye on such behaviours as it cannot advance fast, and its vision will be blurred. It applies to the need for the rights and duties of men and women to be quantitively and qualitatively equal. Otherwise, the progress of society will be hampered and slowed, and production will be scarce and poor. Here, the equation of (abandonment and adoption) is required so that the man gives up some of his rights for the benefit of the woman and adopts some of the duties that were borne by women. The woman must also adopt those rights abandoned by the man and relinquish the duties that she held in favour of the man. This equation accompanies every social change that occurs in society, and without it, no progress or development can be achieved.

The Four Realms Alliance Against the Feminine

The activities of feminist movements in gender equality at the present time can be summarised in four main realms, namely:

1. **The World of the Family:** in which women's demands are limited to:

681

a. Giving her the freedom to choose her life partner for marriage.
b. Giving her the freedom to make her decision to divorce her husband when she is not in harmony and their problems escalate.
c. Allowing her to limit the number of children and the use of birth control and abortion methods.
d. Not to interfere in her housekeeping affairs.
e. Respecting her opinion in family decisions.
f. The husband helps her in housekeeping.
g. Equal to her entitlement to the family inheritance.

2. The World of Work focuses on the following matters:
a. Allow her to occupy a position appropriate to her professional experience and educational attainment.
b. Granting her wages equal to the wages of a man who has the same professional experience and educational attainment.
c. Continuing to pay her salaries or wages when she is entitled to maternity, maternity, and breastfeeding leave.
d. Granting her health insurance for her and her children.
e. Allowing her to return to work after her family vacations.

3. **The World of Social Culture:** which includes the following:
a. Not to subject her to male authority (the patriarch), but rather to allow her to express her opinion and respect it and to make decisions that concern her personal matter.
b. Not giving preference to males over her in consideration of social and family influence.
c. Not to be seen as a tomboy if she works outside the home.
d. Involve them in technology festivals and highlight their creativity.

4. **The World of Politics:** which includes the following:

a. Allow her to vote in elections, like men, in popular, municipal, parliamentary, and presidential councils.

b. No objection to engaging in political and social movements.

c. Allow her to belong to political parties opposed to government policy.

d. Involve her in the foreign-international diplomatic representation.

e. Opening doors for her to occupy sovereign positions.

Upon the realisation of her rights in the four worlds, it can be said that there is gender equality in the society, and such equality cannot be subject to compelling external pressures such as foreign colonialism or occupation, just as America occupied Japan and instituted some reforms not out of love for Japanese women, but because of the need for them in the new phase. Or as happens in modern technological innovations that require the use of the soft element in them, or when they fall, or collapse of a political system occurs in a country as that occurred in the communist camp in Eastern Europe. It is important to mention that such strict and daring external forces do not fully succeed unless they are accompanied by an internal reform movement by national reformers from Men and women who believe in the new change and the need for national labour of both sexes, as happened in Japan, Russia and China. Or when a popular national leader emerges demanding comprehensive and radical change, such as what happened in China during the leadership of (Mao Zedong) and (Lenin) in Russia and (Nehru) in India. The question here is why the woman waits for these external and internal influences in order to do justice to her right, her role, and her national social and

683

cultural status? Why is this exclusion and marginalisation by the national social culture represented by father patriarchal authority and ethnic and religious intolerance, why? Why wait for foreign powers to liberate her from the hegemony of the patriotic authority and man? Is this related to male genes? Or the female genes? Wasn't the woman the mother of the man, his sister, and his wife whom he loves and sanctifies? Didn't she create him as she wanted? Why does he deny her?

Therofore, tho nood for interoots, in partioular tho material, is stronger than the blood ties of the father and the family. Likewise, the personal material interest of employers is stronger and more merciful than the national and social interest, and the opportunist political interest is stronger than the national interest.

It seems that the demand for sexual equality faces many and varied obstacles, collective and individual, political and cultural, familial and partisan, all of whom are united by personal interest rather than collective, factional rather than national, partisan rather than national, material rather than moral, moral and sectarian rather than religious. The women contribute in part to their sexual inequality with men because they also prefer the boy over the girl after they marry and have children, as they wish to give birth to a son over a daughter, and when she gives birth to boys and girls, she takes care of the boys and more than the girls. Culturally and legally, it made men continue to marginalise and enslave them, so it required women to be bold, daring, and defiant, stealing their rights and doubling their domestic, family and community duties.

C. TRANSFORMATION OF GENDER

It is critical to note that when examining the issue of gender in the societies of totalitarian political systems that lack democracy and openness, it is important to dissect all social, cultural, and ruling variables, and to cite the objectives and intentions, because sexuality (gender) does not stem from biological differences (male and female), but rather is issued and is largely imprinted by the society's prevailing culture, its national races, its system of government, and its stage of development.

Whereas the more traditional, conservative, and ancient the culture of society is, the more biological differences prevail over the sexual type (gender), meaning that the rights of the male are more and better than the rights of the female, and his status is higher than her, his income is higher than her income, and her family responsibility is more and broader than his responsibility, and his power and family authority is higher than hers. And vice versa, if the society's culture is urban and technical - materialistic, then the sexual gender (feminine and masculine) is sacrificed equally in rights, duties, positions, and roles. The situation is similar to the case of social culture with ethnic-national diversity, as men's rights become more and better than women's rights and their status is inferior to him, but her family role is broader and more than his role within the family due to the presence of a social majority and social and ethnic minorities that do not prevail in them the justice and the social equality.

And when the political system is totalitarian (the one-party ruling system or clan, feudal or familial), then the rights of man are more and better than the rights of woman, and her duties are broader and more than his duties. And when the social system is patriarchal (man domination over the family), the rights of men be higher than women's rights and duties lower than theirs.

These facts must be noted when examining sexual diversity in human society. But these social facts are not fixed and irreverent. They only change with the change of the society and its transition from a traditional stage to a developmental stage, from rural to civilised, and from feudalism to industrialism. Thus, among the changes that affect society is sexual type (gender) because women as an individual in the society acquire education, culture, aspiration to the future and friction civilisation with other civilisations, which increases her awareness of her restricted and imprisoned reality in cultural, bureaucratic, methodological, ethnic and political stereotypes, which resulted from the liberation of these multiple and diverse stereotypes through learning and worked so that she at least becomes financially independent. Since she represents half of the society or more, the man's fear of her population size and her importance in the reality of the family is great and effective.

Accordingly, it can be concluded from the foregoing that gender is not affected by biological differences between males and females in urban, capitalist, industrial and information societies but is affected by Bedouin, rural, feudal, religious, sectarian, totalitarian, traditional and conservative societies.

So, they are attracted to each other in these societies, but they repel each other in the urban, industrial, capitalist, and informational societies. These are social constants that are obtained through the development of human societies. These inconsistencies stand out between gender and biological differences in the following areas:

1. In education, women are less educated than men.
2. At work, women are less involved in work than men.
3. In the wages of work, women get fewer wages than men.
4. In public participation in scientific and official life, women participate less than men.

But the destroyer of these barriers that exist between men and women are not all from within the community, but from outside it in most cases, such as:

1. Globalisation.
2. Free global trade.
3. Advanced technological development.
4. Instant electronic communications and computers.
5. Democracy.
6. Free competition.
7. Compulsory education.
8. Voluntary people's organisations.

The factors that reinforce the differences and barriers between biological differences and gender are the following:

1. Civil, global, and international wars.
2. Revolutions and military coups.
3. Military rule.
4. The Patriotic System.
5. Unemployment (international economic blockade).
6. The domesticated intellectual and the executioner.
7. The spread of illiteracy.
8. Sectarian rule - religious and ethnic.

Indicators of equal rights and duties of both sexes in human societies are as follows:

1. Women going outside the home to work.
2. Women's financial and economic independence.
3. Making decisions for herself and her family.
4. Stop violence against her by men or society.
5. Obtaining powerful and bureaucratic positions.

6. The freedom to choose her life partner.
7. She is free to make her own decision in the event of her divorce from her husband.

D. LIBERATING THE FEMININE FROM THE CONSTRAINTS OF MASCULINE POWER

To liberate the feminine from the constraints of patriarchal and cultural authority, the Indian Manu laws, and Confucian principles, she is required and must be liberated in the following affairs and matters:

1. Developing and educating the mother's role in raising her children and making family life successful.
2. Reducing the population size.
3. Health education for women.
4. Raising its official and political awareness.
5. Exercising its awareness as a pressure group on the government in family matters (such as what the Indonesian wife did in the matter of polygamy).
6. Reducing the wife's burdens by legalising childbearing, proving her strength in the family, and making her voice heard and not subject to the authority of the man.
7. Stop the violent physical and verbal practices of the man by the man.
8. Her involvement in the trade union - professional.
9. Raising her low wages.
10. Paying her additional wages in the event of her birth and motherhood and granting her leave during menstruation (as the Indonesian wife did).
11. Her transformation from a servant to the husband to an active participant in her family, as happened in China.
12. Granting her the right to divorce and inherit, cancelling the dowry, allowing the widow to marry, and not being

overpowered by the husband (like what happened in China).

It is worth noting when studying gender in different countries that there are wonderful initiatives in their civil and humanity, such as what Indonesian wives have done (in preventing the appointment of employees in state departments to anyone who marries more than one wife so that they do not intersect with Islamic teachings prevailing in the country) and what the government has done Japanese in not violating Japanese cultural taboos filling in the large gaps in the workforce opens the door for foreigners to immigrate to Japan so as not to violate Japanese family, religious and cultural customs and beliefs.

As long as we are within the limits of our purposes, we address the following topic: I should mention as a note that not every government, organisation, or national leader who calls for gender equality is sincere in his call because his saying may not be translated on the ground. Through our study of gender in different countries of the world, we were able to diagnose three types of propositions on this topic:

1. The vocal appeal, or the verbal chants only with it to show that they have free opinions in liberating women from male, cultural and religious restrictions, like all the rulers of Arab and African countries who opened women's agencies calling for the equality of the feminine with the masculine (gender) verbally, but in reality, it is an agency to polish their rule politically and in the media. It does not consider equality, either in terms of rights or duties.

2. A call to silence extremist organisations in liberating women from official and customary restrictions and freezing many feminist movements that were calling for equality with men and mobilising the street (as happened

689

in Indonesia during the rule of Suharto). I mean using the call as a pressure card on the political opposition to silence them and to stop the demand for (feminine) participation in political positions.

3. A sincere call in her words and actions in liberating women from official and customary restrictions, bringing her rights closer to man's rights, and bringing man's duties closer to her duties, such as calling for the United Nations, and in Indonesia after 1998 by the (Men's Power) group, and in China when the reform law was issued in 1980 and the other reforming law in 2001 and the Russian legislation in 1917 that did justice to a Russian woman and the Indian Gelang movement that emerged in the nineteenth century and what (Jawahar Nehru and Gandhi) did in India who gave the woman the rights to inheritance, divorce and vote as well (Andrea Gandhi) and her famous reform in 1984 for equality of woman's rights with man's. Then there are Indian feminist movements that are active in change. Then there are the democratic practices in Japan in 1947 and in 1994 when the Japanese government established a gender department on equality and gender reforms in 1997 and 1999.

REFERENCES

1. Al-Omar, Maan Khalil. 2012 AD. New Crimes. Dar Wael - Amman
2. Al-Omar, Maan Khalil. 2009 AD. "The Science of Victims of Crime". Dar Al-Shorouk – Amman
3. Al-Omar, Maan Khalil. 2016 AD. New Fields in Sociology. Dar Al-Shorouk - Amman
4. Al-Bahrani, Zainab. 2012 AD. "Women of Babylon" translated by Maha Hassan Bahbouh. Medames Publishing Company - Beirut
5. Al-Omar, Maan Khalil. 2000 AD. "The Dictionary of Sociology". Dar Al-Shorouk - Amman
6. Al-Khaqani, Issa bin Abdul Hamid. 2013 AD. "education basics". Prince's House - Beirut
7. Lathakani, Mohieddin. 2012 AD. The female is the lamp of the universe. Midrak Publishing House - Beirut
8. Al-Omar, Maan Khalil. 2013 AD. Islamic Sociology. Dar Al-Zahra – Riyadh
9. Bessant, Judith and Watts, Rob. 2007. "Sociology" Allen and Unwin. NSW – Australia
10. Kendall, Diana. 2012. "Social Problems" Allyn and Bacon Pearson, Boston MA.
11. Anderson, Margret and Taylor, Howard. 2013. "Sociology" Wadsworth Cengage learning, Australia
12. Jenainati, Cathia and Groves, Judy. 2007. "Introducing Feminism" I can books Ltd. UK
13. Vankrieken, Robert and etal. 2006. "Sociology" Harper Collins Pub. Australia
14. Thomsen, Natasha. 2007. "Women's Rights" Infobase Publishing. New York
15. Giddens, Anthony. 1994. "Sociology" Polity Press Blackwell pub. Oxford. UK

691

16. Lehti, Mariti and Aromaa, Kauko. 2002. "Trafficking in Human Beings, Illegal immigration". Helsinki University Press. Helsinki, Finland
17. Glonti, Georgi. 2004. "Human Trafficking" (ed.) Organised Crime. Trafficking, Drugs Nevala, Sami Aramma Kanko Hakapoino OY. Helsinki, Finland
18. Spriggs,Merle and Julina Savulesch. 2006. "Ethics of Surgically assigning for intersex children". In David Benat (ed.) Cutting to the care: Exploring the Ethics of contested surgeries, Canham MD, Rowman and Little Field.
19. Foucault, Michael. 1990. "The uses of pleasure" Volume II of Robert Hurley (trans) the history of sexuality. New York
20. Lindsey, Linds. 2011. "Gender Roles" Prentice Hall. New York.
21. Stearman, Kevin and Boyd, Tony. 2003. "Understanding Political ideas and movement". Manchester University press. New York
22. Healey, Justine. 2014. "Gender Discrimination and Inequality". The Spinney presses. Australia
23. Mawby, R. I. and Gill, M. L. 1989. "Crime Victims". Tavistock pl. London
24. Loraux, Nicole. 1989. "Mother in Mourning" With the Essay, Of Amnesty and Its Opposite carinne poche thaco. N. Y. Cornell University.
25. Clements Barbara Evans, Rebecca Friedman and Dan, Healey (eds.). 2002. "Russian Masculinities in History and Culture". Hound mills, Hampshire. UK. Palgrave.
26. Lindsey, Lindal. 2007. "Impact of globalisation on woman in China". Midwest Sociological Society Chicago.

27. Potts, Malcolm. 2006. "China's one child Policy". The policy that changes the world. British medical journal.
28. Brook, James. 2005. "Fighting to protect her gift to Japanese woman". New York Times, May 28 International.
29. Hori, Haruhiko. 2009. "Labour market segmentation and the gender wage gap". Japan later review.
30. Tsuya, (etal.). 2005. "Is the gender division of later manging in Japan?". Asian population studies.
31. Liddle, Joanna and Sackiko Nokojima. 2000. "Rising Suns Rising Dough Gender". Class and power in Japan. London. Zed.
32. Notter, David. 2000. "Towards a cultural analysis of modern family". Beyond the revisionist parading in trinational Journal of Japanese Sociology.
33. Mitter, Sara S. 1991. "Dharmg's Doughers". Contemporary Indian women and Hindu culture New Brunswick Rutgers University.
34. 26 – Roy, Ranjan. 1994. AIDS explosion fear in India's prostitute. Town's St. Louis Post Piroatch maich
35. Howitt, Bernie and Julinn, Robin. 2009. "Sociology and culture". Pearson Sydney.
36. Anastaskos, Kiki. 2002. "Structural adjustment policies in Mexico and costa Rica in Rakha Datta and Judith Kovnberg (eds.) women in Developing countries Assessing strategies for Empowerment.
37. Mir Hosseini Ziba. 2001. "Iran Emerging Feminist Voices". In Lynn Walter, (ed.). Women Rights a Global View.
38. Nydell, Margaret. 2012. "Understanding Arabs intercultural". Press London

39. Sasson, Levy, Orua. 2003. Feminism and military gender practices: Israeli women soldiers in masculine, sociological Inquiry 73.
40. Bergpvist, Christina and Anita Nyberg. 2002. "Welfare state restructuring and childcare in Sweden in Sonya Michel and Rianne Mahon" (eds.) Childcare Policy at The Crossroads Gender and Welfare State Restructuring,

Lightning Source UK Ltd.
Milton Keynes UK
UKHW020656090223
416720UK00003B/747

9 781915 662453